THE BOOK OF THE TWELVE AND BEYOND

ANCIENT ISRAEL AND ITS LITERATURE

Thomas C. Römer, General Editor

Editorial Board:
Mark G. Brett
Marc Brettler
Corrine L. Carvalho
Tom Dozeman
Cynthia Edenburg
Konrad Schmid

Number 29

THE BOOK OF THE TWELVE AND BEYOND
Collected Essays of James D. Nogalski

James D. Nogalski

Atlanta

Copyright © 2017 by Society of Biblical Literature

All rights reserved. No part of this work may be reproduced or transmitted in any form or by any means, electronic or mechanical, including photocopying and recording, or by means of any information storage or retrieval system, except as may be expressly permitted by the 1976 Copyright Act or in writing from the publisher. Requests for permission should be addressed in writing to the Rights and Permissions Office, SBL Press, 825 Houston Mill Road, Atlanta, GA 30329 USA.

Library of Congress Cataloging-in-Publication Data

Names: Nogalski, James, author.
Title: The Book of the Twelve and beyond : collected essays of James D. Nogalski / by James D. Nogalski.
Description: Atlanta : SBL Press, [2017] | Series: Ancient Israel and its literature ; number 29 | Collection of essays. | Includes bibliographical references and index.
Identifiers: LCCN 2016056525 (print) | LCCN 2016059234 (ebook) | ISBN 9781628371642 (pbk. : alk. paper) | ISBN 9780884142065 (hardcover : alk. paper) | ISBN 9780884142058 (ebook)
Subjects: LCSH: Bible. Minor Prophets—Criticism, interpretation, etc. | Nogalski, James.
Classification: LCC BS1560 .N633 2017 (print) | LCC BS1560 (ebook) | DDC 224/.906—dc23
LC record available at https://lccn.loc.gov/2016056525

Printed on acid-free paper.

Contents

Acknowledgements vii
Original Publication Information ix
Abbreviations xi

Introduction to *The Book of the Twelve and Beyond*:
   Authorial Reflections 1

Redactional Texts

The Redactional Shaping of Nahum 1 for the Book of the Twelve 23

Zephaniah 3: A Redactional Text for a Developing Corpus 33

Zechariah 13:7–9 as a Transitional Text: An Appreciation and
   Reevaluation of the Work of Rex Mason..49

Micah 7:8–20: A Reevaluation of the Identity of the Enemy.....................63

One Book and Twelve Books: The Nature of the Redactional
   Work and the Implications of Cultic Source Material in the
   Book of the Twelve...83

Not Just Another Nation: Obadiah's Placement in the Book of
   the Twelve..115

Thematic Explorations

Joel as "Literary Anchor" for the Book of the Twelve...............................137

The Day(s) of YHWH in the Book of the Twelve 157

Recurring Themes in the Book of the Twelve: Creating Points
   of Contact for a Theological Reading 181

Jerusalem, Samaria, and Bethel in the Book of the Twelve......................195

Intertextuality

Intertextuality and the Twelve 217

Zephaniah's Use of Genesis 1–11..241

Job and Joel: Divergent Voices on a Common Theme............................265

Textual Criticism and Tradition History

The Problematic Suffixes of Amos IX 11 281

Obadiah 7: Textual Corruption or Politically Charged Metaphor?........289

Reading David in the Psalter: A Study in Liturgical Hermeneutics 297

Bibliography...321
Ancient Sources Index..339
Modern Authors Index...361

Acknowledgments

I would like to express my gratitude to the journals and publishers with whom the original editions of the essays in this volume were published for allowing these essays to be published in a collection together: Bloomsbury Publishing, Gorgias Press, SBL Press, Walter de Gruyter Verlag, *Zeitschrift für die alttestamentliche Wissenschaft*, *Vetus Testamentum*, *Interpretation*, *Horizons in Biblical Theology*, and *Hebrew Bible and Ancient Israel*. The full bibliographic information appears on a separate page. Their cooperation and permission to reprint these essays made this book possible.

Original Publication Information

"The Day(s) of YHWH in the Book of the Twelve." Pages 192–213 in *Thematic Threads in the Book of the Twelve*. Edited by Paul L. Redditt and Aaron Schart. BZAW 325. Berlin: de Gruyter, 2003.

"Intertextuality and the Twelve." Pages 102–24 in *Forming Prophetic Literature: Essays on Isaiah and the Twelve in Honor of John D. W. Watts*. Edited by John W. Watts and Paul R. House. JSOTSup 235. Sheffield: Sheffield Academic, 1996.

"Jerusalem, Samaria, and Bethel in the Book of the Twelve." Pages 251–69 in *Die Stadt im Zwölfprophetenbuch*. Edited by Aaron Schart and Jutta Krispenz. BZAW 428. Berlin: de Gruyter, 2012.

"Job and Joel: Divergent Voices on a Common Theme." Pages 129–41 in *Reading Job Intertextually*. Edited by Katharine J. Dell and Will Kynes. LHBOTS 574. London: T&T Clark, 2013.

"Joel as 'Literary Anchor' for the Book of the Twelve." Pages 91–109 in *Reading and Hearing the Book of the Twelve*. Edited by James D. Nogalski and Marvin A. Sweeney. SymS 15. Atlanta: Society of Biblical Literature, 2000.

"Micah 7:8–20: Re-evaluating the Identity of the Enemy." Pages 125–42 in *The Bible as a Human Witness to Divine Revelation: Hearing the Word of God through Historically Dissimilar Traditions*. Edited by Randall Heskett and Brian Irwin. LHBOTS 469. London: T&T Clark, 2010.

"Not Just Another Nation: Obadiah's Placement in the Book of the Twelve." Pages 89–107 in *Perspectives on the Formation of the Book of the Twelve: Methodological Foundations, Redactional Processes, Historical Insights*. Edited by Rainer Albertz, James D. Nogalski, and Jakob Wöhrle. BZAW 433. Berlin: de Gruyter, 2012.

"Obadiah 7: Textual Corruption or Politically Charged Metaphor?" *ZAW* 110 (1998): 67–71.

"One Book and Twelve Books: The Nature of the Redactional Work and the Implications of Cultic Source Material in the Book of the Twelve."

Pages 11–46 in *Two Sides of a Coin: Juxtaposing Views on Interpreting the Book of The Twelve*. AnGor 201. Piscataway, NJ: Gorgias, 2009.

"The Problematic Suffixes of Amos IX 11." *VT* 43 (1993): 411–18.

"Reading David in the Psalter: A Study in Liturgical Hermeneutics." *HBT* 23 (2001): 168–91.

"Recurring Themes in the Book of the Twelve : Creating Points of Contact for a Theological Reading." *Int* 61 (2007): 125–36.

"The Redactional Shaping of Nahum 1 for the Book of the Twelve." Pages 193–202 in *Among the Prophets: Language, Image, and Structure in the Prophetic Writings*. Edited by Philip R. Davies and David J. A. Clines. Sheffield: JSOT Press, 1993.

"Zephaniah 3: A Redactional Text for a Developing Corpus." Pages 207–18 in *Schriftauslegung in der Schrift: Festschrift für Odil Hannes Steck zu seinem 65. Geburtstag*. Edited by Reinhard G. Kratz, Thomas Krüger, and Konrad Schmid. BZAW 300. Berlin: de Gruyter, 2000.

"Zephaniah's Use of Genesis 1–11." *HBAI* 2 (2013): 351–72.

"Zechariah 13:7–9 as a Transitional Text: An Appreciation and Re-evaluation of the Work of Rex Mason." Pages 292–304 in *Bringing Out the Treasure: Inner Biblical Allusion in Zechariah 9–14*. Edited by Mark J. Boda and Michael H. Floyd. JSOTSup 370. London: Sheffield Academic, 2003.

Abbreviations

AB	Anchor Bible
ANETS	Ancient Near Eastern Texts and Studies
AnGor	Analecta Gorgiana
AOTC	Abingdon Old Testament Commentaries
ATD	Das Alte Testament Deutsch
ATSAT	Arbeiten zu Text und Sprache im Alten Testament
BASOR	*Bulletin of the American Schools of Oriental Research*
B. Bat.	Bava Batra
BEATAJ	Beiträge zur Erforschung des Alten Testaments und des antiken Judentum
BETL	Bibliotheca Ephemeridum Theologicarum Lovaniensium
BHS	*Biblia Hebraica Stuttgartensia*. Edited by Karl Elliger and Wilhelm Rudolph. Stuttgart: Deutsche Bibelgesellschaft, 1983.
BiE	Biblische Enzyklopädie
BibS(N)	Biblische Studien (Neukirchen)
BKAT	Biblischer Kommentary, Altes Testament
BN	*Biblische Notizen*
BZAW	Beihefte zur Zeitschrift für altorientalische und biblische Rechtsgeschichte
c	common
C. Ap.	Josephus *Contra Apion*
CAT	Commentaire de l'Ancien Testament
CBQ	*Catholic Biblical Quarterly*
CBQMS	Catholic Biblical Quarterly Monograph Series
CC	Continental Commentaries
ConBOT	Coniectanea Biblica: Old Testament Series
CurBR	*Currents in Biblical Research*
DtrH	Deuteronomistic History
Eng.	English

f	feminine
FAT	Forschungen zum Alten Testament
FOTL	Forms of Old Testament Literature
FRLANT	Forschungen zur Religion und Literature des Alten und Neuen Testaments
HAT	Handbuch zum Alten Testament
HerBS	Herders biblische Studien
HDR	Harvard Dissertations in Religion
HTR	*Harvard Theological Review*
IDBSup	*Interpreter's Dictionary of the Bible: Supplementary Volume.* Edited by Keith Crim. Nashville: Abingdon, 1976.
Int	*Interpretation*
ITC	International Theological Commentary
JBL	*Journal of Biblical Literature*
JETS	*Journal of the Evangelical Theological Society*
JSOTSup	Journal for the Study of the Old Testament Supplement Series
JSS	*Journal of Semitic Studies*
JTS	*Journal of Theological Studies*
KAT	Kommentar zum Alten Testament
KHC	Kurzer Hand-Commentar zum Alten Testament
KUT	Kohlhammer Urban-Taschenbücher
LCBI	Literary Currents in Biblical Interpretation
LHBOTS	Library of Hebrew Bible/Old Testament Studies
LSTS	Library of Second Temple Studies
LXX	Septuagint
m	masculine
MLBS	Mercer Library of Biblical Studies
MT	Masoretic Text
n	neuter
NCB	New Century Bible
NIBCOT	New International Bible Commentary on the Old Testament
NICOT	New International Commentary on the Old Testament
NIDB	*New Interpreter's Dictionar of the Bible.* Edited by Katherine Doob Sakenfeld. 5 vols. Nashville: Abingdon, 2006–2009.
NSKAT	Neuer Stuttgarter Kommentar, Altes Testament
OAN	Oracles against the nations (e.g., Zeph 2:4–15)
OBO	Orbis Biblicus et Orientalis

OTL	Old Testament Library
OTS	Old Testament Studies
p	plural
PRSt	*Perspectives in Religious Studies*
RB	*Revue biblique*
RBS	Resources for Biblical Study
ROT	Reading the Old Testament
RST	Regensburger Studien zur Theologie
s	singular
SamDalp	Sammlung Dalp
SBLDS	Society of Biblical Literature Dissertation Series
SBLMS	Society of Biblical Literature Monograph Series
SBLSP	Society of Biblical Literature Seminar Papers
SBS	Stuttgarter Bibelstudien
ScEccl	*Sciences ecclésiastiques*
SemeiaSt	Semeia Studies
SHBC	Smyth & Helwys Bible Commentary
SJCA	Studies of Judaism and Christianity in Antiquity
SSN	Studia Semitica Neerlandica
SThL	Sammlung theologischer Lehrbücher
SymS	Symposium Series
TLZ	*Theologische Literaturzeitung*
TRE	*Theologische Realenzyklopädie*. Edited by Gerhard Krause and Gerhard Müller. Berlin: de Gruyter, 1977–.
UCOP	University of Cambridge Oriental Publications
VT	*Vetus Testamentum*
VTSup	Supplements to Vetus Testamentum
WBC	Word Biblical Commentary
WMANT	Wissenschaftliche Monographien zum Alten und Neuen Testament
ZAW	*Zeitschrift für die alttestamentliche Wissenschaft*
ZDMG	*Zeitschrift der Deutschen Morgenländischen Gesellschaft*
ZS	*Zeitschrift für Semitistik und verwandte Gebiete*
ZTK	*Zeitschrift für Theologie und Kirche*

Introduction to *The Book of the Twelve and Beyond*: Authorial Reflections

Background

I have been actively involved in the study of the Book of the Twelve since 1985, when I naively decided to begin exploration of this topic for my master's thesis. As I write this introduction in the summer of 2016 realizing I will turn sixty later this year, I am reminded that I have been working on this topic for more than half of my life. This decision to explore the Book of the Twelve was not preplanned. Rather, it took shape gradually as the result of an offhand comment by a seminary professor, some nascent curiosity, and a fortuitous set of circumstances that landed me in an academic context in Switzerland that was uniquely situated to prepare me to deal with such a topic.

Before moving to Switzerland in 1985 to do a ThM in Hebrew Bible, I had the good fortune to take a class that worked through the Hebrew text of Malachi. One day while waxing eloquent on an unrelated topic the professor, J. J. Owens, paused and said, "You know, there is an ancient Jewish tradition that treats the Minor Prophets as a single book, and I have often wondered if there's anything to that." It turns out that his intuition may have been right. Incidentally, Paul House was in that same class, and unbeknown to either one of us, he would also pursue the topic independently of my own endeavors, working from a synchronic literary perspective in the form of a monograph and several essays of his own.[1] At any rate, I remembered that comment, and when it came time to select a thesis topic

---

1. Paul R. House, *The Unity of the Twelve*, JSOTSup 97 (Sheffield: Almond Press, 1990).

several years later, I convinced my thesis advisor to allow me to explore this question even if it might lead to a dead-end.

Looking back, I could hardly have been more fortunate in choosing a context in which to pursue questions regarding how prophetic books attained the shape in which they now exist. Whereas my training in America had provided me with linguistic skills in Hebrew and Greek, along with a strong emphasis upon explaining the final form of the text, it left me with many unanswered historical questions about how these texts came to be. I remain extraordinarily grateful for this early training and more grateful still for the opportunity to study in Europe for six years, where the methodological focus upon the diachronic processes that shaped the text of the Hebrew Bible were receiving renewed, systematic, and rigorous attention. Unknown to me at the time, nowhere was this more in evidence than at the University of Zürich, where the two Hebrew Bible professors, O. H. Steck and H. H. Schmid, conducted a biweekly discussion group (*Sozietät*) among faculty and PhD students exploring topics of mutual interest through the discussion of common readings and formal papers. I was fortunate that they invited me (through my ThM advisor) to participate in these discussions even while I was still a master's student. It was in this academic context that I first met Reinhard Kratz, Eric Bosshard, Hermann Spieckermann, and Konrad Schmid from the University of Zürich in addition to the aforementioned professors Steck and Schmid. Relatedly, I benefited greatly from the tutelage of my master's supervisor Hans Mallau, who first invited me to attend the sessions, and from my colleague Mark Biddle who continued to explore these questions in the context of Jeremiah. I mention these people specifically because we have sometimes been lumped together as the "Zürich School," a name that is both erroneous and significant. We were never a school in the sense that we produced a consistent, unified theory of the development of the prophetic corpus. We were a school, if by that one means that we were a community in conversation asking similar questions, a community that pushed one another, challenged one another, corrected one another, and learned from one another. Theses were put forth during these meetings that would become foundational for the projects we were pursuing at the time. I am grateful to have been a part of this academic crucible. My own ideas about the redactional implications of catchwords were certainly deepened by these conversations.

The work on the Book of the Twelve would not, however, have continued to develop if my work remained just another dissertation consigned to the dusty shelves of an old library somewhere. The broadening of this conversation took off, I believe, for two primary reasons. First, other scholars, working independently, began pursuing questions related to the formation and purpose of the Book of the Twelve. Second, someone had the foresight and the energy to bring these and other people together in the context of an extended conversation that has taken place in the Society of Biblical Literature. That person was John D. W. Watts. At the Annual Meeting of the Society Biblical Literature in 1992, Watts arranged a dinner for more than a dozen scholars from very different backgrounds with the purpose of petitioning the Society of Biblical Literature for a spot on the program. Watts had only recently retired as a full-time faculty member, but he remained actively involved in the work of this group for nearly another decade. The group he assembled included senior scholars like himself, several who already were in the middle of their careers (such as Paul R. Redditt), and others of us who recently completed or were in the midst of completing their own works on some aspect of this topic. This latter assemblage of scholars included Barry Jones (PhD, Duke), Russell Fuller (PhD, Harvard), Aaron Schart (*Habilitationsschrift*, Marburg, Germany), Paul House (a former student of Watts who had already published his monograph in 1990), and myself (Zürich). The Society of Biblical Literature approved our petition and the group has remained an active part of the Annual Meeting program, starting as a consultation, then a seminar, and then a group. From the beginning, this group sought to foster serious dialogue (by proponents and skeptics alike), to include both synchronic and diachronic methods, and to seek participants from geographically diverse locations. Watts and House were keen to make sure that synchronic approaches were represented, and Schart was instrumental in recruiting people from Europe to contribute to our meetings.

These conversations under the auspices of the Society of Biblical Literature led directly to three published collections of essays presented at these Annual Meetings.[2] Further, these sessions and publications led to broader networks of scholars including international seminars in Geneva,

---

2. James W. Watts and Paul R. House, eds., *Forming Prophetic Literature: Essays on Isaiah and the Twelve in Honor of John D. W Watts*, JSOTSup 235 (Sheffield: Sheffield Academic, 1996); James D. Nogalski and Marvin A. Sweeney, eds., *Reading and Hearing the Book of the Twelve*, SymS 15 (Atlanta: Society of Biblical Literature, 2000); and Paul L. Redditt and Aaron Schart, eds., *Thematic Threads in the Book of the Twelve*, BZAW 325 (Berlin: de Gruyter, 2003).

Switzerland (2009) and Münster, Germany (2011). It is in the context of these meetings and publications that a substantial number of the essays in this volume first appeared. Recently, conferences have also taken place in Metz, France (2015) and Louvain, Belgium (2016). Somewhere along the way, the conversations changed from merely whether or not one could meaningfully speak of the Twelve as some type of composite literary unit/collection/anthology/book and began to include questions regarding what happens when one reads these twelve prophetic writings together. Of course, questions about the developmental stages of the Twelve and its component parts remained a vital part of the conversation as well. In addition, I was frequently asked to contribute essays on some aspect of the Twelve for other projects. Many of these essays dealt with issues I was exploring during the decade I devoted to writing my two-volume commentary on the Book of the Twelve (2001–2011).[3] Hence, this collection of essays comes from a broadly distributed series of venues that very few people have seen in their entirety. I am very grateful to SBL Press and to Thomas Römer, the editor of the Ancient Israel and Its Literature series for their willingness to publish these essays together as I near my sixtieth birthday in hopes that as a group they can stimulate conversation regarding the intersection of various methods that have formed the core of Biblical studies (text criticism, source criticism, form criticism, redaction history, tradition history), as well as more recent approaches that have enhanced the discipline (synchronic literary analysis, intertextuality, metaphor theory, and sociological studies—the latter particularly as it relates to the issue of scribal training).

Foundations, Assumptions, and Changes in One Author's Work

In looking back over the work of one's professional life, especially when trying to contextualize essays published over nearly a quarter of a century, one could be tempted to articulate the connections between the essays as though they followed some kind of master plan that proceeded logically and coherently toward a destination. Such was not the case for me for my scholarship probably benefited more from the search than a plan would have allowed. That being said, reflecting upon the essays in

---

3. James D. Nogalski, *The Book of the Twelve: Hosea–Jonah*, SHBC (Macon, GA: Smyth & Helwys, 2011); Nogalski, *The Book of the Twelve: Micah–Malachi*, SHBC (Macon, GA: Smyth & Helwys, 2011).

this collection does allow some patterns to emerge. At least three observations seem worth noting. First, the genesis of my own work was crucial, and clearly the early stages of my scholarship were controlled by questions I was asking in the dissertation. Second, context matters. Third, methodological tools serve a purpose. They are not an end in themselves, but a lens through which diverse aspects of the interpretive process may be explored.

The genesis of my work on the Book of the Twelve, even in retrospect, strikes me as something of a quest. It began simply enough with the need to find a topic for my master's thesis, and I already related how an offhand comment from a professor became the catalyst for selecting this topic. Yet, moving forward required at least three separate, but interrelated, search processes: finding a point of entry, an approach suitable for that entry point, and a voice with which to express it.

Finding a point of entry was a daunting procedure. What drew me to the topic was simply curiosity. What happened to this tradition of the Book of the Twelve? Is there anything that binds these writings together as some kind of book? Researching the former turned out to be far simpler than the latter. Yet, through the process of reading, rereading, and rereading again, I was struck one evening at how frequently the end of one book contained clusters of words that reappeared at the beginning of the next book. I began focusing upon these catchwords as the focal point around which to try to make a contribution. In a sense, the questions that propelled me also structured the work itself. This work attempted to document a historical tradition lost and catchwords found as key components for understanding the scroll of the Twelve Prophets.

Finding an approach, while less daunting than finding a point of entry, proved to be every bit as significant. Since I had been studying the Hebrew Bible for a number of years already, I often resonated with the works of authors that seemed to point at one level in opposing directions: a holistic approach that dealt with the final form of the text, and a fascination with the historical details that suggested a long process of redactional work that shaped the final form of the canon. The work of such scholars were well represented at the time by Brevard Childs and Hans-Walter Wolff.

The work of Childs already began to change the conversation. Childs's *Introduction to the Old Testament as Scripture* appeared in 1979, in which he issued a clarion call to Old Testament scholars around three thematic pivot points: (1) to explain the final form of the text; (2) to recognize that the process that shaped the final form of the book was at its heart a theological process; and (3) to understand that those who shaped the books were themselves members of a community of faith whose commitments shaped how they saw their task.[4] At the same time, Childs grew weary of historical investigations seeking the original forms that may have existed behind the text we currently have. In his process, he essentially insisted that scholars accept the critical consensus—as he understood it—regarding the likelihood that biblical books came about in stages; that they abandon the fruitless search to describe that process; and that they focus instead upon the final form of the text as the real conveyor of theological meaning. Even as a novice scholar of the Hebrew Bible, Childs's emphasis on the final form made sense to me; downplaying the diachronic elements, however, did not.

One of the first critical commentaries I worked through in detail was Wolff's commentary on Joel and Amos.[5] It appeared to me that Wolff largely succeeded in the task of explaining the final form as a theological enterprise, but one that came about in stages that could be isolated and examined. For Wolff, each stage added a new dimension to the final form. These stages included shaping the book as we have it, but also recognizing that the theological convictions of the editors could change radically over time. How else could one describe the series of promises at the end of the book of Amos that differ so drastically from the words of finality and judgment in the remainder of the book? The work of Wolff, it seemed to me, sought historical plausibility and allowed the diachronic processes to be heard as part of the theological meaning one might derive from the book. These processes helped to shape the book, in terms of accounting for collections of sayings as well as longer compositions; in terms of recognizing later materials that commented upon existing texts; and in terms of wrestling with the combination of the divergent voices which this process left behind.

The works of three other authors also had a significant impact upon me as I was fashioning the dissertation. I was exposed to the work of Michael Fishbane and his treatment of inner biblical exegesis.[6] This work

---

4. Brevard S. Childs, *Introduction to the Old Testament as Scripture* (Philadelphia: Fortress, 1979).

5. Hans Walter Wolff, *Joel and Amos: A Commentary on the Books of the Prophets Joel and Amos*, trans. Samuel Dean McBride Jr., Hermeneia (Philadelphia: Fortress, 1977).

6. Michael Fishbane, *Biblical Interpretation in Ancient Israel* (Oxford: Clarendon, 1985).

documents a compelling case that the interpretation of biblical traditions already began within the texts of the Hebrew Bible itself. The instances of texts interpreting other texts that he pulled together provided a systematic glance into some of the interpretive functions served by later commentators who augmented biblical traditions in a number of ways. I found his work within the Torah to be far more developed and comprehensive than his relatively brief chapter treating the prophetic writings as mantalogical exegesis.[7]

Walther Zimmerli published a very insightful article in 1979 that ruminated on the process involved in moving from a prophetic speech to a prophetic book.[8] Zimmerli succinctly described how a significant number of the prophetic writings contain smaller units that moved thematically from judgment to promise. He concluded, quite naturally, that this pattern could hardly be accidental. While a number of scholars point to the shortcomings of his suggestions in terms of not accounting for every detail, his work nevertheless articulated the heuristic value regarding large structures underpinning prophetic literature that often went unnoticed.[9] From Zimmerli, I learned that holistic structures go beyond linguistic arguments alone.

The influence of my mentor at Zürich, Steck, upon my work was profound. A student of Gerhard von Rad, Steck's own work began as an extension of the tradition history project at Heidelberg by tracing the tradition (literarily and chronologically) of the violent destiny of the prophets from its appearance in the Hebrew Bible through the numerous places it occurred in Jewish and Christian literary works produced in the Hellenistic and Greco-Roman periods, including the New Testament. As significant as this work proved to be, Steck made lasting contributions to other significant areas that had a more direct impact upon my own dissertation: his long-standing interest in methodological transparency and his own groundbreaking work on the redaction of the entire Isaiah scroll.

---

7. Ibid., 458–99.

8. Walther Zimmerli, "Vom Prophetenwort zum Prophetenbuch," *TLZ* 104 (1979): 481–96.

9. See, e.g., already the critique by Erhard S. Gerstenberger, "'Gemeindebildung' in Prophetenbüchern? Beobachtungen und Überlegungen zum Traditions- und Redaktionsprozeß prophetischer Schriften," in *Prophet und Prophetenbuch: Festschrift für Otto Kaiser zum 65. Geburtstag*, ed. Volkmar Fritz, Karl-Friedrich Pohlmann, and Hans-Christoph Schmitt, BZAW 185 (Berlin: de Gruyter, 1989), 47–48.

Above all, for Steck, process mattered. If one sought to interpret a text holistically, as Steck's students were encouraged to do, one required a holistic method capable of handling such tasks. The exegetical task began by taking seriously the text-critical evidence, even though at the time work with Septuagint texts as literary products in their own right was not as widely studied as it is today and conversations about the pluraformity of textual traditions behind the MT were only beginning to receive attention.[10] The process of determining whether the final form of a text reflected a homogenous or a heterogeneous piece of literature could not be assumed from the outset. The biblical scholar could only draw such conclusions through a careful intertwining of methodological tasks that included *Literarkritik*, form criticism, tradition history, transmission history, and redaction history. These tools are used analytically and synthetically to first determine as far as possible the shape of the earliest written and oral forms of the material, before making the return trip, putting the pieces back together step-by-step in order to offer explanations for how the text came to be.

The second, and perhaps most fortuitous, area of Steck's expertise that influenced my own work was his ongoing investigation of the book of Isaiah as a redacted whole. For generations, particularly in European programs, scholars recognized three primary settings about which the material in the book of Isaiah was concerned: events from the last third of the eighth century BCE (which appears prominently in chapters 1–39), material from the mid-sixth century BCE that mention Cyrus of Persia by name and hopefully anticipates an imminent return to Jerusalem (which largely comprises chapters 40–55), and material that presumes a functioning Jerusalem temple and exhibits signs of serious disagreements among the population that once again lived in Judah (essentially, chapters 56–66). It remained quite common at this point for scholars to treat these chapters largely in isolation from one another. Steck was one of a handful of scholars at the time who challenged these assumptions, arguing instead that the editorial work actually sought to integrate this material in a way that affected each of the three major blocks. He brought a keen eye to this task, both with his observational skills and his ability to synthesize pertinent observations from the works of others into his own analysis. His

---

10. One has to remember that even by the mid-1980s, study of the Qumran documents was largely controlled by a small cadre of scholars who had the difficult task of trying to piece together thousands of fragments.

ability to draw together profiles of theological agendas that spanned all sixty-six chapters of the book remains impressive. He popularized the idea that "bridge texts" could be composed in key positions by those who added later texts in order to summarize certain thematic elements from the existing corpus while simultaneously foreshadowing the emphases of the new collection that was being added.[11] He also taught his students to ask questions about the literary horizon of a text rather than to assume the text merely represents someone's abbreviated memory of a short prophetic speech that was simply recorded for posterity.

I am cognizant of how deeply the works of these scholars affected my own research. They are certainly not alone, however, for all of us who work in this discipline build upon the work of those who precede us.

The third aspect of the quest upon which I set out for which I had to find a voice was discovering a means to contribute constructively to the discipline. In hindsight, one of the more distinctive aspects of the dissertation that carried over into the essays (especially the early ones) was the tenor of the work as an investigation. I did not recognize this element myself. Rather, a number of people through the years expressed to me their sense that the dissertation read something like a detective novel. I suspect that this quality probably developed because of the nature of the task. I began with a question, not with a theory. Could these recurring words at the literary seams of the Twelve offer insight into how the twelve prophetic writings became a book? I tried, as best I could, to follow the evidence. Undoubtedly, the tenor of investigative inquiry about which several people spoke to me derived not by design, but by the sense that I was beginning a quest. As the project began to extend beyond the dissertation and into the circle of the Society of Biblical Literature Book of the Twelve groups, I frequently found myself in the 1990s thinking in two directions simultaneously: recruitment and progress.

Being part of the steering committees of the Book of the Twelve consultation, seminars, and group I had the good fortune to work with colleagues to carry on extended conversations from year to year. We invited skeptics as well as proponents into the dialogue. Often these discussions were animated, and they were almost always illuminating for those of us

---

11. The most notable example would be his treatment of Isa 34–35 in the relatively thin volume entitled Odil Hannes Steck, *Bereitete Heimkehr: Jesaja 35 als redaktionelle Brücke zwischen dem Ersten und dem Zweiten Jesaja*, SBS 121 (Stuttgart: Katholisches Bibelwerk, 1985).

interested in the formation of the Book of the Twelve. Many of the essays in this volume began first as presentations for these meetings. Early on, one can detect in some of these essays the need to justify the endeavor. I felt as though it was incumbent upon me to explain the tradition of the Twelve as a single book written on a single scroll. Somewhere along the way, however, that changed as others joined the group and the Twelve took its place alongside Isaiah, Jeremiah, and Ezekiel in the program of the Annual Meetings. I do not mean to imply by this statement that suddenly the discipline found consensus on the nature and function of the Book of the Twelve, only that increasingly it became clear that the question of the role of the individual books/collections/writings within the scroll is a topic that could not be swept aside without some comment. In the process of these extended discussions, new avenues of interpretation arose that extended well beyond the question of catchword associations. Scholars began to investigate recurring themes across the Twelve that provided it with a distinctive character, especially when compared with the themes of the other three prophetic scrolls. Relatedly, broader questions engendered considerable exploration concerning the nature of intertextuality, and how one speaks about allusions, echoes, and recurring metaphors in prophetic literature. In a sense, then, my own work moved from the question "is there a *book* of the Twelve" to a related question: "How does one read it?" Finally, in the last decade my work on the Twelve has increasingly turned to sociological and historical questions related to the ways that prophets, their literary legacies, scribes, and cult become intertwined during the Persian period. None of these issues arose in a vacuum, and in many respects were largely shaped by parallel conversations going on elsewhere in the study of the Hebrew Bible. This larger context itself deserves some reflection.

The Larger Conversation

In the early and mid-1990s, diachronic and synchronic debates raged for a number of years in biblical studies. What was unusual, perhaps, concerning the Society of Biblical Literature sessions on the Book of the Twelve was the fact that from the beginning, these sessions created space at the table to have these conversations in a less strident manner than happened in some other contexts.

As indicated above in the discussion of Childs, claiming a goal of the discipline to find ways to explain the final form of the text is a task worthy of extended conversations, evaluation, and proposals. At the same time, speaking of the final form of the text becomes considerably more complicated when dealing with the question of the Book of the Twelve. How does one talk about the final form of Hosea, for example, in the Book of the Twelve without some type of diachronic model? To speak synchronically of the role of Hosea in the Book of the Twelve places Hosea on the same compositional level as Haggai, Zechariah, and Malachi, yet Hosea claims to be a record of the word of YHWH to a prophet in the eighth century BCE, while the last three all presuppose a Persian period setting two to three centuries later. Wrestling with such questions helps one to understand the context of several of the articles in this collection. As someone trained in an exegetical process that began and ended with the final form of the text, I had no difficulty in understanding the importance such studies could have. At the same time, approaching texts in the Twelve only with an eye toward synchronic patterns places severe limitations on what one can say historically, unless one also combines this task with careful diachronic analysis. Some of the problems in these early discussions had to do with clarifying the limits of each approach, even while respecting the perspective each brought to the task. I have certainly found it helpful to explore observations more synchronically on occasion, as is particularly evident in the essays on intertextuality and the "The Day(s) of YHWH in the Book of the Twelve."

It should therefore be clear that from the beginning, I think my work has attempted to take seriously synchronic calls for the importance of the final form, yet I have always resisted the move toward a complete historical skepticism. Prophetic texts did not drop magically from the sky as fully formed pieces of literature. They underwent (sometimes lengthy) processes of preservation, collection, ordering, combining, and updating. Some of the writings in the Twelve probably have their origins in oral settings, but most of the writings in this scroll represent literary reflections, though some of these may be quite early (e.g., the first four visions of Amos that reflect intricate literary patterns of repetition, paronomasia, and climax as a group). I have learned much, for example, from the writings of Ehud ben Zvi whose critiques have pushed me to consider how the process of reading and rereading early traditions shaped the postmonarchic final forms of the text. At the same time, I do not agree with him, as is evident from several of these essays, that this process must be restricted to the final form of the individual writings; nor do I share his rather radical rejection of the task of trying to piece together scenarios through which this process may have taken place.

By the end of the 1990s, a stasis of sorts began to take shape which affirmed the necessity of both the shape of the final form and the historical processes that created them. Conversations in the 2000s gradually shifted from exploring the various ways the individual writings link (or can be linked) to one another genetically and/or contextually to the broader scribal culture that produced the prophetic books.

My own work in this movement benefited not merely from the ongoing conversations of those working on the Book of the Twelve in the Society of Biblical Literature, but from the significant works of other scholars as well. Most importantly, perhaps, my own thinking has been shaped in significant ways by the investigations of three scholars in particular. I was certainly influenced by one of Steck's later works where he extensively dealt with the theological shaping of the book as book.[12] Additionally, the treatments of the development of scribal culture by Karel van der Toorn and David Carr had a profound impact upon my own thinking in ways that I am continuing to develop.[13] To be sure, to speak of a prophetic "book" can be anachronistic because the physical form of a scroll is not the same as a book and because the largely poetic forms of the material within the Twelve defy narrative conventions (e.g., plot) that help other portions of the Hebrew Bible which also draw upon composite forms (e.g., the Torah and the Former Prophets in both their individual forms as scrolls and the collective form often now called the Enneateuch). Nevertheless, Steck's conviction that prophetic books—especially Isaiah and the Twelve—derive meaning from their chronological and epochal flow, as well as a metahistorical perspective implicit in prophetic speech still rings true to me.[14] In short, the message of the whole collection requires recognizing the nature of the final form of the collection and its constituent parts.

The essays in this volume are arranged methodologically and chronologically in the hopes that the arrangement might facilitate dialogue and be helpful for those wishing to use this collection in a classroom setting.

---

12. Odil Hannes Steck, *The Prophetic Books and Their Theological Witness*, trans. James D. Nogalski (St. Louis: Chalice, 2000).

13. Karel van der Toorn, *Scribal Culture and the Making of the Hebrew Bible* (Cambridge: Harvard University Press, 2007); David M. Carr, *Writing on the Tablet of the Heart: Origins of Scripture and Literature* (Oxford: Oxford University Press, 2005); and Carr, *The Formation of the Hebrew Bible: A New Reconstruction* (Oxford: Oxford University Press, 2011).

14. Steck, *Prophetic Books*, 44–52.

The first grouping of articles deals with redactional issues. The majority of these essays deal with particular texts and the redactional role that they play within the individual writing and the larger corpus of the Twelve. The last two essays in this section, however, expand the discussion further into the function of the redactional work in creating meaning among and between the writings. The second section explores several of the collective themes that transcend the individual writings within the Book of the Twelve. These essays dialogue more extensively with the synchronic work of others, as well as a treatment of the changing roles of Jerusalem, Samaria, and Bethel as they appear in the Twelve as a whole. The third section contains three essays involving diverse aspects of intertextuality: an early attempt to clarify some of the terminology regarding the ways in which prophetic texts within the Twelve relate to one another, and two more recent explorations of intertextuality relating texts inside the Twelve to texts outside the Twelve. The first of these texts illustrates an author-centered approach to intertextuality, while the second draws upon a reader-centered intertextuality.[15] The final grouping of essays presents two relatively short text critical articles and a longer study on the role of David in the Psalter.

The two text critical essays illustrate my early fascination with text critical issues in poetic texts. Particularly in the Twelve, I have long suspected that ancient translators and modern scholars alike have struggled to articulate what can appear to be difficult texts by simply rewriting those texts or ignoring the problem. Yet, when compared to Jeremiah and Ezekiel, the text of the Twelve Prophets appears considerably more stable, especially when dealing with unpointed texts. Divergences in the ancient translations do not always require the assumption that the translator was working from a different *Vorlage*. In the case of Amos 9:11, scholars often describe the MT as corrupt because of what at first glance appears to be an incoherent use of three different suffixes referring back to the same antecedent phrase. Yet, I show that, far from representing the earliest reading, the consistency of suffixes in the LXX simply ignores the problem. I then suggest a solution to the problem that recognizes that poetic texts can play with artistic expressions. Concerning Obad 7, I demonstrate that the nearly ubiquitous assumption of modern transla-

---

15. See discussion of these issues in Geoffrey David Miller, "Intertextuality in Old Testament Research," *CurBR* 9 (2011): 283–309. I find intrinsic value can be found in both types of intertextual research so long as one recognizes the difference.

tors of the need for emending the MT creates a largely ignored syntactical problem. By contrast, I suggest that the text of the MT actually makes sense when one recognizes ancient poets could have assumed different associations for certain words than modern commentators typically recognize. In both of these instances, one can see how modern assumptions can actually create problems that did not exist for the ancient authors of these texts.

Some might wonder about the final essay since it seemingly has nothing to do with the formation of the Book of the Twelve. I opted to include this essay for methodological reasons that in many respects illustrate in a targeted way what happens when various methodological tools are applied in controlled dialogue with one another rather than in isolation from other methods. In a real sense, this essay presumes results of redaction history and form criticism, while at the same time exploring the historical and literary implications of ten superscriptions in the Psalter seen diachronically through the lenses of tradition history, intertextuality, and reader-response approaches. Scholars have long treated these superscriptions as scribal additions that were appended after the songs were composed. These superscriptions share a common feature that has rarely been considered in the commentaries on the Psalter. Namely, these superscriptions refer to specific events in the life of David (but these narrative episodes are recounted in the Deuteronomistic History, not in Chronicles).

Scholars are equally convinced that, in all probability, the original composition of these psalms did not occur with the event of David's life in view that appears in the superscription. Rather, the scribes who added these superscriptions want the reader to hear the following psalm in light of the episode from David's life to which it points. The concluding essay in this volume seeks to fill a gap in Psalms scholarship while at the same time implicitly bringing in issues that have arisen in conversations on the Book of the Twelve regarding the shifting dynamics that take place when originally independent poems are deliberately appended to literary works in a new context. The addition of a preexisting psalm is widely recognized to have happened in the process of transmission for Jonah 2, Nah 1, and Hab 3. Further, this case in the Psalter represents explicit forms of ancient intertextuality since the superscriptions in question point specifically to narrative episodes from David's life and asks the reader to draw associations from those stories while reading the psalm. Seen in this light, the superscriptions thus become concrete starting points for intertextuality and reader response, but not in the typical sense where these approaches focus upon the role of the modern interpreter. Rather, this essay asks "how" and "what" questions regarding the ancient reader who added the superscriptions. How would these ancient scribes have read these psalms in order to associate them with the life of David, and relatedly, what picture develops of David when one does so? I hope that by including this essay, it will stimulate discussion about preexisting sources in the Book of the Twelve, not just for the aforementioned psalms but in other cases where preexisting sources play a role in the composition of the books within the Twelve, such as Obad 1–5 (cf. Jer 49:14–16, 9), Mic 4:1–4 (cf. Isa 2:2–4), and other passages where scholars suggest that material existed in written form before its inclusion in its current location within the books constituting the Twelve. Source criticism in prophetic literature has changed dramatically since its origins in the late nineteenth and early twentieth centuries when it primarily functioned as a vehicle attempting (and failing) to reach the *ipsissima verba* of the divinely inspired prophet. Today, the work of source criticism can help isolate the building blocks used to construct prophetic literature as we have it, thereby shedding light upon the agenda of those collecting, arranging, and adapting prophetic collections over time.

What Has Been Accomplished?

It is hard to believe as I write this paragraph that I finished the dissertation a full quarter century ago, in July 1991. Much has happened in the world of the Book of the Twelve during these twenty-five years. Schart has, for years, maintained an online bibliography of the Book of the Twelve in both an alphabetical and a chronological format. In 2007 I was struck when I noticed that my two-volume dissertation that appeared in 1993 fell halfway down the first page of the chronological listing. What surprised me, however, was that the bibliography had grown to over ten pages. This list has continued to grow, as interest in the topic has continued to a new generation. In many respects, this extended concentration of scholarly investigation has produced concrete results. In other respects, such investigations still seem to be in their infancy as new implications, questions, and approaches become part of the conversation. At the same time, other scholars have expressed caution or skepticism concerning such investigations. I have no doubt both of these realities will continue for the near future. I would, however, offer a few brief comments on some of these developments.

First, conversations regarding the Twelve as a corpus of some type are certainly much more embedded within the discipline than they were twenty-five years ago. This statement does not mean unanimity has been achieved, but very few doubt that the question deserves further scrutiny in the quest for clarity. The long-neglected tradition that these twelve writings were written on a single scroll and counted as a single book is now much more widely known, and this knowledge forces every serious scholarly treatment of these twelve writings to mention this tradition.

Second, debate continues regarding the nature of the scroll. For many who have been involved in these investigations, the intertwining of these twelve writings seems best explained as the work of creative scribes involved at various levels in the composition, shaping, and positioning of the writings within the scroll itself. Others prefer to assume the genesis of the books within the Twelve took more isolated routes, but they recognize that the placement of these books within the scroll was not random. I do believe that the recognition of the nonrandom arrangement of these writings represents an enduring legacy, the implications of which will continue to pique the curiosity of scholars.

Third, scholars will continue to explore the question of the stages by which the twelve came to be. A number of proposals emerged in the past decades. New ones may also appear, but the next stage will also likely begin to compare these models with one another, to suggest refinements, and undoubtedly advance the project. My own initial proposal offers a case in point. I built upon the work of others who recognized the common editing of Haggai and Zech 1–8 and referred to this group of two as a "literary precursor" to the Twelve. I was also influenced by a number of studies in the 1970s and 1980s that talked about "Deuteronomistic" editing within the isolated collections of Hosea, Amos, Micah, and Zephaniah, and I intuited that such editing did not likely occur in isolation as those studies assumed. I therefore referred to this group of four as a "Deuteronomistic corpus" that also served as a literary precursor and, together with Haggai and Zech 1–8, provided the chronological skeleton of what came to be the Twelve. This suggestion was both enhanced and critiqued by Schart, Rainer Albertz, and Jakob Wöhrle.[16] At the core of the critique was my unreflec-

---

16. Aaron Schart, *Die Entstehung des Zwölfprophetenbuchs: Neubearbeitungen von Amos im Rahmen schriftenübergreifender Redaktionsprozesse*, BZAW 260 (Berlin: de Gruyter, 1998), 156–233; Rainer Albertz, *Die Exilzeit: 6. Jahrhundert v. Chr*, BiE 7 (Stuttgart: Kohlhammer, 2001), 164–85; Jakob Wöhrle, *Die frühen Sammlungen des*

tive acceptance of the term *Deuteronomistic* as a heuristic term to describe this corpus because some of the editing, in my opinion, showed knowledge of traditions in Kings. Schart, Albertz, and Wöhrle, in different ways, challenged the appropriateness of that term even while accepting the idea that these four writings were transmitted and edited together. As a result, I have adopted the more generic terminology of Albertz, who simply called this corpus "*das Vierprophetenbuch*" (the Four Prophets Book). I remain fascinated by the outlines of this corpus, its integration and contrast of the northern and southern kingdoms, and its juxtaposition of judgment and hope when read against the backdrop of the story of Judah and Israel. The models, agendas, and social settings of this corpus at its various stages, and its relationship to what ultimately became the Twelve beg for further study. I have no doubt that some of this work is already underway. Still, a growing number of scholars now recognize this Book of Four Prophets as a literary context that deserves to be explored.

Fourth, the synchronic shape and recurring themes within the Twelve has drawn the attention of a number of scholars working with decidedly literary methods. These scholars have greatly enhanced our understanding of how this scroll can be read as a composite literary entity capable of conveying meaning in its own right. Within discussions of the Book of the Twelve, the blending and respective limits of synchronic and diachronic approaches have been part of the conversation from the outset. Much conversation in the early years of this work centered on terminology and focus used by the various approaches. Synchronic approaches to the Twelve have become more sophisticated through the years, as they continue to explore the ways in which the final form of the corpus speaks to its readers without necessarily implying that the unifying elements came about as the deliberate act of some grand unifying editor. At the same time, scholars working with more diachronic approaches have benefited from the insights of those who have focused on synchronic readings. Such synchronic approaches continued to push diachronic scholarship to account for the final form of the text and not just hypothetical reconstructions of the stages along the way.

Finally, work on the Book of the Twelve has both influenced and benefited from broader discussions concerning the identities and social settings

---

Zwölfprophetenbuches: Entstehung und Komposition, BZAW 360 (Berlin: de Gruyter, 2006), 19–20, 51–284.

of the scribal groups who were ultimately responsible for the dissemination of the prophetic corpus as a whole. I have already mentioned the extent to which the monographs of van der Toorn and Carr influenced my own thoughts. Both of these authors highlight the need to understand the years of training necessary to gain the knowledge and the skills required to transmit and to shape the scrolls of the Hebrew Bible. In my own understanding, each highlights elements of a dynamic process of training that should force the next generation of scholarship to integrate their ideas of the creation of scrolls as an important element of scribal education. I have a strong sense that the conversations that they have generated should and will change the conversations about the social location of prophetic scrolls in rather profound ways, forcing scholarship to delimit more clearly the ways in which we describe prophetic tradents. Language concerning scrolls as collections dutifully compiled by disciples who studied at the feet of their masters no longer adequately describes the processes—literary and historical—by which these writings came to be. I look forward to the shape these conversations will take in the foreseeable future.

A Word of Thanks

Scholars are often accused of living in ivory towers, and perhaps the accusation holds a smidgen of truth at times. Yet, at least in my case and those with whom I come in contact regularly, the life of a scholar does not rest solely in the isolated musings of social misfits. Rather, the life of a scholar derives its meaning from intellectual engagement with colleagues and students. It is appropriate to conclude, therefore, with several words of gratitude. I have already mentioned Römer, the board of the Ancient Israel and Its Writings series, and the staff at SBL Press. Their willingness to publish this collection, their suggestions of how to shape it, and their collegiality have not only made the volume possible but the process enjoyable.

In the same vein, I wish to express my gratitude to the publishers of the original essays who have given me permission to reproduce those works in this volume. These companies and the original bibliographic data are listed on a separate page for convenience. The willingness of these companies to accommodate this volume is greatly appreciated.

I owe a tremendous debt to my graduate assistant, Nick Werse, who has done the yeoman's share of editing the essays into a consistent style. In some cases digital copies of the essays had been lost through computer crashes through the years. Hebrew fonts had to be checked and changed throughout in order to make them consistent in this volume. In most cases, that comparison meant retyping the Hebrew. The digital copies in my possession had to be compared with the published versions to account for minor editorial changes that were made by various publishers once the article was submitted. He also carefully compared the original publications to those in this volume and added the original page numbers inside curly brackets for ease of reference. He standardized the footnote and the bibliographic forms in this volume for the sake of consistency, and he corrected typographical errors that appeared in the published versions. His attention to detail, his steady progress, and his commitment to the task were nothing but commendable. He is in the process of completing his own work that will contribute to the discipline, and I am grateful that he has helped with this project.

I have great respect and admiration for all of the teachers and colleagues I have had through the years who invested time in me. My students will tell you that I often tell stories about many of them, though most of them have now passed away. While I have noted several above by name who had a hand in shaping the project, I would be remiss if I did not also mention Hans Mallau, the director of my master's thesis. He mentored students with a passion. He took my early drafts of ideas, of which virtually nothing remains, and pushed me in the art of crafting an argument. He patiently read and reread chapters, helping me to see where I had not given my readers enough information, and where I gave them too much. I can still hear his voice when I write today.

I would also like to thank Baylor University and especially my colleagues in the Religion Department. I have experienced the university as a place that values both research and teaching. They have given me time to develop in both areas. The camaraderie one finds in a professional environment can invigorate or debilitate one's intellectual pursuits. My colleagues overwhelmingly fall into the former category. Our graduate students, as well, contribute dynamically to this environment with their intellectual curiosity, strong work ethic, and energy. If these students in any way represent the future of the discipline, it will be in good hands. I also want to thank my three colleagues in Hebrew Bible in the department, Bill Bellinger, Joel Burnet, and Deirdre Fulton, as well as Steve Reid and Dennis Tucker at the seminary. These folks all have their own research agendas, but they make great conversation partners who listen attentively, probe inquiringly, and laugh incessantly. It is a great pleasure for me to serve alongside these colleagues.

Finally, I remain forever indebted to my wife Melanie. She has been there from the beginning. Her encouragement and her engagement are incredible gifts. She has listened to ideas before they were fully baked. She has read countless drafts, attended untold conferences, and befriended many along the way. She has been a partner in this endeavor in every sense of the word, and I am certainly better for it.

Redactional Texts

The Redactional Shaping of Nahum 1 for the Book of the Twelve

The Unity of the Book of the Twelve

Ancient sources provide incontrovertible evidence that the Book of the Twelve was not only transmitted on a single scroll, but counted as a single book, not twelve. Jesus ben Sirach, LXX, Qumran, Josephus, 4 Ezra 14, B. Bat. 13b–15a, and Jerome all attest to the common transmission of these writings.[1] Sirach 49:12 supplies the earliest concrete reference to "The Twelve," meaning that they were already considered a corpus by the beginning of the second century BCE. Fourth Ezra 14 relates Ezra's inspired role in the restoration of the twenty-four canonical books, and Josephus (*C. Ap.* 1.40) counts twenty-two books. While this discrepancy creates some uncertainty over the precise identity of these books, neither total can be reached unless the Book of the Twelve is counted as a single book. Jerome states this unity explicitly in the introductory remarks to his translation of the prophets.[2] Bava Batra {194} 13b–15a categorizes the Twelve differently from the remaining books in the Old Testament with regard to the space between the writings, and when listing the order of the biblical books, it refers to "the Twelve," and does not refer to the prophecies contained within by name. The remainder of the evidence is more indirect, but nevertheless helps demonstrate conclusively that the Minor Prophets have a long history that places them in a common transmission.

---

1. See further the discussions in Dale Allan Schneider, "The Unity of the Book of the Twelve" (PhD diss., Yale University, 1979), 1–4; James D. Nogalski, *Literary Precursors to the Book of the Twelve*, BZAW 217 (Berlin: de Gruyter, 1993), 2–3.

2. "Incipit prologus duodecim prophetarum," in *Biblia Sacra Vulgata* (Stuttgart: Württembergische Bibelanstalt, 1969), 2:1374. Jerome says "unum librum esse duodecim prophetarum."

Modern scholarship has for the most part ignored this evidence, or merely given it token acknowledgment. The few who do treat the question tend to regard the writings as though they had entirely separate transmission histories, implying that only the final form of the individual writing was incorporated into the larger corpus.³ Only a handful of scholars treat the growth of the individual writings in connection with the context of the Book of the Twelve.⁴ {195}

---

3. See, e.g., the theories of Heinrich Ewald, *Die Propheten des alten Bundes*, 2nd ed. (Göttingen: Vandenhoeck & Ruprecht, 1868), 2:74–82; Franz Delitzsch, "Wann weissagte Obadja," *ZTK* 12 (1851): 92–93; Umberto Cassuto, "The Sequence and Arrangement of the Biblical Sections," in *Biblical and Oriental Studies*, trans. Israel Abrahams (Jerusalem: Magnes, 1973), 1:5–6; Curt Kuhl, *Die Entstehung des Alten Testaments*, SamDalp 26 (Bern: Francke, 1953), 217–18; Hans Walter Wolff, *Dodekapropheton 2, Joel und Amos*, 2nd ed., BKAT 14.2 (Neukirchen-Vluyn: Neukirchener Verlag, 1975), 1–2; Wilhelm Rudolph, *Haggai, Sacharja 1–8, Sacharja 9–14, Maleachi*, KAT 13.4 (Gütersloh: Mohn, 1976), 297–98. See also the dissertations by Schneider ("Unity of the Book of the Twelve") and Andrew Yueking Lee ("The Canonical Unity of the Scroll of the Minor Prophets" [PhD diss., Baylor University, 1985]). The work by House (*Unity of the Twelve*) applies a "New Literary Critical" approach and makes the assumption of one literary form programmatic for his treatment.

4. Carl Steuernagel (*Lehrbuch der einleitung in das Alte Testament: Mit einemanhang über die apokryphen und pseudepigraphen*, SThL [Tübingen: Mohr, 1912], 669–72) believes sections of Nahum and Zech 9–14 were added after other sections of their respective writings were already part of the canon. Two scholars attempted redactional hypotheses to explain common transmission which affected the shape of the writings in the Twelve: Karl Budde, "Eine folgenschwere Redaktion des Zwölfprophetenbuchs," *ZAW* 39 (1921): 218–29; and Rolland Emerson Wolfe, "The Editing of the Book of the Twelve," *ZAW* 53 (1935): 90–129. However, the efforts of both Budde and Wolfe were seriously marred by the assumptions of the old source-critical school and have not received favorable treatment in subsequent commentaries. More promising are the observations of Joseph Blenkinsopp, Peter Weimar, and Erich Bosshard: Joseph Blenkinsopp, *Prophecy and Canon: A Contribution to the Study of Jewish Origins*, SJCA 3 (Notre Dame: University of Notre Dame Press, 1977), 106–8; Peter Weimar, "Obadja: Eine redaktionskritische Analyse," *BN* 27 {195} (1985): 94–99; Erich Bosshard, "Beobachtungen zum Zwölfprophetenbuch," *BN* 40 (1987): 30–62. Blenkinsopp notes that a number of the writings have received substantial additions with an eschatological character. Blenkinsopp is not unique in noticing these additions, but he describes them as a common characteristic in the literary history of the Book of the Twelve. Blenkinsopp lists several of these additions, including Amos 9:11–15, Obad 16–21 and Zeph 3:9–20. Weimar briefly considers the question of the growth of the Twelve from the perspective of Obadiah. He argues that Obadiah must be viewed in light of several redactional levels across the Book of the Twelve which

A phenomenon in the Book of the Twelve exists that has not yet been given the attention it deserves, namely, the presence of words at the end of one book that reappear at the beginning of the next. Occasionally, scholars have noted that catchwords play a role in the order of some of the writings, but the definition, extent, and implications of these catchwords remains virtually untreated. The extent of these catchwords is considerable. Anywhere from five to twenty-five words appear in tandem between adjacent writings. The consistency of this phenomenon is even more intriguing, in that those places where it breaks down (Jonah 4; Zech 14) illumine other phenomena. Jonah 4 does not exhibit the catchwords like the endings of the other books, but the long-noted secondary hymn in Jonah 2 does contain catchwords to Mic 1. Additionally, if Jonah is removed from consideration, a strong connection exists between Obadiah and Mic 1. The end of Deutero-Zechariah presents a second inconsistency in this catchword phenomenon. Yet while Deutero-Zechariah does not exhibit the phenomenon, the end of Proto-Zechariah manifests a strong word connection to Mal 1. Both of these inconsistencies therefore raise the question whether these sections were placed into an existing connection.

Three possible explanations can be offered for the *Stichwort* connections. Each option must be evaluated for every "connection" separately, although some generalizing helps to clarify the character of the connections. The three options are: {196}

1. *Accident.* This option is the least satisfying in most instances, because the phenomenon appears too frequently, and because the existence of broader organizing principles (chronological order of the superscriptions, similarity to Isaiah) demonstrates a thoughtful ordering of most of the writings.

2. *Collection.* This option argues that a compiler recognized the similar wording and placed the completed works next to one

---

point to a common history. Weimar mentions one progressive level of redaction on the prophetic collection which produced literary "*Querverbindungen*" through the aid of "*Stichwortentsprechungen.*" He suggests that at this level the "collection" took the shape of a "book." Bosshard documents a strong correlation between the ordering of the writings in the Book of the Twelve and the structuring themes and motifs of Isaiah. His observations most certainly point in the direction of a common tradent, and, taken *en bloc*, present a striking phenomenon that should be considered carefully.

another. This model represents the model traditionally espoused or presumed for the growth of the Book of the Twelve. It is difficult to exclude for every catchword, since one editorial technique appears to have incorporated previously existing material into new contexts. Nevertheless, close analysis of the text often leads to the conclusion that one or both of the books received significant additions in light of the neighboring book, or in light of themes and motifs within the larger corpus. Many times the most significant words in a connection appear in passages long noted as "secondary" or "tertiary" in their respective contexts. One logical assumption is that the secondary portion was added to unite two or more works.

3. *Redaction.* This option provides the best model for treating the texts as a whole. It asks whether the appearance of these catchwords, particularly in those passages which are literarily suspect, should be approached as deliberate changes to the text in view of the context of the Book of the Twelve. Indeed, significant catchwords often take on considerable importance when viewed as part of larger, programmatic work on the prophetic texts. The intentional reworking of material from an expanded literary context often provides a plausible explanation for troublesome syntax and pericopes. The recognition of various techniques for uniting these texts helps to explain a large number of the common words. Such techniques include redactional notes within existing contexts, incorporation of preexisting material, free composition, redactional frames, and superscriptions. Many words and phrases traditionally treated as text-critical problems take on greater significance when viewed from a redactional and literary perspective. {197}

Nahum 1 as Example

A cursory treatment of Nah 1 will exemplify this catchword technique. The phenomenon itself is readily demonstrable, since Nah 1 shares at least thirteen different words with Mic 7:8–20.[5] The words, both nominal and

---

5. Those words in common between Nah 1 and Mic 7:8–20 are: "enemies"

verbal, range from those which are relatively common, such as "river," to those which are quite uncommon, particularly in prophetic literature, such as Bashan and Carmel in the same context.

The chapter may be safely divided into three sections: the superscription (1:1); the semiacrostic theophanic hymn (1:2–8); and the remainder of the chapter (1:9–14). Close inspection of the Hebrew suffixes and addressees in the last section make it difficult to view these verses as an inherent unity. The remainder of the chapter can be further divided into four subsections: the literary transition from the poem to the Nineveh material (1:9–10); the accusation against Nineveh that originally opened the corpus (1:11); a reworked oracle of relief for Zion (1:12–13); YHWH's announcement of the imminent burial of the king of Assyria (1:14).

There are good reasons for arguing that a redactor has expanded earlier material in 1:11–12a, 14. Recent studies on the composition of Nahum arrive at the conclusion that Nahum did not obtain its final form until the postexilic period.[6] There is strong evidence that the poem (1:2–8) and its transition (1:9–10) are postexilic accretions. The remainder of the chapter (1:11, 12–14) blends with 2:1–3 [Eng. 1:15–2:2]{198} and expands an earlier structure. The earlier structure included a parallel core inside a redactional frame. Chapters 2–3 manifest a well-documented parallel structure. The role of 1:11, 12a, and 14 as redactional frame for the early corpus has not been noted, yet its function as *inclusio* with 3:15b–17, 18–19 is readily demonstrable as noted in the following chart (where A = the early redactional frame and B = the parallel core):

(Nah 1:2, 8; Mic 7:8, 10); "anger" (Nah 1:3, 6; Mic 7:18); "dust" (Nah 1:3; Mic 7:17); "sea" (Nah l:4; Mic 7:12); "rivers" (Nah 1:4; Mic 7:12); "Bashan" (Nah 1:4; Mic 7:14); "Carmel" (Nah 1:4; Mic 7:14); "mountains" (Nah 1:5; Mic 7:12); "land" (Nah 1:5; Mic 7:13); "inhabitants" (Nah 1:5; Mic 7:13); "day" (Nah 1:6; Mic 7:11); "passing over" (Nah 1:8; Mic 7:18); "darkness" (Nah 1:8; Mic 7:8).

6. See especially Jörg Jeremias (*Kultprophetie und Gerichtsverkündigung in der späten Königszeit Israels*, WMANT 35 [Neukirchen-Vluyn: Neukirchener Verlag, 1970]), who argues there was a preexilic core to Nahum which received a postexilic expansion; and the more radical views of Hermann Schulz (*Das Buch Nahum: Eine redaktionskritische Untersuchung*, BZAW 129 [Berlin: de Gruyter, 1973]), who views the entire book as a postexilic composition. Klaus Seybold (*Profane Prophetie: Studien zum Buch Nahum*, SBS 135 [Stuttgart: Katholisches Bibelwerk, 1989]) dates the units differently than Jeremias but agrees with him insofar as he also finds evidence of a preexilic core and exilic and postexilic additions.

> A¹ 1:11–12a: The numerical strength of Nineveh will not deliver it from destruction
> A² 1:14: The preparation of the grave of the king of Assyria
>   B 2:4–14: [Eng. 2:3–13] First description of Nineveh's destruction
>   B' 3:1–15: Second description of Nineveh's destruction
> A¹ 3:16–17: The numerical strength of Nineveh will not deliver it from destruction
> A² 3:18–19: Mocking funeral dirge at the grave of the king of Assyria

The later accretions (1:12b, 13; 2:1–3) blend allusions and quotes from Isa 52 as promises to Zion and Judah.[7] Similar Isaianic allusions in the literary transition in 1:9–10 raise the likelihood that the redactional hand responsible for these allusions is the same one that incorporated the semiacrostic poem in 1:2–8.[8] All of these observations, when taken together, reinforce the belief that the semiacrostic poem in Nah 1:2–8 was a preexisting hymn that has been redactionally incorporated into the corpus. The fact that the catchwords to Mic 7:8–20 appear in the hymn deserves consideration.

The semiacrostic poem is broken in four places. Each of these places contains significant words, which also appear in Mic 7, raising the question of whether this repetition is intentional. Recent literature tends to relativize the acrostic elements. A general consensus exists that regards the hymn as never having extended beyond the first half of the alphabet. A reaction to earlier theories of radical emendation attempting to reconstruct the entire poem along acrostic lines, as well as an increasing respect for the integrity of the MT, has caused textual corruption to all but disappear as an explanation for the break in the acrostic character of the poem. The textual corruption model has {199} virtually been replaced by a widely attested opinion that the hymn should be understood as only loosely semi-acrostic in nature.[9]

---

7. Nahum 2:1 quotes Isa 52:7. In addition to the herald formula of Isa 52:7, Nah 1:12–13 contains other allusions to Isa 52 as well. There Zion is admonished to shake her bonds from her neck (Isa 52:2; cf. Nah 1:13), and reference is made to the oppression/affliction of Assyria (Isa 52:4; cf. Nah 1:12).

8. Compare Nah 1:9–10 with the anti-Assyrian polemic in Isa 10:15–19.

9. Such as Simon J. De Vries, "Acrostic of Nahum in the Jerusalem Liturgy," *VT* 16 (1966): 476–81; Ralph L. Smith, *Micah–Malachi*, WBC 32 (Waco, TX: Word Books, 1984), 71–72. By way of contrast, see Duane L. Christensen, "Acrostic of Nahum

The presuppositions of this relativization should be challenged. The presuppositions, which are sometimes stated explicitly, concern the style of the poem and the nature of composition. Proponents believe the acrostic technique is only one of several stylistic devices Nahum uses and that he was so creative that he was not slavishly bound to one single device such as an acrostic pattern. This relativization assumes the acrostic poem as it stands in the MT represents the author's work in its pristine state. In response to these assumptions, it should be noted that the first assumption treats the creation of acrostic poetry too casually. The creation of such poetry requires considerable deliberation and creativity. It is highly improbable that a poet would deliberately choose to write a poem that is *nearly* acrostic. By contrast, an acrostic once recorded is a subtle device which could readily be overlooked or ignored by someone desiring the poem for another purpose. The second presupposition does not consider fully the possibility that the inconsistencies in the acrostic are deliberate changes to the poem. Indeed when viewed from this perspective (within the frame of the catchword phenomenon), these inconsistencies take on considerable significance.

In the case of Nah 1:2–8, this relativization is unwarranted. The breaks in the acrostic pattern can be explained plausibly as deliberate alterations to a preexisting poem. The easiest disruption to explain is the presence of the ו in the י line. Someone incognizant of the acrostic nature of the poem would have readily added the ו to conform the text to more typical syntax.

The addition of the two bicola between the א and ב lines can be explained from the context of the Book of the Twelve. Nahum 1:2b–3a introduces thematic elements that run counter to the main body of the acrostic poem, namely the delay of YHWH's vengeance. This delay functions meaningfully when one understands Nahum's position in the Book of the Twelve. Nahum functions as representative of the prophetic message during the Assyrian oppression. In addition to the {200} basic theme (destruction of Nineveh), its position following Micah and preceding Habakkuk is appropriate for this function. The delay in 1:2b–3a by no means reflects the lack of faith that YHWH would overthrow Assyria. On the contrary it is better understood as a theological reflection upon historical reality. YHWH will ultimately bring judgment upon

---

Reconsidered," *ZAW* 87 (1975): 17–30. Christensen offers a reconstruction based on syllable count that too nearly approaches the old emendation attempts.

his enemies. In addition, the phrases in this expansion quote and adapt Joel 2:13 and 4:21.

The redactor has worked differently in the ד line. Those not opting for the flexibility of a loose acrostic device have been satisfied with either one of two suggestions for emendation, but both pose considerable difficulties.[10] It makes good sense to suppose that a redactor either changed the first half of the ד line on the basis of Mic 7:14 or inserted an entirely new line into the context. The pairing of Carmel and Bashan is not common, appearing only twice elsewhere (Isa 33:9; Jer 50:19), both times in the context of Assyrian oppression. This makes it difficult to believe that the two words appear accidentally in adjacent passages in the Book of the Twelve, particularly in light of the fact that Nah 1:4 breaks the acrostic pattern. Other stylistic observations distinguish this half-verse from the remainder of the poem.[11] {201}

Three possible explanations present themselves for the ז line. The most common explanation argues for the presumed dislocation of לפני from elsewhere in the sentence. Simultaneously most argue that the form was originally לפניו. The problem with this proposal is that it offers no real

---

10. The presence of אמלל breaks the acrostic, leading to the argument that דללו was original. However, LXX never translates דלל with ὀλιγόω, but does use ὀλιγόω with אמלל (Joel 1:10, 12). The second verb, ἐξέλιπεν, does not necessarily imply another text, since it can be used for אמל (cf. Isa 38:14). The Vulgate likewise uses two different words ("infirmatus" and "elanguit"), but this likely relates to the two different subjects. Some have suggested that the verb was originally ראב (e.g., Duane L. Christensen, *Transformations of the War Oracle in Old Testament Prophecy: Studies in the Oracles Against the Nations*, HDR 3 [Missoula, MT: Scholars Press, 1975], 168–69), but it is difficult to perceive how these consonants could have been confused to the point of becoming אמלל, and it could not easily explain the reading in LXX.

11. In addition to the acrostic interruption, several observations set this line apart literarily, making plausible the suggestion that this entire line has been substituted for one that did not adequately serve the redactor's purpose. First, this line is the only line in the entire poem containing no reference to YHWH. Second, the entities Carmel, Bashan, and Lebanon are not intrinsic to Old Testament theophanic material. Third, the passive use of אמלל stands out from the active verbs elsewhere in the hymn, giving this line a *situational* character, rather than one that depicts the reaction to YHWH's appearance. Fourth, the reference to the withering of Bashan, Carmel, and Lebanon takes up literary traditions appearing elsewhere. Scholars typically interpret the withering of these three areas only via traditions associating these regions with fertility. However, this interpretation ignores two essential elements of the metaphor: the political and the literary.

explanation as to how the word became transposed. More likely is a grammatical correction. The verb עמד in the *qal* can take a direct object without a preposition, and be used in the sense of "to stand before."[12] A later hand unaware of the acrostic could very conceivably have added the preposition to conform to more common constructions of עמד. A third alternative suggests the insertion of the phrase "all its inhabitants" in the preceding line could have accounted for the dislocation and the change from לפניו to לפני. The deletion of the phrase, and the change to לפניו, improves the parallelism.[13] The presence of "all its inhabitants" can be explained in light of Mic 7:13, where the phrase appears in similar form. This suggestion is less probable than the simple grammatical change, but still well within the realm of possibility.

Thus, not only can all four interruptions of the acrostic be explained as deliberate changes, but at least two and possibly three are best understood as the work of a redactor operating from a broader literary perspective. This broader perspective demands brief treatment.

The Function of Nahum within the Book of the Twelve

A brief survey of Nahum's structure and literary history confirm that its position and function in the Book of the Twelve has been created with considerable deliberation. The selection of Nahum in its current position, as already noted, coincides well within the historically oriented literary framework of the Book of the Twelve, even though it does not contain the typically Deuteronomistic superscriptions stating the chronology, which themselves probably represent an earlier corpus.[14] {202}

The structure of Nahum in its expanded form, which incorporates the semiacrostic poem, fits a structural pattern beginning in Micah and extending through Habakkuk. This pattern helps explain the selection of

---

12. E.g., Gen 19:27; Jer 48:11; Hab 3:11; Exod 33:9; Josh 20:4. Many of these constructions also have theophanic elements present in the context.

13. The phrase would then have read originally, "And the land is lifted up before him [מפניו] and the world before him [לפניו]."

14. Cf. Hos 1:1; Amos 1:1; Mic 1:1; Zeph 1:1. Similar Deuteronomistic superscriptions that lack reference to the ruling king(s) appear in Joel 1:1; Jonah 1:1; Hag 1:1; Zech 1:1 and are related stylistically to one another, and probably {202} experienced similar transmission histories. They also date the prophet's message by reference to the reign of a specific king.

the theophanic hymn in its current position. Micah, in its latest structural development, begins with a theophanic portrayal (1:2–5), and ends with a lament (7:1–7 [Eng. 8–20]). Nahum also commences with a theophanic portrayal and concludes with a woe oracle and mocking lament. Habakkuk starts with a compositional lament and finishes with a theophanic portrayal which shares vocabulary and outlook, to a certain extent, to Nah 1.

The inserted redactional allusions to Joel in Nah 1:2b–3a coincide with the same phenomenon in Nah 3:15ab, 16b and indicate a considerable probability that Nahum entered the corpus simultaneously with, or subsequently to, Joel. The dating of Joel in the Persian period (at least in the form containing Joel 4) suggests that the Nahum corpus entered the larger corpus after 400, and not closer to the time of Deutero-Isaiah.

In summary, the catchword phenomenon is one facet that should be borne in mind when treating the writings of the Book of the Twelve. In the case of Nahum, this phenomenon simultaneously affords a rationale for the presence of the acrostic pattern.

Zephaniah 3:
A Redactional Text for a Developing Corpus

Scholars increasingly recognize both the incongruence and the unifying tendencies of the final chapter of Zephaniah. The beginning of the chapter (3:1–8) concludes the oracles against the nations (Zeph 2:4–15 = OAN) by dramatically shifting to pronouncement of judgments against Jerusalem. The present form of Zeph 3:9–20 makes theological affirmations concerning YHWH's salvific intention for Judah, Jerusalem, and the nations. No one seriously questions the dominant notion that the placement of these verses balances the theological message of judgment that dominates Zeph 1:2–3:8.

There is little argument concerning the extent of the subunits, but the origin, focus, and function of these units remain debated.

3:1–8a	Judgment against Jerusalem
3:8b	Divine proclamation of judgment against the nations
3:9–10	Divine proclamation of the purification of the nations to serve YHWH
3:11–13	Divine proclamation of the establishment of a humble remnant in Zion by the removal of the haughty
3:14–15	Prophetic proclamation of the removal of YHWH's judgment from Zion
3:16–17	Prophetic proclamation of YHWH's presence in the midst of Zion
3:18–19	Divine proclamation of restoration for Zion's afflicted and her reputation
3:20	Divine proclamation of the restored fortunes of the people

Even a cursory glance at this description demonstrates that, following 3:8, these verses provide variations on the theme of restoration in which the recipients of the salvific acts of YHWH change.

Several stylistic elements add to the impression of cohesion as well as detract from it. The use of first-person common singular forms dominates the chapter after 3:6, connoting YHWH as the speaker. However, Zeph 3:14–17 lack this stylistic feature, suggesting the prophet speaks these verses. Similarly, second-person feminine singular verbs and pronouns in direct address to Lady Zion prevail over much of the chapter, beginning in 3:7. However, these forms periodically disappear.[1] Much of the chapter displays a {208} poetic style, but the last three verses shift toward prose.[2] Finally, changing metaphors and anthropomorphic images for God add to the confusion.[3] Explaining these variations, so typical of prophetic material in general, requires choosing from several models for reading prophetic literature.

Competing Models for Reading Zephaniah 3

Thematic shifts occur abruptly in Zeph 3. These thematic shifts mirror similar shifts in Zeph 1–2. Sometimes these shifts are signaled to the reader, while at other times they occur without warning. Scholars disagree concerning the extent to which one can and should account for them. Before looking more closely at the shifts in Zeph 3, it is necessary to clarify how one interprets prophetic literature in general. At least three models exist for interpreting Zephaniah and other prophetic writings: synchronic harmonizations, diachronic collections, and diachronic development of

---

1. The units treating the purification of the nations (3:8–10) and 3:20 address a group in 2mp. Note also the use of 3fs form to refer to Zion in Zeph 3:18b.

2. See the discussion of the prose particle density of Zephaniah in Byron G. Curtis, "The Zion-Daughter Oracles: Evidence on the Identity and Ideology of the Late Redactors of the Book of the Twelve," in Nogalski, *Reading and Hearing*, 166–84.

3. God is portrayed as judge, king, warrior, bridegroom, and shepherd. See María Eszenyei Széles, *Wrath and Mercy: A Commentary on the Books of Habakkuk and Zephaniah*, trans. George A. F. Knight, ITC (Grand Rapids: Eerdmans, 1987), 106. See also the extended discussion of the shepherd metaphor in Rainer Kessler, "'Ich rette das Hinkende, und das Versprengte sammle ich': Zur Herdenmetaphorik in Zef 3," in *Der Tag wird kommen: Ein interkontextuelles Gespräch über das Buch des Propheten Zefanja*, ed. Walter Dietrich and Milton Schwantes, SBS 170 (Stuttgart: Katholisches Bibelwerk, 1996), 93–101.

literary works. The model selected will greatly affect how one treats the material within this chapter.

Synchronic harmonizations deliberately avoid the question of a text's development for reasons of conviction or convenience. The oft-repeated mantra for this model claims that since only the final form of a given text exists, one may only interpret that form. For those using this model, speculation about earlier forms, or a developing corpus, has no impact upon interpreting the existing text. Some opt for this model out of respect for authorial claims of the text itself, treating Zephaniah (in this case) as the prophet/writer of the book who lived during the reign of Josiah (cf. Zeph 1:1).[4] Others acknowledge that prophetic writings may well contain material from different times, but they reject the premise that identifying earlier material serves any useful purpose for interpreting the text's final form.[5] In either case, synchronic harmonizations {209} downplay changes in perspective within the text as literary devices (e.g., irony), or they argue that recognizing these diverse elements derives from overly complicated critical readings. Synchronic harmonizations prefer, instead, to stress the unifying factors of a given writing.

Those who interpret prophetic writings as diachronic collections recognize that prophetic writings contain material from different time periods. However, proponents of this model see prophetic books as repositories for (independent) prophetic sayings arranged in a loose thematic order. They interpret thematic shifts as new units that reflect alternative proposals for a given topic. This model recognizes that prophetic books contain material of diverse origins, both in terms of authorship and time, but until recently, those working from this model rarely reflected upon its implications for understanding prophetic books.[6] Recent discussions by proponents of this model adopt cautious or skeptical attitudes toward the

---

4. O. Palmer Robertson, *The Books of Nahum, Habakkuk, and Zephaniah*, NICOT (Grand Rapids: Eerdmans, 1990), 40.

5. Adele Berlin, *Zephaniah: A New Translation with Introduction and Commentary*, AB 25A (New York: Doubleday, 1994), 31–47. Berlin acknowledges (42) the likelihood of monarchic traditions, an exilic compositional edition, and perhaps a postexilic edition, but she chooses (20–22) to interpret the existing text as a rhetorical unity whose literary setting is the time of Josiah.

6. See Wolfgang Lau, *Schriftgelehrte Prophetie in Jes 56–66: Eine Untersuchung zu den literarischen Bezügen in den letzten elf Kapiteln des Jesajabuches*, BZAW 225 (Berlin: de Gruyter, 1994); and the reviews by James D. Nogalski (*JBL* 116 [1997]: 127–29) and Odil Hannes Steck (*TLZ* 120 [1995]: 782–86).

idea of labeling prophetic collections as books.[7] They treat prophetic writings as literary products in the sense of thematic anthologies. The original impetus for a collection, it is generally presumed, arose from the sayings of a given prophet. Additions to the collection attest to theological reflections on later experiences, but, for this model, literary shaping means arrangement of the sayings into broad thematic groupings.

A third model preferred in recent redaction historical treatments sees prophetic books as literary works that grew and changed their shape over time. Proponents argue that to understand the character and message of prophetic writings as we now have them, one must attempt to isolate material of diverse origin, explain this material's presence in relative chronological order, and attempt to explain the driving forces (historical, theological, and literary) that compelled the growth of a given writing.[8] This model sees thematic variations as *potential* indicators of the growth or the editorial interests of a given writing. There is a growing tendency to see these changes as the product of a literary elite trained to work on prophetic texts. One frequently finds references to this work as scribal prophecy. Two differences distinguish this model from the model of diachronic collections: the consideration of the relationship between smaller units and the literary horizon of a given unit. Rather than assuming that short units, such as one finds in Zeph 3, merely reflect loosely arranged {210} collections, proponents of the model of literary development also evaluate the extent to which a unit's position in the corpus *could* account for its formulation and/or its placement. This task has become increasingly complex over the last decade as questions about literary horizons have expanded beyond the individual writings. Anyone asking these questions for Zephaniah must also consider the Book of the Twelve, the Latter Prophets, and indeed, the entire Hebrew canon. The remainder of this presentation builds upon recent redactional work by asking, how do the units of Zeph 3 relate to one another?

---

7. Ehud Ben Zvi, "Twelve Prophetic Books or 'The Twelve': A Few Preliminary Considerations," in Watts, *Forming Prophetic Literature*, 125–56; and David L. Petersen, "A Book of the Twelve?," in Nogalski, *Reading and Hearing*, 3–10.

8. See Odil Hannes Steck, *Die Prophetenbücher und ihr theologisches Zeugnis: Wege der Nachfrage und Fährten zur Antwort* (Tübingen: Mohr Siebeck, 1996), 138–45 (Eng. trans.: *Prophetic Books*, 127–34).

Relating the Units of Zephaniah 3

Several clues suggest that the units of Zeph 3 were neither compiled nor composed in a single setting. Simultaneously, several elements provide insight into the intended relationships of the units. These elements include literary position, chronological markers, literary horizons, shifting theological perspectives, and thematic correspondence.

Scholars generally agree that the position of Zeph 3 reflects a general pattern of collection for prophetic literature that moves from judgment against YHWH's people (cf. Zeph 1:4–2:3*), to OAN (2:4–15), to salvific promises for YHWH's people (3:11–20).[9] However, two sections (3:1–7, 8–10) do not coincide with this general arrangement. Zephaniah 3:1–7 deviates from this pattern by pronouncing judgment upon Jerusalem. The position of these verses reflects awareness of the OAN in 2:4–15. Zephaniah 3:1 begins with הוי, like 2:5, near the beginning of the OAN. However, 3:1–7 changes the theme of judgment against the nations to judgment against Jerusalem, and thus relates to the dominant focus of 1:4–2:3*. The deviation in 3:1–7 may also deliberately imitate the technique used in the OAN that begins Amos. Just as Amos 1:3–2:5 culminate in pronouncements of judgment against Israel in Amos 2:6–16, Zeph 3:1–7 climaxes the OAN by pronouncing judgment against Jerusalem in a manner designed to catch the reader/hearer off guard.[10] These observations suggest that Zeph 3:1–7 displays a twofold literary horizon (Zephaniah and Amos) in which the theme of coming judgment upon Jerusalem plays a significant role. {211} The chronological setting created by Zeph 1:1 encourages readers to associate the coming judgment with events from the time of Josiah to Jerusalem's fall.

Accounting for Zeph 3:8–10 requires a shift in focus thematically and linguistically. Zephaniah 3:8a begins with a formal marker ("therefore")

---

9. See Walther Zimmerli, "Vom Prophetenwort zum Prophetenbuch," 481–96.

10. See Nogalski, *Literary Precursors*, 174–75. Note how the enigmatic phrasing of Zeph 2:4 adds to this impression. It effectively begins the OAN in Zephaniah, but it relates formally to the preceding verses (note the use of כי), as though it functions as a transition to the new unit. Zephaniah 2:5 begins with הוי and is directed against the region of Philistia. This transitional verse (2:4) mentions the same four cities as the anti-Philistine oracle of Amos 1:6–8. Moreover, these four cities appear in precisely the same order as Amos 1:6–8. Thus, both the beginning and the end of the OAN in Zephaniah exhibit significant similarities with Amos 1:3–2:16.

that assumes a causal connection to the previous verse. YHWH remains the speaker, but the addressee changes from second-person feminine singular address of Zion to masculine plural imperative ("wait"), formally implying the third-person masculine plural suffix on "*their* deeds" in 3:7 as the intended antecedent. No matter how one reads the last word of Zeph 3:8a, the context implies YHWH's intention to judge a group of people on the day of his rising.[11] However, the judgment assumed in 3:8b is not a judgment limited to Jerusalem. Rather, the judgment in 3:8b will come upon nations/kingdoms/all the earth. This verse presents the difficulty in microcosm for interpreting the shifts that occur in Zeph 3. On the one hand, the change of style and addressee can be understood as change to a new unit. On the other hand, the formal connector ("therefore") and the continuation of the same voice as speaker argue for the continuation of the unit. At the very least, the former provides a literary marker as to how an editor intended 3:8 to relate to the preceding material. By noting the literary horizon and thematic correspondence of this verse, one can adequately explain these elements. Thematically, this verse serves as both a warning to the people of Jerusalem and as a conclusion to the OAN. Jerusalem's population will not escape YHWH's wrath, but they will not be alone. In this respect, the verse demonstrates cognizance of its location in the book. It combines YHWH's coming judgment on the nations and on Jerusalem. It intertwines judgment on Judah and Jerusalem with a universal perspective as in Zeph 1 (cf. especially the abrupt change from the universal to the particular exhibited in Zeph 1:2–3 and 1:4–12).[12]

As with 3:1–7, however, the phrasing of Zeph 3:8 suggests that its literary horizon may be broader than the immediate context, especially at the point of the thematic change in 3:8b. This verse recalls Zeph 1:18 ("in the fire of his jealousy, all the earth will be devoured").[13] However, the phrasing of 3:8b also evokes echoes of language that point back to Nahum and Habakkuk.[14] The echoes of Nahum's theophanic hymn anticipate a coming

---

11. Various proposals have been suggested for reading לְעַד, none of which are without problem. Some have tied the word to עַד (I), "perpetuity," עַד (II), "prey," or to some form of the root עוּד, "testify," or "witness."

12. See also 1:14–18. Scholars working with diachronic models generally interpret this dual focus as the work of more than one person, while those working with a synchronic model interpret the variation as a compositional technique.

13. Unless otherwise stated, all biblical translations are my own.

14. Verbal ties between Zeph 3:8 and elsewhere include: wait (Hab 2:3); gather

day of indignation {212} and burning anger that reflects God's jealousy (Nah 1:2, 6; Zeph 1:18). The connections to Habakkuk pick up a thread in Habakkuk in which the prophet is told to wait for the coming judgment in two stages. In the first stage, YHWH will use the Chaldeans to punish the wicked in Judah (1:5–11) while in the second stage YHWH will punish the Chaldeans for their arrogance (Hab 2:3–5; cf. Hab 3:16 as a response to 3:2–15).[15] These allusions portray judgment against both YHWH's people and against the nations of the earth. They also provide connections to themes in Zechariah's visions (cf. Zech 1:14–17). The judgment against YHWH's people is not removed, but some comfort may be gained from the idea that the nations will not escape.

Zephaniah 3:9–10 changes the focus once again. Steck has demonstrated that, to a large extent, the formulation of Zeph 3:9–10 reflects awareness of Isa 18–19, chapters which treat Ethiopia and Egypt.[16] He bases his argument on the literal citation of Isa 18:1b by Zeph 3:10a, as well as other formulations in the two Isaiah chapters.[17] These thematic associations include other prophetic texts concerning Egypt (e.g., Jer 46:11 and Ezek 30:21) and trigger associations of Egypt, Cush, and Assyria.[18] Steck also argues that the positioning of 3:9–10 makes sense, coming after the announcement of universal judgment on the nations, yet limiting that judgment so that those among the nations can worship YHWH. The verse picks up on the last mentioned nations (Cush and Assyria) in the OAN of Zeph 2:12–15.[19] Assuming, with Steck, that these verses represent a redactional *Fortschreibung* that builds upon existing material in Zephaniah (as

---

nations, collect peoples (Hab 2:5; cf. Hag 2:22); wrath (Nah 1:6); burning anger (Nah 1:6); fire (Nah 1:6); devour the earth (Zeph 1:18; cf. Nah 3:13); jealousy of god (Nah 1:2); fire of jealousy (Zeph 1:18). There is a thematic connection from Zeph 3:8 to Hag 2:22 (overthrow of the kingdoms), but the only lexical connection to that verse is the word "kingdoms."

15. In Hab 2:3, the prophet is told to wait for the vision that will come regarding the arrogant one anticipated in 1:12–17, specifically addressing the prophet's question to YHWH in 1:17. The arrogant one is no longer assumed to be just the wicked in Judah but also the attacker whom YHWH sends (cf. Hab 2:5b, 8). The last chapter of Habakkuk predicts the coming defeat of the enemy, but not before that enemy attacks Judah itself (Hab 3:16).

16. Odil Hannes Steck, "Zu Zef 3:9–10," *BZ* 34 (1990): 90–95.

17. Ibid., 90.

18. Ibid., 91–92.

19. Ibid., 93.

well as the Twelve and the *corpus propheticum*), one can ask how these verses were understood in relation to their context. A formal marker provides the necessary information at the beginning of 3:9 with the words "for then..." (כי־אז) thereby indicating that the pilgrimage of worshipers from the nations described in the remainder of these verses will result from the universal judgment described in the previous verse. As such, 3:9–10 interprets the judgment of 3:8b not as total annihilation, but as a judgment that will purify the nations, enabling those worshiping YHWH among the nations to bring their offering to Jerusalem.

The addressee and theme of the verse shifts again with Zeph 3:11–13. The personified Lady Zion, representing the city of Jerusalem, becomes the primary {213} addressee until 3:20.[20] Thematically, the remainder of the chapter focuses upon several salvific aspects for Jerusalem. A formulaic marker ("on that day") begins Zeph 3:11, signaling a shift in the topic, but also placing the chronology of the next unit at the same time as the preceding unit. Regarding content, three elements come into focus: the removal of Zion's shame (3:11a), the removal of the arrogant ones from Zion (3:11b), and the creation of a pious remnant within Jerusalem (3:12–13). At this point, one can detect tension in the presumed chronology of the context since it is not clear how the pilgrimage of the nations (3:9–10) would take place prior to Jerusalem's cleansing. One can explain this tension by recognizing that 3:9–10 interrupts a stronger logical connection between 3:1–7, 8 and 3:11. The salvific promises of 3:11–20 reverse the judgment against Jerusalem announced in the first part of the chapter. In fact, the literary horizon of 3:11–13 appears cognizant of the Zephaniah context (cf. references to Zion's deeds in 3:7, 11) and, as with 3:1–7, this perspective appears most closely related to the interests of the Deuteronomistic corpus (Hosea, Amos, Micah, Zephaniah).[21]

---

20. Only the parenthetical description of the remnant of Israel in 3:13 (using 3mp), one 3fs statement about Zion in 3:18, and the direct address of the people in 3:20 interrupt this 2fs style.

21. See my discussion how the remnant motif of Zeph 3:12–13 coincides with the introduction of a remnant motif at the end of Amos immediately following pronouncement of the destruction of the Northern Kingdom (Nogalski, *Literary Precursors*, 177). In addition, the concern expressed for the rebellion of Zion (3:11) makes sense in this context since this powerful root appears only within the four books of the Deuteronomistic corpus within the Book of the Twelve (Hos 7:13; 8:1; 14:10; Amos 1:3, 6, 9, 11, 13; 2:1, 4, 6; 3:14; 4:4 [2x]; 5:12; Mic 1:5 [2x], 13; 3:8; 6:7; 7:18; Zeph 3:11). The rebellion of Zion is of particular interest in Mic 1:5, 13, and Zeph 3:11. Debate

Zephaniah 3:11b–13 depicts a situation in which YHWH will remove the arrogant ones while leaving a pious remnant. The arrogant ones who will be removed are to be understood as inhabitants of Jerusalem, not foreign enemies, because they are specifically addressed as Zion's proud and exulting ones (3:11). The removal of this group allows the pious remnant who take refuge in the name of YHWH to "feed and lie down with no one to make them tremble" (3:13 NASB).[22] {214}

A new unit begins in Zeph 3:14 with a change of speaker, though the addressee remains the same. The imperative addresses Zion in 3:14, but reference to YHWH in the third person replaces divine speech.[23] This stylistic variation continues through 3:17, and given the constellations of possible speakers, one should conceptualize the prophet speaking to Zion. Zephaniah 3:14–17 exhibits a carefully constructed thematic parallelism, despite the fact that 3:16 contains a formal marker of a new unit.[24] The unit's shift in speaker combined with the change to imperative verbs suggests a new unit, but 3:14 contains no formal introductory marker. Zephaniah 3:15 states that Zion should rejoice because YHWH has removed his

---

arises among redaction historians concerning the relationship of these verses to the larger context. Schart and Nogalski argue Zeph 3:11–13 owe their existence to redactional continuations of the Deuteronomistic corpus (see Nogalski, *Literary Precursors*, 177; and Schart, *Entstehung des Zwölfprophetenbuchs*, 214). Steck and Bosshard argue that 3:11–13 fit best with the later elements of 3:9–10, 20 (see Odil Hannes Steck, *Der Abschluss der Prophetie im Alten Testament: Ein Versuch zur Frage der Vorgeschichte des Kanons*, BibS[N] 17 [Neukirchen-Vluyn: Neukirchener Verlag, 1991], 45–46; Erich Bosshard-Nepustil, *Rezeptionen von Jesaia 1–39 im Zwölfprophetenbuch: Untersuchungen zur literarischen Verbindung von Prophetenbüchern in babylonischer und persischer Zeit*, OBO 154 [Göttingen: Vandenhoeck & Ruprecht; Fribourg: Presses Universitaires, 1997], 430–31, 444–45) and the later redactions of Isaiah. Here, I would see the reception and (re)interpretation of Zeph 3:11–13 combined with 3:9–10 as distinct from the connection of Zeph 3:8+11–13. The latter also has a parallel in the context of Isa 40–55 (cf. 50:1 following the 2fs address to Zion in the latter portions of Isa 49), with the issue of YHWH's divorce from Zion because of the rebellion of the children.

22. Contra Kessler, "'Ich rette das Hinkende,'" 98–99, who sees the arrogant as the nations as well.

23. The unique combination of verbs of rejoicing draws upon psalmic forms, but also suggests awareness of Isaiah at an advanced stage of its development. See Ihromi, "Die Häufung der Verben des Jubelns in Zephanja 3:14f, 16–18," *VT* 33 (1983): 106–10.

24. Nogalski, *Literary Precursors*, 203. The elements are easily recognizable: the rejoicing of Zion (3:14–15a; 3:17b), YHWH in Zion's midst (3:15bα; 3:17a), and the removal of fear (3:15bβ; 3:16).

judgment, thus building upon the divine pronouncements in 3:11–13. In this respect, Zeph 3:14–17 can be read contextually, but a question arises: What do these verses add that was not already present in 3:11–13? In other words, do these verses merely repeat a promise to Zion? The difference between the content of 3:14–17 and 3:11–13 is subtle. Both sections offer words of promise to Zion, but a shift in metaphors along with a shift in vocabulary indicates that the focus of 3:14–17 shifts away from internal problems and takes up external concerns. The shepherd metaphor in 3:13 gives way to the images of king and warrior. The promise of the removal of fear implies that a military threat to Zion is taken away. The language of fear, YHWH as warrior, and the enemy YHWH will face invoke images of an external threat which YHWH will remove, not the threat of arrogant Judeans who are ignoring YHWH's law (cf. 1:12–13; 3:2–4, 11).

The literary horizon of 3:14–17 extends beyond the immediate context. This promise makes sense when read with a form of Zephaniah that included the OAN (see esp. 2:8b, 9b–10). It is not, however, clear that these verses anticipate the universal elements of the expanded horizons of the day of YHWH on all the earth. Rather, the removal of the external threat focuses on a specific threat to Zion sent as a result of YHWH's verdicts. In spite of the different recipients of divine action, the time frame implicit in this unit should formally be understood as the same as the time of 3:11–13. Zephaniah 3:14 contains no indication of a different time, and 3:16 contains a ביום ההוא formula that places it with 3:11. Nevertheless, this formula places all of these events in the future. If one takes the chronological formulas seriously, none of these promises has yet come to fruition (nor have the judgments for that matter). In the larger context, these verses evoke language of royal psalms, the holy war tradition, and Isaiah, making it difficult to claim a specific text serves as a backdrop for this passage, but also suggesting a fairly late date for the existing {215} unit.[25] The entire passage exhibits a metahistorical perspective in which Zion is encouraged to rejoice because the coming judgment and its constituent threat will be removed. In Hab 3:16, 18–19 the prophet rejoices because YHWH will punish the enemy who attacks his people, although the prophet also trembles because he must also endure the coming day of distress. Similarly, in Zeph 3:14–17, the prophet offers words of hope to Zion that her verdict

---

25. See Günter Krinetzki, *Zefanjastudien: Motiv- und Traditionskritik + Kompositions- und Redaktionskritik*, RST 7 (Frankfurt am Main: Lang, 1977), 157–66.

will be removed, and her enemy defeated, but not before she endures her own punishment.

In Zeph 3:18–20, divine speech again dominates. Zephaniah 3:18–19 continues to address Zion explicitly as indicated by the second-person feminine single forms, while 3:20 shifts to second-person masculine plural, a perspective that marked the transition in 3:8 and the brief reference to Israel in 3:14. Does this shift indicate distinct units, different times of composition, or diverse theological perspectives? In all probability, Zeph 3:18–19 and 20 reflect different times of composition, although neither unit is independent of its context.[26] Zephaniah 3:18–19 addresses a final promise to Zion by speaking about YHWH's salvific action toward the lame and the outcast, and especially by drawing reflectively upon Mic 4:6–7.[27] By contrast, direct address to these groups in Zeph 3:20 builds upon the promise of Zeph 3:18–19 and reflects a broader literary horizon.[28] In addition, the chronological markers and the style of these verses set them apart from the preceding units in Zephaniah. {216}

---

26. See, e.g., Norbert Mendecki, "Deuteronomistische Redaktion von Zef 3,18–20?," *BN* 60 (1991): 27–32. Mendecki argues that Zeph 3:18–20 reflect two to four different layers (all postexilic) based upon an analysis of the vocabulary. He finds an initial redaction that reflects either a pre-Deuteronomistic form in 3:18, 19abc or to the Deuteronomistic redaction that is almost certainly present in 3:19d. This layer uses language from Jeremiah and Ezekiel at a relatively advanced stage of the redaction of Jeremiah. Mendecki finds another redaction in the addition of Zeph 3:20aβ. It builds upon the Zephaniah context, but it also reflects either an Ezekelian redactor or a post-Deuteronomistic redactor who is associated with an expansion school from the book of Jeremiah.

27. Nogalski, *Literary Precursors*, 210–11; Hubert Irsigler, *Gottesgericht und Jahwetag: Die Komposition Zef 1,1–2,3, untersucht auf der Grundlage der Literarkritik des Zefanjabuches*, ATSAT 3 (St. Ottilien: EOS, 1977), 163.

28. See Nogalski, *Literary Precursors*, 212–15. Note that Mendecki ("Deuteronomistische Redaktion von Zef 3,18–20?") does not reflect upon why he finds Jeremianic, Ezekelian, Deuteronomistic and post-Deuteronomistic language within these verses. It does not seem plausible to distinguish four different redactional layers purely upon the provenance of isolated words. By the same token, Curtis seems equally formalistic when he assigns all three verses to a single addition based upon a shift to prose (cf. Curtis, "Zion-Daughter Oracles"). E.g., Curtis associates Zeph 3:18–20 with the Zion oracle in Zech 9:9–10, but he does not account for the very different attitudes toward kingship assumed in those verses compared to the context of Zeph 3. Also, his celeritous elimination of the Greek period context of Zech 9:13 ignores the fact that Greece is depicted as Judah's enemy, not Persia's enemy.

Zephaniah 3:18 returns to divine speech, but this change by itself does not indicate an entirely new unit. Rather, 3:18 draws upon the metaphor of YHWH the shepherd who will retrieve the sheep who have strayed: "Those mourning the appointed feasts I will gather. They were from you."[29] This verse now shifts the focus from YHWH's war against the enemy back to a promise to Zion concerning the inhabitants of Jerusalem (or more properly, the pious remnant). The perspective of this promise presumes both YHWH's restoration and the experience of punishment. YHWH's restorative action only makes sense when one presumes that something has caused the cessation of the appointed festivals.[30] Thus, one sees evidence that these verses presume destruction of the temple even in the promise of restorative activity. In other words, the promise, though ostensibly still set in the time of Josiah (cf. Zeph 1:1), offers a promise to Zion that relates to a period after the temple's destruction.[31]

Zephaniah 3:19 contains new chronological markers, but it is not an independent unit. The first marker uses הנני + a participle that typically indicates a time of imminent action: "Behold, what I am *about* to do with all your oppressors." The second chronological marker confuses the issue with a more vague reference to the future ("in that time"). This chronological marker equates the time frame of this promise with the consequences of the imminent action of Zeph 3:18. Zephaniah 3:19 also presents a thoughtful rewording of the promise of Mic 4:6–7 that reflects awareness of its function in Zephaniah and its location in the developing multivolume corpus that would come to be known as the Twelve.[32] Even the ques-

---

29. Kessler, "'Ich rette das Hinkende,'" rightly demonstrates how the assumption of the shepherd metaphor helps make sense of this very difficult text. I have therefore adopted the accentuation of MT in contrast to my earlier translation (Nogalski, *Literary Precursors*, 49–50). The latter half of this verse still contains difficult syntax because of the third person reference to Zion. Zephaniah 3:18b probably stems from an isolated gloss that comments upon the character of the mourners and presumes a rationale for YHWH's actions: "(They were) a burden upon her, a reproach."

30. See also the arguments on the postmonarchic context of Zeph 3:19 by Ehud Ben Zvi, *A Historical-Critical Study of the Book of Zephaniah*, BZAW 198 (Berlin: de Gruyter, 1991), 257.

31. See the discussion of metahistory in Steck, *Prophetenbücher*, 35–36 (Eng. trans., 32–34).

32. For details concerning the intricate alterations of Mic 4:6–7, see Nogalski, *Literary Precursors*, 209–11. The formulaic introduction of Zeph 3:19 shifts from ביום ההוא to בעת ההיא, already anticipating Hag 1:2, 4, the next writing in the Twelve.

tion of why Zeph 3:19 cites Mic 4:6–7 perhaps reflects awareness of the context of Zeph 3. The promise of Mic 4:7 ends with a purpose statement that "YHWH will rule [מלך] over them on Mount Zion," a promise that ties into an image already noted in Zeph 3:15: "YHWH, the king {217} of Israel, is in your midst."[33] The content of 3:19 promises to remove *all* Zion's oppressors and restore praise and renown to the groups that YHWH has restored. The identity of the oppressors is difficult to place unless one takes the extended context into account, and even then, decisions about the literary horizon affect the manner in which one interprets the oppressors. Given the intertextual nature of this verse, it seems wiser to treat this collective term in the context of an extended historical period.[34]

Zephaniah 3:20 continues the divine speech, but addresses a collective group (using 2mp), presumably the lame and the outcast from 3:19. The chronological marker equates the time frame of 3:20 with that of 3:19.

Zephaniah 3:19 also associates the lame with the remnant in citing Mic 4:7, and equates the mourners with that remnant (cf. Zeph 3:13). Moreover, subtle shifts in wording indicate YHWH's salvific actions toward the lame reflect the expectation that YHWH's actions toward that group will occur more quickly than the actions toward the second group (the outcast).

33. Only five texts in the Twelve combine YHWH and מלך (using either a nominal or verbal form): Mic 4:7; Zeph 3:15; Zech 14:9, 16–17; Mal 1:14. Of these, the first two draw on the context of YHWH's restoration of a remnant in Jerusalem while the remaining three speak about the nations coming to worship YHWH the king in Jerusalem. Thus, the Zephaniah and Micah contexts are related, not only verbally, but on the level of motifs as well.

34. Kessler assumes that this verse has Zephaniah as its primary point of reference and thus includes the inner-Judean group along with external enemies among those whom YHWH will punish as Zion's oppressors ("'Ich rette das Hinkende,'" 100). He sees this imagery consistent with the judgment aspects of shepherd imagery in Old Testament texts. By contrast, I have argued that the prideful Judeans treated elsewhere in Zephaniah (cf. 3:11) would fit better among those considered as the outcasts (see Nogalski, *Literary Precursors*, 204–9). I see the reference to "all your oppressors," with the link to Mic 4:6–7, as suggestive of all external powers who have oppressed Zion beginning with the late Assyrian period. In this respect, the reference would include Assyria, Egypt, and the other nations mentioned in the OAN, as well as Babylon who is not mentioned explicitly in Zephaniah. However, Babylon's inclusion can be assumed from the context of Mic 4–5. Zephaniah 3:11 also provides other arguments against seeing "oppressors" as a reference to Judean leadership. In Zeph 3:11, the prideful and arrogant ones belong to Zion, and are treated as part of her guilt, not part of her punishment. By contrast, Zephaniah speaks of those who oppress Zion, implying this group would be those who took advantage of YHWH's punishment of Zion.

Zephaniah 3:20 concludes with a formula ("says YHWH") that appropriately ends Zephaniah. Apart from the formal change of addressee, 3:20 merely repeats the message of the previous verse with one additional piece of information. Zephaniah 3:20b includes restoration of possessions among the promises. The manner in which this motif is phrased ("when I restore your fortunes") implies knowledge on the part of the reader/hearer that YHWH plans to restore their possessions. The context of such a promise can again be explained by an extended literary horizon, although one can debate whether this context includes only Zephaniah or several writings. This phrase appears five times in the Book of the Twelve but twice in Zephaniah (Hos 6:11; Joel 4:1; Amos 9:14; Zeph 2:7; 3:20). Interestingly, in the Twelve, the phrase appears only in the context of the Deuteronomistic corpus and Joel 4.[35] Only Joel 4:1 and Zeph 3:20 explicitly place {218} this motif in the context of YHWH's universal judgment of the nations. The phrase essentially announces the reversal of judgment.[36] Zephaniah 3:20 certainly functions appropriately within the Book of the Twelve where it is the last verse of the prophetic writings with a preexilic literary setting. Haggai, the next writing in the Twelve not only exhibits a postexilic setting, it starts with YHWH's confrontation of the people whose possessions have been restored. They have built their own houses, but have not rebuilt YHWH's house.

Conclusion

Careful attention to various connecting elements of Zeph 3 provides insight into the important role as a redactional text which this passage played as the Book of the Twelve developed. The units comprising Zeph 3 do not represent independent units. Rather, they build upon one another by combining awareness of their location in Zephaniah and the developing multivolume corpus (as well as the prophetic corpus as a whole). Issues

---

35. In the Twelve, the phrase refers to the restoration of Judah and/or Jerusalem. The phrase is well rooted in its context in Joel and Zephaniah while it appears in updated reworkings in Hosea and Amos. For Hos 6:11, see Jörg Jeremias, *Der Prophet Hosea*, ATD 24.1 (Göttingen: Vandenhoeck & Ruprecht, 1983), 94. Amos 9:14 refers to the restoration of my people Israel who will rebuild the cities and live in them. For a summary of the issues for interpreting Amos 9:11–15 as late additions, see: Wolff, *Joel and Amos*, 352–53.

36. See John M Bracke, "Šûb šebût: A Reappraisal," *ZAW* 97 (1985): 233–44.

related to judgment upon Jerusalem in 3:1–7, as well as texts dealing with a remnant (3:11–13, 18–19) interact with texts and structures of the Deuteronomistic corpus. Texts focusing on the punishment of external enemies (3:8, 14–17) pick up thematic elements that are developed in Nahum, Habakkuk, and Zechariah. Zephaniah 3:20 demonstrates awareness of its function as a transition to Haggai, as well as verbal and thematic links to Joel 4. Finally, Zeph 3:9–10 implants the theme of a remnant for the nations consistent with motifs from Zech 14:16–21.

The chronological markers of this chapter place all of the action in the future. In so doing, they create ambiguity because the verses ascribe very different divine actions to the same time without clearly indicating the expected order of these events: punishment of Jerusalem, restoration of a remnant in Jerusalem, destruction of an enemy threatening Jerusalem, punishment of the nations, and recognition of foreigners worshiping YHWH. Logically, one can presume some order to these diverse elements that can help make sense of the whole. YHWH will use various nations to inflict punishment on Jerusalem before gathering the remnant in Jerusalem. The impression left by the cumulative perspectives is that this gathering is near, and it will institute a time of punishment on the nations that will result in some among the nations recognizing YHWH's power over all the world.

Zechariah 13:7–9 as a Transitional Text: An Appreciation and Reevaluation of the Work of Rex Mason

Nearly thirty years ago, Rex Mason's dissertation, "The Use of Earlier Biblical Material in Zechariah IX–XIV: A Study in Inner Biblical Exegesis," anticipated several of the developments that would take place in the study of the Hebrew Bible in the coming decades. These issues include inner biblical exegesis, the use of allusion and citation, and an emphasis upon explaining the final form of the text (even when recognizing the composite nature of that text). One of the passages to which Mason devotes special attention is Zech 13:7–9. Mason argues that this passage originally formed the conclusion to 11:4–17. This paper will summarize Mason's arguments for Zech 13:7–9; it will survey how scholarship since Mason has reacted to the views he expresses; and finally, it will suggest refining the model to explain the similarities and differences noted by various scholars.

Mason's Treatment of Zechariah 13:7–9

Mason joins those who believe that Zech 13:7–9 originally concluded the shepherd passage of Zech 11:4–17. So confident is he of this function that he places his treatment of 13:7–9 after the chapter on 11:4–17 and before the chapter on 12:1–13:6. The association of 13:7–9 with 11:4–17 also underlies Mason's treatment of the imagery of 13:7–9, since much of the discussion of the three-verse unit develops as a continuation of the chapter on 11:4–17. Still, Mason does not merely assume that the two units are related. He focuses heavily on the tradition-historical background of significant phrases in 13:7 and the formulation of the remnant motif in 13:8–9.

In an earlier chapter, Mason documents numerous points of contact between the Shepherd Allegory of Ezek 37:15–28 and Zech 11:4–17.[1]

---

1. Rex A. Mason, "The Use of Earlier Biblical Material in Zechariah IX–XIV: A

In his chapter on 13:7–9, Mason examines the tradition-historical background of six words and phrases from 13:7. He concludes {293} that the prophetic tradition behind this verse, which is reflected in its imagery, continues the judgment announced in 11:4–17. Mason first explores the background of the use of "sword" as a metaphor of divine judgment that has significant parallels, including Isa 34:5–6, Jer 47:6, and Ezek 21. He next delves into the problem of identifying the background of the shepherd, siding with those who see the term used ironically to refer to an unworthy leader. Third, he cautiously concludes that the word גבר may carry messianic connotations, but, if so, they too are utilized ironically. Fourth, Mason finds the ironic use of the rare word "neighbor" (עמית) in prophetic texts to be significant since the word normally appears in the legal codes of Leviticus. Finally, Mason finds similar reasons for judgment against the leaders in the "smiting" of the shepherd, which leads to the scattering of the flock. He argues that all of these terms portray a decidedly negative attitude toward the leadership of Judah, one that is quite consistent with refutation of the current leadership in 11:4–17.[2]

Mason sees the formulation of the remnant motif of Zech 13:8–9 as another point in which Zech 13:7–9 connotes an outlook similar to Ezekiel traditions.[3] He argues that the three-group division of the people destined for judgment reflects an affinity to Ezek 5, where one-third of the population will be killed inside the city, one-third will be cut down around the city while trying to flee, and the remaining third will be scattered and then killed by Yahweh's sword. Mason notes that Ezek 5 appears to have experienced a revision in Ezek 5:3–4, which reinterprets the scattering to allow for a remnant of the third group to survive. It is this additional action against the final third that solidifies the impression, for Mason, that Zech 13:7–9 draws upon Ezek 5. He also notes that Ezekiel also uses the metaphor of smelting to connote total judgment in 22:17–22.[4] Mason

---

Study in Inner Biblical Exegesis" (PhD diss., University of London, 1973), 135–67. Mason's dissertation was subsequently published in: Rex A. Mason, "The Use of Earlier Biblical Material in Zechariah 9–14: A Study in Inner Biblical Exegesis," in *Bringing Out the Treasure: Inner Biblical Allusion in Zechariah 9–14*, ed. Mark J. Boda and Michael H. Floyd, JSOTSup 370 (London: Sheffield Academic, 2003), 1–208.

2. Mason, "Use of Earlier Biblical Material in Zechariah IX–XIV," 168–79.

3. Ibid., 180–87.

4. The issue of the intratextuality of the smelting imagery will be raised again in the third section of this paper.

notes that Ezekiel's own use of the smelting, however, differs from Zech 13:8–9 in that Ezekiel's use of the imagery of smelting depicts complete destruction, not the creation of a remnant.[5] Finally, Mason suggests that another combination of motifs strengthens the association of the broader context of Zechariah to Ezekiel. Mason notes that the smelting imagery of Ezek 22:17–22 is followed by a message of judgment against the leadership, judgment whose sign is the lack of rain (Ezek 22:23). He believes that the movement from smelting to rain exhibits parallels with the role of cleansing water in the broader context of Zech 9–14 (cf. 10:1; 13:1; 14:8, 17). For Mason, {294}

> The gift of water symbolizes God's cleansing of the community from a corrupt and tainted leadership. It is yet another indication that the section before us belongs to that stream of tradition which sees the re-emergence of a redeemed community following the cleansing process which strikes down the false leadership of the old age.[6]

Thus, for Mason, the judgment and remnant motifs of Zech 13:8 draw upon Ezekiel traditions because they are so closely related to Zech 11:4–17.

The situation changes somewhat with Zech 13:9, as Mason notes, which emphasizes the newness following the cleansing. Mason sees more influence from earlier prophetic traditions in 13:9. He singles out the similarity of Zech 13:9 with Hos 2:25, but also Ezek 37:23, 27 and Zech 8:8. In the end, it is not entirely clear whether, for Mason, Zech 13:9 is citing Hos 2:25 or whether he sees the Hosea text merely as one of several examples of an ongoing line of tradition.[7] At any rate, Mason correctly sees in Zech 13:9 the renewal of covenant language that is only possible because of the judgment which has purified the community.

Mason concludes his treatment of 13:7–9 by observing its relationship to the context of 11:4–17 and to a lesser extent 12:1–13:6. He contends that similarities in language, structure, and especially theme create

---

5. Mason, "Use of Earlier Biblical Material in Zechariah IX–XIV," 184.
6. Ibid., 185.
7. On the one hand, Mason states that the renewed covenant language of 13:9 is "strongly reminiscent of Hos 2:25" (ibid.). On the other hand, Mason goes on to discuss Ezek 37:23, 27 and Zech 8:8 before saying that "It is such *a line of tradition* which seems to lie behind Zech 13:8f." (ibid., 186, emphasis added).

a striking similarity between 13:7–9 and 11:4–17. Mason notes five points of similarity:[8]

1. Both texts utilize shepherd imagery.
2. Both texts mention the place where the sword will strike the shepherd.
3. Both texts allude to smelting.
4. Both texts draw upon covenant concepts.
5. The metrical structure from 11:17 continues in 13:7.

It is these similarities that motivate Mason to discuss 13:7–9 immediately after the chapter on 11:4–17. However, Mason also notes thematic contacts with the tradition block of 12:1–13:6. He notes that both 12:1–13:6 and 13:7–9 refer to a time of general suffering that serves as a prelude to salvation. This suffering will be directed toward the removal of corrupt leadership and those parts of the community that have followed that {295} leadership. At this point Mason suggests in passing the idea that the (re)location of 13:7–9 may not be the result of an accidental misplacement. He notes that while he has focused upon the similarities between 13:7–9 and 11:4–17, he also sees a general connection between 13:7–9 and 12:1–13:6 that "indeed may vindicate its positioning where we find it." Mason does not elaborate how the similarities between 13:7–9 and 11:4–17, on the one hand, and 13:7–9 and 12:1–13:6, on the other hand, could be explained; but he implies the possibility that the relationship is not accidental.[9]

In the intervening period since Mason wrote his dissertation, several studies have appeared that have a direct bearing upon his work. A brief review of four of these works will help to sharpen the issues involved in understanding Zech 13:7–9. While these works show that, in some ways, many of the debates noted by Mason continue unresolved, bringing these four treatments into conversation with Mason also allows one to create a springboard that helps to reconceptualize the model by which one relates 13:7–9 to the broader context.

---

8. Ibid.
9. Ibid., 186–87.

Recent Treatments of Zechariah 13:7–9

The works of Paul Redditt, Stephen Cook, Carol Meyers and Eric Meyers, and David Petersen may be utilized in a constructive dialogue with Mason.[10] Redditt argues that Zech 9–14 reflects two significantly different blocks of material, namely, chapters 9–11 and 12–14, each of which had a separate redaction history.[11] Redditt deduces that the process by which these blocks were brought together can be detected as the work of a redactor who has combined no fewer than six collections of material: (1) a futuristic section with a pro-Davidic empire perspective in 9:1–10; (2) a prounion section demonstrating great concern for the exiles in 9:11–10:1 and 10:3b–12; (3) an antiunion collection consisting of shepherd materials now appearing in 10:2–3b, 11:1–17, and 13:7–9; (4) a pro-Jerusalem collection in 12:1–4a, 5, 8–9; (5) a collection that downplays Jerusalem's elevation over Judah and anticipates a purification of Jerusalem in 12:6–7 and 12:10–13:6;[12] (6) a pro-Jerusalem collection in 14:1–13, 14b–21 that {296} anticipates an attack on Jerusalem by the nations, an attack that is more debilitating for Jerusalem's inhabitants than the one depicted in chapter 12.[13] Redditt later clarifies his argument to indicate that collections three and five in reality supplement existing material, making them better understood as the work of the redactor responsible for the basic shape of Zech 9–14. While collection five comments upon the core of chapter 12 with a decidedly more negative attitude toward Jerusalem, the shepherd materials of collection

---

10. Paul L. Redditt, "Israel's Shepherds: Hope and Pessimism in Zechariah 9–14," *CBQ* 51 (1989): 631–42; Redditt, "The Two Shepherds in Zechariah 11:4–17," *CBQ* 55 (1993): 676–86; Redditt, *Haggai, Zechariah and Malachi*, NCB (London: HarperCollins, 1995); Stephen L. Cook, "The Metamorphosis of a Shepherd: The Tradition History of Zechariah 11:17 + 13:7–9," *CBQ* 55 (1993): 453–66; Carol L. Meyers and Eric M. Meyers, *Zechariah 9–14: A New Translation with Introduction and Commentary*, AB 25C (New York: Doubleday, 1993); David L. Petersen, *Zechariah 9–14 and Malachi: A Commentary*, OTL (Louisville: Westminster John Knox, 1995).

11. Redditt draws upon the insights of Childs, *Introduction to the Old Testament as Scripture*, and Yehuda T. Radday and Dieter Wickmann, "Unity of Zechariah Examined in the Light of Statistical Linguistics," *ZAW* 87 (1975): 30–55.

12. Here following Redditt's later delineation of this unit as stated in his commentary (*Haggai, Zechariah and Malachi*, 103). The delineation of this block in his earlier article cites the {296} material as 12:6–7, 10–12 and 13:6, but later implies that 13:2–6 is also part of this collection ("Israel's Shepherds," 638).

13. Redditt, "Israel's Shepherds," 636–38.

three exhibit a negative attitude toward the leaders in a more general sense. They are the only group of texts noted by Redditt that crosses both chapters 9–11 and 12–14. Redditt argues that "the redactor of 9–14 assembled the four collections and revised them by means of the supplements of 12:6–7, 12:10–13:6 and the shepherd materials."[14] For Redditt, the redactor of Zech 9–14 serves as compiler, arranger, and author who displays a decidedly more pessimistic attitude than the core texts which the redactor also includes. For Redditt, this negative attitude also points to the redactor as a member of a community who probably lived in the Judean countryside outside Jerusalem.[15]

Redditt's work has implications for Mason's presentation. Rather than seeing 13:7–9 as text that has been relocated from its original setting, Redditt argues that the author of 11:4–17 and 13:7–9 was also the editor who placed 13:7–9 in its current context to incorporate the idea of a purging into the cleansing discussed in 12:1–13:6.[16] Mason hints at the possibility that the placement of 13:7–9 functions meaningfully in the context of 12:1–13:6, but Redditt takes this idea a step further. This contextual function also comes into play in the works of Cook, as well as Meyers and Meyers, to explain the verses in their context. However, they take significantly different stands on how 13:7–9 relates to the context.

Cook counters Redditt's claim that the shepherd of 13:7–9 derives from a marginalized community or that the shepherd of 13:7–9 should be interpreted as a negative figure in its *current canonical* context.[17] Cook shapes his arguments in three parts. In part one, he acknowledges that 13:7–9 originally formed the conclusion of 11:4–17, when the shepherd narrative circulated independently.[18] Cook, however, {297} notes that 13:7–9 does not flow as seamlessly when read with 11:4–17 as most people assume. The poetic style is not the same in 13:7–9, and 13:8 begins with a new introductory formula (והיה) that makes it quite likely that one may understand 13:8–9 as a "supplementary elaboration" to 11:4–17.[19] He

---

14. Redditt, *Haggai, Zechariah and Malachi*, 103.
15. Redditt, "Israel's Shepherds," 638–40.
16. Redditt, *Haggai, Zechariah and Malachi*, 136.
17. Cook, "Metamorphosis of a Shepherd," 454, 456–57.
18. Since Ewald in 1840, a significant portion of scholars have argued or assumed that 13:7–9 has been *accidentally* dislocated from the end of 11:4–17 and somehow managed to be placed after 13:6 (ibid., 454, esp. nn. 3 and 4).
19. Ibid., 455–56.

believes, however, that this elaboration occurred while 11:4–17 still circulated as an independent tradition block. Cook also argues that the prophet of 11:4–17 actually portrays two shepherds: one good, the other evil.[20] It is, according to Cook, to this latter figure that 13:7–9 is addressed.[21]

In part two of his article, Cook argues that the relocation of 13:7–9 radically changes its original meaning so that the shepherd figure of 13:7–9 ceases to be an evil figure when the verses are relocated to its new context of Zech 12–14. Cook argues that in this new context the "broad chiastic pattern," which he finds to be the structure of Zech 12–14, now supersedes the original meaning of the text:[22]

    A. The eschatological war and the final victory (12:1–9).
       B. Descriptions of purification and return to God (12:10–13:1).
          C. Cleansing of idolatry and false prophecy (13:2–6).
       B′ Descriptions of purification and return to God (13:7–9).
    A′ The eschatological war and the final victory (14:1–21).

More important than the pivotal involvement of 13:7–9 in this structure, according to Cook, is his claim that 13:7–9 "now mediates the logical contradictions between the descriptions of the eschatological battle at the outer extremes of the Trito-Zecharian chiasm."[23] As appealing as this simplistic chiastic structure might appear to be at first glance, its broad outlines hardly justify Cook's claim that "the shepherd of 13:7–9 is now to be interpreted not as the anti-David in 11:15–17, but as a figure within the context of a more positive messianic expectation (as in Zech 3:8; 6:12–14; 9:9–10; 10:4)."[24] Mason's tradition-historical treatment of the shepherd imagery offers a needed corrective to the Cook's retrofitting of 13:7–9 with the hermeneutic of the New Testament Gospel writers, a move that becomes explicit in the third portion of Cook's article.[25] {298}

---

20. Ibid., 456.
21. For the inherent problems of this interpretation, see Mason's chapter on 11:4–17 ("Use of Earlier Biblical Material in Zechariah IX–XIV," 135–67).
22. Cook, "Metamorphosis of a Shepherd," 460.
23. Ibid., 461.
24. Ibid.
25. Cook's argument is even implicit in his headings: "The New Messianic Meaning of Zechariah 13:7–9" (ibid., 461–63) and "The Use of Zechariah 13:7–9 by Mark and Later Interpreters" (ibid., 463–66). Cook essentially contends that the New Testa-

Nevertheless, Cook makes two significant observations regarding 13:7–9, which should not be overlooked. First, his analysis of the uneven quality of the relationship between 13:7–9 and 11:4–17 illuminates a significant problem for understanding 13:7–9 as an original ending to 11:4–17. He bases his arguments upon stylistic and formal markers (esp. in 13:8–9). These arguments raise questions that require further consideration. Second, Cook underscores the possibility, already implied by Redditt, that the (re)location of 13:7–9 is not the result of accidental misplacement, even though his own explanation of a radically different meaning for 13:7–9 fails to convince.

In their commentary on Zech 9–14 Meyers and Meyers offer several observations regarding the character of 13:7–9 as a piece better suited to its current canonical context than to 11:4–17.[26] They state several rationales for relating 13:7–9 to the context of Zech 13.[27] First, they argue that the fate of the shepherd differs between 13:7 (where the sword of Yahweh will slay the shepherd) and 11:17 (where the sword is only used against the eye and arm of the shepherd). The language of intimacy is also more appropriate for a king than a prophet. Second, they argue that the shepherd of 13:7–9 presumes a ruler (as in Jer 23:1–6 and Ezek 34:1–23), not a prophet (as in 11:4, 15, 17). Finally, they argue that 13:7–9 functions with 13:1 as part of the thematic frame for chapter 13. They note that Zech 13:1 begins a new section, forming the first of three subunits. Zechariah 13:1 introduces a theme of *royal* leadership, a theme to which 13:7–9 returns after the discussion of 13:2–6, that has no "direct thematic links" with the framing material on either side.[28] They recognize that 13:2–6 concerns the removal of false prophets, but it presents this removal in a concrete fashion that is at odds with the abstract notion of the sword of Yahweh. By contrast, the frame of the chapter (13:1, 7–9) relates to the cleansing of the Davidides and the subsequent scattering of the people. Meyers and Meyers

---

ment writers correctly interpreted the messianic overtones from the context of Zechariah.

26. Meyers and Meyers, *Zechariah 9–14*, 384–97, 404–6.
27. Ibid., 384–85.
28. Ibid., 385. Meyers and Meyers do note elsewhere, however, that 13:2–6 contain "striking lexical connections" to 13:7–9 (398) which helps to fashion a subtle cohesion through the idea of the removal of impurities: 13:1 addresses the cleansing of the leadership through a fountain; 13:2–6 speaks of the removal of the impure spirit of the false prophets (cf. 13:2); and 13:7–9 speaks of the purification of the remnant who survive the judgment of devastation and exile.

conclude that 13:7 provides a historical allusion to the end of the monarchy that leads to ultimate restoration of the people: {299}

> This image of the slain shepherd and the consequent scattering of the flock is best understood as retrospective language used to anticipate the future age when the suffering and hardships undergone by the scattered flock will at last prove to have been efficacious in the formation of a new order—a renewed covenant with Yahweh.[29]

Thus, the pronouncement of the smiting of the shepherd in 13:7 begins a process of purification for a remnant that will be tested and found pure.

Meyers and Meyers, like Cook, provide a logical framework for understanding 13:7–9 in its current canonical context. Unlike Cook, they argue against 13:7–9 having originally circulated with 11:4–17. Meyers and Meyers also differ from Cook in that they see the relationship of 13:7–9 focused more narrowly upon chapter 13 than upon chapters 12–14. Also, they see the reference to the shepherd in historical and eschatological, not messianic, terms. In this sense, they concur with Mason's conclusion that this shepherd is not a positive figure. How strong are the arguments of Meyers and Meyers that 13:7–9 are formulated for the immediate context without any strong connection to 11:4–17? To be sure, they illustrate several tensions between 13:7–9 and 11:4–17 that call for serious reflection about the nature of the relationship between these two passages. However, the fact that so many scholars have related 11:4–17 and 13:7–9 to one another makes one wonder if recognition of these tensions is enough to overshadow the powerful connections seen by so many between these passages. Meyers and Meyers argue, for example, that the condemnation of the prophets in 13:2–6 nowhere expresses the idea that the prophets are to be considered as shepherds. For example, they argue that 13:7 begins a new subunit, in part because 13:2–6 condemns false prophets but does not explicitly associate these prophets with shepherds.[30] By contrast, they see in 13:7 a direct connection to the royal figures of 13:1, even though 13:1 also lacks any specific reference to shepherds. The subtle connections argued by Meyers and Meyers for the cohesion of 13:2–6 with 13:1 and 13:7 also do not appear to override the sense that 13:7–9 draws upon 11:4–17 when seen in light of the concrete connections noted by Mason and

---

29. Ibid., 388.
30. Ibid., 385.

others. The work of Meyers and Meyers also requires that one reevaluate the nature of the relationship between 13:7-9 and 11:4-17.

Another work deserves mention at this point, namely, the commentary of Petersen. It also challenges the view that 13:7-9 inherently belongs to 11:4-17. Like Meyers and Meyers, Petersen expresses doubt that 13:7-9 is an original ending to 11:4-17 on form-critical and literary {300} grounds.[31] Form critically, Petersen notes first that 11:4-17 can be seen as a unit without 13:7-9, and second, that 11:4-17 is a narrative report of symbolic actions while 13:7-9 betrays a poetic style that does not fit this genre. Petersen also observes that 13:7-9 not only draws upon a different genre, but merely mentions the shepherd in passing before moving on to a different focus.[32] These observations lead Petersen to argue that 13:7-9 functions "as a proleptic—and mildly sanguine—summary of the events that are described in greater detail in chap. 14."[33] He sees the verses as a poetic transition that involves a sequencing of events to answer the question: will anyone survive the coming judgment of Yahweh? The sequence to which Petersen refers is the sequence of destruction, refining, and restitution. In other words, for Petersen, these verses do not originally function with 11:4-17. Instead, they point the reader forward by introducing Zech 14.[34]

The comparison of more recent presentations with Mason's has elicited several sources of similarity. To be sure, several points of contention remain. It is doubtful that unanimity will ever be achieved for this passage. Still, many of Mason's conclusions continue to carry weight. The shepherd figure is generally viewed as negative. The passage is most often viewed as relating to the theme of the castigation of Judean leadership in some form. The passage is taken by some to reflect a community's concern to place themselves in contradistinction to the leadership of their day. The sense that Zech 9-14 draws extensively upon other biblical texts has certainly been enhanced. Finally, the relationship of 13:7-9 to 11:4-17 continues to play a major role in the discussion of the passage, even though

---

31. Petersen, *Zechariah 9-14 and Malachi*, 88-89.
32. Ibid., 129.
33. Ibid.
34. Redditt makes this point differently ("Two Shepherds," 685). While he focuses more on the relationship between 13:7-9 and 12:1-13:6, he also notes that striking the shepherd and scattering the people prepares the reader for the attack of the nations (14:2) and Yahweh's intervention (14:9).

this relationship must now be viewed more complexly. This complexity of the relationship between 11:4–17 and 13:7–9 appears to be the area of the most significant challenge to Mason's presentation, especially with regard to the need to explain the *current* function of 13:7–9 when it is separated from 11:4–17 by the material in 12:1–13:6. Mason anticipates this question by raising the possibility that the *placement* of 13:7–9 may appear after 13:6 for a reason. Four different presentations have been reviewed in this paper. Redditt sees the shepherd material as a major redactional thread for the tradition units of all of Zech 9–14. Cook argues that the relocation of 13:7–9 to its current location radically altered its meaning. Meyers and {301} Meyers argue that the literary tensions between 11:4–17 and 13:7–9 force one to consider the latter as part of chapter 13 without significant reference to 11:4–17. Petersen sees the primary function as an introduction to chapter 14. At the risk of muddying the waters even more, the remainder of this study will consider a slightly different model for understanding 13:7–9, one that can help to account both for many of the similarities and for the tensions noted by others between 13:7–9; 11:4–17, and 12:1–13:6. This model will explore the implications of viewing 13:7–9 as a redactional composition created for its context in Zechariah *and* in the Book of the Twelve.

Zechariah 13:7–9 as a Redactional Composition with a Broad Literary Horizon

In most discussions of Zech 13:7–9, two points often receive only minimal notice, if any at all. However, these neglected characteristics open the door for understanding 13:7–9 from a different perspective that can perhaps alleviate some of the long-standing issues. These items are the transitional function of these verses and the broad literary horizon they exhibit. In the case of the transitional function, all four of the recent presentations discussed above have suggested that these verses function meaningfully in the current context; nevertheless the emphasis tends to be placed upon the manner in which they comment upon, or are involved with, different portions of Zech 11–14.

When viewed in totality, it is striking how consistently scholarship of the last thirty years has interpreted 13:7–9 as significantly related to the three major tradition blocks near it. Some (e.g., Mason and Redditt) see the primary and/or the original focus of 13:7–9 with 11:4–17. Some (e.g., Cook plus Meyers and Meyers) see 13:7–9 in relationship to all or parts of

12:1–13:6. Some (e.g., Petersen and Redditt) note that 13:7–9 introduces the material to come in chapter 14. All of these perspectives, divergent though they may be, are rooted in textual and contextual observations. The similarities to chapter 11 focus on the shepherd and sword connections in 13:7. The connections to 12:1–13:6 focus on the rejection of the leadership in general, or the royal house in particular, implicit in the smiting of the shepherd in 13:7. The connections to chapter 14 rely upon the introduction of an implicit attack in 13:8 or the remnant motif in 13:8–9.

Perhaps the biggest problem lies in the assumption that an either/or relationship best explains the relationship of these verses to their context. Each of the arguments tends to relate the *primary focus* of these verses to one of the major tradition blocks (11:4–17; 12:1–13:6; or 14:1–21). In {302} reality, these verses have points of connections to *all* of the blocks in the vicinity. It seems plausible in the light of the arguments presented that we need to conceptualize 13:7–9 as a redactional transitional text composed to provide direction for combining the three major blocks around it. Redditt, I believe, comes very close to arguing this point, but he seems to maintain that 13:7–9 originally concluded 11:4–17, a position that Meyers and Meyers as well as Petersen show to be problematic. Conversely, just because 13:7–9 is not original to 11:4–17, does not mean that scholars such as Mason as well as Redditt do not see connections to 11:4–17 that were intended by the author of 13:7–9. I would suggest that Zech 13:7–9 takes up the imagery of the shepherd *from* 11:4–17 through its allusions to the shepherd and the sword, but not as an original conclusion to 11:4–17. The same can be noted for its thematic connections with 12:1–13:6, on the one hand, and with 14:1–21, on the other. The three-verse unit stands out from its context on formal and stylistic grounds, but it also provides a connecting point on lexical and thematic grounds. As such, it guides the reader from the condemnation of the leadership and the annulment of the covenant (11:4–17) to the purification of the leadership (12:1–13:6) and the anticipation of the renewed covenant for the remnant following the day of Yahweh (14:1–21).

Regarding the second point about the character of 13:7–9, the literary horizon of these verses is not limited to Zech 11–14. Rather, I would suggest that the redactional processes involved in combining the latter portions of Zechariah take place in a scribal prophetic milieu that has the coherence of the entire prophetic canon in its purview. The impetus for this argument derives from several observations, especially with respect to the formulations of the remnant motif and the covenant renewal of 13:9.

Several of the scholars surveyed have noted that the covenant language recalls Hos 2:25 (23), among other texts.[35] However, most of these discussions have assumed that the connection to Hos 2:25 derives solely from tradition-historical similarities. Close inspection of Hos 2:25 and Zech 13:9 suggests that the latter is alluding *specifically* to the former. While it is true that several texts rely upon the association of calling on the name of Yahweh to express the covenant idea, none of these other texts share their formulation to the extent that 13:9 and Hos 2:25 do.

> And I will say to Not-my-people, "You are my people." And he will say, "my god." (Hos 2:25 [note ענה in 2:23–24])

> He will call on my name and I will respond [ענה] to him. I will say, "He is my people," and he will say, "Yahweh is my god." (Zech 13:9b) {303}

These are the only two verses in the Hebrew Bible in which the speech of Yahweh alternates with the speech of a prophet to express this idea. Further, this formulation is introduced with "respond" (ענה), a verb used five times in the two verses preceding Hos 2:25. The context of Hos 2:25 is the renewal of the covenant (cf. 2:20 [Eng. 18]) with the children of the prophet introduced in Hos 1–2, the first explicit reference to "covenant" in the Book of the Twelve. It is noteworthy that Zech 13:9b alludes to Hos 2:25.

It is equally noteworthy that Zech 13:9a alludes to the passage containing the last reference to "covenant" in the Book of the Twelve, namely, Mal 3:1. Fewer scholars have noted this allusion, probably because so many have seen the refiner language in Zech 13:9a as part of the continuation of the interplay between Zech 11:4–17 and Ezekiel.[36] However, the coalescence of vocabulary and concepts between 13:9a and Mal 3:1–3 suggests Zech 13:9 alludes to Malachi. Both texts combine images of refining (בחן / צרף in Zech 13:9; טהר / צרף in Mal 3:3), with the concepts of Yahweh's day of judgment and the covenant playing significant roles in the surrounding verses.

---

35. Mason, "Use of Earlier Biblical Material in Zechariah IX–XIV," 185; Redditt, *Haggai, Zechariah and Malachi*, 136; Meyers and Meyers, *Zechariah 9–14*, 396; Petersen, *Zechariah 9–14 and Malachi*, 132.

36. Mason sees 13:8–9 in relationship to Ezek 5:3–4 and 22:17–22 because of the division of the fate of the people into three groups in the former and the smelting imagery in the latter ("Use of Earlier Biblical Material in Zechariah IX–XIV," 182–84). However, the smelting imagery of Ezek 22:17 uses another word.

Further relationships between Zech 9–14 and other prophetic texts suggest these chapters draw upon other prophetic writings with enough regularity to see this as a central part of the character of these chapters. Given that Zech 13:7–9 anticipates Zech 14, as noted by Petersen, and that Zech 14 is a pastiche of sayings concerning the day of Yahweh, it is not surprising that Zech 14 contains its share of allusions and parallels to other prophetic texts. Chief among these would be Joel 4, as noted by Mason and others, and Isa 66 (the beginning book of the Latter Prophets).[37] The end of Malachi also contains an editorial ending that has been seen in recent years as a text that alludes back to the beginning of Joshua (the beginning of the former Prophets). Mason also notes briefly a similarity between the outpouring of the spirit in Joel 3:1 [Eng. 2:28] and Zech 12:10.[38] {304} In short, Zech 13:9 is not the only verse in Zech 9–14 that suggests a broader horizon than the immediate context, a horizon that likely has the entire prophetic corpus in its sights.

Thus, Zech 13:7–9 should be viewed as a redactional text composed to create a literary transition between preexisting tradition blocks. It speaks of the initiation of a process of refinement that begins with Yahweh's judgment upon the leadership, which in turn leads to judgment upon the leader and the people, before a small minority survives to continue the covenant relationship. This sequence reflects the themes of the context of chapter 11, 12:1–13:6 *and* chapter 14, which goes a long way toward explaining the function of 13:7–9 as a redactional and transitional unit.

It is becoming clear that one of the major functions of Zech 9–14 as a whole is its recasting and its dependence upon other prophetic texts. The work of Rex Mason has played no small part in understanding this function of Zech 9–14. If some of his conclusions have been modified over time, it is significant that he was asking many of the right questions long before the discipline as a whole.

---

37. I have discussed these canonical allusions elsewhere (James D. Nogalski, "Intertextuality and the Twelve," in Watts, *Forming Prophetic Literature*, 123–24). See also how Meyers and Meyers explain the differences in Zech 13:9 and Mal 3:3 with respect to the metallurgical processes to which they allude (*Zechariah 9–14*, 394–95).

38. Mason explains this similarity in tradition-historical terms, but in light of Joel's function as a literary paradigm for the Book of the Twelve, this relationship needs further exploration (see James D. Nogalski, "Joel as 'Literary Anchor' for the Book of the Twelve," in Nogalski, *Reading and Hearing*, 91–109).

Micah 7:8–20:
A Reevaluation of the Identity of the Enemy

The Problem

Micah 7:8–20 is unusual among Old Testament texts in that one may speak of a relatively strong consensus on three fronts.[1] First, since Stade, most scholars agree that the passage belongs to the latest compositional level of the book and presumes a postexilic setting in its present form.[2] Second, since Gunkel, most scholars recognize a postexilic liturgical setting, or in more recent literature, at least a liturgical pattern, in Mic 7:8–20.[3] Third, most scholars either presume or argue explicitly that these {126} verses, or

---

* This study is dedicated to the memory of Gerald Shepherd. His untimely death not only robbed family and friends of a valued loved one; it also robbed the discipline of biblical studies of a person whose insights and creativity still had much to offer. He will be missed, but his legacy will endure through his own writings, through the questions he raised, and the people whose lives he touched.

1. This study develops ideas noted in Nogalski, *Literary Precursors*, 144–170.
2. Bernhard Stade, "Streiflichter auf die Entstehung der jetzigen Gestalt der alttestamentlichen Prophetenschriften," *ZAW* 23 (1903): 153–71. Hillers represents a rare exception; see Delbert R. Hillers, *Micah*, Hermeneia (Philadelphia: Fortress, 1984), 89.
3. While variations exists regarding how best to describe the liturgical character, the presence of liturgical elements is widely recognized: Stade, "Streiflichter"; Karl Marti, *Das Dodekapropheton*, KHC 13 (Tübingen: Mohr Siebeck, 1904), 298; Bernhard Duhm, "Anmerkungen zu den Zwölf Propheten II," *ZAW* 31 (1911): 92–93; Hermann Gunkel, "Der Micha-Schluß: Zur Einführung in die literaturgeschichtliche Arbeit am Alten Testament," *ZS* 2 (1924): 145–78; (see also: Gunkel, "The Close of Micah: A Prophetic Liturgy," in *What Remains of the Old Testament and Other Essays*, trans. Alexander K. Dallas [New York: Macmillan, 1928], 115–49); Bo Reicke, "Liturgical Traditions in Mic 7," *HTR* 60 (1967): 349–67; Otto Eissfeldt, "Ein Psalm aus Nord-Israel: Mi 7,7–20," *ZDMG* 112 (1962): 259–68; Theodor Lescow, "Redaktionsgeschichtliche Analyse von Micha 6–7," *ZAW* 84 (1972): 182–212; James Luther Mays, *Micah: A Commentary*, OTL (Philadelphia: Westminster, 1976), 155.

significant portions of them, originated independently from the book in which they now reside.⁴ Evidence for the first two opinions need not be challenged here. There are good reasons for presuming postexilic concerns motivate Mic 7:8–20. The destitution of Zion reflected in Mic 7:8–13 presupposes the time after 587 BCE. Likewise, the text itself clearly indicates the author worked with a liturgical pattern. The dialogical vacillation of speakers in a pattern of address and response requires such a model, and the documentable parallels within Old Testament literature make it the most plausible framework from which to read the text.

The assumption that Mic 7:8–20 originated independently from its literary context, however, creates considerable difficulty for determining the concrete identity of the enemy within these verses. To be sure, the text does not make the identity of the enemy explicit. The only *concrete* references to the enemy appear in 7:8 and 7:10, where the enemy is cited using feminine singular references.⁵ Efforts at determining the *original* identity of this enemy have not succeeded. Three suggestions dominate the literature: Edom, Babylon, and an unspecified collective enemy. Yet each of these suggestions creates problems for understanding 7:8–20.

Edom is the entity most frequently suggested for the enemy mentioned in Mic 7:8–10.⁶ The assumption of a late date for these verses gives rise to this suggestion in light of numerous anti-Edom passages during the exilic and postexilic period.⁷ Despite the frequency with which Edom is suggested, this option is the most unlikely for syntactical reasons. The enemy in 7:8–10 is feminine, but no other Old Testament text refers generically to Edom using feminine address.⁸ Additionally, Edom plays

---

4. E.g., Hans Walter Wolff, *Micah: A Commentary*, trans. Gary Stansell, CC (Minneapolis: Augsburg, 1990), 215–17; Wilhelm Rudolph, *Micha, Nahum, Habakuk, Zephanja*, KAT 13.3 (Gütersloh: Mohn, 1975), 131.

5. The enemy is addressed both directly and in the third person. This change of perspective should be treated as a stylistic variation, however, and is not the result of separate sources.

6. See, e.g., Mays, *Micah*, 158–59, who follows Gunkel and Sellin.

7. E.g., Obadiah; Mal 1:2–5; Jer 49:7–22; Ezek 35, etc. Lescow typified those who understand 7:8–10 as a liturgy of repentance from the exilic period ("Redaktionsgeschichtliche Analyse von Micha 6–7," 205).

8. One noted exception appears in Obad 1, but the parallel in Jer 49:14 makes clear that the original addressee of that oracle was the city Bozrah. See the discussion of the relationship between Obad 1–5; Jer 49:14–16, 9; and Amos 9:1–4 in James D. Nogalski, *Redactional Processes in the Book of the Twelve*, BZAW 218 (Berlin: de

no role elsewhere in the book of Micah, requiring one to assume these {127} verses originated separately from the book, without offering adequate explanations as to how or why they were incorporated into their present location.

Babylon appears elsewhere in feminine singular form, but the assumption of Babylon creates chronological difficulties for the text as a whole.[9] The entire context, but particularly Mic 7:8–10, reflects an enemy in an ascendant position over against Jerusalem.[10] Babylon could hardly have been so described in the postexilic period after its overthrow by the Persians in 539 BCE. Thus, if Babylon were the original enemy in 7:8–10, this portion of the "liturgy" could not stem from the postexilic period. Thus, as with the suggestion of Edom, the assumption that Babylon was the enemy requires that these verses circulated independently of the book, and that someone incorporated them into Micah, together with other preexisting blocks, without making the referent explicit or by deliberately omitting reference to Babylon.

Several recent commentaries contend that the feminine singular reference intends a collective enemy.[11] Several of these commentators even translate the references to the singular enemy in Mic 7:8–10 as plural in order to emphasize the collective nature. While syntactically possible, the feminine *singular* "enemy," appearing in both verbal and pronominal forms, makes this collective explanation unsatisfactory if another explanation can be found. Like both of the other suggestions, proponents of the assumption of a collective enemy typically concede independent origin for Mic 7:8–10 at some point following the destruction of Jerusalem in 587 BCE.[12]

Gruyter, 1993), 61–74. Edom does appear in Lam 4:21 as feminine, but only with the specific title "daughter of Edom."

9. E.g., Wolff believes that the enemy was likely Babylon (*Micah*, 220).

10. Micah 7:8 states, "Though I dwell in darkness." A desolate Zion who waits for deliverance, "Until he (YHWH) pleads my case and executes justice for me," is reflected in Mic 7:9. See also Mic 7:18, "He does not retain his anger forever."

11. See, e.g., Smith, *Micah–Malachi*, 58; Leslie C. Allen, *The Books of Joel, Obadiah, Jonah, and Micah*, NICOT (Grand Rapids: Eerdmans, 1976), 390–91; Hillers, *Micah*, 87; Rudolph, *Micha, Nahum, Habakuk, Zephanja*, 131–32; Marvin A. Sweeney, *The Twelve Prophets*, Berit Olam (Collegeville, MN: Liturgical Press, 2000), 2:408–14.

12. So Allen, *Joel, Obadiah, Jonah, and Micah*, 394. Hillers represents an exception since he wants to date the entire passage in the eighth century. Even Hillers,

66 THE BOOK OF THE TWELVE AND BEYOND

Thus, all three suggestions for the identity of the enemy create substantial problems for a concrete determination of the original enemy and for the current position of Mic 7:8–10. Edom as the enemy is extremely {128} unlikely because of the feminine form of address. The assumption of Babylon as the original enemy requires a date prior to 539 BCE. The supposition of a collective enemy requires that one explain away the clear singular forms. None of these suggestions adequately explain why Mic 7:8–20 found its way into the book of Micah.

The Intertextual Phenomenon

All three of the suggestions mentioned above presume that Mic 7:8–10 originated independently from the book. Additionally, many presume or argue explicitly that 7:8–10 originated independently of the remainder of the component parts of 7:8–20. As a prelude to challenging this assumption, it is necessary to document the existence of an extensive intertextual phenomenon between Mic 7:8–20 and Isa 9–12. This intertextuality will then serve as the basis for understanding 7:8–10 as an integral part of Mic 7:8–20 and for seeing the entire complex as a literary construct created explicitly to conclude Micah.

As the following table indicates, almost every verse in Mic 7:8–20 contains elements that also appear in the anti-Assyrian polemic of Isa 9–12.

Micah 6:16; 7:1–20		Isaiah 9–12	
6:16	Statutes of Omri	10:1	Evil statutes
7:1	Woe is me	10:1	Woe to those who enact
7:2	There are no godly/upright ones	10:2	The unjust acts of YHWH's people
7:3	Bribe of prince, judge	10:1	Unjust legal decisions
7:4	Day when punishment and confusion will come	10:3	Day of punishment
7:5–6	There is no one to trust	10:3–4	There is nowhere to turn for help
7:7	I will wait for the God of my salvation.	12:2	Behold, God is my salvation

however, is cautious about doing so, since he states: "I prefer to hold that it fits conditions of Micah's time, but to leave open the possibility of later origin" (*Micah*, 89).

7:8	Do not rejoice my enemy Though I am in darkness YHWH is my light.	9:1–2	The people who dwell in darkness will see a great light, and will rejoice.
7:9	I will bear YHWH's indignation (his anger)	10:25	Soon my indignation against you will be spent, and my anger will turn to their (Assyria's) destruction.
7:10	My enemy said where is your God?	—	(But cf. Isa 36:18–20 = 2 Kgs 18:32b–35)
7:10	My enemy will be trampled down like mire of the streets	10:6	Assyria was sent against the people of my fury to trample them down like mud in the streets
7:11	A day for building your walls your boundary will become distant	9:9 10:13 10:3	The bricks have fallen, but we will rebuild with smooth stones (cf. especially 2 Chr 32:5) Assyria says I removed the boundaries of the peoples Destruction will come from afar
7:12	He will come from Assyria and the cities of Egypt	10:6, 12 10:24 10:26	I sent Assyria against a godless nation and Jerusalem Assyria will strike you like a rod in the way Egypt did God will raise the sea with his staff as he did in Egypt
	unto the river (Euphrates) and the sea and the mountains	—	(cf. Isa 11:11–12)
7:13	And the land becomes desolate	10:23	There will be complete destruction in the midst of the whole land
7:14	Shepherd your people with your rod	10:5	Assyria is the rod of my anger (cf. also 10:15, 24)
	A forest	10:18	YHWH will destroy the glory of Assyria's forest
	in the midst of Carmel	10:19 10:34	and his thicket [כרמל] and the rest of the trees of his forest will be reduced YHWH will cut down the thickets of the forest

7:15	YHWH's going forth from Egypt	10:26	Parting of the sea when leaving Egypt
7:16	Nations will see YHWH's noisy deeds and be ashamed of their own might	10:33	YHWH will destroy Assyria noisily and any other nation of stature
7:18	The remnant of his possession will survive his anger	10:20–22	A remnant will remain from the destruction of Israel. (cf. 11:11: YHWH will recover the remnant of his people a second time)
7:19	He will again have compassion [רחם] on us.	12:1	Although you were angry with me, your anger is turned away, and you comfort [נחם] me.

These common elements represent a wide variety of vocabulary and motifs, and it is striking that they occur with such regularity in these two diverse passages. The question, of course, arises as to the explanation for these common elements. Do they represent coincidental similarities to which one may not attach any interpretive weight? Does one passage manifest a dependency upon the other, and if so, how does one characterize that dependency? Which text draws from which, and for what reason?

It is doubtful that the occurrence of these elements may be attributed to chance. These elements are too extensive, and their backgrounds are too diverse to suggest credibly that such an integrated series of parallels would occur by happenstance. These parallels include specific vocabulary, and common motifs which are not natural counterparts in two unrelated passages. Both passages combine such terms as darkness and light with rejoicing (Mic 7:8 // Isa 9:1–2); trampling the enemy like mire/mud in the streets (Mic 7:10 // Isa 10:6); the verb "to build" (Mic 7:11 // Isa 9:9); the "rod" of YHWH (Mic 7:14 // Isa 10:5, 15, 24); "forest" and "Carmel" (Mic 7:14 // Isa 10:18); the anger of YHWH (Mic 7:18 // Isa 10:25). Additionally, very close synonyms buttress the common vocabulary, such as with the appearance of YHWH's indignation (זעף in Mic 7:9) and rage (זעם in Isa 10:25); complete destruction (Isa 10:23) and desolation (Mic 7:13). {131[13]}

Finally, the diversity of motifs appearing in both passages cements the conclusion that the combination of these elements is no accident: rejoic-

---

13. This chart was initially displayed on pages 129–30 in the original printing.

ing at the eventual deliverance of YHWH, despite the current situation (Mic 7:8 // Isa 9:1-2); YHWH's anger and indignation against his own people will lead to the punishment of the enemy (Mic 7:9-10 // Isa 10:6, 25); rebuilding of city structures (Mic 7:11 // Isa 9:9); reference to the exodus from Egypt (Mic 7:15 // Isa 10:26); defeat and fear of the nations (Mic 7:16 // Isa 10:33; 11:14-16); survival of a remnant (Mic 7:18 // Isa 10:20-22); YHWH will again have compassion despite his anger (Mic 7:19 // Isa 12:1). Thus, the remarkable consistency of common vocabulary, themes, and motifs argue strongly that a relationship exists between these two passages.

Given the existence of a relationship between these two texts, scholarly consensus requires that any dependency must be on the part of the author of Mic 7:8-20. While no one doubts that Isa 9-12 contains diverse material in its own right, there is likewise little doubt that the vast majority of these chapters had attained written form long before the destruction of Jerusalem. By contrast, scholarly consensus argues that Mic 7:8-20 presupposes Jerusalem's destruction. Hence, there is no reason to doubt that Mic 7:8-20 draws from Isa 9-12, and not the other way around.

How then does one characterize the dependency of Mic 7:8-20 upon Isa 9-12? Before turning to a specific proposal, it is necessary to point out one other phenomenon, because it offers another clue as to how the author of Mic 7:8-20 works. Two significant motifs in Mic 7:8-20 exhibit a distinct similarity to portions of the Hezekiah narratives. Micah 7:10 quotes Zion's enemy asking the taunting question: "Where is your God?" Second Kings 18:32b-35 (= Isa 36:18-20) depicts a speech delivered by the messenger of the "king of Assyria" (2 Kgs 18:31 = Isa 36:16), who delivers a speech to the people of Jerusalem in the time of Hezekiah just prior to Sennacherib's siege. This speech utilizes the question, "Where is the god of 'X'?" as a refrain to claim that the gods of other countries were of no value to them when Assyria's military machine was turned against them. This refrain climaxes with a question regarding the power of Jerusalem's god (2 Kgs 18:35 = Isa 36:20), which essentially parallels the question in Mic 7:11.

A second noticeable motif in Mic 7:8-20 appearing in the Hezekiah traditions relates to the phraseology of Mic 7:11. In this verse YHWH promises the personified Zion the building of walls and extension of the boundary. Second Chronicles 32:5 reflects an interesting tradition attributed to Hezekiah, namely, that in response to the threat of attack from Sennacherib, Hezekiah rebuilt the city wall that had fallen down, and {132} built another wall *outside* it, effectively extending Jerusalem's boundary prior to the siege. Thus, in addition to the awareness of the anti-Assyrian polemic of Isa 9–12, Mic 7:8–20 contains echoes of two specific motifs which appear in the Hezekiah traditions.

A Proposal Concerning the Intertextual Significance

The discussion above demonstrates that Mic 7:8–20 reflects the awareness of an anti-Assyrian polemic from Isa 9–12 and evidences motifs specifically found in traditions surrounding Hezekiah. How does one characterize this dependency upon these elements? The intertextuality operating within Mic 7:8–20 provides strong evidence that this so-called liturgy did not arise independently but that it was created with full awareness of its *position in Micah*. The anti-Assyrian polemic and the connection to the motifs from the Hezekiah traditions form a natural *inclusio* to Mic 1:1, where it is stated that Micah preached during the reigns of Jotham, Ahaz, and Hezekiah. The extent of the intertextuality suggests that the entire passage should be read as though it were set in this time period, as though it comments upon the entire Assyrian period. When one does so, not only does such a reading make sense, but it illuminates several enigmatic elements which have puzzled scholars concerning Mic 7:8–20. Reading 7:8–20 with these echoes not only allows one to ascertain the hermeneutical movement running through 7:8–20, it illuminates the qualification of promissory elements within the liturgical framework. The liturgical framework and the presupposition of an Assyrian period setting (created by a postexilic author) must be kept in mind constantly when interpreting 7:8–20.

The constellation of this passage incorporates a three-fold movement within a liturgical framework, one which is created by the change in *speakers* evident in the text. This liturgical pattern may be outlined as follows: (1) Mic 7:8–13, Zion's song of confidence and YHWH's response; (2) Mic 7:14–15, the prophet's intercession and YHWH's response; and (3) Mic 7:16–20*, the people's response.[14] Understanding how the {133} presump-

---

14. One portion of this final movement does not conform to this pattern. Micah 7:19b cannot be a speech of the people, because it addresses the people using a third-person masculine *plural* reference: "And you will cast all of their sins into the depths of the sea." The identity of the masculine singular referent is obviously YHWH, since only YHWH could cast the sins into the depths of the sea. The speaker cannot be the

tion of an Assyrian setting on the part of the author effects the interpretation requires a closer look at these verses.

The first constellation involves the personified Zion's song of confidence in Mic 7:8–10 and the divine response offering a qualified promise in 7:11–13. In 7:8–10, Zion affirms her confidence in YHWH, despite the current situation which Zion accepts as punishment for sin (7:9). The verses are addressed to an unspecified feminine enemy. Having already noted the problems inherent in typical suggestions of the identity of this enemy, several interrelated observations allow one to postulate that Nineveh personified is *presumed* as the enemy in these verses. Micah 7:8–10 involves the conception of two feminine entities. One feminine entity speaks to and about another feminine enemy. The identities of these speakers may be *deduced* as Zion and Nineveh personified. The identity of the personified Zion as the speaker is evident on the basis of Old Testament tradition-historical considerations, from the immediate context, and from broader phenomena in Western Semitic culture.[15] Indeed, Zion is almost universally recognized as the speaker in these verses, although

---

people since elsewhere in this section, the people speak using first-person common plural references (Mic 7:17, 19). This elimination allows only two possibilities. Either the liturgy is so created that the prophet breaks in for a short speech, or else this verse represents a later editorial insertion. Tradition-critical and redaction-critical evidence {133} points strongly toward the latter, because this half-verse clearly takes up the language of Jon 2:4, drawing a parallel between the "salvation" of Jonah and the salvation of the congregation in Mic 7:19b. For further development of these thoughts, see Nogalski, *Literary Precursors*, 152–53. For reasons listed there, Mic 7:19b will not be included in the discussion that follows.

15. The personified Zion as city appears elsewhere in Old Testament texts such as Isa 60–62; Zeph 3:11–20; Ezek 16; 23; etc. The immediate context reveals the speaker is considered a city since the promise in 7:11 involves the rebuilding of her walls. Within the broader phenomenon of Western Semitic culture, capital cities were often personified. See evidence and interpretations in Aloysius Fitzgerald, "Mythological Background for the Presentation of Jerusalem as a Queen and False Worship as Adultery in the OT," *CBQ* 34 (1972): 403–16; John J. Schmitt, "The Motherhood of God and Zion as Mother," *RB* 92 (1985): 557–69; Mayer I. Gruber, "The Motherhood of God in Second Isaiah," *RB* 90 (1983): 351–59; Mark E. Biddle, "The Figure of Lady Jerusalem: Identification, Deification and Personification of Cities in the Ancient Near East," in *Biblical Canon in Comparative Perspectives*, ed. William W. Hallo, K. Lawson Younger, and Bernard F. Batto (Lewiston, NY: Mellen, 1991), 173–94; Odil Hannes Steck, "Zion als Gelände und Gestalt: Überlegungen zur Wahrnehmung Jerusalems als Stadt und Frau im Alten Testament," *ZTK* 86 (1989): 261–81.

the conceptualization of Zion is often muted into that of the congregation rather than allowing the force of the metaphor and the tradition of Zion as personified city to permeate the text.[16] {134}

For many of the same reasons, Nineveh appears as the most likely enemy portrayed in these verses. The immediate context has many parallels indicating awareness of Isaiah's anti-Assyrian polemic. The broader background of Western Semitic culture demonstrates it was common for capital cities to be personified as women. The specific personification of Nineveh as a woman appears in other Old Testament texts, in Nah 2–3. Finally, the *assumption* of Nineveh as the enemy eliminates one of the primary enigmas of this passage, namely anonymity of the enemy. Traditions regarding the identity of the prophet Micah categorically portray him as a prophet in the Assyrian period.[17] Any redactional continuation of Micah in the postexilic period could hardly have been ignorant of the historical associations of that prophet. Likewise, Sennacherib's siege of Jerusalem during the reign of Hezekiah would naturally spring to mind as the threat to which Zion alludes in Mic 7:8–10. All of these observations imply the enemy in these verses is the personified Nineveh.

The divine response to Zion's confidence appears in Mic 7:11–13. These verses also appear most coherent when read as a commentary upon the Assyrian period *if* one is to maintain the unity of the verses. Formally, these verses presuppose their context, but the speaker changes. Micah 7:11–12 address Zion explicitly, indicating Zion can no longer be the speaker as in Mic 7:8–10. The nature of the promises in these verses indicates YHWH is now understood as the speaker, as he affirms that Zion's confidence is not unfounded. The divine response continues formally through 7:13, since the speaker changes again in 7:14. Yet, despite a consistent divine speaker, these verses (7:11–13) evidence considerable tension with one another.

Formally, Mic 7:11 clearly announces a promise to Zion, which apparently continues without interruption in 7:12. Micah 7:13, however, just as clearly announces desolation. How does one account for the change from promise to destruction within the same divine response? One could, of

---

16. See, e.g., Allen, *Joel, Obadiah, Jonah, and Micah*, 394; Smith, *Micah–Malachi*, 58.

17. Not only does the Deuteronomistic superscription of Mic 1:1 place Micah's ministry in the reigns of Jotham, Ahaz, and Hezekiah, but also Jer 26:18 locates the prophet in the reign of Hezekiah.

course, postulate an interpolation from a later hand, but clear rationale for such an interpolation is unclear. Micah 7:11–12 continue the second-person feminine singular suffixes and references from the immediate context, leaving 7:13 as the most likely candidate for interpolation, yet the decisive judgment pronouncement of this verse makes it very difficult to believe someone would have added it to a context of salvation. As with {135} the song of confidence in 7:8–10, the presumption that the postexilic author is writing about the Assyrian period, combined with careful observations concerning the promises in 7:11–13, alleviates the tension within these verses considerably.

Micah 7:11 is clearly promissory in nature. It promises Zion that the walls will be rebuilt and the boundary expanded. Typically, this verse is interpreted in light of Jerusalem's destruction in 587 BCE as evidence that the verses were composed prior to Nehemiah. Indeed, when 7:11 is so read, the next verse adds to the impression of a promise of Zion's restoration. Micah 7:12 continues the thought of 7:11 when it promises "and he will come unto you from Assyria even to Egypt, and from Egypt even to the Euphrates, and from sea to sea, and mountain to mountain." Under the influence of the promise in Mic 7:11, this verse is normally interpreted as a reference to the return of the diaspora Jews from Assyria, Egypt, Babylon, and all the regions to which YHWH's people had been exiled. Certainly, this reading is possible syntactically. The problem comes with the attempt to incorporate Mic 7:13 into the picture, since it speaks in no uncertain terms of desolation: "And the land [הארץ] will become a desolation because of its inhabitants, on account of the fruit of their deeds."[18] The sins of the inhabitants have already been depicted in 1:7, 9, 13; 2:1–11; 3:1–12; 6:1–16.

Three interrelated observations, which challenge conventional readings of 7:11–13, may be submitted to clarify the thought progression. First, as already stated, 7:13 refers to the desolation of the land, not universal desolation. Second, this pronouncement of desolation upon the land in Mic 7:13, contrasts *intentionally* with the promise to Zion in 7:11, reflecting an awareness of the historical aftermath of the Assyrian period. The Northern Kingdom was destroyed, and its capital sacked. Much of Judah

---

18. Typically, scholars translate ארץ in Mic 7:13 universally. Tradition-critically, the association of "desolation" with ארץ elsewhere refers to the land, and not the entire world. Note the interpretive translation of the LXX for example. See further discussion in Nogalski, *Literary Precursors*, 148–49.

came under Assyrian control. The fact that Jerusalem remained intact physically and politically coincides with the promise in 7:11. In fact, when one notes the explicit parallels to the Chronicler's Hezekiah tradition, one may even understand the phraseology of 7:11 as specifically related to the events surrounding Sennacherib's siege. It is Jerusalem which receives the promise for the rebuilding and expansion. This promise to (re)build the walls and expand the boundary coincides remarkably well with the Chronicler's account in which Hezekiah {136} rebuilds one wall and builds another wall outside it, thereby expanding the boundary of *Jerusalem*, not the entire land.[19]

Third, while Mic 7:12 is tied syntactically to 7:11, it does not necessarily follow that this verse promises the return of the exiles. The verse announces only that *he will come to you*, but does not explicitly state either the identity or the purpose of the one who comes. The formulation of עַד + בוֹא, normally understood to refer to the return of the diaspora, also

---

19. The question of the date and historicity of the Chronicler's account plays no major role in this observation. There are now a considerable number of supporters for an early version of the Chronicler's history which was already compiled in the sixth century, meaning it would have been available in written form at the time of composition of Mic 7:8–20. If the older theory that the Chronicler's account was not composed prior to the end of the fourth century continues to hold up, the likelihood that the Chronicler would have drawn upon an older tradition that Hezekiah expanded the walls of Jerusalem implies that this tradition would have been known earlier in the postexilic period as well. It appears that something approaching a consensus is emerging that 1 and 2 Chronicles themselves have protracted redaction histories, which predate the attachment of these works to Ezra and Nehemiah, with the earliest version appearing around the end of the sixth century. The catalyst for this theory is due in large part to the article by Frank Moore Cross, "Reconstruction of the Judean Restoration," *JBL* 94 (1975): 4–18 (esp. 11–14). Cross argues for three versions of Chronicles, with initial composition containing 2 Chr 20:1–30 set shortly after 520 BCE. Cross's second redaction occurred following Ezra's mission around 458 BCE, and the third appeared around 400 BCE. While some disagreement may still be noted, most recent commentators seem to accept the basic thrust of his arguments for a relatively early and separate version of the Chronicler's history. See discussions in Roddy L. Braun, *1 Chronicles*, WBC 14 (Waco, TX: Word, 1986), xxv–xxix; David L. Petersen, *Late Israelite Prophecy: Studies in Deutero-Prophetic Literature and in Chronicles*, SBLMS 23 (Missoula, MT: Scholars Press, 1977), 68–77, 100–102; Magne Sæbø, "Chronistische Theologie/Chronistisches Geschichtswerk," *TRE* 8:74–87 (esp. 79–80). Some, especially in the German-speaking realm, date the written version of Chronicles considerably later. See Reinhard Gregor Kratz, *The Composition of the Narrative Books of the Old Testament*, trans. John Bowden (London: T&T Clark, 2005).

appears in Old Testament texts to describe military campaigns.[20] The LXX interprets 7:12 as an announcement of judgment. In addition, the order in which the political entities are mentioned in 7:12 poetically {137} outlines the political history of the one hundred plus years following the siege of Sennacherib. Assyrian domination of the region was followed by Egyptian control. Egyptian control gave way to the despotic rule of Babylon, which in turn left Israel open to scavenging attacks from the likes of Tyre and Edom during the exilic period. Hence, while this verse is correctly taken as evidence of a postexilic situation, it need not be treated as a promise of restoration. Rather, it makes more sense as a reflection upon the foreign domination of the seventh and early sixth centuries.

One may thus state with certainty that Mic 7:12 *can be* read as an announcement of the political domination to come in the years following Hezekiah. Does it necessarily follow, however, that the verse *should be* read in this manner? In response, one may note that such a reading smooths the transition to 7:13 dramatically. Micah 7:12–13 announces the coming political domination (7:12) which, in turn, *results in* the desolation of the land (הארץ). But does this reading of projected desolation in 7:12–13 not leave the promise of 7:11 as a conceptual straggler? The answer is no, when one remembers that the promise in 7:11 can be read in light of the preparatory actions of Hezekiah prior to the arrival of Sennacherib. Jerusalem is not promised eschatological peace, but is promised time to fortify herself prior to Assyrian attack. One should neither lose sight of the fact that 7:8–11 offers the divine response to *Zion's* affirmation in 7:8–10, nor that they announce the land will be desolated on account of the sins of its inhabitants in 7:13.

The next major section of the passage is the prophetic intercession and divine response, which begins with the change of speaker in Mic 7:14 and concludes with a short response of YHWH in 7:15b. One may isolate the prophet and YHWH as the participants in the constellation from the text itself. The intercession in 7:14–15a is addressed to YHWH directly in the second-person masculine singular. Theologically, only YHWH

---

20. The formulation in Mic 7:12, the verb בוא + עד, can be used to describe a military campaign. Compare, e.g., Judg 7:13; 9:52. For a partial understanding of the combination of the entities, see Lam 5:6, 9, which specifically mentions submission to Egypt and Assyria as reasons for Babylon's ability to destroy Jerusalem. It also depicts difficulties following the destruction of Jerusalem which arose from the surrounding regions.

could perform the deeds requested in these verses. The speaker of the intercession must be deduced from the context. Given the intercessory form of 7:14–15a, one could make a case for either the prophet or the people as the speaker. However, the divine response to the intercession in 7:15b states explicitly, "I will show him miracles."[21] This masculine singular reference in the third person clearly intends "people" in 7:14, syntactically and conceptually. Thus, by simple process of elimination, one may confidently determine the prophet as speaker, interceding to YHWH on behalf of the {138} people. YHWH responds with an affirmative message about the people. A careful evaluation of the content of this intercession, particularly when read against the intertextual background of Isa 9–12, provides a very different slant to the interpretation than is normally understood.

The opening phrase of the intercession ("Shepherd your people with your rod") is almost universally understood in purely positive terms as a prophetic intercession to a benign shepherd figure who is called upon to tend his flock. Several observations contest this interpretation. First, the intertextuality of this entire passage creates a much more negative impression when YHWH's rod (שׁבט) is read in conjunction with Isa 10:5, 15, 24. The same word appears in that context as a highly charged metaphor signifying the punitive powers of Assyria under the commission of YHWH. Assyria is YHWH's rod of punishment. Second, the immediate context in Mic 7:13 calls for the desolation of the land, and it is in this context that the need for petition should be read. Third, an identical syntactical construction (the use of the verb shepherd + an object + the preposition ב + an instrument) appears in Mic 5:5, where the negative connotations of the phrase are clearly recognizable. Fourth, while most associate the shepherd imagery with positive traditions, several Old Testament passages use shepherd imagery negatively.[22] Fifth, the images of *YHWH's* rod and staff appear overwhelmingly with negative connotations in the Old Testament.[23] Sixth, Zion's affirmation in Mic 7:8–10 includes both a recognition of pun-

---

21. So MT. The frequent suggestion to emend Mic 7:15b on the basis of the LXX ignores the interpretive nature of the entire context in the LXX. It is highly dubious that any emendations based upon the LXX carry much weight in these verses.

22. E.g., Ezek 34:13; Zech 11:4; Ps 49:14.

23. Only one exception can be found. Ps 23:4 mentions the "rod" and "staff" of YHWH positively.

ishment and an acknowledgment that the punishment was deserved.[24] It is not surprising, therefore, to find an *implicit* acceptance of YHWH's punishment in the petition of the prophet. Thus, intertextually, contextually (both immediate and broader), syntactically, and tradition-historically, the phrase "Shepherd your people with your rod" implies an *acceptance of punishment*, not a request to a benevolent shepherd who ignores the sins of his people.

How do these negative images relate to that which follows, where the prophet asks for a return to the former relationship between YHWH and the people? Again, tradition-historical observations go a long way toward explaining the remainder of the petition. Three geopolitical entities play a role in the prophetic petition of Mic 7:14–15a. These three entities, Carmel, Bashan, and Gilead, have periodically prompted the suggestion that the "liturgy" has a northern provenance because they comprised {139} substantial portions of the Northern Kingdom.[25] However, the call for the restoration of these northern regions makes perfect sense when read in light of the contextual awareness of the Assyrian period and its aftermath. Contextually, the only promise delivered to this point in the text is a qualified promise, delivered to Jerusalem following her confession (7:11). By contrast, YHWH has announced desolation for the land (הארץ) in 7:13, so it is not surprising that the prophet petitions for a restoration of the people "as in the days of old." Just as significant is the fact that the regions cited in 7:14 have considerable attestation in prophetic literature as precisely those regions which were lost to the "king of Assyria."[26] The oracle against Babylon in Jer 50:17–19 unites the punishment of the "king of Assyria" and the "king of Babylon," incorporating precisely those areas mentioned in the prophetic petition of Mic 7:14:

---

24. The punishment is recognized in Mic 7:8 ("Though I dwell in darkness"), and it is acknowledged as proper in Mic 7:9 ("because I have sinned against him").

25. See, e.g., Francis Crawford Burkitt, "Micah 6 and 7: A Northern Prophecy," *JBL* 45 (1926): 159–61; Eissfeldt, "Ein Psalm aus Nord-Israel: Mi 7,7–20."

26. See Magnus Ottosson, *Gilead: Tradition and History*, ConBOT 3 (Lund: Gleerup, 1969), 236–38. Biblical passages reflecting both the awareness of this loss, and hope for a change in the status of these regions add weight to the suspicion that many of those restoration movements of the postexilic period desired reunification of northern and southern territories. See Amos 9:11–12; Obad 19–21; Isa 10:16–18; 19:23–24; 29:17; 32:15–16; 33:9; 37:24; and particularly Jer 50:17–19. For a fuller treatment of the relationship of these passages to a Carmel/thicket tradition which plays on the loss of this territory, see Nogalski, *Literary Precursors*, 159–61.

Israel is a scattered flock, the lions have driven them away. The first one who devoured him was the king of Assyria, and this last one who has broken his bones is Nebuchadnezzar, king of Babylon. Therefore, thus says the Lord of hosts, the God of Israel: "Behold I am going to punish the king of Babylon and his land, just as I punished the king of Assyria. And I shall bring Israel back to his pasture, and he will graze on Carmel and Bashan, and his desire will be satisfied in the hill country of Ephraim and Gilead." (Jer 50:17–19 NASB)

Thus, these regions were considered forfeitures to the Assyrian military machine. Their presence in Mic 7:14, when read in light of the punitive character of the opening phrase, simultaneously *functions* as an implicit acceptance of YHWH's punishment and a petition that this punishment not be one of total annihilation. The verses implore YHWH to leave at least a remnant of his flock (the one dwelling alone).[27] YHWH then promises to show miracles to the people. What is significant about this {140} petition and response between the prophet and YHWH is that it presumes YHWH's miraculous deliverance, but it *does not* rescind the punishment. The punishment will still occur, but YHWH will ultimately bring deliverance. Micah 7:8–10 manifests a similar dialectic of the affirmation of YHWH's deliverance in the midst of punishment. It will become evident in the response of the people which follows that they likewise affirm YHWH's ultimate deliverance, despite the fact that the current situation contradicts this hope.[28]

The final unit of the passage, Mic 7:16–20*, portrays the grateful response of the people.[29] Just as the prophetic petition in 7:14–15a reacted to the destruction announced in 7:13, so the response of the people expounds upon YHWH's positive affirmation in 7:15b, where YHWH announces he will show the people miracles. Immediately thereafter, the people describe the future in terms which explicate the "miracles" announced in 7:15b. Despite the fact that 7:16 contains no explicit markers denoting the speaker, one may confirm the people as the speaker on the basis of 7:17, where the reference to "*our* God," together with the direct

---

27. See also the parallel expression in Mic 7:18: "the remnant of his possession."

28. Micah 7:19 states explicitly that YHWH "will again have compassion on us," with the clear implication that the compassion has not yet manifested itself in historical events.

29. Micah 7:19b is excluded in this discussion. For the rationale, see above discussion and 70 n. 14.

address to YHWH ("They will be afraid before *you*" [NASB]), unequivocally requires the people as speakers.[30] Formally, the presence of an *inclusio* between 7:14 and 7:20 ("as in/from the days of old") unites these verses on more than a casual basis. Thematically, this response of the people has two parts, which correspond chiastically to the themes of the prophetic intercession (7:14–15a) and the divine response (7:15b):

Speaker	Unit and Content
Prophet	vv. 14–15a: Petition: Despite punishment, restore your people as in the days of old
YHWH	v. 15b: Response: I will show him miracles
People	vv. 16–18: We will see the nations come trembling to YHWH
	vv. 18–20: YHWH will have compassion as in the days of old {141}

YHWH's announcement of miracles is interpreted as the military overthrow of the nations, while the people affirm that YHWH will ultimately restore the relationship with his people.

Several observations relate this response to the first part of the "liturgical" constellation as well. First, the interpretation of YHWH's miracle as having a dramatic effect upon the nations coincides with the announcement of the military attacks in Mic 7:12. Since the land will be attacked by a series of nations (7:12), it is fitting that these nations will come to YHWH in fear and trepidation as a result of the deeds which he will perform. Second, the present situation is viewed as the result of the sinful act of YHWH's people in 7:18, which corresponds to the same presumption on the part of Zion in 7:9. Third, 7:18 presumes forgiveness follows the punishment as does Zion's affirmation in 7:9. The people speak from the situation of punishment with the confidence of change for the better ("He does not retain his anger forever.... He will *again* have compassion upon us" [NASB, emphasis added]).

---

30. There is no reason to follow *BHS* in claiming the phrase "to YHWH our God" is secondary. The very next phrase with its direct address to YHWH means that Mic 7:16–17 cannot be a continuation of the divine speech in Mic 7:15b. Since YHWH is being addressed in 7:17, and since 7:17 is tied syntactically to 7:16, one may state confidently that already in 7:16 one should picture the people addressing YHWH.

Another unifying factor for this portion of the "liturgy" is the fact that the intertextual parallels to Isa 9–12 continue in Mic 7:16–20* in a manner which sheds interesting light upon the context. Isaiah 10:33 helps to explain the phraseology of Mic 7:16. Micah 7:16 states that the nations "will see and be ashamed of all their might." This fear is understandable in light of the pronouncement in Isa 10:33–34, where the prophet predicts the destruction of Assyria and any other enemies of stature. These verses utilize a tree metaphor for Assyria, but also threaten any other resplendent "trees."[31] Knowledge of the message of Isa 10:33–34 may be detected in Mic 7:16, despite the fact that the metaphor of the trees is not picked up. When Mic 7:16 states that the nations "will be ashamed of all their might," its phraseology is highly suggestive that the nations realize it is their might which threatens them before YHWH. This shame corresponds to the abasement of the lofty trees (= mighty nations) in Isa 10:33.

A second major parallel appears in the concluding verses. In terms of form and vocabulary, Mic 7:18–20 bears a striking resemblance to Isa 12:1–6. Both passages offer thanksgiving for YHWH's future deliverance.[32] Both conclude extended passages regarding threats from the nations sent by YHWH as punishment to a recalcitrant people. In both {142} cases, Assyria plays the primary role of YHWH's instrument, but it is not the sole nation intended. Both passages take consolation in YHWH's compassion and comfort.

Summary

The preceding analysis provides substantial evidence challenging the assumption that Mic 7:8–20 arose independently from the book of Micah. Recognition of an intertextual relationship between this passage, Isa 9–12, and traditions surrounding Hezekiah allows one to trace the operative hermeneutic of the *postexilic* author of Mic 7:8–20 who composed this "liturgy" for the corpus set in the Assyrian period, as though it was foreshadowing events to come. This assumption of an Assyrian period perspective derives from the time in which the prophet Micah preached (see Mic 1:1).

---

31. Hence, "Those who are tall in stature will be cut down, and those who are lofty will be abased" (NASB).

32. The majority of Isa 12:1–6 is expressed as thanksgiving for comfort already received, but the introductory ביום ההוא formula makes clear that the events themselves still lie in the future.

The "liturgical" constellation comprises three subunits: Zion's song of confidence and YHWH's qualified response (Mic 7:8–13); the prophet's intercession and YHWH's affirmative response (Mic 7:14–15); and the grateful response of the people (Mic 7:16–20*). A personified Nineveh is the dominant enemy of Zion in Mic 7:8–10, while the remainder of the verses incorporate a broader historical outlook, but one which still draws upon the anti-Assyrian polemic in Isaiah. Jerusalem is promised time to prepare for the oncoming attacks (7:11–12), but punishment for the land is not rescinded (7:13). The prophet petitions YHWH in a manner which simultaneously accepts YHWH's punishment while calling for restoration of significant portions of the Northern Kingdom originally lost to the Assyrians (7:14–15a). Following YHWH's affirmative response (7:15b), the people express their confidence that YHWH will deliver a remnant from the power of the nations (7:16–17) and restore the relationship to the way it was before the sinful acts of his people (7:18–20*).

One Book and Twelve Books:
The Nature of the Redactional Work and the Implications of Cultic Source Material in the Book of the Twelve

A spate of redactional studies since 1993 has made progress in developing a comprehensive reconstruction of the redactional history of the Book of the Twelve. The first section of this paper will explore these recent discussions in three sections: areas where progress toward a consensus has been made, followed by a response to some of the objections raised about the task, and an assessment of the nature of the redactional work which isolates four areas of continuing debate. The second portion of the essay will focus on a fresh proposal which, it is hoped, will stimulate discussion that will move the discussion of redactional work on the Book of the Twelve forward. Namely, it will be argued that the role of cultic source blocks redactionally incorporated into the Book of the Twelve has not been adequately appreciated. The extent of this cultically oriented material should invite a reevaluation of the function of cultic material in the literary context and the implications of the use of this material for understanding the tradents. {12}

Recent Redactional Investigations on the Book of the Twelve

Progress Toward a Consensus

It is now widely accepted that the Book of the Twelve should be treated as a redactional unit. Progress toward a consensus has occurred on three fronts: the deliberative nature of the order of the writings, the priority of the MT sequence over the LXX, and the extended transmission of two

---

* I wish to thank Paul Redditt, Aaron Schart, and Roy E. Garton for commenting on a draft of this paper, thereby strengthening its presentation, though they are not responsible for any confusion which may remain.

preexisting corpora. First, there is wide agreement that the ordering of the twelve writings is hardly inadvertent. Chronology plays too clear a role in the placement of the writings to be accidental. Dated superscriptions create a chronological frame that unfolds across the Twelve. These dated writings move from those writings attributed to eighth-century prophetic figures (Hosea, Amos, Micah) to a seventh-century figure (Zephaniah). This group is followed by writings with a late sixth-century focus on the rebuilding of the temple (Haggai, Zechariah).

Four additional writings tie directly into this chronological movement. Malachi assumes a Persian period setting *after* the temple has been reconstructed, which secures its position after Haggai and Zechariah. Nahum and Habakkuk deal with a theological portrayal of the seventh century, requiring that they come after Micah, the last eighth-century prophetic figure. Jonah, on the other hand, presents a narrative about a prophet who lived in the days of Jeroboam II, and this requires that Jonah be placed prior to Micah since the three kings mentioned in Mic 1:1 all postdate the time of Jeroboam II. Thus, ten of the Twelve owe their location to a chronological framework.

In addition to chronology, themes, catchwords, and citations play a role in the location of many of the writings in the Twelve. Two of the clearest examples of these contextual links appear in Joel and Obadiah (ironically, the two writings which do not exhibit the chronological orientation of the other ten). The last few verses of Joel contain citations of Amos. Joel 4:16 draws on Amos 1:2 (the opening verse of Amos after the superscription), and Joel 4:18 parallels Amos 9:13 (the third to the last verse in the book). Synchronically speaking, then, Joel effectively encompasses the beginning and end of Amos. Similarly, the essential theme of Obadiah is already anticipated in Amos 9:12. {13}

Several of the writings which presume the chronological framework also make sense thematically in their setting. By way of example, the fall of Assyria in Nahum and the rise of Babylon in Habakkuk will be explored later in this paper. Malachi deals with issues of the postexilic community after the temple has been rebuilt wherein they must once again confront problems related to improper sacrifice. Some have argued (or assumed) the thematic overlap was the result of choices in positioning more or less completed writings, but most have seen some degree of editorial work evident in the process of arranging these twelve writings.[1]

---

1. This issue will be discussed in more detail below.

A second, and related, area of relative consensus concerns the priority of the MT sequence of writings when compared to the LXX. Conversations over the last fifteen years have tended to conclude that the MT represents the oldest order, though questions about the rationale for the LXX's changing the order have not been entirely resolved.[2] Occasional arguments for LXX priority have proven incapable of convincing the overwhelming majority that the LXX order takes priority in the case of the Twelve. More importantly for future study, a sustained treatment of the LXX has not been undertaken to explore the implications of the changes in sequence by treating the LXX as an entity in its own right, though Sweeney has suggested that a significant shift in emphasis on the nations occurs for the reader when the sequence is {14} changed.[3] Others have been satisfied to note that the change of sequence can be explained simply as a decision to group the three eighth-century prophets (Hosea-Amos-Micah) together, which then leaves Joel-Obadiah-Jonah in the same sequence as the MT.[4]

A third area of widespread agreement appears in the suggestion that two preexisting collections created the foundation for what comes to be the Book of the Twelve. One group comprises most of Hosea-Amos-Micah-Zephaniah, while the other contains Haggai-Zechariah 1–8. Each of these

---

2. The order of the MT (Hosea, Joel, Amos, Obadiah, Jonah, Micah) and LXX (Hosea, Amos, Micah, Joel, Obadiah, Jonah) differ among the first six writings, while the last six are identical in both traditions. One other sequence may be exhibited in one Qumran manuscript that seems to present Jonah after Malachi, but this order is idiosyncratic to this point and there is no conclusive proof that other writings from the Twelve were included on the same scroll. For a more complete discussion of these issues, see Russell Fuller, "The Form and Formation of the Book of the Twelve: The Evidence from the Judean Desert," in Watts, *Forming Prophetic Literature*, 86–101; Barry Alan Jones, *The Formation of the Book of the Twelve: A Study in Text and Canon*, SBLDS 149 (Atlanta: Scholars Press, 1995), 6–7, 237–39; Odil Hannes Steck, "Zur Abfolge Maleachi–Jona in 4Q76 (4QXIIa)," *ZAW* 108 (1996): 249–53.

3. Marvin A. Sweeney, "Sequence and Interpretation in the Book of the Twelve," in Nogalski, *Reading and Hearing*, 49–64.

4. See already Schneider, "Unity of the Book of the Twelve, 224–25; Nogalski, *Literary Precursors*, 2–3. Schart implies the connections between Hosea, Amos, and Micah go even further, especially given the similar dates in the superscriptions, as well as other similarities of content between these three writings. See Aaron Schart, "Reconstructing the Redaction History of the Twelve Prophets: Problems and Models," in Nogalski, *Reading and Hearing*, 37–38. See also Schart, *Entstehung des Zwölfprophetenbuchs*, 218–20.

collections were "published" and edited together prior to their association with the remaining writings.

The first of these collections has been called by various names, but it includes Hosea, Amos, Micah, and Zephaniah. Nogalski called it the Deuteronomistic Corpus because of certain similarities these writings share with the theological perspective of the Deuteronomistic History.[5] Schart concurred with the idea of a common redactional history shared by these four writings, but he qualified Nogalski's observations in at least two significant ways. First, he delineated the common history more carefully (arguing that Hosea and Amos shared a history prior to the incorporation of Micah and [only later by including] Zephaniah). Second, Schart concludes that "Deuteronomistic" is not the best term, in part because {15} so many of the phrases typically considered to be distinctively Deuteronomistic elsewhere are lacking in this group of four. Schart, therefore, suggests the term D-corpus as a means of distinguishing this corpus from "Deuteronomic/Deuteronomistic" materials that use Deuteronomic phraseology more consistently.[6] Others, such as Albertz, prefer a more neutral term and simply speak of the Book of the Four Prophets (*Vierprophetenbuch*).[7] Most recently, the reason for the debate has been clarified considerably with the work of Wöhrle (who also calls this corpus the Book of the Four Prophets). He shows that the "Deuteronomistic" flavor points to a phenomenon whereby these writings periodically, but specifically, allude to the accounts of Hezekiah and Josiah in 2 Kgs 17; 20; 22–25.[8] As a result of these conversations, the idea that these four writings were shaped together over time now rests on fairly stable ground.

The second preexisting corpus arises from the common editing of Haggai and Zechariah 1–8. Since this suggestion had already been proposed in Old Testament scholarship prior to recent investigations of the

---

5. See the summaries in Nogalski, *Literary Precursors*, 276–80; and Nogalski, *Redactional Processes*, 274–75.

6. Schart, *Entstehung des Zwölfprophetenbuchs*, 156, 218–33.

7. See Rainer Albertz, "Exile as Purification: Reconstructing the Book of the Four (Hosea, Amos, Micah, Zephaniah)," in *Society of Biblical Literature 2002 Seminar Papers*, SBLSP 41 (Atlanta: Society of Biblical Literature, 2002), 213–33. For a discussion of the background issues, see Rainer Albertz, "In Search of the Deuteronomists: A First Solution to a Historical Riddle," in *The Future of the Deuteronomistic History*, ed. Thomas C. Römer, BETL 147 (Leuven: Leuven University Press, 2000), 1–17.

8. See the charts and summary in Wöhrle, *Frühen Sammlungen des Zwölfprophetenbuches*, 269–70, 275–82.

Twelve as a corpus, it is not surprising that this idea has received strong endorsement among Book of the Twelve scholars.[9] A few remain skeptical, but the majority of scholars now see editorial connections, at least, between Haggai and Zechariah {16} 1–8.[10] The background of these two writings shows concern for explaining the prophetic role in the rebuilding of the temple and in the leadership of society in the late sixth century.

To summarize, progress has been made toward a consensus in three areas: (1) recognizing that the arrangement of the Twelve writings in the corpus is both deliberate and reflects significant editorial work; (2) the LXX order derives from changes made to the MT sequence; (3) two pre-existing multivolume corpora, when combined, not only account for the chronological framework across the growing Book of the Twelve; they also provide the substance of many of the connecting motifs. These three areas have been treated from various perspectives, and significant points of agreement have been isolated. However, before moving to discuss the nature of the redactional material, it should be noted that scholars have also voiced skepticism or caution concerning common redactional work among the writings of the Book of the Twelve, or at least about modern scholarship's ability to reconstruct this activity.

Doubts about the Task

Alongside progress toward a consensus, doubts concerning the process of finding "*Buchübergreifende*" redactions have been expressed in works by Ben Zvi, Beck, and Petersen. Ben Zvi voices two reasons for taking a cautious approach to the issue of common redaction in/among the writings

---

9. See especially the seminal works of W. A. M. Beuken, *Haggai-Sacharja 1–8: Studien zur Überlieferungsgeschichte der frühnachexilischen Prophetie*, SSN 10 (Assen: Van Gorcum, 1967); and Rex A. Mason, "Purpose of the 'Editorial Framework' of the Book of Haggai," *VT* 27 (1977): 413–21.

10. See recent commentary discussion in David L. Petersen, *Haggai and Zechariah 1–8: A Commentary*, OTL (Philadelphia: Westminster, 1984), 37–39; Carol L. Meyers and Eric M. Meyers, *Haggai, Zechariah 1–8: A New Translation with Introduction and Commentary*, AB 25B (Garden City, NY: Doubleday, 1987), xliv–xviii. A few have argued for the inclusion of Malachi and/or Zech 9–14 with this corpus, but most reject these arguments. The first to make this argument in a sustained fashion was Ronald W. Pierce, "Literary Connectors and a Haggai/Zechariah/Malachi Corpus," *JETS* 27 (1984): 277–89.

of the Book of the Twelve: the lack of a single title, and the lack of control for parallels.[11] {17}

First, Ben Zvi claims the Book of the Twelve contains no title indicating it presents itself as a single work.[12] In so doing, Ben Zvi puts his finger on an important characteristic of the Twelve, but his concerns do little to address the issue of common redaction. Ancient traditions concerning the Twelve as a single corpus were not an invention of twentieth-century critical scholarship. These traditions appear to be based on intertextual interplay between these twelve writings. Further, evaluation of other Old Testament works shows that titles are only one way that editorial connections were made. The Torah has no titles as such, but few would doubt the interconnectedness of the edited works. Chronicles leads to Ezra by repeating two verses, thereby joining the end of Chronicles (2 Chr 36:22–23) with Ezra (1:1–2).

Consider evidence from the Leningrad Codex. The book of Psalms has no unifying title for the corpus in the Leningrad Codex. It does have superscriptions that set off many of the individual Psalms, though most of the superscriptions do not appear on a line by themselves.[13] Despite these superscriptions at the beginning of individual psalms, the Psalter is widely recognized to have undergone editorial work on *groups* of psalms which are not named as editorial units in the corpus as we have it.[14] The nature, history, {18} and function of this editorial work is still a matter

---

11. Ben Zvi, "Twelve Prophetic Books," 125–56; See also Martin Beck, *Der "Tag YHWHs" im Dodekapropheton:* {17} *Studien im Spannungsfeld von Traditions- und Redaktionsgeschichte*, BZAW 356 (Berlin: de Gruyter, 2005), 17.

12. Ben Zvi, "Twelve Prophetic Books," 137.

13. Individual psalms are separated from the preceding psalm with one blank line in the codex. The superscriptions are usually followed by a gap of 3–10 letters, like the divisions between any other verse. Some psalms (e.g., Pss 15; 50) do have the superscription on a line by themselves, but this is not typical.

14. Beginning with the influential work of Gerald H. Wilson (*The Editing of the Hebrew Psalter*, SBLDS 76 [Chico, CA: Scholars Press, 1985]), work on the editing of the Psalter has been ongoing. See a good summary of the redactional growth of the Psalter in Klaus Seybold, *Die Psalmen: Eine Einführung*, KUT 382 (Stuttgart: Kohlhammer, 1986), 36–54. See also the recent discussion in Joel S. Burnett, "A Plea for David and Zion: The Elohistic Psalter as Psalm Collection for the Temple's Restoration," in *Diachronic and Synchronic: Reading the Psalms in Real Time; Proceedings of the Baylor Symposium on the Book of Psalms*, ed. Joel S. Burnett, William H. Bellinger, and W. Dennis Tucker Jr., LHBOTS 488 (London: T&T Clark, 2007), 95–113; for an example of reading an extended section of the Psalter, see also William H. {18}

ONE BOOK AND TWELVE BOOKS   89

of discussion, but its existence is largely assumed in recent studies of the Psalter. Moreover, none of the prophetic books in the Leningrad Codex have their own title; they merely start after a gap of a few lines.[15] There are, however, Masoretic notes at the end of the Twelve and at the midpoint of the corpus which do treat the Book of the Twelve as a unit in its own right.[16] Thus, Ben Zvi's argument about the lack of a unifying title for the Twelve carries little weight on the issue of common redaction, but evaluating manuscripts does provide evidence that favors treating the Twelve as a corpus, not just twelve disconnected writings. The existence or absence of a title is not indicative of common editorial work.

Ben Zvi offers a second word of caution about reconstructing common redactional work among the writings of the Twelve when he argues that many of the observations regarding the interplay between two texts lack controls to establish them as parallels and links.[17] Ben Zvi raises a valid concern, but only to a point. More attention has been paid to this issue in literature subsequent to his essay.[18] Still, one has to recognize that very few editorial connections {19} in the prophetic canon could meet all of the criteria laid out by Ben Zvi. It is the nature of the connections that they demand a high degree of awareness of the content on the part of the reader *and* editor. Moreover, he ignores the fact that these connecting devices are used within the context of redactional studies in other

---

Bellinger, "Reading from the Beginning (Again): The Shape of Book I of the Psalter," in Burnett, *Diachronic and Synchronic*, 114–26.

15. It should be noted that the number of lines separating the writings of the Book of the Twelve from one another is smaller than the number of lines separating the book of Isaiah, Jeremiah, and Ezekiel from their neighboring books. This pattern appears to conform to the rules described in b. B. Bat. 13b. Thus, even the separation of the writings of the Book of the Twelve illustrate they were treated differently.

16. Consider the Masoretic note in the margin beside Mic 3:12. It reads: "One half of the scroll by verses." The notes at the end of the Twelve (right after notes concerning Malachi) reference the total number of verses for the Book of the Twelve (1,050) and cite Mic 3:12 as the midpoint of the corpus. Simple arithmetic shows that the numbers used in these verse counts are accurate.

17. Ben Zvi, "Twelve Prophetic Books," 135–37, 139–42.

18. See, e.g., evaluations of the catchword connections proposed by Nogalski as assessed by Schart and others in later works. Not every argument has proven convincing, but these evaluations do not negate the use of catchwords as a technique. See, e.g., Schart, *Entstehung des Zwölfprophetenbuchs*, 97 (positively), or 230 (negatively). See also several of the essays in {19} Erich Zenger, ed., *"Wort Jhwhs, das geschah—" (Hos 1,1): Studien zum Zwölfprophetenbuch*, HerBS 35 (Freiburg: Herder, 2002).

"scrolls" or "writings." These methods are not limited to the Book of the Twelve. Using his criteria, for example, one must eliminate *eo ipso* any connections created by common words *because* they are common, but some thematic lines of connection *are* created by *combinations* of relatively common words.[19] In the end, it should be the interpretive contributions to the task and the convincing power of the proposals (including the evaluation of whether recurring words appear by accident) which determines the usefulness of a proposed link. The interest generated by redactional studies of the last fifteen to twenty years and the intersection of results make the task promising.

Ben Zvi also calls for a more careful process of defining words like audience and tradents. He is correct that more attention needs to be paid in this area. The study of prophetic tradents still stands at the front end of a very complicated task. The task of defining tradents more carefully will be addressed in more detail below by exploring the role of cultic texts and cultic concerns in the growth of the Book of the Twelve, especially in those six writings where more debate exists.[20]

Ben Zvi's cautions are taken further by Beck, who presents a sustained, skeptical counterargument against the idea of an extended redactional history affecting the Book of the Twelve as a corpus.[21] He contends that the Book of the Twelve is really an anthology highlighting the day of YHWH, but that the writings were {20} only connected in two stages at a very late date (the Hellenistic period), first as a book of ten. Later, Jonah and Malachi were added to make the Book of the Twelve. Thus, the writings were independently transmitted until quite late according to Beck. Catchwords are dismissed as too unconvincing or unprovable. Quotations are explained away as shared tradition history or citations so limited in scope as to have no literary value when trying to understand the corpus. He denies these texts have an expanded literary horizon. He is very similar to Ben Zvi in this regard. He frequently challenges the conclusions of those who have argued for connective redactional implantations by systematically discounting the

---

19. In the Book of the Twelve, the most prominent example is the recurring motif of the fertility of the land which is often signaled by combinations of common words connoting the presence or absence of agricultural bounty: wine, vine, grain, and fig tree. See James D. Nogalski, "Recurring Themes in the Book of the Twelve : Creating Points of Contact for a Theological Reading," *Int* 61 (2007): 128–30.

20. See part 2 of this essay ("Form and Function of the Redactional Work").

21. Beck, *"Tag YHWHs" im Dodekapropheton.*

observations of Nogalski, Schart, Bosshard-Nepustil, and others. In the end, he rejects so many of the arguments as failing to meet his list of criteria that one almost wonders why he speaks of the Book of the Twelve at all.

Like Ben Zvi, Beck makes some valid points about the need to argue carefully and account for opposing views consistently. However, Beck falls into many of the same traps (perhaps unavoidably) of those he critiques when he begins making his own case for the importance of the day of YHWH. For example, he argues that the day of YHWH language in both Joel and Zephaniah could be more easily explained as Joel drawing upon Zephaniah than the implanting of Joel language into Zephaniah. However, he concludes that the *best* explanation is to deny there are any strong connections between the two writings since Exodus traditions and Zion theology so prominent in Joel are lacking in Zephaniah.[22] Both of these claims are problematic. His argument assumes connections to Exodus traditions are present in Joel, but documenting these links to the Exodus traditions utilizes some of the very same methods he denies are sustainable in editing the Book of the Twelve.[23] Beck is not clear why he thinks Zion tradition {21} is lacking in Zephaniah. Given the fact that much of Zeph 3:8–20 explicitly addresses Lady Zion, one can only assume he has some predetermined idea of what constitutes Zion tradition which could account for his assertion. Further, his own evidence for dating the combination of independent writings in the Greek period in order to form the Twelve is not as convincingly presented as his literary critical arguments.

In addition to Ben Zvi, Beck raises the issue of the random growth of writings as something that could account for (at least some of) the editorial additions. He notes that additions containing similar themes do not automatically require common redactional work. Such cautions are well heard by those working in this area. However, part of this critique, too, is limited by one's predisposition. The nature of the connections is such that, if one determines in advance to approach the issue skeptically, one will likely not be convinced that such connections are present. In many cases, Beck argues against connections which others have seen but argues for connec-

---

22. Ibid., 117.
23. Links between Joel and Exodus are most thoroughly and creatively demonstrated by Siegfried Bergler, *Joel als Schriftinterpret*, BEATAJ 16 (Frankfurt am Main: Lang, 1988). Bergler, however, makes extensive use of allusion via combinations of isolated words to make the case. Beck ignores the fact that the same kinds of techniques used by Bergler appear in discussion of redaction in the Book of the Twelve.

tions between texts which would strike others as questionable. In the end, such a skeptical approach does not adequately account for the nature of the ancient traditions that the Twelve was counted as a single book.[24]

A third scholar expressing caution about the task is Petersen. Petersen raises questions regarding how one's terminology connotes something about the presumed model of compilation and its significance for interpretation.[25] Petersen makes an important contribution regarding terminology. To call the corpus "The Book of the Twelve" conveys something to those who approach this question for the first time. Undoubtedly, modern readers bring presuppositions regarding what constitutes a book. The Book of the Twelve is certainly not a modern novel; nor is it merely a catalog of prophetic sayings arranged with a single, consistent organizing principle. Distinctions must be made between what modern readers associate with the word "book" and the unifying functions found within the Book of the Twelve. Petersen recognizes a complex history of the Twelve, and he thinks that the best way to approach {22} the unifying elements is from the perspective of theme. He believes that "the day of YHWH" is an appropriate theme for speaking about the dominant literary features of the Twelve because of the frequency of the phrase and because the time span covered by the Twelve is larger than any other prophetic corpus. Petersen is less clear about how one speaks of theme without dealing with how the theme "unfolds" or with why some texts exhibit this theme while others do not.

Other terms have also been used in attempting to avoid the problem of the presumptions associated with "book," but these terms also connote some semblance of commonality as well as a lack of continuity (be it literary, chronological, or theological). Some of these terms include collection, corpus, compendium, or "thematized anthology" (Petersen's own term). Terminology requires careful delineation by anyone working in this area.

Petersen is correct. It is important to keep the character of the Book of the Twelve in mind when speaking about the whole. The terms "anthology" and "compendium" can be used effectively to accent certain elements of the corpus in order to describe parts of its character, but these terms do not go far enough to convey the sense of intentionality that is implicit in the chronological arrangement or evidenced between *some of* the editorial links which show a cognizant exploration of an issue or theme across

---

24. See Nogalski, *Literary Precursors*, 2–3.
25. Petersen, "Book of the Twelve," 3–10.

multiple writings. This issue will be discussed in more detail below by reflecting on the nature of redaction.

The Nature of the Redactional Work in the Book of the Twelve

Questions have also been asked by sympathetic proponents of the Book of the Twelve as a redactional entity about how to characterize the redactional work transcending the individual writings in the Twelve, leading to new models for the growth of the corpus and a need to evaluate the nature of the redactional processes themselves. In contrast to the skepticism of Beck, Wöhrle seeks a more comprehensive model that can account for the development of all the writings in the Book of the Twelve. Wöhrle is correct when he argues that the convincing power of such a redactional model would be increased dramatically if it could account of the growth of each {23} writing.[26] However, such a comprehensive model has not yet been put forward.

Wöhrle adds constructively to the conversation, but his own 467-page analysis, in the end, only offers a *tentative* theory for some of the twelve writings. He does not have room in this volume to analyze Hosea, Obadiah, Nahum, Habakkuk, Malachi, or Zech 9–14 (though he does give some hints as to where he thinks these works may fit). He only studies Joel, Amos, Micah, Zephaniah, Haggai, and Zech 1–8 in detail.

Wöhrle raises at least two issues with his model that require comment: Joel's development and the role of Hosea. Wöhrle contends that much of the previous scholarly work has either assumed the essential unity of Joel (Nogalski, Schart) or approached Joel as a writing which has grown over time (Bosshard-Nepustil) without laying the groundwork carefully.[27] Wöhrle sides with the latter group, though he thinks both groups have approached the growth of the book through a faulty starting point.

---

26. Wöhrle, *Frühen Sammlungen des Zwölfprophetenbuches*, 24–27, 466–67. See also his extensive review of recent redactional studies, pp. 12–24. Wöhrle has recently released his second volume that extends his model into the remaining sections of the Twelve, though still does not deal with Hosea. Time does not allow incorporation of the second volume, but neither does it change the points raised in this discussion to any great degree. See Jakob Wöhrle, *Der Abschluss des Zwölfprophetenbuches: buchübergreifende Redaktionsprozesse in den späten Sammlungen*, BZAW 389 (Berlin: de Gruyter, 2008).

27. See the following in Wöhrle, *Frühen Sammlungen des Zwölfprophetenbuches*: on Nogalski, 12–14; on Schart, 16–18; on Bosshard-Nepustil, 15–17.

Nevertheless, Wöhrle concludes that Joel's involvement with other writings of the Book of the Twelve requires that one account for the growth of Joel and the growing multivolume corpus simultaneously.[28] This assertion raises an important question affecting several of the writings, not only Joel. Specifically, how does one account for the shape of the writings? Wöhrle points to very few substantive tensions not already noted in previous scholarship. The differences in the models hinge upon when and how the independent units were combined. Specifically, how one answers two questions dictates how one explains Joel's compositional history: First, did the bulk of {24} Joel 1–2 exist independently, or did an early version of these chapters already serve as the bridge to other writings in what would come to be the Book of the Twelve? Second, how does one explain the relationship of Joel 1–2 to Joel 3–4? Wöhrle's model for Joel suggests six distinct layers of redactional activity, though the first two are more extensive than the others.[29] According to his analysis, Wöhrle finds numerous connections in the foundational layer to the *subsequent* writings in the exilic version of the Book of the Four (Amos, Micah, Zephaniah), but not to the preceding writing, Hosea.[30]

The lack of connections from Joel to Hosea, according to Wöhrle, leads to another important issue in his model, one where Wöhrle stands alone: the role of Hosea. Wöhrle argues that the incorporation of this early corpus of Joel literally replaced Hosea as the opening book of the multivolume corpus.[31] For at least two reasons, this suggestion appears to be even less convincing than his diachronic hypothesis. First, the physical changes this theory would require of the scroll would be hard to envision. Of course, ancient editors could and did omit material as even a cursory comparison of Chronicles and Kings would confirm. However, such a model of the redaction of the Book of the Twelve seems highly implausible. It would require that the redactors take a collection which begins with Hosea in the first position, then eliminate Hosea in favor of Joel, only to replace Hosea back in the first position at a later point. One would have to account for someone maintaining Hosea as an independent scroll for an indeterminate period before it was reintroduced into the multivolume corpus. One would also have to explain why someone deemed Hosea inadequate for

---

28. Ibid., 436–53.
29. See his summary in ibid., 428–35.
30. Ibid., 436–49.
31. Ibid., 450–53.

inclusion yet a subsequent version returned Hosea to its place of prominence as the first writing of the corpus.

A second reason for rejecting the inclusion/exclusion/reinclusion hypothesis for Hosea would be the recognition of Hosea's *continuing* role in the function of the growing corpus. The mention of several illustrations will have to suffice in this venue. To begin, Wöhrle himself suggests that the superscription of Joel {25} imitates the "word pattern" of the Book of the Four.[32] However, the superscription of Joel is closer to Hosea than to Amos. It would seem odd to imitate the superscription (word of YHWH versus words of Amos), but to drop the writing.

Additionally, the communal call to repentance comprising the end of Hosea and the beginning of Joel is a powerful parallel that makes better sense when both are present than it would if Joel was the only exemplar. Relatedly, much of the material within Hos 4–13 contains accusations against the people of YHWH (primarily Israel, but with periodic [often redactional] applications to Judah as well), whereas Joel contains no accusatory material to explain the guilt of the people.

Finally, several intratextual links exist between Hosea and Joel, and other writings, which Wöhrle either ignores or too quickly dismisses. In addition to the presumption of guilt in Joel (see Schart,[33] and Nogalski[34]) and the parallel calls to repentance in Hos 14 and Joel 1–2, connections have been noted between Joel and Hos 2 (Nogalski[35] and Braaten[36]), and the involvement of the quote of Exod 34:6–7 in the Book of the Twelve with the themes of the names of the children of Hos 1 (Van Leeuwen[37]). It seems unwise to ignore these connections in a model of the growth of the Book of the Twelve.

Nevertheless, Wöhrle's discussion does highlight an important distinctive concerning the way that Joel functions in the Book of the Twelve hermeneutically and theologically. Joel dramatically shifts the focus of the

---

32. Ibid., 38–39.
33. Schart, *Entstehung des Zwölfprophetenbuchs*, 266–67.
34. Nogalski, *Redactional Processes*, 15–18.
35. Nogalski, "Recurring Themes in the Book of the Twelve," 128–30.
36. Laurie J. Braaten, "God Sows: Hosea's Land Theme in the Book of the Twelve," in Redditt, *Thematic Threads*, 108–11.
37. Raymond C. Van Leeuwen, "Scribal Wisdom and Theodicy in the Book of the Twelve," in *In Search of Wisdom: Essays in Memory of John G. Gammie*, ed. Leo G. Perdue, Bernard B. Scott, and William J. Wiseman (Louisville: Westminster John Knox, 1993), 31–49 (esp. 34–36).

96   THE BOOK OF THE TWELVE AND BEYOND

multivolume corpus at the time it is incorporated. Specifically, whereas Hosea and Amos periodically apply the message of those writings to Judah, that application remains a {26} rather sparse portion of the message—until Joel is incorporated. At that point, reference to the priests, Zion, and the temple highlight Judah and Jerusalem. To be sure, Joel *assumes* the guilt of Israel has been applied to Judah, but Joel explicates the implications for Judah in a way that Hosea and Amos do not. Moreover, the paradigm of "history" that unfolds in Joel has a much broader scope, especially with respect to the future of Zion, than does Hosea and Amos.[38]

Wöhrle's treatment underscores the extent to which the model one develops affects how one deals with the texts. There is a difference in quantity and character of the editorial connections in the editorial work on the various writings in the Book of the Twelve. The present form of some writings appears to have been compiled using preexisting material with awareness of their context in the Book of the Twelve. This awareness affects the sources chosen, their combination, and the links connecting them. Other writings appear to be presumed (like Hosea, contra Wöhrle), yet they have had little in the way of editorial additions in later stages of the growth of the Twelve. Generally, the six dated writings have had redactional glosses added, short insertions into existing literary texts which function as *invitations* to compare one text with another within the Book of the Twelve.[39] They have not, however, been radically reshaped when other writings were added to the multivolume corpus.

More importantly, the six writings not included in the two preexisting corpora are still the focus of debates regarding the extent of material incorporated into individual writings for the Book of the Twelve. The role played by each writing's *location* in the Book of the Twelve needs more attention as a contributing factor to its final form.

Nogalski argues Joel and Obadiah essentially owe their shape to their location in the Book of the Twelve. For Joel, Nogalski, following Bergler, suggests that three compositional (source) blocks were brought together by a redactor who shaped and supplemented the materials in light of the existing literary context of Hosea on {27} one side and Amos on the other.[40] These sources included a composite call to repentance (Joel 1–2*), a description of the enemy attack on the day of YHWH (2:1–10), and an

---

38. Nogalski, "Joel as 'Literary Anchor,'" 91–109.
39. Nogalski, *Literary Precursors*, 276–77.
40. Nogalski, *Redactional Processes*, 1–6.

eschatological call to judgment on the nations (Joel 4*). He intimates that Joel 3 was added with a different focus.[41] Schart agrees that Joel owes its form to its location in the Book of the Twelve. In his seminal work, Schart only suggests a few redactional supplements (4:4–8 and 1:2–3) for Joel, yet he demonstrates connections to both Hosea and Amos (as well as Zephaniah and Obadiah).[42] By contrast, Bosshard-Nepustil and Beck see Joel as a composition which grows diachronically with the Book of the Twelve.[43]

For Obadiah, Nogalski also assumes three source blocks (a composite text in 1–9; 10–14+15b; and 15a, 16–21*) have been adapted structurally with particular attention to Amos 9.[44] Others see the tensions in Obadiah as signs of more sources, with Weimar finding six and Wehrle finding as many as seven redactional layers in this short twenty-one verse writing.[45]

Nahum and Habakkuk probably existed prior to their incorporation into the Book of the Twelve but were significantly expanded with preexisting hymnic material (along with other redactional comments) when they were incorporated into the Book of the Twelve. Broad agreement exists that Nah 1 and Hab 3 were added to their respective writing to adapt these two writings for the multivolume collection. In this case, major "redactional" {28} material was added to these writings, but it was not all composed originally for the Book of the Twelve.

Jonah creates difficulty. On the one hand, its genre characteristics make it stand out from other writings in the Book of the Twelve, and its theological agenda (the willingness of YHWH to show compassion to the nations) are in many respects antithetical to those of Joel and many of the writings of the Book of the Twelve. On the other hand, recent studies have also demonstrated thematic or verbal links to other parts of the Twelve: thematic ties to Zech 8:20–23 and Mal 1:10–14; intratextual relationships with a series of texts playing off of Exod 34:6–7; the antiprophetic stance in Mic 4:2–4 and Zech 13:1–6; and the citation of Jon 2 in conjunction with

---

41. Ibid., 27–28 n.74.
42. Schart, *Entstehung des Zwölfprophetenbuchs*, 261–282 (esp. 278).
43. Bosshard-Nepustil argues for four stages in *Rezeptionen von Jesaia 1–39*, 277–83; Beck, *"Tag YHWHs" im Dodekapropheton*, 142–51, 178–82.
44. See Nogalski, *Redactional Processes*, 89–92, 74–78.
45. Weimar, "Obadja," 35–99; Josef Wehrle, *Prophetie und Textanalyse: Die Komposition Obadja 1–21 interpretiert auf der Basis textlinguistischer und semiotischer Konzeptionen*, ATSAT 28 (St. Ottilien: EOS, 1987).

Mic 7:19.[46] To what extent do these connections affect our understanding of Jonah's role in the Book of the Twelve?

Malachi remains perhaps the least well defined, both in terms of the point of incorporation relative to Zech 9–14 and in terms of its function in the Book of the Twelve. A strong consensus exists that its opening and concluding sections relate to other themes in the Book of the Twelve, but no consensus has been reached regarding the form of the book prior to its inclusion in the Book of the Twelve[47] or regarding the relative point when Malachi was added to the Book of the Twelve (before, with, or after Zech 9–14).[48] {29}

One critique that has been leveled against the task of determining the outlines of the formation process is that the practitioners of this task have approached the question with a narrow focus. This charge of a narrow focus has been or could be leveled at most of those who have written on the formation of the Book of the Twelve: De Vries, Beck, Nogalski, Schart, Bosshard-Nepustil, Schwesig, Wöhrle.[49]

---

46. See, e.g., Martin Roth, *Israel und die Völker im Zwölfprophetenbuch: Eine Untersuchung zu den Büchern Joel, Jona, Micha und Nahum*, FRLANT 210 (Göttingen: Vandenhoeck & Ruprecht, 2005), 167–71.

47. Some of the same problems relative to the use of source material in the composition process in Joel come into play with Malachi as well. Thus, Bosshard and Kratz argue for a diachronic and developmental model consisting of several layers of editorial activity, while Schart sees the writing as a more unified compilation. See Erich Bosshard and Reinhard Gregor Kratz, "Maleachi im Zwölfprophetenbuch," *BN* 52 (1990): 27–46; and Schart, *Entstehung des Zwölfprophetenbuchs*, 293–95.

48. See, e.g., Schart, *Entstehung des Zwölfprophetenbuchs*, 291–303; and Nogalski, *Redactional Processes*, 210–12, who treat Malachi as a nearly completed composition. Schart, however, thinks it is added after Zech 9–14, while Nogalski believes it comes into the corpus prior to Zech 9–14. Bosshard-Nepustil sees the inclusion of the core of Malachi prior to Zech 9–14 (*Rezeptionen von Jesaia 1–39*, 426–28). See also Steck, *Abschluß der Prophetie im Alten Testament*, {29} 33–34, 42–55. Steck sees the early layers of Malachi (similar to those described by Bosshard and Kratz [see previous note]) as a *Fortschreibung* to Zech 8, prior to the inclusion of Zech 9–14, while he believes other sections of Malachi were added with major sections of Zech 9–14.

49. Simon J. De Vries, *From Old Revelation to New: A Tradition-Historical and Redaction-Critical Study of Temporal Transitions in Prophetic Prediction* (Grand Rapids: Eerdmans, 1995); for a summary of his conclusions relative to the Book of the Twelve, see also Simon J. De Vries, "Futurism in the Pre-exilic Minor Prophets Compared with That of the Postexilic Minor Prophets," in Redditt, *Thematic Threads*, 252–72; Beck, "*Tag YHWHs*" *im Dodekapropheton*; Nogalski, *Literary Precursors*; Schart, *Entstehung des Zwölfprophetenbuchs*; Bosshard-Nepustil, *Rezeptionen von Jesaia 1–39*; Paul-Ger-

Nogalski has been critiqued for focusing too heavily upon the "seams" of the writings (i.e., the opening and concluding verses) in order to evaluate the presence of catchwords as a redactional linking device. Schart has been critiqued for working from Amos outward and trying to associate too much of Amos's redactional formation with redactional work on other writings in the Twelve. Bosshard-Nepustil has been critiqued for relying too heavily upon parallels between the Twelve and Isaiah. De Vries, writing on the Nevi'im as a group, focuses his technical investigation exclusively on the formulaic elements used to signal statements about the future. Beck and Schwesig focus upon the Day of YHWH, as they reconstruct {30} it, with Beck basing his study almost exclusively on the presence of the phrase, while Schwesig focuses upon those passages he terms day of YHWH poems. Wöhrle focuses on what he considers the "early" collections of the Twelve. What gets lost in these critiques is the degree of overlap which has resulted in these investigations, providing a significant number of checks and balances, as well as a confusing array of combinations. To be sure there is more in common between some of these presentations than others, but in many ways, some clarity has begun to emerge as a result of the multiple starting points.

This brief overview thus shows that much work remains to be done, especially for the six undated writings. At least four prominent points of disagreement have not been resolved by the various redactional studies. Without additional investigations and proposals, these four points in particular represent areas where disagreements appear to have stalled progress toward reconstructing the development of the corpus and describing the group(s) responsible for the development. First, most studies agree that Joel plays a pivotal role in the Book of the Twelve, but there is genuine disagreement regarding its unity and the point of its incorporation into the Book of the Twelve. Is the character of Joel that of a composite writing created in relatively short order or a writing that reaches its current shape over an extended period? Second, there is no clear agreement as to whether Malachi was joined to Zech 1–8 before Zech 9–14 was were added, or whether Malachi was added to the collection after Zech 9–14 was added to Zech 1–8. Third, the nature of the Day of YHWH in the Book of the Twelve remains a subject of debate. Finally, the role that a

---

hard Schwesig, *Die Rolle der Tag-JHWHs-Dichtungen im Dodekapropheton*, BZAW 366 (Berlin: de Gruyter, 2006); Wöhrle, *Frühen Sammlungen des Zwölfprophetenbuches*.

writing's *Sitz im Buch* plays in its formation is too often left unexplored. It is this last issue to which I would like to devote the remainder of this essay.

Form and Function of the Redactional Work

The Role of a Writing's *Sitz im Buch* Can Affect Its Form

What role does a writing's *Sitz im Buch* play in its formation? More attention needs to be given regarding how the inclusion of source blocks in one writing for a particular function in the Book of the Twelve can create literary tensions with another portion of the Twelve. The process of determining the growth of the Book of the Twelve becomes far more complicated when source material reflecting {31} one historical setting is used in the Book of the Twelve for a literary purpose different than originally intended. Consider the case of Nahum and Habakkuk.

It seems clear that somehow Nahum and Habakkuk are intended to function in the Book of the Twelve as prophetic reflections upon YHWH's role in the downfall of Assyria and the rise of Babylon. This function makes sense of the placement of Nahum and Habakkuk between Micah and Zephaniah, and several scholars have argued they are interconnected editorially.[50] In this sense, these two writings seem to presuppose the chronological frame created by the interconnected superscriptions of Hosea-Amos-Micah-Zephaniah. However, as some have noted, these two writings also create certain tensions within the content of the writings in sequence.[51] For example, Nineveh/Assyria appears to be swept aside at the

---

50. Childs already makes this connection. See Childs, *Introduction to the Old Testament as Scripture*, 454. See also the very different presentations of Schart, *Entstehung des Zwölfprophetenbuches*, 246–51; and Bosshard-Nepustil, *Rezeptionen von Jesaia 1–39*, 393–97, who nevertheless see Nah 1 and Hab 3 in close association with one another.

51. This use of source material also affects how one understands the unnamed city in Zeph 3:1–8. Originally, Zeph 3:1–8 almost certainly reflects an oracle delivered against Jerusalem, but some want to interpret its function in Zephaniah as a continuation of the anti-Assyrian oracle in 2:13–15 (such as Wöhrle, *Frühen Sammlungen des Zwölfprophetenbuches*, 219–20, 226–27, who also notes the Syriac version does the same thing by referring in 3:1 to the "city of Jonah" rather than just "the city"). Others argue that the original addressee, Jerusalem, makes better sense as an ironic ending to the collection of oracles against foreign nations in Zephaniah (see also Nogalski, *Literary Precursors*, 175–78).

end of Nahum while Habakkuk anticipates Babylon's imminent rise. However, the Assyria oracle in Zeph 2:13-14 returns to anticipating Assyria's downfall. Moreover, if the analyses are correct, the biggest portions of Nahum and Habakkuk that were added to the existing form of those writings are *not* the portions which deal explicitly with Assyria in Nahum or with Babylon in Habakkuk. Rather, the largest editorial accretions in Nahum and Habakkuk are the theophanic hymns in Nah 1:2-8 and Hab 3:1-19, neither of which mention the respective enemy by name. The theophanic hymn of Nah 1:2-8 mentions enemies (1:2) and {32} adversaries (1:8), not Assyria. Habakkuk 3 mentions the "head of the wicked house" (3:13) and "the people who attack us" (3:16 NRSV), but it does not mention Babylon or the Chaldeans (see Hab 1:6). In both cases, however, good reasons exist for assuming that those shaping the writings intended these enemy references to be interpreted as Assyria in Nahum and as Babylon in Habakkuk. It must, however, be noted that the redactors did not feel compelled to add the specific reference to the hymns when they were incorporated into the respective writings.

This anomaly has implications for interpreting *both* the theological agenda of the editors of this phase *and* for extracting data regarding the identity of the tradents. First, consider the implications of the use of hymns (and other cultic material) as a major source for expanding the growing corpus. There is wide agreement that this cultic material is not typical for the role of a prophet in ancient society. And yet, such cultic genres are hardly unique in the Book of the Twelve. The theophanic hymns in Nah 1* and Hab 3* play an integral role in the expansion of those writings. The thanksgiving hymn of Jonah 2 offers another case in point. Whether or not one agrees that the hymn was added for the incorporation of Jonah into the Book of the Twelve, the thanksgiving hymn in general and this one in particular have undeniable cultic connections. Seen in this light, the communal call to repentance at the core of Joel 1-2* also looms large, as do the cultic concerns underlying confrontation with the priests and people in Malachi. Additionally, the concerns of several of the night visions in Zech 1-6 reflect as much or more concern for the *priestly* role of Joshua as the focus at the end of the Haggai does for the *political* role of Zerubbabel. I am certainly not suggesting that this cultic connection comes from a single hand, or is all cut from a single cloth. I do suspect, however, it has not been given adequate attention in discussions of the prophetic tradents. Somehow, concern for the cult—its proper execution, its personnel, and its modes of expression—

needs to be taken seriously in developing a model to explain the growth of the corpus.

Second, one must consider carefully the difficulty of delineating a consistent and coherent theological agenda on the part of the editors who are shaping these writings when so much of the material they incorporate draws from sources they themselves did not compose. This dichotomy likely plays a major role in understanding {33} why so much disagreement continues around the six debated writings, all of which have significant relationships to cultic materials. This use of cultic source blocks *both* says something about *and* complicates the task of understanding the intentions of the editors/compilers of the Book of the Twelve. This revelation and complication are two sides of the same coin.

On one side of the coin, the evidence suggests editors had access to *cultic texts*, access which results in the use of a wide array of forms associated with the cult and which lasts some considerable time. This access could perhaps be understood as a tradition out of which the various author/editors operate, or (and in my opinion more likely) it could be understood as evidence that the editorial use of this material was possible because the compilers had access to physical sources with which they could work. What, then, would be the nature of these sources and how do they relate to the final form of the writing?

This question leads to the other side of the coin. How does one deduce editorial intention when a *prophetic* writing incorporates preexisting source material with a *cultic* background? Some observations are in order concerning the ways in which tensions are created and ignored in this process. Something in the source block draws the editor's eye, but tensions with the broader context are not necessarily eliminated. Nahum 1:2–8 and the incorporation of Nahum into the Book of the Twelve offers an illustration. The focus of this theophany (prior to its attachment to Nahum) accentuates the role of YHWH in punishing the wicked. One can safely assume this motif manifests an important theological affirmation for the editors. The fact that the same topic plays a prominent role in Hab 3 further solidifies this assumption. However, given the broad chronological outline of the Book of the Twelve, one cannot deduce from this theology that the editors were interested in *replacing* the focus on Assyria with a focus on *the nations* (contra Roth, for example).[52] Rather, it works the

---

52. Roth, *Israel und die Völker im Zwölfprophetenbuch*, 289–90.

other way around. In order to affirm that YHWH is the one responsible for the downfall of Assyria, the theophanic hymn accentuates YHWH's role in the events that follow. For this reason, the material focusing upon Assyria's downfall (the bulk of Nah 2–3) receives a theological emphasis in {34} the form of an introductory theophany focusing upon the power of YHWH. Without the theophanic hymn (Nah 1:2–8), and its editorial transition (Nah 1:9–2,1*), the preexisting collection of anti-Assyria oracles would be far less theologically oriented since YHWH would be almost completely absent from the early corpus.[53] Nevertheless, when incorporating Nahum into the collection, the relatively brief Assyria oracle in Zeph 2:13–15 was not eliminated from Zephaniah, and this decision (or oversight) created a literary tension within the Book of the Twelve that did not exist earlier. The decision to include Nahum and Habakkuk recognized an important gap in the existing Book of the Four. Specifically, the focus upon Israel and Judah in Hosea-Amos-Micah-Zephaniah does not deal with the issue of foreign occupation or the change from one foreign overlord to another. By contrast, the inclusion of Nahum-Habakkuk takes on this issue more in theological than historical or literary terms. By presenting Assyria's demise as an act of YHWH's justice and not just the downfall of a hated enemy, the expanded form of Nahum intones YHWH's power. YHWH is far more than a territorial deity focused exclusively upon the fate of the small kingdom of Judah. Moreover, Nahum portrays YHWH not only as a God powerful enough to bring Assyrian hegemony to a close, but as a God who holds foreign powers to a standard of conduct which imposes limits upon their ability to terrorize other nations.[54] In this respect, the point of combining the theophany hymn with the celebration of Assyria's downfall comes very close to reiterating (or extending) major themes in Isa 10.

In Isa 10:5–6, YHWH announces his intention to utilize Assyria as the means by which YHWH will punish Judah and Israel. YHWH famously refers to Assyria as "the rod of my anger" (10:5) as the tool he will use to punish Judah. Immediately thereafter, {35} YHWH demonstrates

---

53. Concerning the editing of Nahum for the Book of the Twelve presumed here, see James D. Nogalski, "The Redactional Shaping of Nahum 1 for the Book of the Twelve," in *Among the Prophets: Language, Image and Structure in the Prophetic Writings*, ed. Philip R. Davies and David J. A. Clines (Sheffield: JSOT Press, 1993), 193–202. See also Schart, *Entstehung des Zwölfprophetenbuchs*, 242–44, 246–51.

54. See Nogalski, *Redactional Processes*, 105–6, 149–50, 181; Schart, *Entstehung des Zwölfprophetenbuchs*, 248–49.

YHWH's own awareness that Assyria does not know its actions are controlled by YHWH:

> ⁵ Ah, Assyria, the rod of my anger—the club in their hands is my fury! ⁶ Against a godless nation I send him, and against the people of my wrath I command him, to take spoil and seize plunder, and to tread them down like the mire of the streets. ⁷ But this is not what he intends, nor does he have this in mind; but it is in his heart to destroy, and to cut off nations not a few. ⁸ For he says:
> > "Are not my commanders all kings? ⁹ Is not Calno like Carchemish? Is not Hamath like Arpad? Is not Samaria like Damascus? ¹⁰ As my hand has reached to the kingdoms of the idols whose images were greater than those of Jerusalem and Samaria, ¹¹ shall I not do to Jerusalem and her idols what I have done to Samaria and her images?"
> ¹² When the Lord has finished all his work on Mount Zion and on Jerusalem, he will punish the arrogant boasting of the king of Assyria and his haughty pride. (Isa 10:5–12, NRSV)

Immediately after announcing the use of Assyria as a tool to punish Judah, this passage makes two rhetorical points in 10:6–12 which both bear on the role of Assyria and Babylon in the Book of the Twelve. First, not only is Assyria unaware of YHWH's plans, but YHWH knows Assyria's king has his own intentions, to expand Assyria's power (10:7). Second, once YHWH's use of Assyria to punish Judah is complete, YHWH will punish the king of Assyria (10:12). In this respect, Isa 10 "anticipates" Assyrian hegemony as a product of Assyrian arrogance and greed which YHWH allows for a time. A third point connecting Isa 10 and Nahum appears in the speech of the Assyrian king's litany of rhetorical questions designed to accentuate Assyrian power over Judah (Isa 10:8–11). These rhetorical questions stand out as an ironic parallel in light of the confrontation of Assyria with a similar rhetorical question introducing Nah 3:8–11, in the mouth of YHWH, designed to accentuate the absurdity of Assyria's claim of strength in comparison to the intentions of YHWH. YHWH asks Lady Nineveh whether she is better than Thebes—a river city deemed impenetrable because it used the river as a significant portion of its defenses. The rhetorical {36} question in Nah 3:8 functions to condemn Assyrian weakness rather than create an impression of Assyrian power. This ironic twist is accentuated further by the fact that Assyria was the power which defeated Thebes, but the context of Nah 3:8–11 assumes YHWH, not Assyrian might, was the ultimate source of Thebes's downfall.

The point here is not whether Nahum draws upon Isaiah, though one could make that case. The point is the way in which two very similar theological statements are made. Isaiah 10:5–12 makes its points through a speech of YHWH, and YHWH's quote of the Assyrian king within that speech. By contrast, a virtually identical "story line" is created by Nahum's *Sitz im Buch* and Nahum's compositional form by utilizing source blocks rather than a redactor's composition.

Regarding the *Sitz im Buch*, the last two chapters of Micah (whose literary setting concludes in the time of Hezekiah if one takes Mic 1:1 as a clue to the reader), presents three lines of thought rhetorically speaking: (1) following extensive accusations against Judah, YHWH condemns Judah for following the paths of Omri and Ahab (6:16–7:6); (2) Lady Zion anticipates punishment from "an enemy" who gloats over her, but who will herself soon be destroyed (7:8–10); and (3) Jerusalem will eventually be delivered, but punishment of the enemy will only come following Jerusalem's punishment (7:7, 9, 13). Thus, Mic 6–7 sets up a scenario quite similar to Isa 9–10 by anticipating Assyrian occupation as punishment from YHWH. However, the Book of the Twelve's version of this story line does not present its view as foreshadowing this process from the end of the eighth century (as does Isa 10:5–12). Instead of merely eliciting a perspective from a time of Hezekiah (via Isaiah and Micah), the impression from *reading* the Book of the Twelve moves the reader along chronologically when Nahum focuses upon the end of the process—nearer Assyria's punishment. The reader of Nahum assumes a later time period than the one found in Micah because the vivid focus on Assyria's destruction in Nahum forces a shift in the reader's perspective.

The addition of Nahum and Habakkuk creates a more elongated unfolding of these elements in the Book of the Twelve. This elongation adds texture to the chronological frame created by the superscriptions of Hosea-Amos-Micah-Zephaniah. By continuing beyond the promise of the enemy's destruction (Mic 7:8–20), the {37} reader of Nahum in the Twelve senses YHWH's affirmation that Assyria will not go unpunished. Hence, as with Isa 10:5–12, YHWH plans to punish Assyria when he is finished using her. YHWH's punishment of the wicked is affirmed via the incorporation of a theophanic hymn (Nah 1:2–8*) and the editorial transition (1:9–2:1 [Eng. 1:9–1:15]) onto the preexisting pronouncement of Assyria's destruction so much a part of the core material in Nah 2–3. This affirmation of punishment of the wicked also becomes an experience of an impending promise for Judah/Lady Zion (Nah 2:1 [Eng. 1:15]; note also the similarity to Isa 52:7).

This pronouncement does not, however, end the story line in the Book of the Twelve because, at the beginning of Habakkuk (1:2-4), the description of the problems of the people is remarkably similar to the accusations of Mic 7:1-6: violence, bloodshed, and the perversion of justice abound in Judean society. Habakkuk 1:2-4 and the foundational material in 1:12-17 present these accusations largely in the form of an individual complaint song (another cultic form). Because of Judah's problems, Hab 1:5-11 announces YHWH's use of yet another enemy, Babylon, who will punish Judah. This description of the Chaldeans contains elements which present Babylon's strength in markedly similar (but stronger) terms to the description of Assyria in Nahum.[55] In the case of Habakkuk, the redactional expansions to the preexisting material identify Babylon as the enemy (1:6) and equate the actions of the oppressor with the country YHWH will send.[56] Thus, a second enemy nation is sent by YHWH (1:5-6) because, despite Assyria's downfall, Judah has not turned toward YHWH.[57] Nevertheless, the incorporation of the theophany and prayer in Hab 3 serves as a promise from the prophet that *after* YHWH punishes Judah and Jerusalem (using Babylon), YHWH will destroy Babylon (the "people {38} who attack us" in 3:16) and restoration will then be possible (3:16-19). This connection backwards in Habakkuk is strengthened by the affirmation in Hab 3:18 which parallels the prophet's response in Mic 7:7: "I will wait for/ exult in the God of my salvation."

When comparing Isa 10 with Micah, Nahum, and Habakkuk, the commonalities are clear. In Isaiah (10:1-2) and the Book of the Twelve (Mic 7:1-6; Hab 1:2-4), the society of Judah is described as one of bloodshed and the perversion of justice. In both contexts, YHWH reveals his decision to punish Judah with a foreign power. In both contexts, the foreign power has no knowledge of YHWH's purpose. It has its own agenda and thinks it is operating from its own strength. In each case, however, the reader learns this strength is an illusion when compared to the power of YHWH.

---

55. See Nogalski, *Redactional Processes*, 146-50.
56. Based upon the redactional observations in ibid., 140-46, which delineates the wisdom-oriented material as source material and the Babylonian commentary as the redactional comment.
57. Note also the similarity of Hab 1:6 ("Behold, I am about to raise the Chaldeans") to introduce the arrival of Babylon against Judah in the Book of the Twelve and Amos 6:14 ("Behold, I am about to raise a nation") to introduce punishment for Israel by the Assyrians.

In the Book of the Twelve, this process unfolds not once, but twice. The prophet acknowledges a dual-stage punishment (first Judah, then the foreign power) which leads to the prospect of restoration (waiting for the God of salvation). In Nahum, Judah's punishment is implicitly ongoing, while Nineveh's demise in portrayed as imminent. In Habakkuk, Judah's punishment is imminent but its sin is ongoing while the punishment of Babylon must wait until Judah's punishment is over. Thus, the transitions from Micah to Nahum to Habakkuk exhibit considerable coherence which derives from a redactional agenda to portray a prophetic message using source blocks. This segment of texts presents a theological reflection upon the seventh century decline of Assyria and the rise of Babylon as the work of YHWH, even while confronting YHWH's own people.

Unlike the presentation of Assyria in Isa 10, this twofold process, which accounts for Assyrian *and* Babylonian control of Judah in the Book of the Twelve, largely relies on the use of preexisting material—arranged, amplified, and connected—to present this story line. Yet, the character of the preexisting material has stronger connections to what has traditionally been perceived as cultic forms rather than prophetic forms: theophanic hymns in Nah 1 and Hab 3, and the underlying complaint of Hab 1.

The connections to the Book of the Twelve isolated in this process serve two functions: to heighten correlations to the immediate literary context and to the broader corpus. These cases have {39} largely been made in earlier discussions and, though there have been some questions raised, the assertions have also found considerable support. Catchwords between Mic 7 and Nah 1 strengthen a sense of connectivity between these two texts, but they were not written by the same hand. The Habakkuk theophany's use of Joel imagery echoes the sense of an impending judgment which will make the land infertile before YHWH delivers his people. The way that Nah 1 connects with Joel is equally important. The citation of Exod 34:6–7 in Nah 1 presents the flip side of Joel's citation of Joel 2:13. Joel 2:13 cites Exod 34:6, focusing upon YHWH's חסד, patience, and desire for repentance, while Nah 1:2b–3a (inserted into the acrostic poem) evokes Exod 34:7: YHWH's promise to punish the wicked. In so doing, this citation functionally parallels the allusions to Exod 34:7 in Joel 4:21 (Eng. 3:21) noted by several scholars.[58] Further, this separate invocation of Exod 34:6 and later 34:7 in Joel 2:13 and 4:21 corresponds to the allusions to Exod

---

58. See Van Leeuwen, "Scribal Wisdom," 41.

34:6 in Mic 7:18–19 and to Exod 34:7 in Nah 1:2b–3a. Thematically, Joel's use of Exod 34:6–7 deals both with YHWH's patient, long-suffering grace toward those who repent *and* the eventual punishment of the guilty. The transition from Micah to Nahum does the same when it incorporates both Exod 34:6 and 34:7.

How then does one explain this phenomenon of the use of preexisting *cultic* texts in redactional work shaping *prophetic* writings to reflect upon *history*? This is not an easy question, but there do seem to be two avenues from which to begin a conversation on this topic. First, one can ask what group(s) would have access to these texts associated with the cult? Second, one should also ask, whose interests are served in compiling this reflection upon history that exhibits theological admonitions, cultic forms, the framing of history, and a developing eschatological (and protoapocalyptic) perspective? The remaining section of this essay will explore one possibility: identification of the Levites as a group associated with the collection of the Twelve in its latter stages. {40}

The Functions of the Levites in Chronicles, Ezra, and Nehemiah

The books of Chronicles, Ezra, and Nehemiah represent Persian period narrative literature. As such, these books offer important insights into traditions of the past filtered through the lens of Persian period reality, along with some level of historical revisionism. These writings do not represent a seamless narrative from the hand of a single author, but at some level they have been edited together by persons sharing a substantially similar perspective. At the very least, they are intended to be read in conjunction with one another, as evidenced by the fact that the last two verses of Chronicles (2 Chr 36:22–23) are the same as the opening verses of Ezra (1:1–3a) and that Ezra functions as a major character in both Ezra and Nehemiah.[59]

The role of the Levites, and especially their relationship to the Zadokite and the Aaronide priests, has been a subject of some discussion for understanding the Persian period world of Judah.[60] This question is

---

59. Ezra and Nehemiah, of course, are much more integrally connected to one another than to Chronicles. For a summary of the similarities, see the evidence (ancient and modern) for connecting Ezra and Nehemiah more closely in Hugh G. M. Williamson, *Ezra, Nehemiah*, WBC 16 (Waco, TX: Word, 1985), xxi–xxiii.

60. See, e.g., Antonius H. J. Gunneweg, *Leviten und Priester: Hauptlinien der*

complex because of conflicting data, the sparsity of sources, divergent numbers, and the difficulty of sifting through the various genealogical presentations. However, for the purposes under discussion in this essay, the exact historical relationships of the passages to one another need not be resolved in their entirety in order to appreciate the breadth of cultic functions associated with the Levites. The variety of functions assigned to the Levites in these texts suggests this group (however the network of families was constituted at any given time) may well have been a pivotal factor in the production of texts for use in the temple. {41}

A survey of the functions attributed to the Levites across these books suggests they are the only group mentioned in these postexilic narrative texts who had the resources, access, and intellectual wherewithal to compile the writings of the Twelve which demonstrate so many connections to cultic source blocks. These functions include specific tasks in four broad areas that impinge upon their ability to compile literary collections: (1) access to the temple itself, (2) training in musical composition and performance, (3) access to the means of production for scrolls, and (4) training in scribal duties (both for writing and for teaching).

(1) Physical proximity to the temple is beyond dispute for the Levites. The genealogical material in 1 Chr 9:18, 26–27 mentions that Levites guarded the temple gates, closed them at night and opened them again in the morning. According to Chronicles, an aging David assigned Levites several roles in the temple after it is no longer necessary for the Levites to carry the ark of the covenant since it will have a new place inside the temple (1 Chr 23:26–32).[61] These tasks included "care of the courts and chambers, the cleansing of all that is holy, and any work for the service of the house of God" (1 Chr 23:28, NRSV).

In Chronicles, a number of texts also indicate the Levites guarded the temple gates themselves, while other texts mention the Levites and

---

Traditionsbildung und Geschichte des israelitisch-jüdischen Kultpersonals, FRLANT 89 (Göttingen: Vandenhoeck & Ruprecht, 1965); Menahem Haran, *Temples and Temple-Service in Ancient Israel: An Inquiry into the Character of Cult Phenomena and the Historical Setting of the Priestly School* (Oxford: Clarendon, 1978), 99–111.

61. These narratives and others combine sources from different time periods, but in their final form represent the agenda of organizing temple personnel in the late postexilic period under the authority of ancient traditions. It is not always easy to determine which texts reflect the later realities and which an ideal order for the Chronicler. See Williamson, *Ezra, Nehemiah*, 18–19.

gatekeepers separately, but in close proximity to one another. Levites are named as gatekeepers in 1 Chr 26:17, which lists the number of Levites stationed around the temple gates each day: six in the east; four in the north; four in the south; four (two + two) at the storehouse; and four in the west (two + two at the colonnade).

Levites also serve as guards of the treasuries where tithes and cultic contributions are stored (1 Chr 26:20). Relatedly, it is the Levites who are depicted as collecting temple taxes, offerings, and other contributions: 2 Chr 24:5–6 (for temple repair during the {42} reforms of Joash); 35:7–9 (during the reforms of Josiah); Ezra 2:68–70; 8:29–30; 8:33 (note that the gifts are also counted by Levites).

According to Neh 13, the second temple had a storage room which was the responsibility of the Levites themselves. While Nehemiah was away, the room was given by the chief priest to Tobiah, his relative and Nehemiah's nemesis. This move cost the Levites their ability to support themselves from the temple treasury according to 13:5, 10. As a result, the Levites (along with the singers) had been forced to return "to their fields."

The functions attributed to the Levites in the programmatic list of duties assigned by David included temple cleansing and repair: 1 Chr 23:28; 2 Chr 29:4–19 (Hezekiah); Ezra 1:5 (rebuilding temple); 3:8–9 (oversight of temple workers). Relatedly, purification of the Levites was an important expectation and shows up in various ways. In Ezra 9:1, the people, priests, and Levites need purification because they have married foreign women, so in 10:5, 15 the priests and Levites divorce their foreign wives. In Neh 9:38, various leaders, including Levites, sign Nehemiah's covenant of purity (10:9 lists the names of the heads of Levites who sign). Other texts focus on the general purity of the Levites (Neh 10:28; 12:30; 13:22).

(2) Chronicles, Ezra, and Nehemiah collectively suggest a close (but admittedly complex) association of Levites with temple music, both in terms of performance and presumably also its composition. Levites are frequently associated with singing and playing instruments during cultic celebrations (1 Chr 15:16–24; 2 Chr 5:12; 7:6; 8:14–15; 29:25–26, 30; 30:21–27; 34:12; 35:5, 14–18; Ezra 3:10; Neh 12:8; 12:24–25; 12:27). Invocation, praise, and thanksgiving become expressions for leading temple singing (1 Chr 6:31, 48; 9:33–34; 16:4; 2 Chr 20:19; Neh 9:4–5). The guild of Asaph (1 Chr 15:16–24; 2 Chr 20:14; Ezra 2:40; 3:10; Neh 7:43–45) and the Korahites (2 Chr 20:19) appear with, or are counted among, the Levites. These

groups are credited with significant collections of the Psalter.[62] Numerous texts mention the Levites with temple {43} singers (1 Chr 9:33; 15:16, 27; 2 Chr 35:15; Ezra 2:70; 7:7, 24; Neh 7:1, 73; 10:28; 11:22; 12:47; 13:5, 10). Many of these references point to divisions of the two secondary clerical functions, but some also associate this activity with the Levites themselves.

(3) The probability that Levites have access to the means of production for scrolls can be deduced from several texts. Pasturelands are given to the Levites at the command of David, an act which implies they own lands used for cattle throughout the country (1 Chr 6:64;[63] 13:2). The Levites run into trouble with Jeroboam I when they refuse to help with sacrifice at the new Northern Kingdom sites and thus lose these fields because of their commitment to worshiping YHWH only (2 Chr 11:13–14). Clearly, this episode is recounted to bolster their claim to lands in the postexilic community. When they lose their place at the temple in Nehemiah, the Levites have "fields" to which they can return (Neh 13:10).

The skinning of animals offered as sacrifice is a task attributed to the Levites during the monarchy (2 Chr 29:34; 35:11) and/or Persian period (assuming that part of the rationale for the Chronicler is to root the cultic practices of his day in the authority of David). Over time, this task may have been assigned to other temple servants, but presumably under the oversight of the Levites. At any rate, these skins would provide the Levites with ongoing control of the hides essential for producing scrolls.

Thematically, several texts also intimate that the Levites had a vested interest in the fertility of the land because their livelihood depended upon it (1 Chr 9:31; 23:24, 29; 2 Chr 31:4–5; 32:28; Ezra 7:13–18; Neh 5:1–11; 10:31–39). Some even use the same stock formulaic groupings which appear in fertility texts in the Book of the Twelve (vine/wine, grain, and oil).

(4) Levites are also portrayed as scribes and teachers. Scribal groups and activities associated with Levites would reflect the tasks {44} they

---

62. Two small collections of Asaph and Korahite psalms appear together in Pss 42–49 (Korahites) + 50 (Asaph) and 73–83 (Asaph) + 84–88 (Korahites) in books 2 and 3 of the Psalter.

63. The entire chapter points to a composite use of sources, including some clear relationships to Josh 21, which also associates these pasturelands with the Levites (21:3, 8, 27, 34, 41). For a thorough discussion of the composite nature of the chapter and the interplay with Joshua, see Sara Japhet, *I and II Chronicles: A Commentary*, OTL (Louisville: Westminster John Knox, 1993), 145–62 (esp. 145–49). These lands around the city are not conceptualized merely for planting, but for tending cattle as well (see Josh 14:4).

needed to fulfill. Scribes would have had to count and record the gifts brought to the temple. Scribes would be needed to write, or at least record in written form, the songs which the Levitical groups performed. These could have been recorded and stored in rooms in the temple to which the Levites had access. One finds references to certain Levites as scribes (1 Chr 24:6; 2 Chr 34:13), and exiled Levites play a central (though at times reluctant) role in the book of Ezra, whose chief character is the scribe of scribes (see the account of the recruitment of Levites in Ezra 8:15–20).

The role of Levites as teachers plays prominently in Chronicles and Nehemiah. This teaching involves understanding the Torah and application to the history of YHWH's people (2 Chr 17:8; 35:3; Neh 8:7–11). This task involved the study of Torah and other texts, which one may safely presume were available to them at the temple. The association of Levites with the study of Torah, and with the collection (and production) of psalm texts, at least significantly raises the possibility that the Levites also had access to prophetic scrolls.[64] This prophetic connection is increased when it is recognized that Haggai and Zechariah traditions play a significant (albeit confusing) role in Ezra's narrative of the early restoration period.[65]

One text in particular, Neh 9:32, stands out thematically in reference to the teaching of the Levites because of its correlation with the interests of the Book of the Twelve in general and the six debated writings in particular. In the context of Ezra's teaching, with the help of Levites (see Neh 9:4–5), Ezra recounts Israel's history with God, summarizing the time from Moses through the monarchy. In the end, Ezra accents God's compassion in delaying the punishment of his people, a punishment that begins to unfold from the incursions of the Assyrians in the eighth century: {45}

> Now therefore, our God—the great and mighty and awesome God, keeping covenant and *steadfast love*—do not treat lightly all the hardship that has come upon us, upon our kings, our officials, our priests, our prophets, our ancestors, and all your people, *since the time of the kings of Assyria until today*. (Neh 9:32, NRSV, emphasis added)

---

64. While problematically referring to the text as a "Levitic sermon," Beuken's observations concerning the similarity of Zech 1:3–6 and 2 Chr 30:6–9 are also instructive at this point because of the reflection on prophets and history in Zech 1:3–6. See Beuken, *Haggai-Sacharja 1–8*, 110–15.

65. Ezra 5:1; 6:14. See discussion of the narrative framework in Williamson, *Ezra, Nehemiah*, 73–74.

This verse, in its literary context, introduces a final challenge to the people of Nehemiah's day by interpreting history from the eighth century to the late Persian period. In one sense, this verse could summarize portions of the book of Kings, but it also describes the main theological emphases of the Book of the Twelve: punishment of YHWH's people begins with the time of the kings of Assyria (Hosea, Amos, Micah). God's fidelity and compassion delay punishment (see the earlier discussion of the quotations of Exod 34:6–7 in the Book of the Twelve), but once the punishment begins (Nahum and Habakkuk), it continues into the postexilic period (Malachi). To be sure, the form of the story is presented differently in the Book of the Twelve, but the essential outlines assumed in Neh 9:32–37 and the collected writings of the Book of the Twelve are very similar in this respect.

Several texts imply that the duties and fate of the Levites shifted over time, but not always in ways which improved their status.[66] In this regard, early postexilic optimism regarding the temple may have periodically given way to a sense of marginalization in relating to the power structure of the temple. One of the recurring suggestions for the move from prophetic eschatology to apocalypticism has long involved the suspicion of this deep sense of alienation.[67]

Further, a group associated with Levites would certainly have had interest in the proper role of the cult in society. Themes of cultic purity were associated with Levites in the narrative texts. They would have been well schooled in the ancient traditions regarding {46} the fertility of the land which could have accounted for the ongoing interest in the state of the agricultural products used in cultic feasts. Relatedly, the "sons of Levi" appear to be the group in need of reforming and restoring who are mentioned in Malachi (2:4, 8; 3:3; see also Zech 12:13).[68]

---

66. See, e.g., the summary description of delineated views within P material in Gunneweg, *Leviten und Priester*, 185–88.

67. See, e.g., Paul L. Redditt, "The Book of Joel and Peripheral Prophecy," *CBQ* 48 (1986): 225–40. Redditt sees the marginalized group behind Joel as "separatist, exclusivistic, and nonmessianic" (238), but as prophetic rather than priestly in its orientation.

68. Redditt argues that a non-Zadokite Levite is responsible for composing Malachi, but extending this suggestion to the group responsible for compiling the Book of the Twelve in its final form needs careful consideration. See Redditt, *Haggai, Zechariah and Malachi*, 151–52.

In sum, these observations concerning the functions performed by Levites in postexilic narrative literature offer a tantalizing web of connections between those functions and the resources (physical and intellectual) needed to produce the corpus of the latter stages of the Book of the Twelve. To be sure, this picture needs further development, refinement, and probably correction in places. However, no other group mentioned in these biblical texts comes close to having the variety of skills, assets, training, and networks necessary to pull together a prophetic collection combining the kinds of source material present in the latter stages of the Book of the Twelve. The cultic connection of the six debated writings merits more attention than it has heretofore received, both in terms of its literary function in the Book of the Twelve and the implications for the production of the corpus. The Levite teachers portrayed in Ezra/Nehemiah represent a group that had interests in interpreting history from the eighth century. It seems plausible to postulate that the cultic circles in which the Levites moved inherited the Book of the Four/Deuteronomistic Corpus (which was probably transmitted in Palestine) after the rebuilding of the temple, and that this group had already begun to be influenced by those groups associated with those repatriated by the Persians who controlled the temple. The fate of this group changed over time, sometimes having a more privileged status, while at other times they were more marginalized within the power structure. This changing status could also help account for the more pessimistic attitudes for society as a whole in the latter portions of the Book of the Twelve.

Not Just Another Nation:
Obadiah's Placement in the Book of the Twelve

I recently suggested that finding agreement (or at least narrowing the disagreements) for dating the editorial work of the six writings in the Book of the Twelve whose superscriptions do not contain dates needed to explore more fully the use of "cultic source blocks" to accomplish editorial agendas.[1] That essay explored how the editorial adaptation and the placement of preexisting theophanic hymns at the beginning of Nahum and the end of Habakkuk served the redactor's literary and theological agenda. Recognizing the editorial elements produces a coherent rhetorical function in reading Micah, Nahum, and Habakkuk sequentially.

The current essay continues this line of investigation by considering the composition of Obadiah in light of its location in the Book of the Twelve. Doing so raises a methodological question: Have models of the redactional growth of the corpus that comes to be known as the Twelve moved too quickly to explain literary and theological tensions within the writings by postulating "redactional layers" without fully considering whether these tensions may be explained by the adaptation of source material for a writing's *Sitz im Buch*?

Unlike Nahum and Habakkuk, the editorial work in Obadiah does not involve the attachment of a cultic hymn to a preexisting corpus. Nevertheless, the book of Obadiah almost certainly represents an adaptation of source material that was initially composed for another purpose. The reason, however, for the selection and arrangement of this material has not been given the attention it deserves. This essay shall explore this question from two directions. First, it will delineate evidence for understanding Obadiah as a

---

1. See James D. Nogalski, "One Book and Twelve Books: The Nature of the Redactional Work and the Implications of Cultic Source Material in the Book of the Twelve," in *Two Sides of a Coin: Juxtaposing Views on Interpreting the Book of The Twelve*, AnGor 201 (Piscataway, NJ: Gorgias, 2009), 30–39.

composite piece of literature that combines (through ordering, editing, and composition) at least three brief units, at least two of which originated in another context. Second, {90} the essay will argue that the motivation for arranging these units derives not from a desire to record the sayings of an anonymous prophet, but that this arrangement instead owes its shape to its literary location, its *Sitz im Buch*. Further, by taking seriously the idea that the Book of the Twelve represents the literary context for understanding Obadiah, one can plausibly understand many of the book's literary abnormalities, its macrostructural flow, and its role in the broader corpus. Fundamentally, these assertions recognize the role of Edom in Obadiah does not merely, or even primarily, serve as a cipher for any nation. Rather, in Obadiah, Edom means Edom.[2]

Structural and Thematic Parallels Between Obadiah and Amos 9

The Placement of Obadiah

In the history of scholarship, a few scholars have noted that the placement of Obadiah in the Book of the Twelve resulted from a *compiler's* decision to place it beside Amos because of the fortuitous reference to the "possession" of "Edom" in Amos 9:12, two keywords which also appear in Obad 17–18. In many respects, this combination, they argue, could represent a thematic summary of Obadiah as a whole.[3] Consequently, these scholars assume correctly that the context in the Book of the Twelve influenced the location of Obadiah.

However, assuming an editor merely copied a completed collection of anti-Edom sayings onto a scroll at the end of Amos because one verse contained two key concepts in Obadiah does not provide an adequate explanation for Obadiah's placement for two reasons: (1) the parallels between Amos 9:12 and Obad 17–18 only begin to scratch the surface of

---

2. Contra those who see Edom primarily as a type for all nations, such as Philip Peter Jenson, *Obadiah, Jonah, Micah: A Theological Commentary*, LHBOTS 496 (New York: T&T Clark, 2008), 7; House, *Unity of the Twelve*, 82; Douglas Stuart, *Hosea–Jonah*, WBC 31 (Waco, TX: Word, 1987), 421–22. One should take full account of the references to Edom when interpreting Obadiah. For a comparative example, see Ursula Struppe, *Die Bücher Obadja, Jona*, NSKAT 24.1 (Stuttgart: Katholisches Bibelwerk, 1996), 52–53.

3. E.g., Cassuto, "Sequence and Arrangement," 5–6.

the common motifs, wording, and structural components of Amos 9 and Obadiah; and (2) the idea that a completed Obadiah was placed beside a completed Amos based upon the presence of two common words begs a larger question: namely, why these two words? More should be said about both of these reasons: documenting parallel vocabulary, structural components, and themes between Amos 9 and {91} Obadiah, on the one hand, and considering the possession of Edom in the postexilic context, on the other.

Given the difference in genres between Amos 9 and Obadiah, as well as the history of interpretation that has largely treated the individual writings in the Book of the Twelve as entirely independent of one another, one can hardly be surprised that these two passages are rarely treated together. However, the sheer volume of lexical and thematic parallels, combined with observations regarding the transitional markers of Obadiah that match those of Amos 9, requires an explanation that goes beyond coincidence.

Amos 9

One first needs to consider Amos 9 as a composite literary entity in its own right. Amos 9 begins the fifth and final "vision" of Amos (9:1–4) in which the prophetic spectator envisions the destruction of Israel. While scholars have often noted the uniqueness of this vision compared to the first four visions, no one doubts that 9:1–4 plays a key role in the book by demonstrating with finality God's judgment upon the Northern Kingdom. Together with the concluding doxology (9:5–6), these verses once likely concluded Amos prior to the addition of 9:7–15*, verses whose promissory nature stands in stark contrast to anything that has preceded in Amos.[4] This promissory material, in its current form, reflects two units: the first (9:7–10) reflects a debate about the nature of election and a remnant in which two sides of the debate are presented; the second unit (9:11–15) represents a composite eschatological promise that God will restore the Davidic kingdom and provide for the land's fertility. In short Amos 9 begins with destruction and ends with promise: the destruction of Israel and the promise of a restored Davidic kingdom.

---

4. Amos 9:7–10 and 9:11–15 represent additions to the chapter. See the more detailed explanation of the complex unity of these verses in Wolff, *Joel and Amos*, 245–46; Nogalski, *Literary Precursors*, 104–21.

While Amos 9 almost certainly reflects more than one hand in shaping its final form as the conclusion to Amos, two verses stand out for their thematic connections forward to Obadiah (Amos 9:12) and backward to Joel (Amos 9:13b, which cites Joel 4:18a). The promise to restore the Davidic kingdom by rebuilding it reads more smoothly if these short comments were not present, so one can easily imagine these two verses as an editor's parenthetical foreshadowing (9:12) and rehearsal (9:13) of Obadiah and Joel respectively. {92}

Amos 9 and Obadiah: Structural and Thematic Parallels

Thus, Amos 9 has its own literary integrity, composite though it may be, which generally makes sense within the developmental history of Amos. Nevertheless, a comparison of Amos 9:1–15 with Obadiah reveals a number of significant parallels that go well beyond the thematic foreshadowing of Amos 9:12, as can be seen in the following chart.

Structural and Thematic Elements		Amos	Obadiah
Vision		9:1	1
Five אם ("if/though") clauses		9:2–4	4–5
No escape from YHWH: "From there I will bring them/you down"		9:2	4
Destruction & remnant motifs (using agricultural imagery)		9:7–10	5
Thematic shifts/text markers:	הלוא "Is it not"	9:7 (2x)	5 (2x) 8 (1st word)
	ביום ההוא "on that day"	9:11	8 (2nd word)
	נאם יהוה "utterance of YHWH"	9:7,8,13	8 (3rd word)
Day(s) of *Judah's* restoration/destruction		9:11 (ביום ההוא) 9:13 (ימים באים)	11–14 (ביום 10x)
Introduction with eschatological "day" of punishment on nations and restoration of Judah		9:11	15
Allusion to destruction of Jerusalem		9:11	16

Restoration of Davidic kingdom	9:11–12	19–20
"Possession" of Edom and other nations	9:12	17–18; 19–20
Restoration of captivity/exiles	9:14	19–20
Concluding promise for restoring the kingdom	9:15	21

To understand these parallels, one should see them in light of their rhetorical function in Obad 1–5, 8–9, 10–14+15b, and 15a,16–21.

Obadiah 1–5

Comparing the differences between Obad 1–5 and its parallel in Jer 49:14–16, 9, one can plausibly explain most of the variations between the Jeremiah and the Obadiah parallel as changes in Obadiah's sources that reflect elements from Amos 9:1–4. First, Amos 9:1–4 {93} contains five concessive clauses constructed with משם ... אם ("though ... from there"). While Obad 1–5 contains only one clause with this construction, it does contain five clauses that begin with אם. The parallel text and Jer 49 contains only two such clauses. The phrase "from there I will bring them down" in Amos 9:2 parallels the same phrase in Obad 4, except the latter has a second-person masculine singular pronoun ("from there I will pull you down). This phrase, "from there I will pull them/you down" appears in only one other text, namely, Jer 49:16, the very passage (Jer 49:14–16) that parallels Obad 1–4.

Second, the superscription in Obad 1 labels Obadiah as a "vision," even though the subsequent verses do not conform to what one would traditionally expect as a vision. By contrast, no one doubts that Amos 9:1–4 should be interpreted as a vision.

Third, after Obad 1–4 closely parallels Jer 49:14–16, Obad 5 reaches backward and picks up Jer 49:9 but inverts the order of the two halves of the verse by placing 49:9b prior to 49:9a.[5]

Jer 49:9b	... or [אם] thieves at night, would they destroy [שחת] their sufficiency?
Obad 5a	If [אם] thieves come

---

5. See Nogalski, *Redactional Processes*, 66.

	to you—or [אִם] destroyers [שֹׁדְדֵי] at night—how [אֵיךְ] you would be ruined [נִדְמֵיתָה]—would they not [הֲלוֹא] steal their sufficiency?
Obad 5b	or [אִם] grape harvesters come to you, would they not [הֲלוֹא] leave gleanings?
Jer 49:9a	If [אִם] grape harvesters came to you, (would they) not [לֹא] leave gleanings?

Obadiah 5 (= Jer 49:9b, a) uses agricultural metaphors to depict the thematic content of the destruction and (the lack of) a remnant for Edom. Amos 9:7, 8–10 also uses agricultural metaphors to explain Israel's destruction (Amos 9:7 // Obad 5a) and the existence of a remnant (Amos 9:8–10 // Obad 5b). In essence, the compiler of Obadiah draws upon and yet inverts Jer 49:9b, a to create a thematic parallel to Amos 9:7–10, although the application of these thematic elements to Edom, as opposed to Israel, means that the parallel also displays a hermeneutic of ironic reversal. Whereas Israel will be destroyed (Amos 9:7), a remnant will remain (Amos 9:8–10). By contrast, the agricultural metaphors of Obad 5 articulate a situation in which Edom will be destroyed (Obad 5a) but *no* remnant will remain (Obad 5b). This hermeneutical perspective will reappear in several places in Obadiah. {94}

Thus, these five verses in Obadiah draw upon a parallel text (Jer 49:14–16, 9), but they do so in a way that suggests a deliberate, intentional mirroring of the vocabulary, structure, and thematic development of Amos 9:1–10. Nevertheless, these similarities should not hide differences in the rhetorical aims of Obad 1–5 and Amos 9:1–10 that: whereas both Israel and Edom will be destroyed, a remnant will remain for Israel (Amos 9:7–10, 11–15), but not for Edom.

These thematic and structural parallels between Amos 9 and Obadiah do not stop with the parallels of Obad 1–5. Much of the remaining material in Obadiah also exhibits structural or thematic parallels with Amos 9.

Obadiah 8–9

The syntactical and transitional markers in Obadiah represent essentially the same markers, and in roughly the same order, as those in Amos 9. As already noted, the term "vision" in the superscription of Obad 1 essentially evokes and summarizes the final vision of Amos (9:1–4). Relatedly, the presence of משם ... אם along with a fivefold use of אם in Obad 1–5 corresponds to the five משם ... אם clauses in Amos 9:1–4.

Beyond Obad 1–5, the syntactically cumbersome triple formula beginning the transitional verse in Obad 8 ("Surely, on that day, utterance of YHWH") mirrors the same transitional markers in Amos 9, where "surely" (הלוא) appears twice in Amos 9:7; "on that day" appears in Amos 9:11; and "utterance of YHWH" appears in 9:7, 8, 13.

This transitional trio marks the beginning of a saying (Obad 8–9) that essentially functions as an *inclusio* to the entire, composite anti-Edom collection of Jer 49:7–22.[6]

Obad 8	Jer 49:7
[8] On that day, says the LORD, I will destroy *the wise out of Edom*, and understanding out of Mount Esau. (NRSV)	Concerning Edom. Thus says the LORD of hosts: Is there no longer *wisdom in Teman*? Has counsel perished from the prudent? Has their *wisdom* vanished? (NRSV)
Obad 9	Jer 49:22
[9] Your *warriors* shall be shattered, O Teman, so that everyone from Mount Esau will be cut off. (NRSV)	Look, he shall mount up and swoop down like an eagle, and spread his wings against Bozrah, and the heart of the *warriors of Edom* in that day shall be like the heart of a woman in labor. (NRSV)

{95}
Hence, not only does Obad 8–9 contain the same structural elements as Amos 9:7–15, the content of these two verses also alludes to the first and last Edom oracle in the Jeremiah collection of 49:7–22: the destruction of the wise (Jer 49:7) and the warriors (Jer 49:22) of Teman/Edom. This is the same collection, needless to say, where the parallels to Jer 49:14–16, 9 appear.

Obadiah 10–14

A subtle thematic and phonetic phenomenon appears with Amos 9:13 and Obad 10–14. Amos 9:11 combines the sound of ב with the word יום in the word ביום that begins the verse (on that day; ביום ההוא). Amos 9:13

---

6. Ibid., 67; Paul R Raabe, *Obadiah: A New Translation with Introduction and Commentary*, AB 24D (New York: Doubleday, 1996), 97.

transitions to a new promise with the phrase "behold the days are coming." The days to which Amos 9:13 alludes refers to a time of promise for Israel as the coming days, ימים באים, a phrase that also combines the sound of ב with the word יום- albeit in reverse order.

Interestingly, ten times Obad 10–14 uses the singular form of "day" preceded by the preposition ב, which means that in Amos 9:11, 13 the coming days (ביום ההוא ;ימים באים) of promise for God's people are contrasted in Obadiah with ten references to something happening "on a day" (ביום) of judgment.[7] Thus, even the eschatological day phrases in Amos 9:11 and the plural ימים באים of Amos have a parallel in Obadiah, except that the "day" of judgment in Obad 10–14 refers to Judah's punishment (as opposed to Judah's restoration in Amos 9:13), while condemning Edom's behavior. Rhetorically, these verses serve as (implicit) accusations against Edom—as will be discussed below.

Obadiah 15a, 16–21

The thematic parallels continue in Obad 15a, 16–21, where the "day" of Judah's judgment in Obad 10–14 gives way to a promise concerning the day of YHWH as punishment on the nations and restoration of Judah. Nevertheless, restoration presumes destruction, further underscoring the need for Obad 10–14: to explain the reason for Edom's judgment *and* to convey the relationship of Edom's judgment to the judgment on Judah.

These verses have long been recognized in many circles as an independent unit artfully attached to Obad 10–14, 15b. Not only does 15a, 16–21 change subject, it changes the dominant style of address. The preceding verses consistently refer to Edom in the second-person singular, whereas Obad 15a, 16–21 address Judah using second-person masculine plural forms. This block of verses also coalesces thematically with Amos 9:11–15.

Amos 9:11 introduces the final promissory unit of Amos with the editorial transition ("on that day" of restoration) while Obad 15a begins {96} with a reference to the "day of YHWH" against "all the nations." Amos 9:12 further explicates "that day" as a time when the fallen booth of David will possess Edom and "all the nations" called by YHWH's name.

Amos 9:11 alludes obliquely to the destruction of Jerusalem in terms of the fallen booth of David that will be restored and rebuilt, while Obad

---

7. The forms include: ביום + עמד, שבות, אח, נכר, אבד, צרה (2x), and איד (3x).

16 refers to Jerusalem's destruction using the "cup of wrath tradition" that plays a prominent role in Jeremiah's oracles against the nations (OAN). Amos 9:11–12 articulates its promise as restoration of the Davidic kingdom (fallen booth of David, rebuilt as in the days of old, all the nations over whom my name is called). Restoration of the Davidic kingdom, using different terminology and specifying surrounding regions, also underlies the articulation of the promise of Obad 19–20 (possession of Esau's mountain, Philistine territory, Samarian territory, Gilead, etc.).

Amos 9:12 calls for the "possession" of Edom and other nations, while Obad 17 refers to Jerusalem's "possession" of those who dispossessed them. Obadiah 18 goes on to identify these enemies as the "house of Esau." The possession of Edom by Israel leads directly to possession of other nations and territories in Obad 19–20, so that the exiles who are reclaiming territory essentially reconstitute the idealized borders of David's kingdom with Jerusalem at the center. The repossession of these territories essentially surrounds Jerusalem in Obad 19–20:

And the Negeb will possess the Mountain of Esau,
And the Shephelah (will possess) the Philistines.
And they will possess the field of Samaria,
And Benjamin (will possess) Gilead.
And the exiles of this force belonging to the sons of Israel
who are among the Canaanites as far as Zarephath.[8]
And the exiles of Jerusalem who are in Sepharad (Sardis),
they will possess the cities of the Negeb. {97}

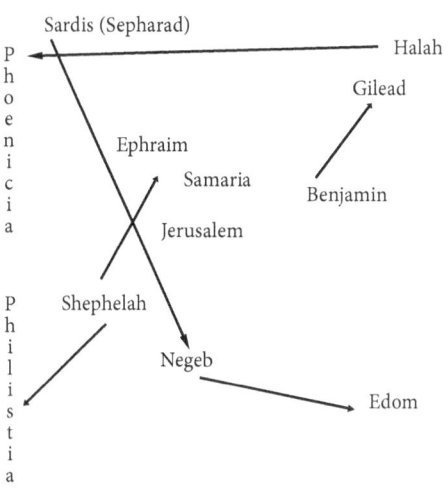

The first wave (v. 19) describes the retaking of territory that had been lost, with Jerusalem essentially in the center. The second wave describes reinforcement of territory that was vacated during the first wave (Negeb) or the second wave (Phoenicia).

---

8. Alternatively: The exiles of the Israelites who are in Halah [will possess] the Canaanites [Phoenicia] as far as Zarephath.

Amos 9:14 promises to "restore the fortunes" and rebuild the cities while Obad 19-20 promises the retaking of the territory in the return of the exiles to Judah. Amos 9:15 offers a concluding promise of enduring restoration of the people to the land while Obad 21 offers its concluding promise of the restoration on Mount Zion and rule over Esau as signs of YHWH's enduring kingship.

The parallels between these two texts are clear but admittedly of a different character than those between Obad 1-5, 8-9 and Jer 49:7-22. How does one account for these similarities between Amos 9 and Obad 1-21?

Source Material, Adaptation, and Composition

Obadiah reflects at least three sources blocks (1-9; 10-14 + 15b; and 15a + 16-21), adapted or composed by the compiler to fit the literary context and to serve a rhetorical purpose.[9] Several observations about the adaptation of the source material and the function of these sources to the rhetorical aims of Obadiah in general are now in order.

Obadiah 1-5, 6-9

As noted, Obad 1-5 draws from Jer 49:14-16, 9, but the verses have been adapted when compared to that text. The direction of borrowing derives from the compiler of Obadiah borrowing and adapting Jeremiah's Edom oracle (49:7-22). While some suggest we cannot determine the direction of borrowing, recent redactional studies are largely united in suggesting that Obadiah borrows from Jeremiah.[10] The evidence {98} for this asser-

---

9. The extent of the parallels between Obadiah and Amos make it highly unlikely that the similarities can be explained merely by the placement of one completed text next to another, contra John Barton, who relies on Ben Zvi to ascribe similarities to unintentional verbal echoes of other prophetic texts (John Barton, *Joel and Obadiah: A Commentary*, OTL [Louisville: Westminster John Knox, 2001], 116-17; Ben Zvi, "Twelve Prophetic Books," 130-38).

10. Barton doubts the dependence can be determined (*Joel and Obadiah*, 125-26), despite the work of Raabe, who evaluates numerous allusions to Jeremiah and concludes: "The hypothesis that Obadiah reused and adapted material from Jeremiah best accounts for the evidence" (*Obadiah*, 31, see also 22-31). Ehud Ben Zvi also remains skeptical (*A Historical-Critical Study of the Book of Obadiah*, BZAW 242 [Berlin: de Gruyter, 1996], 53). For those who conclude Obadiah is dependent upon Jeremiah, see Nogalski, *Redactional Processes*, {98} 61-74; Schart, *Entstehung des Zwölfproph-*

tion does not rely exclusively upon the parallels to Amos 9 created by the compiler.

The strongest single piece of evidence derives from the third-person feminine singular pronominal suffix in Obad 1 whose antecedent must be Edom: "Rise up! Let us rise against it (3fs) for battle." The command, "rise up," contains a masculine plural imperative, followed by a first-person cohortative ("let us rise") in which the speaker identifies himself as part of the group who is called to attack "it." The word "it" represents the feminine singular pronominal suffix as the object of the preposition. The antecedent in Obad 1 can only refer to Edom, but countries normally take a masculine singular gender, and nowhere else does Obadiah refer to Edom with a feminine pronoun. By contrast, the parallel text (Jer 49:14) also has a feminine singular pronominal suffix, but this suffix has as its antecedent the city Bozrah in 49:13. Cities, in contrast to countries, do normally take feminine singular antecedents. As such, the pronoun in Jeremiah makes perfect sense, whereas its presence in Obadiah is syntactically unique.

A second line of evidence for Obadiah's use of Jeremiah appears in the expansionary elements in Obad 4 (compared to Jer 49:16) and in the expanded sentence in Obad 5a (compared to Jer 49:9b). Obadiah 4 inserts a poetic line that complicates the syntax while presuming the subject, verb, and direct object of the simpler line. It also changes the introductory particle from כי to אם. The result of this insertion is twofold: it adds two אם particles in comparison to the Jeremiah source text, and the inserted line elevates the parallelism to the stars rather than merely assuming a high nest (as in Jer 49:16). This parallel comes closer to the comparative heights of Amos 9 (esp. the mention of "heaven" in 9:2; and in the doxology of 9:6). This heightened contrast into the stars introduces the verbal parallel with Amos: "from there I will bring you down." This phrase appears five times

---

etenbuchs, 270–71; Jörg Jeremias, *Die Propheten Joel, Obadja, Jona, Micha*, ATD 24.3 (Göttingen: Vandenhoeck & Ruprecht, 2007), 63–65; Sweeney, *Twelve Prophets*, 1:282; Jakob Wöhrle, *Der Abschluss des Zwölfprophetenbuches: Buchübergreifende Redaktionsprozesse in den späten Sammlungen*, BZAW 389 (Berlin: de Gruyter, 2008), 195–201. Artur Weiser gives little attention to the issue, but simply seems to presume Obadiah borrows from Jeremiah (*Das Buch der zwölf kleinen Propheten I: Die Propheten Hosea, Joel, Amos, Obadja, Jona, Micha*, ATD 24 [Göttingen: Vandenhoeck & Ruprecht, 1949], 207). Jeremiah scholarship also generally concurs on this point. See especially, Jack Lundbom, *Jeremiah 37–52: A New Translation with Introduction and Commentary*, AB 21C (New York: Doubleday, 2004), 325.

in Amos, but elsewhere only in Jer 49:16 and Obad 4. It likely sparked the compiler's interest in the Edom oracles of Jeremiah in the first place.

The compiler of Obadiah inverts the parallel between Obad 5a, b and Jer 49:9b, a. In so doing, the Obadiah compiler borrows the verb from Jer 49:9a to introduce 49:9b (whereas that verb is assumed by Jer 49:9b in the Jeremiah context). The use of Jer 49:9 also adds the final three אם particles, including two in the source text and one in the inserted {99} material of Obad 5. This additional אם particle brings to five the number of אם particles in Obad 14–16, the same number as in Amos 9:2–4, while the Jeremiah parallels have only two such particles.

These observations account for many of the differences between Obadiah and its Jer 49 parallels. The compiler chose a compatible text as a starting point, but made minor adjustments to the text to strengthen parallels with Amos 9.

Obadiah 15a, 16–21

Obadiah 15a, 16–21 also appears to be an originally independent oracle that has been attached to Obad 1–14, 15b. The reasons why it represents a new unit are widely recognized.[11] First, the forms of address change from the singular direct address of Edom that dominates 1–14 to masculine plural forms that address the people of Judah.

Second, the theme of the day of YHWH introduced by Obad 15a differs from 1–14, where the reference to the day of YHWH alludes to Jerusalem's day of reckoning (10–14), although it is not incompatible with the reference in Obad 8 to "on that day" when the wise and discerning of Edom will be destroyed. Obad 8, it was already suggested, comes from the hand of the compiler.

Third, the target of the oracle is not merely Edom, unlike the focus on Edom in Obad 1–14. The target of the day of YHWH, according to Obad 15a, is "all the nations."

Fourth, Obad 16–21 presumes Israel will attack Edom. By contrast, Obad 1 introduces the first unit in a way that announces that the nations will punish Edom.

---

11. See Wilhelm Rudolph, *Joel, Amos, Obadja, Jona*, KAT 13.2 (Gütersloh: Mohn, 1971), 296; Hans Walter Wolff, *Obadiah and Jonah: A Commentary*, trans. Margaret Kohl (Minneapolis: Augsburg, 1986), 37–38; Barton, *Joel and Obadiah*, 118–19.

Despite wide acceptance that 15a, 16–21 represents a preexisting unit, several commentators dispute the cohesion of the verses, mostly with respect to the second wave of attacks in Obad 19–20. For example, Wolff describes 15a, 16–21 oddly. On the one hand, in his commentary he refers to 1–14, 15b as a as "a single unit, in spite of a number of difficulties," and he separates 15a, 16–21 as a "passage."[12] On the other hand, he does not mean an author's singular composition by these designations. He seems to assume a model whereby individual sayings were compiled in written form after becoming fixed in oral transmission. When describing the "form" of Obad 15a, 16–21, Wolff refers to the "rhetorical unit" as being comprised of *two* sayings (15a, 16–17 and 18), {100} a "two-stage addition" (19–20), and a conclusion to the book (21).[13] Rudolph sees 15a, 16–18 as a unit from Obadiah, while he labels 19–21 as *Anhänge* (additions), but he also describes Obad 21 as consistent with genuine Obadiah speech material.[14] Barton divides 15a, 16–21 into two parts (15a + 16–18 and 19–21).[15] Raabe extensively details the wide variety of divisions of units in Obadiah, delineating three models of composition that result in at least nine different explanations of the various units.[16] Consequently, Raabe opts to treat the entirety as a single composition, preferring to consider the endeavor

---

12. Wolff, *Obadiah and Jonah*, 37.
13. Ibid., 62.
14. Rudolph, *Joel, Amos, Obadja, Jona*, 311–18.
15. Barton, *Joel and Obadiah*, 150–58, respectively, for the two units, and he also dates 15a, 16–21 to the late Persian or early Hellenistic period (123) even as he dates 1–14, 15b to near the time of Jerusalem's destruction. In other words, he dates the passages approximately 250 years apart from one another. He offers no real motivation for what caused this addition other than a general propensity to add eschatological material to the end of prophetic collections. William Schniedewind makes a compelling case that support for the collection of literature changes from royal patronage to cultic centers in the Persian period (*How the Bible Became a Book: The Textualization of Ancient Israel* [Cambridge: Cambridge University Press, 2004]). However, when he argues (139–64) that only a small amount of material was produced in the Persian period, he overstates the case since he does not adequately deal with the possibility of Mizpah as a place where religious scribes relocated following the loss of the temple. See Albertz, *Exilszeit*, 65–68; Albertz, *A History of Israelite Religion in the Old Testament*, trans. John Bowden, 2 vols., OTL (Louisville: Westminster John Knox, 1994), 241–42, 370–73.
16. Raabe, *Obadiah*, 14–18.

of determining its sources as too speculative to be reliable or to produce a coherent reading.¹⁷

Barton, who otherwise is not particularly receptive to the idea of the Book of the Twelve affecting the shape of individual writings, offers a very interesting take upon Obad 19–20:

> The oracle thus spells out in detail the hopes probably implied in Isa 55:4–5 and Amos 9:11–12. One could see Obad 19–20 as a kind of commentary on or detailed working out of the underlying oracle that appears toward the end of the book of Amos (itself regarded by most commentators as a postexilic addition to the words of Amos).¹⁸

In fact, Barton is more correct than he realizes in that the entire act of compiling Obadiah owes its shape to Amos 9. The structural, lexical, and thematic parallels between Amos 9 and Obadiah, once observed, require more explanation than typically provided. Obadiah 19–20 does not merely serve as a commentary to portions of Amos 9. Rather, the entire {101} book adapts preexisting anti-Edom sayings to draw a parallel between the destruction of the Northern Kingdom and the anticipated destruction of Edom.

In addition to these critical assessments, one should also note the curious reference to the day of wrath tradition, which connects Obad 15–17 conceptually to the OAN of Jeremiah (especially in the LXX version). Obadiah 15a announces the nearness of the day of YHWH on all the nations. The reason for the pronouncement is given is Obad 16: "because you [2mp] have drunk upon my holy mountain, all the nations will drink [3mp] continually." The plural "you" must be interpreted as an address to Judah in this verse. Consequently, Obad 16 presumes a situation in which prior judgment against Judah inaugurates judgment on the nations.

The "drinking" in Obad 16 draws upon the "cup of wrath tradition" which assumes judgment will come upon Jerusalem, but that judgment will not stop when Jerusalem's punishment is complete. Rather, Jerusa-

---

17. Raabe states, "Despite the amount of diversity displayed in it [Obadiah], the book does present itself as a literary and structural unit, a unity that invites the reader to make coherent sense of the book's contents by interpreting the parts as integrally related to each other rather than as self-contained and self-defining units" (ibid., 18).

18. Barton, *Joel and Obadiah*, 157. Compare his skepticism elsewhere about the Twelve's editing affecting the shape of the writings: ibid., 116–17.

lem's judgment will inaugurate a series of judgments as the day of YHWH begins to unfold. This cup of wrath imagery plays a prominent role in Jeremiah's oracles against the nations. This tradition finds its fullest expression in Jer 25:15–29 (the original conclusion to Jeremiah's OAN that appears in the MT at the end of the corpus), but it also appears in Isa 51:17–23 (where the cup's effects are first described and then removed by passing to unnamed tormenters). It also appears in Ezek 23:31–32 (where personified Lady Jerusalem receives the cup from her sister Samaria); Lam 4:21 (against Edom); Hab 2:12 (against Babylon); and within Jeremiah in the oracles against Edom (49:12) and Babylon (51:7).

Thus, in both Jeremiah and the Twelve, the cup of wrath to be drunk by the nations is applied both to Edom and Babylon. This connection between the refrains of Jeremiah's Edom and Babylon oracles increases the likelihood that the dependence upon Jeremiah by the Obadiah compiler had access to a version of Jeremiah in which the OAN were still in the middle of the book. One cannot, of course, prove this case absolutely, but this cup of wrath imagery is certainly suggestive.[19] {102}

Obadiah 10–14

Obadiah 10–14 may constitute a third preexisting source, but it more likely represents the longest compositional element from the compiler of Obadiah.[20] However, no one disputes its function in Obadiah. It provides the reason why Edom will be punished, but the formulation of these accusations is expressed as a future event to be avoided: "You shall not gloat, rejoice," and so on (Obad 12–14). These vetitive forms represent a classic "*vaticinium ex eventu*" (prophecy after the fact).

Literarily Obadiah *anticipates* Edom's destruction on the day of YHWH at a point in the Book of the Twelve where Israel's destruction has just been documented (Amos 9:1–4). At the end of the Twelve, Mal 1:2–5

---

19. The case is complicated, of course, and requires further exploration. See, e.g., the discussion of the uncharacteristic extra wording in the LXX version of Jer 49:16 and Obad 4 in Ben Zvi, *Historical-Critical Study of the Book of Obadiah*, 67–68.

20. It has a thematic parallel to Amos 9, though the parallel comes via the relentless combination of ב and יום. Caution is warranted at this point, however, because the dovetailing of 15b and 15a suggests two preexisting units were "woven" together. If so, then 10–14 could be the continuation of 1–9, as a kind of midrash on Jer 49:7–22, combined with images from Ezekiel.

presumes that Edom's punishment is under way,[21] while Obadiah largely presumes the punishment has not yet happened—even though the reason for Edom's punishment has occurred.

This dichotomy is quite similar to the dichotomy of Jerusalem's destruction in the Book of the Twelve and in Isaiah.[22] These prophetic scrolls either "anticipate" Jerusalem's destruction in Hosea–Zephaniah, or its aftermath is presumed in Haggai–Malachi. In the same way, Obadiah "anticipates" Edom's destruction while Mal 1:2–5 presumes its judgment has begun.

The same dynamic happens in Isaiah with the destruction of Edom and Jerusalem. Isaiah 34–35 anticipates Jerusalem and Edom's destruction, where Isa 40–55 presumes Judah's punishment as a past event (replaced by restoration) while Isa 63:1–6 narrates Edom's destruction by YHWH as a past event.

Why Edom and When Was Obadiah Compiled?

Positive and negative traditions regarding Edom can be found in biblical traditions. Positive traditions include (1) theophanies related to YHWH's appearance in Edom, (2) Edom as a home for wisdom, and (3) traditions about Edom's "brotherhood" with Israel through their respective progenitors Esau and Jacob. {103}

(1) Texts depicting Edom as the home of YHWH include Deut 33:2; Judg 5:4; and Hab 3:3. All three present a theophany that associates YHWH with Edom, the first two even using Seir and Sinai in parallel. This theophanic connection attests to an ancient association of the worship of YHWH in Edom. Habakkuk 3:3 is often cited as ancient poetry.[23] The other two passages existed by the end of the seventh century. External evidence for the ancient association of YHWH with Edom also appears in two inscriptions from Kuntillit Ajrud (late ninth century or early eighth

---

21. Cf. Ruth Scoralick, "The Case of Edom in the Book of the Twelve: Methodological Reflections on Synchronic and Diachronic Analysis," in *Perspectives on the Formation of the Book of the Twelve: Methodological Foundations, Redactional Processes, Historical Insights*, ed. Rainer Albertz, James D. Nogalski, and Jakob Wöhrle, BZAW 433 (Berlin: de Gruyter, 2012), 35–54.

22. See James D. Nogalski, "Teaching Prophetic Books," *PRSt* 36 (2009): 252–53.

23. John E. Anderson, "Awaiting an Answered Prayer: The Development and Reinterpretation of Habakkuk 3 in Its Contexts," *ZAW* 123 (2011): 58–59.

century). Together these inscriptions show an intriguing connection between the worship of YHWH in Samaria and in Edom:[24]

The inscription on Pithos A testifies:

"Say to Yehal[lel'el] and to Yo'asah and [to Z]: I bless you by *Yahweh of Samaria* and by his asherah."

Inscription 2 on Pithos B from the same site reads:

"Amaryau says: say to my lord: Is it well with you? I bless you by *Yahweh of Teman* and by his asherah. May he bless you and keep you and be with my lord."

This evidence has no direct connection to Obadiah, but it demonstrates that traditions rooted in the worship of YHWH have a long history, one that precedes the textual traditions of biblical texts. The fact that Obadiah inverts this theophanic tradition after 587 shows how long these common traditions lingered, even if the details are too obscure to postulate the exact circumstances. These traditions also suggest that ancient associations between Edom, Israel, and Judah help explain the location of Obadiah in the Book of the Twelve and why it may have been important to insert a literary work that drew attention to the parallel fates of Israel and Edom.[25]

(2) Edom also connotes wisdom. Job 1:1–3 claims that Job comes from Uz (associated with Edom in Lam 4:21). In Job, Eliphaz comes from Teman, located in Edom.

(3) Brother traditions include the Jacob cycle and Deut 2:4. The Jacob cycle relates the story of Esau and Jacob as the twin sons of Isaac and Rebekah (though the story resolves through an uneasy truce). Compared to the stories of the Ammonites and Moabites (Gen 19:30–38), these stories operate with a different set of assumptions. Deuteronomy 2:4–5 {104}

---

24. Judith M. Hadley, *The Cult of Asherah in Ancient Israel and Judah: Evidence for a Hebrew Goddess*, UCOP 57 (Cambridge: Cambridge University Press, 2000), 121–29 (translations on 121 and 125); see also William G. Dever, "Asherah, Consort of Yahweh: New Evidence from Kuntillet ʿAjrûd," *BASOR* 255 (1984): 32–34 nn. 5, 27, 45.

25. In most assessments of the order in which the writings were incorporated into the Twelve, Jonah represents a late arrival to the corpus. See Nogalski, *Redactional Processes*, 270–73; Schart, *Entstehung des Zwölfprophetenbuchs*, 289–91; Wöhrle, *Abschluss des Zwölfprophetenbuches*, 396.

alludes to Esau's descendants as Jacob's brothers, implicitly explaining why Israel does not take Edomite territory when it conquers the promised land.

Negative traditions reverse these same motifs in prophetic literature as a whole, with Obadiah transposing more of these positive characteristics than any other writing. Isaiah 63:1–6 inverts the Edomite theophany tradition. This late text depicts YHWH coming from Edom (63:1) with blood on his garments after destroying Edom and "the peoples" (63:3, 6) on the "day of vengeance" (63:4). This text almost certainly alludes to Isa 34, which anticipates "the day of vengeance" (34:8) directed against Edom (34:5) and the peoples (34:1).[26]

Several prophetic judgment oracles reject the wisdom of Edom tradition. Significantly, both Jer 49 and Obadiah do so, though the material is not a direct citation (Jer 49:7–8; Obad 7, 8–9). In both prophetic texts, the wisdom of Edom evaporates as the wise will be destroyed.

Edom and brotherhood serve as the backdrop for two denunciations of Edom's betrayal. Amos 1:11–12, often considered an exilic addition to the OAN of Amos, condemns Edom for "pursuing his brother with the sword." Obadiah 10–14 expresses similar ideas by condemning Edom's behavior toward its brother on the day of Jacob's (= Judah's) calamity. Malachi 1:2–5 describes Esau's (= Edom) misfortune as punishment from YHWH to affirm YHWH's preference for Jacob (= Judah).

Within prophetic writings, the combination of Edom's wisdom and brotherhood appears only in the Book of the Twelve. Jeremiah (49:7) refers to Edom's wisdom, but does not refer to Edom as a brother. Isaiah and Ezekiel do neither. Obadiah combines a wide range of punishments against Edom. It reverses the positive traditions of Edom as brother and as the home of wisdom. Ezekiel's anti-Edom statements accuse Edom of participation in Jerusalem's overthrow, like Obadiah.

When was Obadiah compiled? In Ezek 25:12–14, the text anticipates Israel taking vengeance for YHWH against Edom (Obad 18) because they grievously injured the "house of Judah" and "my people Israel." Ezekiel 35:5 accuses Edom of retaliation because they "gave over the people of Israel to the power of the sword at the time of their calamity" (איד; see Obad 13),

---

26. Odil Hannes Steck, "Zu jüngsten Untersuchungen von Jes 56,9–59,21; 63,1–6," in *Studien zu Tritojesaja*, ed. Otto Kaiser, BZAW 203 (Berlin: de Gruyter, 1991), 209–11.

and according to 35:10, Edom also tried to "possess" Israel, making Israel and Edom one nation, but under Edomite rule.[27] {105}

The adaptation of Jeremiah's OAN by Obadiah, probably occurred at a time before the expanded MT version moved those OAN out of their original location following Jer 25:13. Dating the oracles in Jer 49:7–22 depends upon several factors.[28] Nevertheless, most commentators do not

---

27. Dating Ezek 35 can be done only in general terms. The situation described in Ezek 35:10 assumes Edomite incursion. According to Karl-Friedrich Pohlmann, the bulk of Ezek 35 entered the corpus with the *gola*-oriented redaction responsible for most of the book, though the date of the source material in Ezek 35:5, 10–11 is earlier (*Das Buch des Propheten Hesekiel [Ezechiel] Kapitel 1–19*, ATD 22.1 [Göttingen: Vandenhoeck & Ruprecht, 1996], 34). {105} Pohlmann dates this redaction to some point near the end of the fifth century. By contrast, Walther Zimmerli gives more credence to the date formulae in fourteen superscriptions, that date oracles between 593–571 BCE, and he thus dates the book around that time (*Ezekiel: A Commentary on the Book of the Prophet Ezekiel, Chapters 1–24*, trans. Ronald Clements, Hermeneia [Philadelphia: Fortress, 1979], 9–11). More specifically, Zimmerli argues that Ezek 35–36 was collected prior to the return of exiles with Zerubbabel (*Ezekiel: A Commentary on the Book of the Prophet Ezekiel, Chapters 25–48*, trans. James D. Martin, Hermeneia [Philadelphia: Fortress, 1983], 234). By contrast, Steven Tuell emphasizes the allusions to the ancestor stories (*Ezekiel*, NIBCOT 15 [Peabody, MA: Hendrickson, 2009], 241–42), but he considers the final editing of the book to have taken place in the fifth century, during the latter half of the reign of Darius II (522–485; ibid., 2–3). Hence, the date of Ezek 35 can be confidently fixed between 571 and 400, though Tuell's position of the early fifth century probably reflects more of a consensus at this point.

28. Lundbom, *Jeremiah 37–52*, 325, argues that scholars typically date Jer 49:7–22 too late because they read these verses "through the refracted lens of Obadiah and other OT passage of late date." He avers that nothing in these Edomite oracles requires that one assume the oracles postdate Jerusalem's destruction. His observations should raise caution. Nevertheless, he overstates the case since it is hard to imagine that 49:12 does not already presume Jerusalem's destruction. Edom did not experience Babylonian devastation at the same time as Jerusalem, but evidence suggests they did experience Babylonian attacks during the reign of Nabonidus (556–539). See ibid., 331. It is difficult to say with certainty at what date the proto-MT and the LXX source material were separated from one another. Some see this division as quite early; so Jack Lundbom, *Jeremiah 1–20*, AB 21A (New York: Doubleday, 1999), 57–62, who thinks one copy of the Jeremiah corpus was taken to Egypt (by Baruch) and another was taken to Babylon, with the Babylonian version undergoing more editorial activity thereafter. By contrast, most others see the division coming in the late Persian period; so, Louis Stulman, "Jeremiah, Book of," *NIDB* 3:220–24. In either case, an early sixth-century date for the oracles themselves means they would have been available, though it makes more sense that these oracles were preserved in Judah than in Babylon or Egypt.

date these materials too far into the sixth century.[29] The Obadiah adaptations were made in light of Amos 9 at a point after the expansions of 9:7–10 and 9:11–15*, which suggests the early Persian period as the *terminus ante quem*, but before the proto-MT of Jeremiah relocated the OAN to the end of that corpus. Malachi 1:2–5 presumes Edom's punishment is underway, and alludes to Obadiah, marking the *terminus ad quem*. The collection of OAN for prophetic texts could perhaps stem from a point after Ezra/Nehemiah reforms which emphasized the need for separatism from other nations. Edom plays no role, however, in Ezra-Nehemiah, suggesting Edom could have already been in decline during the time of Ezra-Nehemiah. Of course, even this relative chronology only limits the dates somewhat for Obadiah because the dates of Malachi and Ezra-Nehemiah are very much in dispute.

---

29. Douglas Jones, *Jeremiah*, NCB (Grand Rapids: Eerdmans, 1992), 512–13.

Thematic Explorations

Joel as "Literary Anchor" for the Book of the Twelve

A strong consensus appears to be developing regarding two aspects of the shape of the Twelve. First, the chronological framework created by the dated superscriptions provides one element unifying the corpus. The six writings with dated superscriptions/incipits provide the framework that moves deliberately from the eighth-century Assyrian period into the postexilic Persian period.[1] Second, recurring words, images, and phrases also play a role in linking the writings of the Twelve, leaving one with the impression that more must be said than just that the Twelve progresses chronologically. After these statements, however, the consensus breaks down quickly. Are these unifying elements created redactionally or simply decisions of positioning? How, if at all, does the chronological framework relate to the recurring words? Do these recurring words overlook, ignore, presume, or transcend the chronological frame? This essay, from the perspective of Joel's pivotal function, seeks to open a dialogue on the literary aim(s) of the larger corpus.

To understand the discussion, it will be necessary to note in advance that two basic models for reading prophetic literature—the synchronic and the diachronic—operate in the various approaches to the Twelve. Synchronic models have the advantage of keeping questions of literary shape in the foreground without hypothesizing about the date(s) and order in which the writings were incorporated. Conversely, in order to treat the literary nature of the whole, they have the disadvantage of having to treat the *entire* corpus as a single entity. In other words, synchronic {92} models do not provide a means by which one may determine which aspect(s) should more important for reading the Twelve. Diachronic models have the advantage of being able to account for multiple theological perspectives by seeing divergent opinions as part of a writing's transmission whose

---

1. See the following discussions: Nogalski, *Literary Precursors*, 85; Schart, *Entstehung des Zwölfprophetenbuchs*, 36–46.

formulation originated before, during, or after it entered the larger corpus. Diachronic models have difficulty, however, talking about the literary aims of the larger corpus because they get bogged down in issues of development. This essay addresses one aspect of this last problem for the diachronic models by building on my previous suggestion that Joel serves as the "literary anchor" for the Book of the Twelve.

In so doing, I argue that Joel forms a necessary (but not the only) interpretive key for unifying major literary threads in the Twelve, as seen in at least three ways: dovetailing genres, recurring vocabulary, and the presumption of a "historical paradigm" that "transcends" the chronological framework of the dated superscriptions. Joel deliberately creates a transition between Hosea and Amos by dovetailing genres. Hosea ends with an extended call to repentance, while Joel begins with the same genre. Joel ends with an extended pronouncement of eschatological judgment against the nations, while Amos begins with an extended group of oracles against the nations. Recurring vocabulary takes place in Joel's reinterpretation of images in subsequent writings. This use of Joel in other contexts provides the clues for determining the transcended "historical" paradigm which shapes the Twelve. I have elsewhere labeled this formative literary development as "the Joel-Related Layer."[2]

What Kind of "Book" Is the Twelve?

In the last century, scholarly research into the prophets and prophetic literature has focused on numerous issues, including biographies of the prophets, historical settings of the various units, the theology of a given prophet, prophetic forms, and the development of the book. Only relatively recently has serious attention turned to the question of the message conveyed by prophetic books rather than the individual oracles.[3] When the question {93} of message is asked of the Book of the Twelve, however, the difficulties of the task increase dramatically, for this collection is composed of twelve books (or writings). To what degree should the meaning of the individual writings determine the message of the Twelve as a whole? How does one find those passages which have more direct bearing upon the meaning of the Twelve than the meaning of the writing? One must

---

2. See the summary in Nogalski, *Redactional Processes*, 275–78.
3. See, e.g., Steck, *Prophetenbücher*, 2–14. {93} (Eng. trans., 3–13).

make some basic (yet also preliminary) decisions about the character of a particular prophetic book before one can proceed in the task of reading it. To do so, one should note how the Book of the Twelve differs from the other three prophetic books in how it presents itself.

First, the other three prophetic books mention only a single prophet explicitly. Whether one works diachronically or synchronically, this simple observation creates a significantly different perception for a reader of the corpus. The Book of the Twelve presents itself as YHWH's word to twelve different persons. Second, the Book of the Twelve, like Isaiah, presents itself in a way that covers a lengthy period of time from the time of Uzziah/Jeroboam to the Persian period (and beyond). This observation differentiates the purpose of the Book of the Twelve from the more limited time frames of Jeremiah, which concerns the time leading up to Jerusalem's destruction, and Ezekiel, which concerns the time from the first exile onward.

The combination of the first two differences leads to a third distinction: the presumed setting of the text. Isaiah mentions only one prophet, which creates its own difficulties for conceptualizing how the prophet "speaks" in contexts which obviously presume a Persian setting.[4] In the end, one is forced to hear the prophet as anticipating the events of later generations from an eighth-century prophetic "persona," or one must presume different prophetic voices.[5] Thus Isaiah, in some sense, anticipates the events from the eighth-century into the postexilic period. By contrast, the Book of the Twelve "walks the reader through" this same period with prophetic voices more clearly delineated. The twelve prophetic writings alternate between documenting YHWH's message to various groups and anticipating the outcome of the people's failure to respond appropriately. {94}

How does this change of prophetic voices affect the reader of the Twelve? The reader must pay careful attention to the change of the *Sitz im Buch*. The texts within these writings sometimes address different groups, which vary according to chronological, geographical, literary, and attitudinal considerations. When reading the Twelve, whether synchronically or diachronically, one must take these differences seriously. References to

---

4. See discussions in Christopher R. Seitz, "How Is the Prophet Isaiah Present in the Latter Half of the Book? The Logic of Chapters 40–66 within the Book of Isaiah," *JBL* 115 (1996): 219–40; Steck, *Prophetenbücher*, 45–61.

5. See the discussions in Seitz, "How Is the Prophet Isaiah Present," 224–28.

Israel, Samaria, Bethel, or Ephraim in Hosea, Amos, and Micah should not evoke the same images as references to Judah, Jerusalem, and Zion.[6] Even though the prophets are roughly contemporary, the geographical distinctions (along with the theological message) require different messages from YHWH. Similarly, the group from Bethel in Zech 7:1–7 does not represent the same group in Amos, because the chronological situation has changed. Nevertheless, one must also ask whether the reader should presume knowledge of YHWH's message to Bethel in Amos.[7] Documenting the ways in which the writings in the Twelve presume the message of other works presents a monumental task, which has only recently begun to be explored.[8] This task is generally easier to conceptualize for writings containing the dated superscriptions, but the undated writings should be given careful consideration from this perspective as well. The remainder of this essay looks at some of the ways that Joel presumes its location in the Book of the Twelve and ways in which Joel is cited by other writings in that corpus.

Dovetailing Genres from Hosea to Joel to Amos

Studies of Joel over the last several years correctly portray it as a highly integrated work, but they have generally not asked how Joel relates to the Book of the Twelve. When this question is raised, the sophisticated nature of the book of Joel's integration becomes all the more astounding. {95} One important dimension of Joel's relationship to the larger literary context arises when one notes the way in which the genres of Joel coincide with those of the writings on either side. Hosea ends with an extended call for Israel's repentance, the outcome of which is not narrated.[9] In prophetic literature, only Joel begins with a call to repentance.

---

6. Note the complicated task of determining the identities of groups given such names as "Jacob," "Joseph," "House of Jacob." See the discussion, e.g., in Schart, *Entstehung des Zwölfprophetenbuchs*, 139.

7. Several commentators have noted Zech 1:2–6 as evidence that Zechariah is presuming knowledge from outside that writing. See, e.g., the discussion in Petersen, *Haggai and Zechariah*, 132.

8. E.g., Schart, *Entstehung des Zwölfprophetenbuchs*; Bosshard-Nepustil, *Rezeptionen von Jesaia 1–39*; Helmut Utzschneider, *Künder oder Schreiber? Eine These zum Problem der "Schriftprophetie" auf Grund von Maleachi 1,6–2,9*, BEATAJ 19 (Frankfurt am Main: Lang, 1989); Bergler, *Joel als Schriftinterpret*; Nogalski, *Redactional Processes*.

9. Jeremias, *Prophet Hosea*, 169–70. By contrast, Stuart, *Hosea–Jonah*, 211–18. Stuart treats this passage as a promise to the future Israel.

But, as well as dovetailing with Hosea, the end of Joel, an eschatological oracle against the nations, dovetails genres with Amos. Other prophetic writings close with pronouncements against the nations, but the way in which Joel and Amos are related through quotations, indicates an intentional association.[10] These overlapping genres deserve closer analysis.

Hosea 14:2-9 [Eng. 1-8] comprises a two-part call to repentance. Hosea 14:2-4 [Eng. 1-3] advances the call proper, culminating in a specific prayer of repentance that presupposes Israel's sins involving (1) political dependence on nations rather than YHWH and (2) idolatry. These accusations do not appear for the first time in chapter 14.[11] In that prayer, the people are told to say:

> Assyria will not save us. We will not ride on horses. Nor will we again say, "our god" to the works of our hands, for in you the orphan finds mercy. (14:4 [Eng. 3] NASB)

Hosea 14:5-9 [Eng. 4-8] then changes to divine speech and offers words of promise.

> I will heal their apostasy, I will love them freely, for my anger has turned away from them. I will be like the dew to Israel; he will blossom like the lily, and he will take root like Lebanon. His roots will sprout, and his beauty will be like the olive tree, and his fragrance like Lebanon. Those who live in his shadow will again raise grain, and they will blossom like the vine. His renown will be like the wine of Lebanon. O Ephraim, what more do I have to do with idols? It is I who look after you. I am a luxuriant cypress. From me comes your fruit. {96} (NASB)

These verses have often been interpreted as the divine "response" to the prayer of 14:3 (Eng. 2). However, Jeremias convincingly demonstrates that, in fact, one should *not* presuppose the prayer of 14:3 (Eng. 2) has been expressed.[12] Instead, 14:5-9 (Eng. 4-8) offers the foundational

---

10. See discussions in Nogalski, "Intertextuality and the Twelve," 105–8; Schart, *Entstehung des Zwölfprophetenbuchs*, 219; Van Leeuwen, "Scribal Wisdom," 41.

11. For the theme of depending upon Assyria and Egypt rather than YHWH, cf. 5:13; 7:11; 7:16; 8:9; 9:3; 10:6; 11:5, 11; 12:1; 13:4. The anti-idolatry theme appears in virtually every chapter.

12. Jeremias, *Prophet Hosea*, 169. Jeremias notes three ways that the text itself argues against the presumptions that the prayer has already been expressed. First, the

promise of YHWH's salvific intention, on which the call to repentance is built. This promise is not offered *because* Israel has repented; it offers the reason *why* Israel should repent. The significance of the call to Israel and its position at the end of the writing lies in the open-ended nature of the invitation. It becomes a type of divinely initiated RSVP to which Israel is called to respond, but no response is narrated. In fact, the final verse of the book indicates that the open-ended nature of the call is transferred to the reader:

> "Whoever is wise, let him understand these things; whoever is discerning, let him know them, for the ways of YHWH are right, and the righteous will walk in them, but transgressors will stumble in them." (14:10 [Eng. 9] NASB)

In short, the promise of 14:5–9 becomes part of the invitation to repent, but the reader is "left hanging" with respect to the response.

If one wishes to determine how Israel responded to this invitation, one must broaden the literary horizon beyond Hosea. In a very real sense, the "story" must continue. But how does it continue? Interpreters in bringing resolution to Hosea often mention Samaria's destruction, noting the tragedy of Israel's failure to respond. However, one should note that reference to the events of 722 requires knowledge that goes beyond Hosea alone. One must assume a reader's knowledge of the history of the Northern Kingdom in order to make this association. But how does a "reader" gain this knowledge? Generally, knowledge of the events of 722 is assumed by interpreters, but the *literary* continuation of this open-ended invitation is not addressed. By enlarging the literary horizon beyond Hosea, the multivolume prophetic work that came to be known as the Book of the Twelve provides the literary resolution, albeit in more than one interpretive avenue.

Following the chronological framework of the Twelve that orders the eighth-century prophetic writings, Amos demonstrates conclusively that Israel (the Northern Kingdom) does not respond positively to the invita-

---

divine speech of 14:5–9 (4–8) speaks of Israel in the third person. YHWH does not address Israel directly, as one would assume if YHWH were responding to the prayer. Second, the healing of Israel's disloyalty (משבה) would require repentance from Israel, but such is not the case here. Third and most significant, Hos 14:9 (8) presupposes a time prior to the repentance.

tion {97} in Hosea. These associations have begun to be explored, but it is not my purpose at this time to explore the ways in which this literary thread continues in Hosea and Amos.[13] Instead, in this section of the paper and the next, I will investigate what happens when Hosea's call to repentance is read with the extended call to repentance in Joel.

Joel's call to repentance differs from Hos 14:2–9 (Eng. 1–8) in several pivotal respects, including its addressees, the presumption of guilt, the threat of punishment, and the eschatological dimension. Hosea 14:2–9 (Eng. 1–8) should be read as addressing the people of the Northern Kingdom of the eighth-century. By contrast, Joel lacks specific chronological markers, and addresses "all the people of the land" (1:2) in a way that, as it becomes increasingly clear, focuses on Judah and Jerusalem (see esp. 1:13–16; 2:1–24). While Hosea 14:2–9 [Eng. 1–8] treats the people as a single entity, Joel challenges several specific groups throughout the first chapter (1:2, 5, 11, 13). Moreover, while Hosea delineates specific accusations against Israel within the prayer of 14:4 (Eng. 3), no such accusations appear *explicitly* in Joel. The threatened punishment in Hosea, as with the promise, appears to lie in the future. By contrast, the punishment in Joel is both current and future. The land is (and/or will be) devastated from a composite series of threats: a series of locust plagues, drought, and enemy attack. This element leads to one of the most obvious differences between Hos 14:2–9 (Eng. 1–8) and Joel 1–2. The threat in Joel contains an eschatological dimension to the threat which is not matched in Hosea. Hosea 14:2–9 (Eng. 1–8) presumes YHWH will punish Israel but does not describe that punishment in detail. Joel anticipates on the day of YHWH an enemy attack (2:1–11) that causes the devastations of the locusts and drought imagery to pale in comparison.

Hosea 14:2–9 (Eng. 1–8) and Joel 1–2 differ. However, two particular similarities between the calls to repentance in Hos 14:2–9 and in Joel 1–2 deserve attention as well. First, as with Hosea, Joel contains a critical passage in which the call to repent is grounded with a promise of bounty, without ever stating explicitly that the prayer of repentance was executed. Joel 2:12–27 contain a series of admonitions to gather the people to repent in an attempt to avoid the coming day of destruction (2:12–16), including

---

13. For the growing evidence that the Hosea/Amos connections have a long, common redactional history that presupposes a reader's knowledge of both writings, see the discussions in Jörg Jeremias, "The Interrelationship Between Amos and Hosea," in Watts, *Forming Prophetic Literature*, 101–55.

the prayer which was to be spoken by the priests (2:17). Subsequently, {98} the promise of YHWH's positive actions appears in 2:18–27, but as with Hos 14:5–9 (Eng. 4–8), the restoration still lies in the future and the reader is never explicitly told whether the people repent.[14] These promised actions include: (1) the return of the agricultural bounty (2:19, 21, 24) and (2) the removal of the army (2:20), (3) the restoration of the rains (2:22), (4) recompense for the years of the "locusts" (2:25), (5) removal of the famine (2:26–27). These actions reverse the punishments and threats of 1:2–2:11 in much the same way that Hosea's promissory section resolve the problems mentioned earlier in Hosea.

Second, between the two calls to repentance vocabulary recurs in quotations and strong allusions to agricultural fertility images, whereby Joel adapts a major motif of Hosea. In Hosea's call to repentance, the fertility images appear in the promise and offer resolution to the anti-Baal/anti-idolatry polemic, which admonishes Israel for failing to recognize YHWH as the source of its abundance (e.g., 2:10, 15; 9:10; 11:2; 13:1). In Joel's call to repentance, the fertility imagery refers to things that have been devastated. In Joel 1:2–2:11, these fertility elements have been removed or destroyed by locusts, drought, and enemy attack; they will only be restored following repentance of all the inhabitants (2:12–26). Even the introductory verse of Joel 1:2 takes on a larger perspective as a transitional element than an independent summons to attention.[15] {99} Most convincingly, Joel

---

14. Note especially the formulation in 2:19 with the quote from YHWH cited using *vav*-consecutive constructions, followed by the statements of what YHWH is about to do (participle + הנה).

15. Joel 1:2 is typically treated as a teacher's "call to attention" because commentators presume an independent existence for Joel. This interpretation creates at least three difficulties that can be resolved if one sees the verse as a deliberate reference to Hos 14. First, this call to attention appears more frequently in prophetic literature than in wisdom literature. More important, in prophetic literature the phrase generally plays a *connecting* role. Second, when Joel 1:2 is treated as an independent introduction, "this" has no antecedent, requiring the presumption of two *different, proleptic antecedents* ("Hear this *word* … has this *locust plague* happened in your days or the days of your fathers?"). Third, the rhetorical question makes no sense literally. When the question is asked—"Has this happened in your days, or in the days of your fathers?—the implied answer is no. Yet, when "this" is interpreted as a reference to the locust plague(s), a comparative preposition must be presumed (Has *anything like* this happened in your days?). If one asks what happens if Joel 1:2 is read in conjunction with Hosea, all three problems disappear. First, "Hear this" plays a connecting function that is typical for prophetic examples of this phrase. Second, "this" has one (not

2:24 specifically alters Hos 9:2 by changing it from a description of punishment to a promise of fertility. It will be necessary to treat the recurring vocabulary in the next section of this paper, but first it will be helpful to look briefly at the transition between Joel and Amos created by overlapping genres.

Joel 4:1–21 (Eng. 3:1–21) presents a message of eschatological judgment on the nations. Thematic structure holds the chapter together as a composite unit.[16] It is formulated to serve a dual function as the conclusion to Joel (esp. in 4:18–21 [Eng. 3:18–21]) and as an eschatological transition to Amos (hence the quote of Amos 1:2 in Joel 4:16 [Eng. 3:16] and the use of Joel 4:18 [Eng. 3:18] in Amos 9:13 to bracket the beginning and end of Amos).[17] I will not explore the manner in which Joel 4 (Eng. 3) shapes the reading of Amos, since Schart has already done this at considerable length.[18] I simply make several observations regarding how Joel causes the reader to hear Amos differently.

First, unlike Amos, Joel's message to the nations does not utilize a refrain to address individual nations in succession. Joel does highlight specific nations for specific crimes (Tyre, Sidon, and the regions of Philistia in 4:4 [Eng. 3:4] for their enslavement of Judeans and Jerusalemites, and Edom and Egypt in 4:19 [Eng. 3:19]), but the majority of the chapter focuses on YHWH's retribution against "all surrounding nations" (4:11, 12 [Eng. 3:11, 12]), a phrase that takes on greater significance when seen as a transition to Amos 1–2. Second, in keeping with Joel's overall message, Joel 4:1–21 (Eng. 3:1–21) presents a judgment that, with its emphasis on the Day of YHWH, creates an eschatological framework. Schart even

---

two) concrete (not proleptic) antecedent in Hosea's call to repentance (and foundational promise): "has this *repentance* occurred?" Third, the rhetorical question makes sense because the expected negative answer is consistent with the subsequent description. No, this *repentance* has not happened, and, as a result, the land is devastated.

16. See my discussion in Nogalski, *Redactional Processes*, 26–41. Some of the unifying elements of this chapter include the thematic chiastic structure, and the reversal of the destruction of chapters 1–2 (through citation of verses and catchwords from those passages).

17. See particularly the discussions in Schart, *Entstehung des Zwölfprophetenbuchs*, 81; Nogalski, *Redactional Processes*, 36–37; and Nogalski, *Literary Precursors*, 104–5, 116–22.

18. Schart, *Entstehung des Zwölfprophetenbuchs*, 220–23. See also my discussion of the "eschatologization" of Amos 1:2 in Nogalski, "Intertextuality and the Twelve," 105–8.

suggests that Joel's concentration upon the "day of YHWH" provides a concrete antecedent for the suffix "it" in the refrain of Amos (I will not take "it" back).[19] Third, the link from Joel 4:16 (Eng. 3:16) to Amos 1:2 places the accent upon the Zion tradition, meaning that these nations represent the nations who will attack Jerusalem. Fourth, {100} this enlarged perspective also carries over into the remainder of Amos (see esp. 1:2; 4:6–11; 7:1–4; 9:13).

To summarize, Joel at the beginning dovetails genres with Hosea and Amos at the end. In so doing, Joel adds two dimensions to both preexisting contexts. First, Joel emphasizes the Zion context as compared with the northern contexts of Hosea and Amos. This Zion emphasis occurs both with the call to repentance of Joel 1–2 (cf. Joel's temple imagery and 2:1) and with Joel's pronouncement to the nations (4:1, 16, 17, 21 [Eng. 3:1, 16, 17, 21]). Second, in both instances Joel adds a transcendent eschatological dimension not present in the preexisting forms of Hosea and Amos. The enemy attack in Joel 1–2 not only lacks the concrete references to political entities present in Hosea (cf. Hos 14:3 [Eng. 2] with Joel 1:6), it also portrays the enemy in cosmic terms (2:1–11). This cosmic dimension also characterizes the judgment against the nations present in Joel 4:1–21 (Eng. 3:1–21) (see 4:9–17 [Eng. 3:9–17], and the adapted citation of Amos 1:2 in Joel 4:16 [Eng. 3:16]). In short, the overlapping genres allow Joel to shape the reader's perspective by providing a transition from Hosea to Joel to Amos that transcends the eighth-century chronological framework, and that emphasizes Zion as the central geographical (and theological) lens.

The Recurring Fertility Language of Joel

As mentioned previously, the recurring vocabulary of Joel can be noted in (1) Joel's use (and often adaptation) of images and phrases from earlier writings; and in (2) the redactional implantation of Joel's vocabulary into other contexts. Both of these elements require exploration, but it is also important to note that this recurring vocabulary centers around four

---

19. Schart, *Entstehung des Zwölfprophetenbuchs*, 222. Note also the similar technique created by the introduction of Joel 1:2, in which "this" can be read as a reference to Hosea's promise of 14:5–9 (Eng. 4–8). See above, 144 n. 15. See also Van Leeuwen, "Scribal Wisdom," 41–42. Van Leeuwen argues that Joel 4:21 (Eng. 3:21) "has no real function other than to link Joel and Amos in a manner that contrasts Judah (4:16–20) and Israel, the primary topic of Amos."

interrelated motifs held together by their relationships to the historical paradigm introduced in Joel and played out in the remaining writings of the Twelve: agricultural fertility (or the lack thereof), the centrality of Judah and Jerusalem, the day of YHWH, and theodicy. Alan Cooper and Van Leeuwen have explored the theodicy language of Joel.[20] The Day-of-YHWH language will only be mentioned briefly by way of illustration. The centrality of Judah and Jerusalem pervades almost every writing in the Twelve.

I want to focus on the fertility motif and its relationship to Joel's {101} transcendent historical paradigm. This motif is not selected randomly but extends observations on ideas that recur in redactionally significant passages detailed in my previous work.

The fertility imagery of Joel already entered the above discussion of the overlapping genres. Joel's call to repentance adapts the agricultural imagery promised in the call to repentance of Hos 14:2–9 (Eng. 1–8). More can be said, however, since the fertility images already begin with the anti-Baal polemic of Hos 2:10–25 (Eng. 8–23). In Hos 2:10–15 (Eng. 8–13), the wife (Israel) takes her agricultural bounty and gives it to her lovers (other gods). Since she does not recognize that the grain, wine (תירוש), and oil come from YHWH, YHWH determines to remove these elements and others from the land to shame her as punishment for the days she worshiped Baal (2:10–15 [Eng. 2:8–13]). YHWH will then take her to the wilderness so that he might win her back to a faithful relationship (2:16–22 [Eng. 2:14–20]). Once the fidelity is restored, YHWH will restore grain, wine (תירוש), and oil (2:24 [Eng. 2:22]). When this imagery reappears in Hosea, it becomes clear that the people are not capable of the fidelity demanded by YHWH. In the woe oracle of Hos 7:13–14, Ephraim only laments to receive the grain and wine, not because of a change of heart.

> Woe to them, for they have strayed from me! Destruction is theirs, for they have rebelled against me. I would redeem them, but they speak lies against me. And they do not cry to me from their heart when they wail on their beds. They assemble themselves for the sake of grain and wine [תירוש]. They turn away from me.

---

20. Alan Cooper, "In Praise of Divine Caprice: The Significance of the Book of Jonah," in *Among the Prophets: Language, Image, and Structure in the Prophetic Writings*, ed. Philip R. Davies and David J. A. Clines, JSOTSup 144 (Sheffield: Sheffield Academic, 1993), 144–63; Van Leeuwen, "Scribal Wisdom," 31–49.

In other words, there has been no change on the part of Ephraim. As a result, the vats and the threshing floor will no longer feed them (9:1-2). Against this background the promise of 14:5-8 (Eng. 4-7) takes on added dimension. If the people speak honestly (14:3-4 [Eng. 2-3]), YHWH will heal their apostasy and the fertility will return to the land so that, "the inhabitants will return in his shade. They will grow grain and they will blossom like the vine" (Hos 14:8a [Eng. 7a]).

When one follows this fertility imagery beyond Hosea, one cannot escape the sense that Joel presumes knowledge of this motif, juxtaposing the current situation with the promise of Hos 14:5-9 (Eng. 4-8). Joel 1:2 asks whether "this" has happened in a construction that implies it has not, and then describes the present, in which the fertile land lies in ruins because the people have not repented (cf. the imperatives for repentance).[21] The ruin of the land stems from locusts, drought, and enemy {102} invasion. The specific combination of "grain, wine, and oil" occurs in Joel 1:10; 2:19; 2:24, but Joel 1-2 is rife with agricultural images, in which the land has ceased to produce until the people return to YHWH. This combination of "grain, wine, and oil" also appears once in a logical sequence which forces one to see Joel and Hosea together. First, "grain, wine, and oil" appear in the description of the devastated situation (1:10): "For the grain is ruined. The wine has dried up. The oil has failed." Second, these same three elements appear in the promise of their restoration (2:19): "And YHWH *will answer*, and will say to *his people* (cf. Hos 2:23-25 [Eng. 21-23]), 'Behold, I am about to send you the grain, the wine, and the oil and you will be satisfied.'" Finally, "wine" and "oil" appear with a synonym for grain in the affirmation of Joel 2:24 that explicitly reverses the judgment of Hos 9:1-2: "And the threshing floors will be full of wheat [בר], and the vats will overflow with wine [תירוש] and oil." Use of Joel language to express images of fertility is not limited to this combination of grain, wine (תירוש), and oil, but this combination illustrates how Joel extends and reinterprets the paradigm of Hosea.

Other texts in the Twelve use Joel's fertility language. Haggai 1:11 and 2:19 show how Joel's fertility imagery has been "harvested" redactionally as part of the continuing message of the Twelve. In Haggai, the first writing set in the postexilic section of the Twelve, 1:10-11 state:

---

21. Note also how the fertility motif is tied to the promises of the exodus in Bergler, *Joel als Schriftinterpret*, 247-94.

JOEL AS "LITERARY ANCHOR" FOR THE BOOK OF THE TWELVE   149

¹⁰Therefore, because of you the sky has withheld its dew and the earth has withheld its produce. ¹¹And I called for a drought on the land, on the mountains, on the *grain, on the wine* [תירוש], *on the oil,* on what the ground produces, on men, on cattle, and on all the labor of your hands. (emphasis added)

Haggai 1:11 extends the description of the punishment with a litany of items which the drought has affected, including the three elements of the grain, wine (תירוש), and oil.

Haggai 2:19 includes an example of related images from Joel, which are also combined to help develop the fertility motif. The verse contains a rhetorical question that has been expanded by references to Joel that make no sense in Haggai.²²

Is the seed still in the granary? *Or has even the vine, or the fig tree, or the pomegranate,* or the olive tree not born fruit? (emphasis added)

This combination also evokes the devastated elements of Joel 1–2 in much the same manner as the grain, wine, and oil (note also that Hag {103} 2:17 quotes Amos 4:9 in a way that also touches upon this same imagery). One should probably differentiate the fertility idioms that ultimately have their "roots" in the fertility traditions of the promised land (as, e.g., in Deut 8:8), and the specific literary references to the repentance paradigm of Hosea/Joel. Joel demonstrates awareness of Hosea in other ways than just the use of fertility imagery, and other combinations of these images could be named, but time and space do not permit full explorations. The subject does require that we look at another important aspect of Joel's fertility motif, namely the locusts.²³

---

22. See my discussion in Nogalski, *Literary Precursors*, 228–29. Not only does this expansion create syntactical difficulties, it also provides a strange picture to placing a vine, fig tree, a pomegranate, and an olive tree in an underground storehouse.

23. As an example of other links in imagery, reference to the "virgin" (Israel) in Joel 1:8 takes up the language of Hos 2:1–25 (Eng. 2:1–23). See discussion in Nogalski, *Redactional Processes*, 18–22. Multiple combinations of these terms appear in at least the following passages within the Twelve: "grain," "wine," and "oil" (Hos 2:10 [Eng. 8]; 2:24 [Eng. 22]; Joel 1:10; 2:19, 24; Hag 1:11); "grain" and "wine" (Hos 2:11 [Eng. 9]; 7:14; 9:1–2; 14:8; Zech 9:17); other combinations (Hos 4:11; 14:7–8 [Eng. 6–7]; Joel 1:12; 2:22; Amos 4:9; Mic 4:4; 6:15; Hab 3:17; Hag 2:19). Undoubtedly, not all of these passages were created for the Book of the Twelve, but when read carefully, some

Joel's locust imagery functions in two ways: to depict the destruction of fertility and to anticipate enemy attacks. Elsewhere, I have stated my reasons for arguing that Joel's locusts are not literal references to actual locust plagues but are metaphors for natural disasters and the hordes of attacking armies who invade the land in succession.[24] Not only does Joel itself make this association, but locust images in Amos, Nahum, Habakkuk, and Malachi are interpreted in this way, often through explicit allusions to Joel. Schart argues that Amos 4:9* includes at least one phrase that cites Joel.[25] The drought language of Joel is thus taken up as another example of Israel's failure to heed YHWH's warning and call to repentance. Amos 4:9 presumes the drought of Joel has been sent, but that the people have *not* returned/repented. Nahum 3:15aγ ("It will {104} devour you like the locust" [NRSV]) and 3:16b ("The creeping locust [ילק] strips and flies away" [NASB]) incorporate Joel's vocabulary and interpret Assyria and Babylon as locusts of great numerical strength and power.[26] Habakkuk 1:9, using a different word than Joel, elicits images of Babylon as a locust "horde"; nevertheless, the passage is also associated with the redaction of the developing corpus.[27] The passage forms part of a description of Babylon that takes many of the images that Nah 3 uses for Assyria, but makes them more threatening by applying them to Babylon. In addition, one can hardly ignore the way in which Habakkuk's description of Babylon's destructive

---

exhibit other criteria that suggest the allusions were intentionally created as part of the book's unification (see esp. Hos 2:10, 24 [Eng. 8, 22]; Amos 4:9; Hab 3:17; Hag 2:19).

24. See my discussion in Nogalski, *Redactional Processes*, 2–6, 23.

25. See the discussion in Schart, *Entstehung des Zwölfprophetenbuchs*, 61. Schart argues that ותאניכם וזיתיכם יכל הגזם alludes to Joel 1:6–7, based upon the references to the fig tree and olive tree, as well as the use of גזם for locust. However, since גזם appears in 1:4, and since the earlier portion of the verse refers to both scorching (east wind) and mildew, it is also plausible that the entire verse summarizes the drought imagery from Joel. Amos 4:9 is a self-contained verse that fits the context, making a precise determination of the genetic relationship difficult. The relationship is complicated further by the fact that Hag 2:17 cites Amos 4:9, without the phrase in question. The missing reference to the locust could have been the intention of the redactor (in most other redactional insertions, the locust language refers to attacking nations), or could be explained by Schart's contention that Haggai entered the multivolume corpus prior to Joel, but after Amos.

26. Nogalski, *Redactional Processes*, 120–21.

27. Ibid., 146–50. Schart argues the inclusion of Nahum and Habakkuk predates the addition of Joel (and Obadiah). Details of this argument cannot be treated here. See Schart, *Entstehung des Zwölfprophetenbuchs*, 204–51.

force (1:6–11) coincides with the images of the attacking enemy in Joel 2:1–11. Malachi 3:10–11 also employs images from Joel, thereby offering a final promise of "agricultural fertility" (this time to the righteous remnant) if the people will use the fruits of the land for true worship of YHWH:

> ¹⁰Bring the whole tithe into the storehouse, so that there may be food in my house and test me now in this says the LORD of hosts, if I will not open the windows of heaven for you, and pour out a blessing for you until there is no more need. ¹¹Then I will rebuke *the devourer* for you, so that it may not destroy the fruits of the ground; nor will your vine cast (its grapes) in the field, says the LORD of Hosts. (NASB, emphasis added)

The reference to the devourer is generally interpreted as a locust, even by those not reading the Twelve as a unit. Here, one sees the convergence of Joel's fertility promises (cf. 1:17; 2:24), YHWH's blessing of rain (2:23), and the removal of the locusts (2:25).

The Day of YHWH and Theodicy in Joel

Before moving to the paradigm of history presented by Joel, it is necessary to mention briefly three additional unifying threads that run through Joel and the Twelve: the Day-of-YHWH sayings, theodicy, and repentance. The centrality of the Day-of-YHWH language in Joel adds to the impression of Joel's function as literary anchor for the Book of the Twelve. This language deserves a more detailed treatment than I can give here; that treatment will have to wait for another study. I will mention only one particular aspect of Joel's Day-of-YHWH language in this context. This motif can be recognized by the phrase "the Day-of-YHWH," or the related phrases, "in that day," and "in those days." When one isolates the Day-of-YHWH {105} references in Joel, virtually every one has a close (if not verbatim) parallel in the Twelve. The following chart will demonstrate this relationship more clearly than a narrative description. Interpreting the significance of these parallel formulations is no simple task, but their presence does further solidify the impression that Joel is the writing through which all the major themes of the Twelve must travel. One must also mention Joel's role in creating a discussion of theodicy that plays out across the Book of the Twelve.[28]

---

28. The following chart initially appeared on p. 106 in the original published version of this paper. All translations are NASB.

	Joel		Parallel
1:15 (2x)	Alas for the day! For the day of YHWH is near, and it will come as destruction from the Almighty.	Zeph 1:14	Near is the great *day of YHWH*, near and coming very quickly; listen the day of YHWH! In it the warrior cries out bitterly.
2:1	Blow the trumpet in Zion; sound the alarm on my holy mountain! Let all the inhabitants of the land tremble, for *the day of YHWH is coming*, it is near.	Hos 9:7(?)	The *days* of punishment *are coming*; the *days* of retribution *are coming*.
2:2 (2x)	a day of darkness and gloom, a day of clouds and thick darkness!	Zeph 1:15	A day of wrath is that day, a day of trouble and distress, a day of destruction and desolation, *a day of darkness and gloom, a day of clouds and thick darkness*
2:11	Truly the day of YHWH is great; terrible indeed—who can endure it?	Mal 3:23	Behold, I am going to send you Elijah the prophet, before the coming of the *great and terrible day of YHWH*
3:2	Even on the male and female slaves, in those days, I will pour out my spirit.		No parallel
3:4	The sun shall be turned to darkness, and the moon to blood, before the great and terrible day of YHWH comes.	Joel 2:10b	The sun and the moon grow dark, and the stars lose their brightness. (cf. Joel 2:11)
4:1	For then, in those days and at that time, when I restore the fortunes of Judah and Jerusalem	Zeph 3:20	At that time I will bring you in, even at the time when I gather you together; Indeed, I will give you renown and praise among all the peoples of the earth when I restore your fortunes before your eyes, says YHWH
4:14	Multitudes, multitudes, in the valley of decision! For the day of YHWH is near in the valley of decision.	Joel 1:15	See Joel 1:15 above

4:18	In that day *the mountains shall drip sweet wine, the hills* shall flow with milk, and all the stream beds of Judah shall flow with water; a fountain shall come forth from the house of YHWH and water the Wadi Shittim.	Amos 9:13	Behold, the days are coming declares YHWH, when the plowman will overtake the reaper, and the treader of grapes him who sows seed; *when the mountains shall drip sweet wine and all the hills* will be dissolved.
Other Occurrences of "Day" in Joel			
1:2 (2x)	Hear this, O elders, give ear, all inhabitants of the land! Has such a thing happened in your days, or in *the days of your fathers*?	Mal 3:7	From *the days of your fathers* you have turned aside from my statutes, and have not kept (them). Return to me, and I will return to you says YHWH of hosts (cf. also Joel 2:13)

Cooper and Van Leeuwen have documented the presence of a series of texts in the Twelve that delves into the implications of the theodicy language of Exod 34:6–7 regarding the fate of Israel and Judah.[29] Their works, together, demonstrate that at least two fundamentally different responses to the question are deliberately incorporated in the Book of the Twelve. Neither author attempts to explain how this motif was incorporated redaction-historically, but they do demonstrate its intentional interplay with the Exodus text and with the other texts in the Twelve. More needs to be done to situate this motif within the development of the Twelve as a whole, since the motif is not isolated. Cooper, particularly, demonstrates how this motif is also associated with an ongoing discussion about God's response to repentance, as seen in the divine responses and the interplay between Jonah and Nahum. Van Leeuwen, on the other hand, also highlights the manner in which this theodicy language is associated with the Day of YHWH, and the sense in which Joel serves as the essential interpretive backdrop for this language in the Twelve. In this light, I suspect it is no accident that this particular theodicy language appears only within the first seven writings of the Twelve, while other images are used in the remaining writings.

---

29. Cooper, "In Praise of Divine Caprice," 144–63; Van Leeuwen, "Scribal Wisdom," 31–49.

Joel's Paradigm of History

Now it is time to return to one of the first questions raised in this study: How does one incorporate one or more of these recurring concepts into a comprehensive analysis of the literary intention(s) of the Twelve? While in a very real sense, this task still seems daunting, I would nevertheless attempt to correlate several observations in the hopes of at least advancing the dialogue. First, one must cease thinking of Joel as a collection of unrelated postexilic messages, and investigate its role in the Book of the Twelve more closely. This statement does not argue that {107} Joel is a preexilic creation. Rather, its literary cohesion, its deliberate overlapping of forms, its use of images from Hosea and Amos all serve to anchor Joel into *this literary context*, despite the fact that Joel is *almost* universally considered one of the Twelve's later writings.[30]

Second, Joel's presence between Hosea and Amos does not ignore the chronological context. It transcends it. It introduces or transforms many of the theological emphases of the Book of the Twelve. Subsequent allusions to Joel in the Twelve tend to regard him as having predicted events of that time. For example, Amos 4:9 presumes YHWH has sent the drought and locust attack presumed in Joel 1, and that YHWH has now decided to bring an end to Israel. The locust imagery of Joel is taken up by redactional associations in Nah 3:15-17 to indicate that one "locust" (Assyria) who has invaded the land will be destroyed by another (Babylon); hence the "horde" mentioned in Hab 1:9 that is reminiscent of Joel 2:1-11.

Third, Joel offers a paradigm of history which "plays out" as one reads the Book of the Twelve, simultaneously providing the prophetic revelation and the reading clues necessary for a cohesive reading. As one encounters Joel's language across the Twelve, the realization is that one is not experiencing something unexpected. A cohesive reading which uses Joel as the anchor ultimately does two things. It explains why the history of YHWH's people occurred in the way it did, and it offers hope to the readers that they will endure only by turning to YHWH. A few observations about

---

30. A few writers date Joel in the early postexilic period between Haggai/Zechariah and Malachi (e.g., Redditt, "Book of Joel and Peripheral Prophecy," 225-40), but most date Joel well into the Persian period. See discussions in: Leslie C. Allen, *The Books of Joel, Obadiah, Jonah, and Micah*, NICOT (Grand Rapids: Eerdmans, 1976), 19-25; James L. Crenshaw, *Joel: A New Translation with Introduction and Commentary*, AB 24C (New York: Doubleday, 1995), 21-29.

some of the major thematic themes will perhaps provide impetus for continued reflection.

Joel extends Hosea's call to repentance by juxtaposing the promissory images of fertility with the "current" situation, in which a series of "locust" plagues (1:4, 7), drought (1:5–20), and a locust/enemy attack of unparalleled proportions (2:1–11) will continue until and unless the people repent. *If* the people repent, YHWH will become zealous for his land again and restore what the drought has destroyed and what the "locusts" have eaten (2:12–25).[31] Afterward, the centrality of Zion will {108} be restored (3:1–5; 4:1, 16, 17, 21 [Eng. 2:28–32; 3:1, 16, 17, 21]). Throughout this period (note 4:1 [Eng. 3:1] has "in those days" and "at that time"), the nations will be judged for their actions against YHWH's people (4:1–21 [Eng. 3:1–21]).

Note how Joel's language is then incorporated within this paradigm in other writings in the Twelve. Amos 4:9 uses Joel's fertility images to make the point that the people did not repent, even though they had been warned.[32] Israel is punished (Amos), although fertility and restoration are promised afterward (Amos 9:13, citing Joel 4:18 [Eng. 3:18]). Micah offers the same choice to Judah and Jerusalem (Mic 1:5–9; 3:12), but the south continues in the path of the Northern Kingdom (6:1–7:20). Micah reiterates promises to Judah that presume it will first experience punishments (4:1–4; 7:7–8). Nahum picks up Joel's threads again with the affirmation that YHWH punishes the guilty (Nah 1:3a) and in Nah 3:15–17, which interprets Assyria and Babylon as locusts, who themselves will soon be punished.[33] Habakkuk depicts the unprecedented nature of Babylon's attack by heightening the parallels between Assyria and Babylon[34] and through subtle allusions to Joel 2:1–11.[35] Further, when discussing the fate of the people, Hab 3:17 returns to the (lack of) fertility imagery of Joel

---

31. This passage demands more attention since the text contains considerable tensions about the extent to which the situation is reversed. Certain portions seem to imply restoration of the fertility has begun (2:21–23), but the majority of the text still anticipates the need for restoration (e.g., 2:19, 25).

32. Cf. also Joel 2:12, with the emphatic nature of the call to repentance: "Yet even now, return to me."

33. Note that both of these references are short redactional comments inserted into an existing context. See my discussions in Nogalski, *Redactional Processes*, 104–7 and 120–21.

34. Ibid., 146–50.

35. Note especially the similarities between Hab 1:7–10 and the description of Joel 2:4–9.

to anticipate the coming destruction. Zephaniah draws upon the Day-of-YHWH sayings from Joel (cf. Zeph 1:7, 14, 15) as well as in Zeph 3:19–20, the eschatological promises of Joel and Micah.[36] Haggai returns to the fertility imagery, rooted in Joel, by confronting the returned exiles with the land's infertility. Haggai confronts this people and challenges them to rebuild the temple as a sign they are ready to return to YHWH, so that YHWH will himself begin to restore the blessings of the land. Note how this is accomplished in Hag 2:17, 19* with the citation of Amos 4:9 and Joel 1, respectively. In Zech 1:2–6, this generation finally repents, leading to the statement that YHWH is now jealous for his land (Zech 1:15; cf. Joel 2:18–19 also with Hag 1:11; 2:17, 19). Zechariah 8:12 draws upon the fertility images of Joel, this time with reference to the rain as well (cf. Joel 2:23).[37] Thus, YHWH will save the remnant of this people {109} (or, the house of Judah and the house of Israel) that they will be a blessing rather than a curse among the nations (Zech 8:12–13). With Malachi, however, the people return to the same idolatrous behavior that they exhibited at the beginning. Hence one finds "catchwords" between Zech 8 and Malachi that juxtapose promise and reality, in precisely the same way as the catchwords in Hosea and Joel.[38] Interestingly, and I suspect not accidentally, the last chapter of Malachi presupposes that until the people repent (again), the devourer will remain (3:7, 10). In the end, only those who fear YHWH—not the entire nation—respond to this message (3:16–18).

Diachronic questions will continue to draw my attention, but the side sympathetic with synchronic approaches could not resist attempting to offer a reading of the Twelve that, to me, reflects plausible reading strategies of the editors who brought these writings together. These authors/redactors, by using recurring language related to the fertility and infertility of the land, the repentance of the people, and God's punishment of the guilty (within and outside Israel), compiled and shaped Joel as the literary anchor for a historical paradigm.

---

36. Nogalski, *Literary Precursors*, 181–215; Nogalski, *Redactional Processes*, 47–48.

37. Note also the way in which Zech 8:13, 15 takes up the comfort of the salvation oracle with the command "do not fear." This command appears only four times in the Book of the Twelve, in Joel 2:22; Hag 2:5; Zech 8:13, 15.

38. See my discussion in Nogalski, *Redactional Processes*, 197–200.

The Day(s) of YHWH in the Book of the Twelve

In 1997 Rolf Rendtorff presented a paper in the Society of Biblical Literature Formation of the Book of the Twelve Seminar in which he argued that the concept of the day of YHWH showed significant promise as a unifying theme of the Book of the Twelve.[1] He also suggested that it was unwise to limit the concept merely to those texts that specifically use the construct chain יום יהוה. Twenty-five years earlier, Joseph Everson and others carried on a rather lively debate about the extent to which the background of יום יהוה required that one study only those texts that contained this term.[2] Dissenters exist, but the majority of scholars concurred with Everson that other terms could refer to this day and that the day in question could lie in the past as well as the future. This paper will attempt to investigate these suggestions systematically by asking two questions. First, if other expres-

---

1. Rolf Rendtorff, "How to Read the Book of the Twelve as a Theological Unity," in *Society of Biblical Literature 1997 Seminar Papers*, SBLSP 36 (Atlanta: Scholar's Press, 1997), 420–32. The article also appeared in Nogalski, *Reading and Hearing*, 75–87.

2. A. Joseph Everson, "The Days of Yahweh," *JBL* 93 (1974): 329–37. Other works preceded Everson's article and responded to it. A selection of these writings is mentioned here: Gerhard von Rad, "Origin of the Concept of the Day of Yahweh," *JSS* 4 (1959): 97–108; Klaus D. Schunck, "Strukturlinien in der Entwicklung der Vorstellung vom 'Tag Jahwes,'" *VT* 14 (1964): 319–30; Paul-Émile Langevin, "Sur l'origine du 'Jour de Yahvé,'" *ScEccl* 18 (1966): 359–70; Patrick D. Miller, "Divine Council and the Prophetic Call to War," *VT* 18 (1968): 100–7; Klaus D. Schunck, "Die Eschatologie der Propheten des Alten Testaments und ihre Wandlung in exilisch-nach-exilischer Zeit," in *Studies on Prophecy: A Collection of Twelve Papers*, ed. Daniel Lys, VTSup 26 (Leiden: Brill, 1974), 116–32; Cornelis van Leeuwen, "The Prophecy of the Yōm YHWH in Amos v 18–20," in *Language and Meaning: Studies in Hebrew Language and Biblical Exegesis*, ed. James Barr, OTS 19 (Leiden: Brill, 1974), 113–34; Douglas K. Stuart, "The Sovereign's Day of Conquest," *BASOR* 221 (1976): 159–64; Yair Hoffman, "The Day of the Lord as a Concept and a Term in the Prophetic Literature," *ZAW* 93 (1981): 37–50; Hermann Spieckermann, "Dies irae: Der alttestamentliche Befund und seine Vorgeschichte," *VT* 39 (1989): 194–208.

sions potentially evoke the concept of יום יהוה, how does one recognize which terms do and which do not? Second, how does one evaluate the possibility that this recurring concept provides an avenue into the unifying elements of the Twelve? {193}

Once one opens the door to other terms, one must decide which terms to include. An attempt to investigate the literary cohesion must look at any text that could have been interpreted as a day of YHWH text by those compiling the Twelve. I have therefore assessed those texts which refer to a day of divine intervention in the Twelve for reasons discussed below. This decision greatly increased the number of texts to be evaluated, and it forced a limitation of the discussion in two ways. First, the study was limited to the first four writings of the Twelve. Advantageously, this limitation includes two writings with superscriptions claiming eighth century settings (Hosea and Amos) and two nondated writings (Joel and Obadiah), which the discipline generally dates later than Jerusalem's destruction. Second, I chose to focus the discussion upon passages where multiple terms were present. The volume of texts and the intricacy of the interrelationships make it impossible to treat every text in the space available.

Identifying Day of YHWH Texts

Any study of the day of YHWH must include more than the phrase יום יהוה. This construct chain appears fifteen times in the Hebrew Bible, but this statistic only begins to tell the story.[3] All fifteen references appear in the Latter Prophets, and thirteen of fifteen appear in the Twelve. In addition, a closely related expression, "the day of the wrath of YHWH," occurs three times, and two of these references appear in the Twelve.[4] A third syntactical variant contains the *lamed* preposition before YHWH, the day (belonging) to YHWH (יום ליהוה). This form appears exclusively in the Latter Prophets *when referring to the day of YHWH*, but a close parallel (היום ליהוה) appears elsewhere and refers to a day of ritual celebration.[5]

---

3. Isaiah 13:6, 9; Ezek 13:5; Joel 1:15; 2:1, 11; 3:4; 4:14; Amos 5:18, 20; Obad 15; Zeph 1:7, 14 (2x); Mal 3:23.

4. Zephaniah 2:2, 3; Lam 2:22.

5. The phrase יום ליהוה, when referring to the day of YHWH, appears in Isa 2:12; Ezek 30:3; 46:13; Zech 14:1. This phrase appears five times (Exod 16:25; 32:29; Lev 23:34; Deut 26:3; 1 Chr 29:5) in narrative texts, always with the definite article (היום ליהוה). This latter form refers to a particular day of ritual celebration.

In short, "day of YHWH" appears in variant forms, and these forms demonstrate a remarkably consistent association with the Latter Prophets, and especially with the Twelve.

However, other formulas and idiomatic expressions can refer to the day of YHWH and its effects. Two formulas, "on that day" (ביום ההוא) and "in those days" (בימים ההם), manifest conceptual similarities. Prophetic {194} usages of these phrases differ from their use in other parts of the canon. These phrases can refer to a day when YHWH acts or days which manifest the effects of YHWH's activity and thus relate to the day of YHWH. The expression "in those days" appears thirty-nine times in the Hebrew Bible, and the twenty-five instances outside the Latter Prophets always refer to the past.[6] By contrast, the phrase appears fourteen times in the Latter Prophets, and all but two refer to the future when the effects of YHWH's action will be operative.[7] These formulaic phrases should be evaluated with the same criteria as other יום sayings.

The second formula, "on that day" (ביום ההוא), also functions distinctively in the Latter Prophets. The phrase occurs 206 times in the Hebrew Bible with a significant number (170) in the *Former and Latter Prophets*. The phrase occurs in the Latter Prophets 107 times where it overwhelmingly anticipates a future event. By contrast, outside the Latter Prophets, the phrase typically refers to past events. This phrase is far more prominent in Isaiah (45x, with all but 1 appearing in Isa 1–31) and the Twelve (40x) than in Jeremiah (10x) or Ezekiel (12x). With only a few exceptions, ביום ההוא refers to a past event in narrative literature and a future event in the Latter Prophets. Only 6 times (out of 107) does the formula not refer to the future.[8] References outside the Latter Prophets are even more instructive. In the Torah, DtrH, and the Ketuvim, only 10 of the 99 do not refer

---

6. Genesis 6:4; Exod 2:11; Deut 17:9; 19:17; 26:3; Josh 20:6; Judg 17:6; 18:1 (2x); 19:1; 20:27, 28; 21:25; 1 Sam 3:1; 28:1; 2 Sam 16:23; 2 Kgs 10:32; 15:37; 20:1; Esth 1:2; 2:21; Dan 10:2; Neh 6:17; 13:15, 23; 2 Chr 32:24.

7. Isaiah 38:1; Jer 3:16, 18; 5:18; 31:29; 33:15, 16; 50:4, 20; Ezek 38:17; Joel 3:2; 4:1; Zech 8:6, 23. Isaiah 38:1 refers to the past, but it utilizes 2 Kgs 20:1 as its source. Zechariah 8:6 uses this expression to refer to the present. The remaining texts refer to future events.

8. Jeremiah 39:10 uses the phrase in a narrative account about a past event. Ezekiel 20:6; 23:38, 39 use the phrase in a divine speech to refer to a past event. Zechariah 6:10 implies the present day or the very near future. Isaiah 22:12 refers to the past action of YHWH.

160   THE BOOK OF THE TWELVE AND BEYOND

to past events.[9] Five of these 10 references occur in DtrH or Chronicles, and always in the mouth of a prophet. All 5 pentateuchal references occur in prophetic speeches by Moses. Conversely, several future references within the Latter Prophets occur in prophetic oracles within *narrative* contexts (e.g., Jer 39:16, 17; Hos 1:5). This phrase, when referring to future events, connotes prophetic activity. The two meanings of this phrase (past or future) do not vary because one predominates in narrative literature (versus poetic), but because the future references carry prophetic connotations. {195}

In addition to the formulas, references to a day of YHWH's intervention using idiomatic expressions appear in over one hundred texts.[10] These expressions include terms for YHWH's destructive activity (e.g., wrath, vengeance), the effect of that activity (your overthrow), or the name of the recipient (e.g., Egypt, Midian). The majority of these terms refer to contexts of judgment and punishment, but both the idiomatic expressions and the formulas also appear in contexts which speak of salvation or deliv-

---

9. Exodus 8:18; 13:8; 31:17 (2x), 18; 1 Sam 3:12; 8:18 (2x); 1 Kgs 22:25; 2 Chr 18:24.

10. These idiomatic expressions include at least the following: the day (Mic 7:4, 12; Zech 14:1; Jer 30:7; 31:6; 47:4; Mal 3:19; Ezek 7:7, 12, 19; 12:23; 30:2, 18; 39:8; Zeph 2:2), your day (Ezek 22:4; Jer 50:31), one day (Isa 10:17; 47:9; Zech 3:9), the latter days (Isa 2:2; Jer 23:20; 49:39; Mic 4:1; Jer 30:24; 48:47). In addition, the following construct chains also refer to the "day of x," where x = battle (Amos 1:14; Hos 10:14; Zech 14:3), bitterness (Amos 8:10), building your walls (Mic 7:11), calamity (Jer 12:3; 18:17; 46:21; Amos 6:3), clouds (Ezek 30:3; Joel 2:2; Zeph 1:15), darkness (Joel 2:2; Zeph 1:15), destruction (Obad 12; Zeph 1:15), disaster (Jer 17:17, 18; Obad 13), distress (Isa 37:3; Jer 16:19; Obad 14), Egypt (Ezek 30:9), his burning anger (Isa 13:13); his coming (Mal 3:2), his disaster (Obad 13), his misfortune (Obad 12), his preparation (Nah 2:4), his rebellion (Ezek 33:12), his sin (Ezek 33:12), his turning from wickedness (Ezek 33:12), indignation (Ezek 22:24), its (Assyria) going to Sheol (Ezek 31:15), Jezreel (Hos 2:2), light (Amos 8:9), Midian (Isa 9:3), my rising (Zeph 3:8), my visiting (Jer 27:22), panic (Isa 22:5), punishment (Isa 10:3), rebuke (Hos 5:9), salvation (Isa 49:8), sickliness (Isa 17:11), strangers carrying off his wealth (Obad 11), east wind (Isa 27:8), great slaughter (Isa 30:25), trouble (Nah 1:7; Zeph 1:15), trumpet and battle cry (Zeph 1:16), vengeance (Isa 34:8; 61:2; 63:4; Jer 46:10), woe (Jer 17:16), wrath (Zeph 1:15), YHWH's anger (Zeph 2:2, 3), YHWH's sacrifice (Zeph 1:8), your fall (Ezek 26:18; 32:10), your brother (Obad 12), your overthrow (Ezek 27:27). Plural construct chains also appear that require examination, including phrases that are translated "the days of...," punishment (Hos 9:7), retribution (Hos 9:7), the Baals (Hos 2:15), your slaughter (Jer 25:34), and my dealing with you (Ezek 22:14).

erance. To what extent are these phrases associated with the concept of the day of YHWH? In several cases, these phrases occur as parallel expressions for the day of YHWH, meaning that one cannot eliminate these terms without careful reasoning from a discussion of the day of YHWH.

How does one recognize references to the day of YHWH if one cannot isolate these references based solely on terminology? All prophetic day of YHWH texts presume a point of divine intervention into human events. This intervention may be anticipated, recounted, or interpreted. The divine intervention may be direct or it may involve YHWH's use of some entity to accomplish a given task. By collating multiple qualities referring to a day when YHWH intervenes, one can develop a composite picture of the expectations and explanations of what will happen or has happened. These qualities include the following: the type of action, the recipients of the intervention, the reason for the intervention, the time of the intervention, and potential literary connectors. {196}

Two basic types of action can be noted, positive and negative, but individual texts display a wide variation regarding how the desired action will be achieved. Negative actions essentially involve judgment, but the judgment can be framed as total annihilation, as a purification that will leave a remnant, or as punishment designed to last until specific behavior changes. Positive actions can be portrayed as salvation, deliverance, or restoration.

The recipients of the divine intervention also vary significantly. Not only can the day of YHWH be directed toward YHWH's people or toward foreign nations, but distinctions within these general categories carry different connotations. Intervention may be directed toward Israel or Judah for different reasons, at different points. Foreign nations may also be cited for specific reasons.

The time of the intervention can be past or future. Past references tend to be used as illustrations to coerce some type of change on the part of the current addressee. Future references may imply the distant future or the very near future.

Reasons for divine intervention usually relate to some transgression which YHWH will not tolerate. However, the accusations involve cultic, ethical, or military activities. Sorting through these rationales can provide insights into the theological and literary agendas associated with various texts.

Potential literary connectors also demand reflection. The passage's form and context affect how one interprets a reference. Other indicators may provide clues about the literary horizon of a given passage. Does one text quote or allude to another? Does a text refer to the day of intervention by using idiomatic or formulaic language? Do the anticipated events "recur" in another text?

Evaluating these characteristics can help to determine how the "day of YHWH" functions within the Twelve, where the proliferation of יום texts, when compared with other writings, suggests common transmission or at least a shared orientation on the part of the tradents of these twelve writings. However, without additional validation, repetition of יום יהוה, the phrase or the concept, does not necessarily provide evidence of literary cohesion for the corpus. The remainder of this paper will investigate texts in Hosea through Obadiah that refer to a day of divine intervention as a step toward clarifying the role of the day of YHWH in the Twelve. Time and space dictate that several texts function as focal points of the investigation because they contain multiple references to a "day" of divine intervention.[11] {197}

Hosea 2

Hosea 2 contains the second of three extended units which utilize a marriage metaphor to convey a message that moves from judgment to restoration. However, Hos 2 depicts YHWH, not the prophet, as the husband. It becomes increasingly clear that the wife is the land (of Israel) personified as mother and wife. This role parallels the role played by the personified Lady Zion in other prophetic texts, but Hos 2 reflects its context.[12] Both

---

11. Hosea 2:9; Joel 1–4; Amos 5:18–20; 8–9; and Obadiah. If space permitted, other passages meeting these criteria could be treated: Mic 4–5; 7:8–20; Zeph 1:2–2:3; Zeph 3; Zech 8; 12; 13; 14; Mal 3. In addition to texts containing multiple references to a day of divine {197} intervention, isolated references to a day of divine intervention also occur (e.g., Mic 2:4, Hab 3:17; Zech 2:15, etc.). A complete study would need to evaluate these texts as well.

12. Several prophetic texts express Jerusalem's relationship to YHWH by personifying Lady Zion (e.g., Isa 60; Jer 30:12–17; Ezek 22; Mic 7:8–13; Zeph 3:14–19). Increasingly, the role of Lady Zion as the consort of YHWH and the mother of the children of Jerusalem has come into focus. For the background of this concept, see the writings of Fitzgerald, "Mythological Background for the Presentation of Jerusalem," 403–16; Biddle, "Figure of Lady Jerusalem," 173–94; Julie Galambush, *Jerusalem in the Book of Ezekiel: The City as Yahweh's Wife*, SBLDS 130 (Atlanta: Scholars Press, 1992); Schmitt, "Motherhood of God and Zion as Mother," 557–69.

THE DAY(S) OF YHWH IN THE BOOK OF THE TWELVE   163

the judgment sayings and the salvific promises of Hos 2 draw upon the names of the children mentioned in Hos 1:1–9.

Hosea 2 illustrates how the aforementioned qualities can help to characterize days of divine intervention. "Day" appears eight times in the chapter (2:2, 5, 15, 17 [2x], 18, 20, 23), but only four times (2:2, 18, 20, 23) does יום refer explicitly to a period of divine intervention. All four instances refer to the future. Three of these four texts explicitly anticipate divine intervention, while the fourth implies intervention by using an easily recognized allusion to the literary context. Hosea 2:2 refers to a future time when Israel and Judah will be reunited under one king, hence a time of political restoration. This verse contains no *explicit* reference to divine intervention, but its concluding statement calls the time the "day of Jezreel." This unique phrase alludes to the interpretation of the name of the first son in Hos 1:5: "And it will happen *on that day* that I will break the bow of Israel in the valley of *Jezreel*." (emphasis added). Hosea 1:5 thus interprets the name Jezreel as anticipating a day of divine judgment against Israel, while Hos 2:2 alludes to that action as the "day of Jezreel," but reinterprets the action as a promise of political restoration when Israel and Judah will be united under a single king. {198}

Hosea 2:18, 20, and 23 all refer to future intervention using the formula "on that day." Hosea 2:18–19 anticipates a restoration of the relationship between YHWH and Israel "on that day." The restoration results from YHWH's intervention: "For *I* will remove the names of the Baals from her mouth so that they will no longer be mentioned by their names" (emphasis added). This reference reflects its context, essentially contrasting the future restoration "on that day" with the past "days of the Baals" in 2:15.

Hosea 2:20 uses the ביום ההוא formula to introduce a short promise of a restored relationship. The verse draws upon creation language (cf. Gen 1:30) to reverse the judgment pronounced in Hos 2:14. In the larger context, this creation imagery appears again in Hos 4:3; 7:12; and Zeph 1:2–3, within pronouncements of judgment against Ephraim and Judah respectively. In 2:20, YHWH restores the relationship between mother Israel and the animal realm, but YHWH serves as the mediator of the covenant, not one of the covenant partners.

Hosea 2:23 introduces a promise (2:23–25) that has intratextual connections and provides an added thematic dimension. YHWH's response will restore the course of nature for Israel: "It will happen *on that day* that I will respond to the heavens and they will respond to the earth, and the earth will respond to the grain, the new wine, and the oil, and they will respond to Jezreel" (Hos 2:23-24, emphasis added). As with the other promises, "that day" reverses judgments pronounced in the extended context. This promise restores elements from nature which YHWH had removed earlier in the chapter (2:10-11). The concluding reference to Jezreel in 2:24b not only refers back to the name of the first son, it also introduces word plays in 2:25 which reverse the judgment symbolized in the names of all three children: "I will sow [זְרַע] her for myself in the land, and I will have compassion [רחם] on her who had not obtained compassion [לֹא־רֻחָמָה], and I will say to those who were not my people [לֹא־עַמִּי], you are my people" (NASB). This promise also serves as the source text for a promise in Joel 2:19, following predictions of the day of YHWH against Zion.

In summary, references to a day of divine intervention in this chapter are contextually bound to Hosea as seen by their awareness of the names of the children and their reversal of earlier pronouncements of judgment. Hosea 2:23 is cited in Joel 2:19. These texts expand restoration promises to the political, religious, and natural realms.

Hosea 9

Hosea 9 contains five references to יום (9:5 [2x], 9:7 [2x], 9:9), but only three refer to days of divine intervention, albeit to different events. {199} Hosea 9:7 refers to the immediate future as "the days of punishment" (יְמֵי הַפְּקֻדָּה) and "the days of retribution" (יְמֵי הַשִּׁלֻּם) for Ephraim. Both terms appear in similar forms in other prophetic literature.[13] The third term (the days of Gibeah) alludes to intervention in the distant past as narrated in Judg 18-21.[14] Hosea 9:9 announces judgment upon Ephraim (cf. 9:3) for its "iniquity" like the "days of Gibeah." Hosea 10:9 uses this same phrase to

---

13. Isaiah 10:3 uses the singular form "day of punishment" to refer to an attack commissioned by YHWH from which there is no escape. Jeremiah uses the phrases the "time of their punishment" (10:15; 48:44; 50:27; 51:18) and the "year of their punishment" (11:23; 23:12) to refer to YHWH's intervention against Judah and/or foreign nations. Isaiah 34:8 uses the term "year of retributions" in synonymous parallelism with "day of vengeance."

14. The reference alludes to the account of the punishment of Gibeah and the sons of Benjamin in Judg 19-21 by the sons of Israel following the rape of the Levite's concubine. Note especially the successive consultations of YHWH over three *days* in Judg 20:18, 23, 26-28. Hans Walter Wolff, *Hosea: A Commentary on the Book of the Prophet Hosea*, trans. Gary Stansell, Hermeneia (Philadelphia: Fortress, 1974), 158;

mark the length of time that the people of Israel had sinned while anticipating a future battle when YHWH will cause the nations to attack. Hosea 9:6-8 refers to Ephraim, Israel, Samaria, and Bethel (*Aven*), indicating that this passage concerns the Northern Kingdom. Both the related passage in 10:9 and the allusion to Judges imply that the punishment will come in the form of an enemy attack, with the presupposition that YHWH will instigate the enemy to attack (cf. especially 10:10).

Hosea 9:7-9 thus anticipates a period in the near future when YHWH will intervene for judgment against Israel. Hosea 9:9 draws upon knowledge of traditions from Judg 19-21 (cf. esp. 20:18-28) to affirm both the extent of Israel's guilt and YHWH's ability to accomplish the judgment. Hosea 9:7-9 is linked to another text (Hos 10:9-10) by the unusual phrase "days of Gibeah" as well as the reaffirmation of YHWH's decision to chastise Israel by sending other nations against Israel (the Northern Kingdom) to punish it for its failure to worship YHWH properly. The remaining phrases in 9:7, "days of punishment" and "days of retribution," do not find direct citations elsewhere in the Book of the Twelve, although very similar phrases occur in Isaiah and Jeremiah. The presence of the word pair punishment (פקדה) and retribution/recompense (שלם) appear in reverse order in Mic 7:3-4 in a judgment oracle against the people of Jerusalem.[15] Amos 3:14 uses a similar phrase "on the day I punish Israel" to refer to YHWH's {200} impending judgment on Israel. Amos 3:14 may represent one of several examples of knowledge of the message of Hosea appearing in Amos.[16] Hosea 9:7-9 can function meaningfully within a coherent reading of the Twelve, but does not provide direct evidence that it plays a role in shaping the corpus literarily. This finding differs from the more direct citation of Hos 2:22 by Joel 2:19.

Jeremias, *Prophet Hosea*, 118; Wilhelm Rudolph, *Hosea*, KAT 13.1 (Gütersloh: Mohn, 1966), 179-80.

15. Micah 7:3-4 use the two terms in close proximity. Micah 7:3 uses the term שלום (meaning recompense in the sense of bribery) as an accusation and "your *punishment* [פקדתך] will come on a day of your posting a watchman" (emphasis added) (cf. Hab 2:1?).

16. The use of the writing of Hosea in Amos occurs in virtually every level of the transmission of Amos. See Jörg Jeremias, "Die Anfänge des Dodekapropheton: Hosea und Amos," in *Congress Volume: Paris, 1992*, ed. J. A. Emerton, VTSup 61 (Leiden: Brill, 1995), 87-106; also in *Hosea und Amos: Studien zu den Anfängen des Dodekapropheton*, FAT 13 (Tübingen: Mohr Siebeck, 1996), 34-54.

Joel

Joel contains eleven יום texts that refer specifically to divine intervention and use a significant variety of phrases: the day (1:15), the day of YHWH (1:15; 2:1, 11; 3:4; 4:14), day of darkness and gloom (2:2), day of clouds and thick darkness (2:2), in those days (3:2 [Eng. 2:29], 4:1 [Eng. 3:1]), and on that day (4:18 [Eng. 3:18]). More significant than the terms themselves, the type of action anticipated in these contexts reflects the movement of Joel from presumed judgment to a call for repentance, to promised restoration, to judgment on the nations who oppressed Judah and Jerusalem. This observation suggests that the meaning of similar terminology changes based upon the literary intention of the immediate and extended context (for Joel and the Twelve). The intended recipients of the day of divine intervention also play a significant role in the changing terminology within Joel.

Joel 1 opens with an extended communal call to repentance. Various groups among the inhabitants are singled out and addressed directly (cf. 1:2, 5, 11, 13). These calls *presume* the guilt of these people and describe how the devastation of the land affects each group.[17] The first explicit mention of the day of YHWH comes in 1:15, which warns that a military attack on Jerusalem and Judah will follow the devastation of the land. Subsequent texts in Joel explicate the form of that judgment, especially 2:1–11, which describes the day of YHWH as the attack of an army of unprecedented strength. This army is depicted using the extended metaphorical imagery of a locust plague, but the recipients of the attack are people of the city, not the crops. The description also carries cosmic overtones (2:10–11).

This expectation that the devastation of nature will be followed by a divinely initiated military attack corresponds to the manifestation of divine intervention in the two יום texts from Hosea. Hosea 2 anticipates YHWH's {201} removal of resources from Israel that can lead to a time of restoration while Hos 9:7–9 predicts a military attack against the Northern Kingdom by an army of nations whom YHWH assembles. Joel 1–2 mirrors the essential thematic movement of the day of divine intervention in Hosea with one exception. The recipients in Joel are the people of Judah and Jerusalem, not the Northern Kingdom. Could the compilation of Joel

---

17. For a treatment of how Joel 1 presumes the accusations of guilt from Hosea, see my treatment of the context in Nogalski, *Redactional Processes*, 17–18.

THE DAY(S) OF YHWH IN THE BOOK OF THE TWELVE   167

reflect its literary context? Joel's quotations of Hos 2:23 (Eng. 21) (Joel 2:19), Amos 1:2, and 9:14 (Joel 4:16, 18 [Eng. 3:16, 18]) point in that direction. Could the thematic similarity of the day of YHWH merely result from a limited number of ways that divine judgment was portrayed in these ancient texts? Perhaps, but the multiplicity of the links between Joel and its context in the Twelve must be taken into account. When one sees the extent of thematic development, the dovetailing of genres, the use of catchword connections, and direct citations in Joel, the probability of Joel's cognizance of its *literary* context between Hosea and Amos becomes more plausible than the presumption of coincidence piled upon coincidence.[18]

Joel uses several terms to announce days of divine intervention, a remarkable percentage of which appear elsewhere in the Twelve.[19] These parallels function as markers for Joel's paradigm of history that transcends, but does not replace, the chronological shape of the Twelve. This paradigm provides an eschatological perspective (reinforced by periodic notes to the reader of the Twelve) that Joel's predictions have occurred or are in the process of unfolding. The utilization of Joel imagery in the Twelve occurs with several motifs, not just the day of YHWH.[20]

The character of the days of divine intervention in Joel changes after 2:11, in keeping with this writing's literary movement. The remaining "day" texts promise intervention on Judah's behalf. These promises include {202} the outpouring of YHWH's spirit, deliverance on the day of universal judgment, and judgment of the nations. All of these texts presume this positive intervention will come *if and when* the call to repentance in 1:2–2:17 is accepted (although Joel never states whether that repentance occurs). Joel 3:2 (Eng. 2:29) (with 3:1 [Eng. 2:28]) promises the universal outpouring of YHWH's spirit at a point in the distant future. The outpouring of YHWH's spirit is chronologically more vague (cf. "afterward" in

---

18. The distance between the two ideas in the day of divine intervention texts of Hosea 2 and 9:7–9, when compared with the interweaving of the ideas in Joel argues that Joel is combining ideas already present in Hosea. See also Nogalski, "Intertextuality and the Twelve," 102–24.

19. Ten of the eleven references appear in citations, close parallels, and verbal parallels elsewhere in the Twelve. Compare the following parallels: Joel 1:15 // Zeph 1:14; Joel 2:1 // Hos 9:7 (verbal combination); Joel 2:2 // Zeph 1:15; Joel 2:11 // Mal 3:23; Joel 3:4 // 2:10b and Mal 3:23; Joel 4:1 // Zeph 3:20; Joel 4:14 // Joel 1:15 and Zeph 1:14; Joel 4:18 // Amos 9:13. Only Joel 3:2 has no close parallel elsewhere in the Twelve. See the chart and my discussion of these parallels in Nogalski, "Joel as 'Literary Anchor,'" 106.

20. See ibid., 91–109.

3:1 [Eng. 2:28] and "in those days" in 3:2 [Eng. 2:29]). The divine intervention is directed toward "all flesh," sons and daughters, the youth, the elderly, and even the slaves. No direct verbal connections tie this text to others within the Twelve, though thematic similarities to other texts exist. Zechariah 8:23 and Mal 1:11-14 offer similar positive orientations toward people beyond the borders, as does the book of Jonah, but one cannot establish these connections via the day of divine intervention.

The promissory nature of that time of divine intervention takes an ominous twist in Joel 3:3-5 which anticipates a "great and terrible day of YHWH." The reference to the "great and terrible day of YHWH" in 3:4 occurs in only one other place, at the conclusion of the Twelve, in Mal 3:23.[21] In addition, similar wording occurs in Zeph 1:14-15 which contains several terms from Joel concerning the imminent destruction of Judah and Jerusalem on the great day of YHWH.[22] Like Joel 2:1-11, the day of YHWH anticipated in 3:4 (Eng. 2:31) draws upon cosmic images, even quoting 2:10b. One may extrapolate the recipients of judgment as those *not* calling on YHWH's name, since 3:5 (Eng. 2:32) states that those who call on YHWH's name will be saved in a verse that appears to cite Obad 17.

Joel 4:1 (Eng. 3:1) again uses the phrase "in those days," formally linking it with 3:1-5 (Eng. 2:28-32). The divine intervention of 4:1-21 (Eng. 3:1-21) continues the dual focus of the restoration of Judah and Jerusalem and the punishment of the recalcitrant nations. The chronological formula and the promise in Joel 4:1 (Eng. 3:1) are cited in Zeph 3:19-20, the last verses which separate the "preexilic" portion of the Twelve from the postexilic section. Zephaniah 3:19-20 promises restoration to Judah and judgment upon the nations who took advantage of Judah by taking up the language of Mic 4:6-7 and Joel 4:1 (Eng. 3:1) respectively. Immediately thereafter, the Twelve presumes that YHWH's people are back in the land after the exile. In the larger context of the Twelve, Zeph 3:19-20 implies that Joel's promises of restoration and recompense were not immediately fulfilled. When one reads Joel as an eighth century prophetic

---

21. The word pair "great and terrible" occurs in eight other contexts, but refers to the wilderness (Deut 1:19; 8:15), God (Deut 7:21; Dan 9:4; Neh 1:5; 4:8), God's name (Ps 99:3), or God's actions (Deut 10:21).

22. Zephaniah 1:2-2:3 demonstrates the same blending of images that combine a day of YHWH against Judah and Jerusalem on the one hand, and against all creation on the other.

voice, based on its context in the Twelve not the date of its composition, then the chronological {203} markers of Joel 3:1, 2, 4 (Eng. 2:28, 29, 31); and 4:1 (Eng. 3:1) do not indicate the immediate repentance of the people following Joel 2:17. In other words, while an isolated reading of Joel often assumes that the people repent following 2:17, the Twelve does not narrate the repentance of YHWH's people prior to the generation of Haggai and Zechariah.[23]

Joel 4:14 mentions the day of YHWH as a day of judgment against the nations. It functions within a larger unit (4:9–17) that promises divine intervention. Joel 4:14–16 present a series of quotations which adapt judgment pronouncements against Judah into pronouncements against the nations. Joel 4:14 repeats the threat of the imminent day of YHWH from Joel 1:15 except Joel 4:14 portrays the nearness of the day of YHWH against the nations, not Judah. Joel 4:15 (Eng. 3:15) cites 2:10 with a similar change, and Joel 4:16a (Eng. 3:16a) quotes Amos 1:2 thereby linking the upcoming oracles against the nations in Amos with the eschatological emphasis of Joel.[24] These quotes culminate in an explanation (4:17 [Eng. 3:17]) that this divine intervention will demonstrate YHWH's beneficence toward Zion and Jerusalem.

Joel 4:18 (Eng. 3:18] contains the final specific reference to a day of divine intervention in Joel. It links Joel with the end of Amos by the citation of Amos 9:13. This citation introduces the final literary unit of Joel, a unit which reverses the devastation of Joel 1–2 by using catchwords to previously mentioned elements. The formula "on that day" places the expected time frame in conjunction with the promised judgment of the nations in the remainder of the chapter.

The images of days of divine intervention in Joel are diverse yet interwoven with the immediate and extended contexts. Joel's use of self-quotes helps move the reader from judgment against Judah to potential restoration and then to judgment against the nations. However, these references to days of divine intervention also provide threads of cohesion within the Twelve. By means of thematic combinations and direct citations, the days of divine intervention present a complex picture that picks up where Hosea leaves off and moves to Amos. References back to

---

23. Not until Zech 1:2–6 does a prophetic text in the Twelve clearly indicate that the people repent. The superscription in Zech 1:1 precedes the date of the last messages in Haggai (see Hag 2:10, 20). Elsewhere only the Ninevites in Jonah repent.

24. See Schart, *Entstehung des Zwölfprophetenbuchs*, 292–95.

170   THE BOOK OF THE TWELVE AND BEYOND

Joel's language associated with divine intervention also play a significant role in the Twelve at key points (cf. especially Zeph 1:14–15; 3:19–20; and Mal 3:23). {204}

Amos

Amos 5:18–20, 8:4–14, and 9:11–15 anticipate days of divine intervention with more than a single reference to the day. Amos 5:18–20 is often cited as the earliest text in the Hebrew Bible specifically using יום יהוה. The three uses of this phrase polemically contrast two different perceptions of the day of YHWH. Through a series of rhetorical questions, the voice of the prophet tells those who anticipate a day of divine intervention on their behalf that they are mistaken. The day of YHWH will bring darkness (חשך) and gloom (אפל) rather than light (אור) and brightness (נגה). These verses thus make two affirmations about the day of YHWH: (1) it will come as a day of judgment against the Northern Kingdom and (2) when the day comes, escape will be impossible.

Amos 5:18–20 existed within Amos long before Joel's composition, but at least two indicators suggest they should be read with Joel by the reader of the Twelve. Joel 4 (with its expectation of a day of divine judgment against the nations) contains quotations that link that chapter to the beginning and end of Amos. To this extent, one can say that Joel anticipates and interprets Amos literarily, though Joel's composition is much later than the core of the Amos material. Moreover, Joel 2:2 links to Amos 5:18–20 via the explicit reference to the day of YHWH as a day of darkness (חשך) and gloom (פלה). In fact, Amos 5:18–20 appears as the second of three texts in the Twelve which use this phrase.[25]

For the reader of the Twelve, the link between Amos 5:18–20 and Joel 2:2 provides evidence of deliberate association, but for what purpose? Does anything in the Amos context account for Joel's citation apart from the reference to the day of YHWH? One should not miss three intriguing associations. First, in Amos 5:16–17, the unit immediately preceding Amos 5:18–20, one finds several thematic and verbal links with the mourning of the farmers (cf. Joel 1:10–11) and the wailing "in all the streets" and "in all the vineyards" (cf. Joel 1:12; 2:12). Second, in the context preceding Amos 5:18–20, the chapter begins with the pronouncement of a dirge following

---

25. See Zeph 1:15. See also the discussion in ibid., 220–22.

a divine report of Israel's repeated refusals to return to YHWH using the refrain "yet you did not return to me," also used in Joel 2:12 as an admonition, "yet even now, return to me." Third, the context of Amos relates the dirge (5:1) and the proclamation of the imminence of the day of YHWH (5:18–20) to the destruction of the House of Israel with particular reference to Bethel and Gilgal (5:5). {205}

When reading Hosea, Joel, and Amos sequentially, an interesting phenomenon occurs. Hosea ends with an open call to repentance to the Northern Kingdom, and Joel begins with a call to repentance for Judah and Jerusalem before the arrival of the day of YHWH. The day of YHWH in Amos 5:18–20 is again directed toward the Northern Kingdom, but it presumes the day of judgment will result from *Israel's* refusal to return to YHWH. By contrast, Zion receives a temporary reprieve (cf. Mic 7:8–20) before the day of YHWH pronouncement in Zeph 1:14–15 shows that Jerusalem will suffer the same fate on the day of YHWH just as Joel 2:2 had warned.

Amos 8 uses יום six times in the context of a day of divine intervention (8:3, 9 [2x], 10, 11, 13). Amos 8:3 contains the formula "on that day," but it refers to a day of judgment rather than a promise. The phrase in 8:3 refers to the day of judgment which will bring an end to Israel. It appears within the explanation of the fourth vision. The verse is thus closely tied to its immediate context.

Amos 8:9–10 contains three references to יום. Amos 8:9–10 stands out as a small subunit by the introductory formula and the change of speaker to divine first person speech. While this speaker continues in 8:11–14, those verses signal a new paragraph by another introductory formula in 8:11. Amos 8:9 uses ביום ההוא as an introductory formula to refer to a day of divine intervention for judgment upon Israel. "Day" also appears in reference to YHWH's divine intervention that will make the sun grow dark in the middle of the day. Amos 8:10 refers to this coming day of judgment as a "day of bitterness," a phrase which has its closest parallel in Zeph 1:14, a text which also played a role in the connection between Amos 5:18–20 and Joel.[26] Three things stand out about these verses. First, 8:9 uses ביום ההוא to introduce motifs already explicated within Amos 5:16–17, 18–20, 21–23. The darkening of the day sounds very much like 5:18, 20, and the

---

26. Zephaniah 1:14–18 contains several terms for the day of YHWH from elsewhere in the Twelve.

festivals/songs turned to mourning in 8:10 recalls 5:21-23. Second, this association confirms a presumption noted at the beginning of this paper that the phrase "on that day" *can be* conceptually related to the concept of the day of YHWH. Third, the verbal links in this verse point to the larger context of Amos and to a lesser extent the (developing) Book of the Twelve. Amos 8:9-10 refers to the day of YHWH context of Amos 5, but it also contains echoes of language from Hosea, Micah, and Zephaniah.[27] However, these images cannot be unambiguously labeled as direct citations. {206}

Amos 8:11-12, 13-14 contains two additional formulas introducing a day of divine intervention. In 8:11, "Behold, the days are coming" offers a new introduction, but the images used in these verses do not explicitly link with the motifs of Amos 5 or to the broader context of the Twelve. Amos 8:11 refers to a famine in the *coming days*, but it is YHWH's word, not agricultural elements, that is lacking. Amos 8:13 contains another ביום ההוא formula which formally looks back to the time of the famine mentioned in 8:11. This verse does use images that appear in Amos 5. The verse refers to the *virgins* (בתולות) and the young men (הבחורים) who will faint from thirst. It leads to condemnation of "those who swear by the guilt of Samaria ... who will fall and not rise again" (NASB). Similarly, Amos 5:2 refers to "the Virgin Israel [בתולת ישראל] who has fallen and will not rise."

In summary, the references to a day(s) of divine intervention in Amos 8 show a strong awareness of texts from Amos 5. This link is significant since it correlates day of YHWH statements with ביום ההוא formulas. The "day" references in Amos 8 also contain images from the larger context of the Twelve, with links to Joel 2 and Zeph 1:14-15 being the strongest. As with the references to the day of YHWH in Amos 5, these verses also anticipate judgment upon the Northern Kingdom.

Amos 9:11-15 uses יום twice to refer directly to divine intervention. Amos 9:11 contains two references to "day." One uses ביום ההוא to refer to YHWH's future restoration, and one compares this future day to the ideal "days of old." In its current form, this promise continues through 9:12 and vows to restore the kingdom under a single ruler. The promise in 9:11 links thematically with other royal restoration texts (e.g., Hos 2:2 [Eng.

---

27. In addition to the day of bitterness connection to Zeph 1:14, the "mourning for an only son" sounds much like YHWH's attitude toward Ephraim in Hos 11, although the term {206} "only son" does not appear there. The term "baldness" appears only in Amos 8:10 and Mic 1:16 within the Book of the Twelve.

THE DAY(S) OF YHWH IN THE BOOK OF THE TWELVE   173

1:11]), although the link does not have strong verbal connections, making the question of deliberate association difficult. The image of restoration evoked by this promise functions on multiple levels. First, the promise presumes the destruction of Jerusalem, not just the split of the Northern and Southern Kingdoms, as can be seen from the language of rebuilding the city walls.[28] Since the setting of Amos is placed in the eighth century by the book's superscription, the promise of 9:11-15 serves a metahistorical function.[29] Second, the anticipated restoration of the kingdom goes beyond the reunification of the two kingdoms {207} since 9:12a also anticipates the retaking of "the remnant of Edom and all the nations who are called by my name." Amos 9:12 summarizes the message of Obadiah by announcing Edom's destruction (Obad 1-15) and the restoration of the Davidic kingdom by the combined house of Jacob and house of Joseph (Obad 18) as it (re)possesses Edom and the surrounding territory (Obad 19-21).[30] Again, ביום ההוא and יום יהוה are linked.

Amos 9:13 contains a new introductory formula, "behold the days are coming," followed by a promise of astounding fertility (9:13) and restoration of the cities and crops (9:14-15). Several indicators point to editorial expansion of this short unit. The promise of continual agricultural abundance makes the promise of normalcy seem anticlimactic. Also, the explicit citation of Joel 4:18 in Amos 9:13b creates the suspicion that this reference has been added to establish the concluding link to Joel in Amos. By contrast, the promise of 9:14-15 presumes the devastation of the land and its cities will be restored with the return of "my people," the rebuilding of the cities, and a return to the land's ideal fertile state. The character of the divine intervention implied in these verses does not have the aggressive political overtones of 9:11-12. Apart from the direct link to Joel, the underlying promises in the two parts also have thematic links with the promises of Hos 2:1-25 where one finds the names of Hosea's children used to combine promises of political reunification (2:2), devastation

---

28. See discussion in James D. Nogalski, "The Problematic Suffixes of Amos ix 11," *VT* 43 (1993): 411-18; and Nogalski, *Literary Precursors*, 105-8.

29. On the concept of metahistory, see Steck, *Prophetenbücher*, 50-54; (Eng. trans., 49-52).

30. This association, when noted, was explained by the assumption that two completed works were placed side by side. Recent work suggests this association was created redactionally by inserting part of this verse. See Nogalski, *Literary Precursors*, 217, 115-16; Schart, *Entstehung des Zwölfprophetenbuchs*, 271-72.

(2:14), exile to the wilderness (2:16), and restoration of the relationship that leads to normal agricultural patterns for "my people" (2:23–25).

The promises of divine intervention in Amos 9:11–15 connect thematically to the promises of Hos 2:2–25, but they also contain verbal links backward to Joel and forward to Obadiah. This multiplicity of connections gives Amos 9:11–15 the feel of a pastiche, combining several images of what will happen once YHWH intervenes on the people's behalf. This passage suggests that the day of divine intervention functioned as a stack pole for creating meaning across the multivolume corpus as it developed.

Obadiah

The Hebrew word יום appears twelve times in Obadiah, and all twelve relate to a day of divine intervention. When one analyzes the events of those various days, one notes that the actual intervention combines more than one image. The terms begin with ביום ההוא (Obad 8) and end with a specific reference {208} to the day of YHWH (Obad 15) on all the nations. The ביום ההוא formula introduces a pronouncement of a divinely guided destruction of the wise and the mighty (Obad 9) on the mountain of Edom.

In the remaining instances, ten idiomatic expressions refer to the day of Jerusalem's destruction, accusations about Obadiah's role in that destruction, and the resulting punishment of Edom on the day of YHWH.[31] These idiomatic expressions can be noted in Obad 10–15, which address Edom directly:

> [10]For the violence (done to) your brother Jacob, you will be covered with shame.
> And you will be cut off forever.
> [11]*On the day* you stood far off,
> *On the day* when strangers captured his wealth,
> And foreigners entered his gates and cast lots over Jerusalem,
> Moreover, you were like one of them.
> [12]Do not look *on the day* of your brother, *on the day* of his calamity.
> Do not rejoice about the sons of Judah *on the day* of their destruction.

---

31. For a discussion of יום יהוה in Obadiah, see Fanie Snyman, "Yom (YHWH) in the Book of Obadiah," in *Goldene Äpfel in Silbernen Schalen: Collected Communications to the XIIIth Congress of the International Organization for the Study of the Old Testament, Leuven 1989*, ed. Klaus D. Schunck and Matthias Augustin, BEATAJ 20 (Frankfurt am Main: Lang, 1992), 81–91.

And do not boast *on the day* of distress.
¹³Do not enter into the gate of my people *on the day* of their disaster.
Do not look, especially you, on his wickedness *on the day* of his disaster.
Do not loot his wealth *on the day* of his disaster.
¹⁴And do not stand in the crossroad to cut off his fugitives.
And do not deliver up his survivors *on the day* of distress,
¹⁵because the *day of YHWH* is near on account of all the nations.
Just as you have done it will be done to you.
Your recompense will return upon your own head. (emphasis added)

Unlike Obad 8, the יום sayings in 11–15 allude to the destruction of Jerusalem as the day of divine intervention while warning Edom not to participate in Judah's punishment lest the same fate befall Edom on the day of YHWH for all nations. These verses convey this message using linguistic forms that display a bifurcated sense of time. On the one hand, the accusations against Edom presume knowledge about Edom's role in Jerusalem's destruction. On the other hand, most of the יום sayings use formulations which presume those events have not yet taken place. Obadiah 12–14 uses the syntax of negative commands אל) + imperfect), whose chronological perspective assumes they are issued prior to an event. However, Obad 11 and 15 demonstrate knowledge that Edom *has already* done what verses 12–14 say not to do. This dichotomy is overcome when one understands the metahistorical perspective of Obadiah. Like Joel, Obadiah demonstrates awareness of its literary {209} location when it was compiled. Obadiah's position among the eighth-century prophets in the Twelve functions as a warning that justifies YHWH's punishment of Edom for indifference and/or its active participation in Jerusalem's destruction.[32] The Jacob/Esau language of Obadiah implies Edom should have known better because of its lengthy relationship with YHWH's people. From the perspective of the Twelve, Edom receives a warning which paralleled the warning given to the Northern Kingdom.[33]

The יום sayings in Obadiah contain verbal and thematic ties to other Edom texts in the Latter Prophets, although it can be difficult to classify

---

32. See Nogalski, *Redactional Processes*, 218, 89–92.
33. See my discussion of the parallel structure of Obadiah and Amos 9 in ibid., 61–68; and Nogalski, "Jeremiah and the Twelve: Intertextual Observations and Postulations" (paper presented at the Annual Meeting of the Society of Biblical Literature, Orlando, FL, November 1998).

every link as idiom, parallel, allusion, or citation. One example of these idiomatic expressions illustrates the difficulty. The phrase "day of distress" occurs in Obad 12 and 14. This phrase occurs some fifteen times in the Hebrew Bible.[34] The phrase appears almost as often in the Writings (6x) as in the Prophets (8x), even though the phrase occurs more often in the Twelve (5x) than any other book.[35] The phrase could thus be a common idiom that has no definable role when reading the Twelve. However, it is striking that the phrase appears in texts with ties to the broader context of the Twelve and to the punishment of foreign nations in retaliation for their role in threatening Jerusalem.

This contextual connection provides a certain cohesiveness to the recurring phrase as one reads the Twelve. However, despite the verbal similarity, one cannot say that the phrase was always originally used with the Twelve in mind. In Nah 1:7 the phrase already existed in the acrostic poem that was modified and incorporated into Nahum with an eye toward the context of the developing multivolume corpus.[36] It was thus not written for the Twelve, but the phrase could have served a role in selecting the theophanic hymn to be placed at the start of Nahum. *In that context*, Nah 1:7 functions {210} as the threat of a day of divinely delivered distress upon Assyria because they have threatened Judah. Similarly, the theophanic hymn in Hab 3:16 refers to the day of distress against Babylon *after* they attack Jerusalem.[37] However, in both instances, one would not *hear* these verses in the same way if these hymns appeared in Psalms (cf. Pss 20:2;

---

34. Genesis 35:3; 2 Kgs 19:3 = Isa 37:3; Jer 16:19; Obad 12, 14; Nah 1:7; Hab 3:16; Zeph 1:15; Pss 20:2; 50:15; 77:3; 86:7; Prov 24:10; 25:19.

35. In comparison, the phrase appears does not appear in Ezekiel and appears only once in Jeremiah (16:19). The only time it appears in Isaiah (37:3), it appears in the parallel to the Hezekiah story from 2 Kgs 19:3.

36. Exactly when these hymns were incorporated into Nahum and Habakkuk is a matter of some debate. I have argued that they entered with the Joel-related layer (see Nogalski, *Redactional Processes*, 218) while Schart (*Entstehung des Zwölfprophetenbuchs*, 234–51) and Bosshard-Nepustil (*Rezeptionen von Jesaia 1–39*, 269–432) raise significant arguments that (portions of) Nahum and Habakkuk entered the developing corpus prior to Joel.

37. The prophetic first-person response in Hab 3:16–19 to the theophanic description of 3:3–15 does not presume that the threat of the day of distress has been removed, only that God will provide strength and salvation. The context of the hymn in Habakkuk virtually demands that the reader should associate Babylon with the attacking enemy.

50:15; 77:3; 86:7) or Proverbs (24:10; 25:19). The odds are higher, however, that Obad 12, 14, and Zeph 1:15 were written specifically for a larger, developing corpus. In both contexts one finds the dual association of a threat to Jerusalem followed by a day of divine judgment against the nations. The fact that Zeph 1:14–18 contains links to Joel, Amos, and Obadiah makes it likely that these verses (along with other parts of Zeph 1:1–2:3) functioned as a collecting point for phrases related to the coming day of YHWH's intervention. The greatest difference in these "day of distress" texts comes in the identity of the nation who threatens Jerusalem and who will subsequently be judged. Yet, even this difference makes sense when viewed within the metahistorical framework of the Twelve. The pronouncements against Edom, Assyria, and Babylon depend upon their location in the Twelve. Nahum and Habakkuk function within the chronological framework of the Twelve to anticipate YHWH's use of Assyria and Babylon to confront the people of Judah, while at the same time affirming that YHWH will remove these powers from the scene because they overstep the role which YHWH sent them to perform. Obadiah transcends the chronological framework by virtue of its location among the eighth-century prophets, but its composition deliberately creates structural and thematic parallels to Amos 9, thereby comparing the ultimate fate of Edom with Israel (the Northern Kingdom) while still anticipating Jerusalem's punishment. The complexity of the "day of distress" applies to other phrases as well.

The day of YHWH saying in Obad 15 functions similarly. This verse transitions to a day of divine intervention on the nations (esp. those of the Davidic Kingdom) that will play out *after* Edom has been judged (Obad 18) and possessed (Obad 19) by the "house of Jacob" and the "house of Joseph." The careful reader of the Twelve recognizes that the expression "the day of YHWH is near" has occurred in Joel. It reappears again in Zeph 1:7, 14.[38] Two observations raise questions about the function of the day of YHWH sayings in the Twelve. First, the particular form of "near" (קרוב) {211} appears only in conjunction with day of YHWH texts (Joel 1:15; 2:1; 4:14; Obad 15; Zeph 1:7, 14 [2x]).[39] Second, this phrase does not appear in any of the writings that function as "postexilic" writings in the

---

38. The same formulation כי קרוב יום יהוה appears in 1:15; 4:14. See also the closely related formulation in 2:1.

39. Compare the fact that this phrase appears elsewhere only three times in the Latter Prophets (Isa 13:6; Ezek 7:7; 30:3), while the adjective קרוב appears some seventy-two times in the Hebrew Bible.

Twelve. In other words, this phrase does not appear in Haggai, Zechariah, or Malachi.[40]

The identity of those whom YHWH will use to destroy Edom in Obad 18 should not be overlooked. The combination of the house of Jacob and the house of Joseph denotes a reunified kingdom. The phrase "house of Joseph" is particularly instructive. It appears seventeen times in the Hebrew Bible, but only three times in the Latter Prophets and never in the Writings.[41] The Former Prophets identify the term with the territory of Ephraim and Manasseh (see Josh 17:17, 2 Kgs 11:28). All three uses of the term in the Latter Prophets appear in the Twelve. Amos 5:6 uses the same metaphor of the consuming fire to pronounce judgment upon the house of Joseph that Obad 18 uses to depict judgment upon Edom. The house of Jacob appears twenty-one times, most frequently in the Isaiah corpus (9x) and in the Twelve (6x).[42] In Isaiah and Micah the phrase refers to Judah, which makes the most sense in Obad 17–18 because of the combination of the house of Jacob/Joseph. The term appears twice in Amos with 3:3 referring to the Northern Kingdom as the house of Jacob while 9:8 refers to the remnant of the kingdom as the house of Jacob. The combination of these two entities appears only in Obad 18, and connotes restoration that reflects the reunification of the Davidic kingdom.

Obadiah's role in the literary context of the Twelve and the prophetic corpus should be noted. First, Obadiah was compiled for its position in the Twelve. Its careful structural, thematic, and verbal imitation of Amos 9 make this perspective plausible (and in my mind probable).[43] Second, Obadiah's threefold movement of the day of divine intervention also plays a role in Malachi, the final writing in the Twelve. Obadiah anticipates a day of judgment on Jerusalem that will lead to a day of judgment on Edom as the first of the surrounding nations to be judged on the day of YHWH against the nations. In the Twelve, Edom receives periodic mention in Joel

---

40. Those writings tend to portray a day of divine intervention differently, in a manner that suggests awareness of their postexilic function in the Twelve, but that is the subject of another paper.

41. Genesis 39:22; 43:17, 18, 19, 24; 44:14; 50:8; Josh 17:17; 18:5; Judg 1:22, 23, 35; 2 Sam 19:21; 1 Kgs 11:28; Amos 5:6; Obad 18; Zech 10:6.

42. Genesis 46:27; Exod 19:3; Isa 2:5, 6; 8:17; 10:20; 14:1; 29:22; 46:3; 48:1; 58:1; Jer 2:4, 20; Ezek 20:5; Amos 3:13; 9:8; Obad 17, 18; Mic 2:7; 3:9; Ps 114:1.

43. See Nogalski, *Redactional Processes*, 61–68; and Nogalski, "Jeremiah and the Twelve."

{212} and Amos, and is the subject of extensive treatment in Obadiah, but it is not mentioned again until Malachi.[44] More interestingly, the threefold movement of the day of divine intervention in Obadiah is presumed to be in process in Malachi. Elsewhere I have demonstrated how Mal 1:2–5 displays knowledge of Obadiah, not just nebulous traditions about Edom, except both the judgment on Jerusalem and the desolation of Edom are now in the past.[45] Thus, two of the three "days of divine intervention" anticipated in Obadiah have come to pass, while the third movement is not mentioned in Mal 1:2–5. However, reference to the day of YHWH virtually concludes Malachi with the citation of Joel 3:4 in Mal 3:23: "Behold I am going to send you Elijah the prophet before the *coming of the great and terrible day of YHWH*" (NASB, emphasis added). The coming day of YHWH in Mal 3:23 will be directed at the wicked, not just the nations, but this alteration reflects the situation presented by Malachi where YHWH's people as a whole have returned to false worship practices just as at the beginning of the Twelve, while some of "the nations" have begun turning toward YHWH (cf. Mal 1:11–14). Thus, Jerusalem has been punished, Edom has been destroyed, and on the coming day of YHWH, the righteous will defeat the wicked (Mal 3:21). One sees a similar dynamic in the Isaiah corpus (cf. Isa 34:5–6, 63:1–6) where verbal links unite two widely separated texts in the expectation of the divine warrior's victory on the day of recompense against the nations (cf. Isa 34:8) that begins with Edom's destruction.

In summary, the day of divine intervention in Obadiah appears as a sequence of days of judgment with three recipients: Edom, Judah, and the nations. Judah's punishment (destruction and exile) is presumed (Obad 10–15, 20), even though the event is set in the future, and the reason for the punishment is never addressed. Edom's punishment is portrayed as a future event that will occur *after* Jerusalem's destruction as a result of Edom's hostility toward Jerusalem.

Conclusion

Significant verbal and thematic links show that the concept of a day of divine intervention provides literary cohesion to the writings of Hosea

---

44. The Twelve specifically mentions Edom in Joel 4:19; Amos 1:6, 9, 11; 2:1; 9:12; Obadiah; and Mal 1:4.
45. Nogalski, *Redactional Processes*, 218, 190–91.

through Obadiah. These links suggest that the other writings of the Twelve {213} are also involved. These links include more than the phrase יום יהוה. All four writings demonstrate thematic links, while the later writings (Joel and Obadiah) show more explicit signs of deliberate verbal links which combine references to days of divine intervention across the writings of the Twelve.

Recurring Themes in the Book of the Twelve: Creating Points of Contact for a Theological Reading

Four themes have surfaced in the discussion of the Book of the Twelve as deserving of exploration for the role they play in providing a lens for reading the Book of the Twelve as a composite unity.[1] These four themes (the day of YHWH, fertility of the land, the fate of God's people, and the theodicy problem) show signs of editorial activity, literary development, and/or diverse theological perspectives. These themes intersect with one another in places, but they also each tell portions of a story on their own. As such, they deserve to be heard.

The Day of YHWH

The day of YHWH functions as a recurring concept in the Book of the Twelve more prominently than in any other prophetic corpus.[2] However, two caveats require comment. First, the day of YHWH in the Book of the Twelve is not a single, final judgment as one finds in later apocalyptic writings. Second, the day of YHWH in the Book of the Twelve does not fall neatly into a single, systematic view of this concept. Writings in the Twelve conceptualize "the day" differently, and in fact, more than one event may be classified as the "day" in the same writing. For example, both Joel and Obadiah envision a day of YHWH's intervention first as the day of judgment against YHWH's own people, and as a broader day of recompense

---

1. See the guest editorial: James D. Nogalski, "Reading the Book of the Twelve Theologically: The Twelve as Corpus; Interpreting Unity and Discord," *Int* 61 (2007): 115–22.
2. So, e.g., Rendtorff, "How to Read the Book of the Twelve as a Theological Unity," 75–87; James D. Nogalski, "The Day(s) of YHWH in the Book of the Twelve," in Redditt, *Thematic Threads*, 192–213.

{126} for the surrounding nations, particularly those who have taken advantage of Judah during its time of punishment.

When dealing with the recurrence of the day of YHWH in the Book of the Twelve, three issues require evaluation: the target, the time frame, and the means. The day of YHWH describes a dramatic point of YHWH's intervention in the affairs of this world. The *target* of this intervention may be YHWH's people or foreign nations. The *timeframe* of the day can refer to some point in the immediate future that is soon to be actualized; or, it can refer to a point in the more distant future. For example, the target of the impending day of YHWH in Joel 2:1-11 is Judah and Jerusalem and the time frame is imminent, unless the people's repentance can persuade YHWH to change course. The *means* of judgment on this day is an attacking army led by YHWH himself (2:11). By contrast, Joel 4 depicts the day of YHWH in more distant temporal terms (see 3:1; 4:1 [Eng. 2:28; 3:1]) as a day of judgment on the (surrounding) nations whom YHWH will judge as a means of restoring Judah and Jerusalem. The change between these two days in Joel 2 and 4 presumes the promise of restoration based upon the positive response to a call to repent (Joel 1; 2:12-17). In other words, *if* the people repent, YHWH will restore the fertility of their land and remove the foreigners from the land so that Jerusalem will once again serve as the center of YHWH's created world. While one can debate whether to read the people's response as having occurred or whether Joel leaves the response hanging, one thing is certain: the day of YHWH in Joel 4 has not materialized by the end of Joel.

By contrast, the effects of the day of YHWH anticipated in the distant future in Joel 4 largely serve as a backdrop for *imminent* action in Zech 1. Zechariah 1:2-6 confronts the people who have returned from exile with the need for repentance, and it narrates that repentance (1:6). Thereafter, Zechariah's first vision announces that YHWH has become "very jealous for Jerusalem and for Zion" (1:14 NRSV), phraseology that is quite similar to the pivotal verse in Joel (2:18) that begins YHWH's extended response to the repentance. This vision focuses upon the impending wrath of YHWH toward the nations (1:15) and his compassion toward Jerusalem and Judah (1:17): "My cities shall again overflow with prosperity; the Lord will again comfort Zion and again choose Jerusalem" (NRSV). This change of expectations from the distant future to an imminent decision of God conveys a sense of expectation to the reader of the Twelve that a day of YHWH's intervention on behalf of Judah and Jerusalem is now possible following the repentance of the people in 1:6, in spite of the fact that the phrase "day of YHWH" does not explicitly appear. Nevertheless, YHWH tells the messenger of YHWH's intention to act on behalf of Judah and Jerusalem. In a sense, the reader of the {127} Book of the Twelve receives an invitation to contemplate YHWH's restoration of Jerusalem as a warning to the nations.

The day of YHWH's intervention can also anticipate the destruction of Jerusalem in 587. Such a meaning derives from the reader's knowledge of the story of Judah and Israel. It comes into the prophetic writings of the Book of the Twelve in Obad 11-14, which refers to the (distant) destruction of Jerusalem as the day of (its) distress and calamity. The same dynamic appears in Hab 3:16, where the impending destruction by the Babylonians is also cited as the day of calamity. Zephaniah 1:7-8, 14-16 make similar allusions to Jerusalem's destruction as the day of YHWH, combining even more terms.

The day of YHWH in the postexilic section of the Book of the Twelve takes another track. Like Joel 4, the day of YHWH in Haggai, Zechariah, and Malachi focuses upon the nations as targets of YHWH's intervention. Often, but not always, the reason for YHWH's action reflects punishment against the nations for their role in attacking Jerusalem and Judah. Zechariah 7-8 (dated two years after 1:1, 7), tells a delegation from Bethel to rejoice (7:1-3; 8:18-19) because the time of punishment is over and restoration has begun (8:9-15). This reprieve is short-lived as nations prepare to attack Judah and Jerusalem, but this time YHWH announces an intention to fight on the side of Jerusalem (9:9-13). Zechariah 12-14 contains an array of oracles depicting scenes from a distant day of YHWH when God will beat back the surrounding nations who threaten Judah and Jerusalem (12:2-9), though Jerusalem itself will also experience cleansing in this process (12:10-13:9). Nevertheless, this day of YHWH will demonstrate YHWH's power over the nations and will vindicate YHWH's selection of Jerusalem as a place of holiness (Zech 14:1-21). In the meantime, Malachi makes clear that the people have reverted to old patterns, and he confronts the people and the priests for the insincerity of their worship and their unwillingness to remain loyal to YHWH. The day of YHWH once again becomes a day that threatens YHWH's people, beginning in Mal 3. Yet something is different in the day of YHWH in Malachi. To be sure, it is a day of purification and cleansing (3:2-3), but Malachi's day of YHWH presumes a distinction will be made between the righteous and the wicked (4:1-3 [Eng. 3:19-21]). Given Malachi's relative openness to the nations (1:11,14), this distinction marks a decided theological shift in that the day of YHWH will no longer decimate the entire nation, or indiscriminately target merely foreign nations. Rather, the day of YHWH focuses upon those who reject YHWH's call to return (3:7b), and those who do not use YHWH's "book of remembrance" (3:16) to learn how to distinguish once again between the righteous and the wicked (3:18). {128}

Fertility of the Land

The fertility of the land becomes a recurring topic early in the Book of the Twelve, where Hosea depicts the land's produce as a gift from God that Israel has squandered on the worship of other deities (Hos 2).[3] As a result, God threatens to withhold the produce from the people as punishment (Hos 2; Joel 1; Amos 4:6-11). This punishment affecting the land's fertility takes two basic forms: natural calamity and the aftermath of war.

Several places depict YHWH sending, or threatening to send, natural calamities against Israel and/or Judah. These calamities include drought, blight, mildew, and locusts. Joel 1:2-2:17 and Amos 4:6-12 provide the most extensive passages of this type for Judah and Israel respectively. However, the impression left by these two passages, and their contexts, suggests very different fates await these two political entities. In Joel, Judah receives the opportunity to repent as a means of restoring fertility. While this opportunity is not explicitly actuated, the promise remains in effect. By contrast, Israel is given a chance to repent at the end of Hosea, but Amos, from the outset, assumes Israel's chance has passed. This assumption is conveyed explicitly in 4:6-11 as the result of a series of natural calamities that YHWH has used unsuccessfully to try to change Israel. Despite YHWH's attempts, the people have not returned.

This issue returns in the last three writings of the Book of the Twelve, as the issue of restoration unfolds in stages. First, Haggai assumes the land is suffering because the temple has not been restored, which means the punishment is still in effect at the beginning of Haggai (1:6,10-11) until work on the temple has begun (2:15-19). Not coincidentally, this report that temple reconstruction has begun in Haggai comes shortly after the repentance described at the beginning of Zechariah (note the date formulas in Hag 2:10, 20; Zech 1:1, 7).

Several texts also presume that the land will suffer as a result, or in the aftermath, of military invasions (Joel 1:6-7; 2:1-11; Amos 9:14; Hab

---

3. See also the contributions of Braaten, "God Sows," 104-32.

3:16-17). With the disruption of agricultural life and processes that result from war, a presumption of aggravated devastation is not surprising. This motif also plays a role in several texts where locusts and military invasions coincide, where it is difficult to distinguish which is intended. For example, Joel 1-2 refers to a series of locust plagues (1:4; 2:25), but it also refers to the same events as the result of an invading "nation" (1:6-7). Joel also portends the imminent arrival of judgment as an army attacking on the day of YHWH (2:1-11). The language of Joel, and the image of an attacking nation/locust/swarm reappears at several points in the Twelve via catchwords identifying different nations as locusts. In context, these "locust" allusions identify Assyria, Babylon, and Persia as powerful forces who have invaded the land. In Nah 3:15-17, both {129} Assyria and the enemy who will destroy it (Babylon) are compared to locusts. Habakkuk 1:9 portrays Babylon as a swarm or horde (of locusts) whose forward march cannot be stopped, an image eerily similar to the description of YHWH's army in Joel 2:4-10. Finally, Mal 3:10-11 promises restoration of rain and the removal of the "devourer" only after people bring the tithe to the temple. The "devourer" has frequently been interpreted as locust imagery. While the latter does not specifically mention Persia, the context makes this identification clear. Other images in Mal 3:10-11 evoke the promises of Joel.

The restoration of fertility after punishment (Hos 2:14; Joel 2:12-27; 4:19; Amos 9:13-14; Haggai; Zechariah; Malachi) is a sign that the relationship with YHWH has been restored. This restoration is not limited to a single redactional layer; nor can its recurrence be ignored. Hosea 2 metaphorically depicts YHWH and the land as husband and an unfaithful wife, whose infidelity involves giving her gifts to other lovers without acknowledging that YHWH was the one who had given them to her. These gifts included grain, wine, and oil (2:10 [Eng. 2:8]), which YHWH will withhold from her as punishment (2:11-15 [Eng. 2:9-13]) until such time as she faithfully recognizes YHWH as her husband and YHWH restores fertility to the land (2:23-25 [Eng. 2:21-23]). At the end of Hosea, restorative symbols of the olive tree, grain, and the vine (14:7-8 [Eng. 14:6-7]) function as signs of what YHWH will do if the people will only repent.

Joel 1-2 presents a similar dynamic wherein the current infertility of the land has affected the produce, which includes grain, wine, and oil, but which YHWH may restore if the people repent (2:12-17). Following YHWH's judgment of the nations on the day of YHWH, restoration in Joel 4:9-21 [Eng. 3:9-21] includes (grain) harvest, full vats of wine (3:13), and wine dripping from the mountains (3:18). The latter image reappears at the end of Amos (9:13), along with the hope that people will replant and rebuild (9:14).

Habakkuk also portrays the infertility of the land (3:16–17) following the invasion of the enemy as a necessary consequence of divine displeasure until YHWH chooses to destroy the enemy (3:18, referring back to YHWH's destruction of the enemy in 3:2–15). The message of Haggai claims that the rebuilding of the temple begins a time of fertility (2:15–19), but two years later (see the date in Zech 7:1), the message of Zech 8:9–12 portrays this agricultural restoration as part of a process. The current situation is better than it was "before those days" (8:10) when the temple foundation was rebuilt, because "now" (8:11) YHWH deals with the remnant differently, but "there will be" (8:12) better times still when there is peace, fruit on the vine, produce from the ground, and rain from the sky. The infertility of the {130} land in Mal 3:8–11 presupposes that even though the temple has been rebuilt, the people are once again trying to cheat YHWH by withholding their tithes and sacrifices. Only when they change their behavior, will YHWH restore the blessings of the land for the nations to see.

The Fate of God's People

In the Book of the Twelve, one finds sin, repentance, and salvation treated by means of prophetic accusations, calls to repentance, and eschatological promises of deliverance. The calls to repentance are closely associated with motifs concerned with the fertility of the land, and YHWH's restoration of the land. The land's infertility is portrayed as punishment for unethical actions (esp. against the poor) and rebellion against YHWH (esp. in worship abuses). Calls for repentance to Israel and Judah go unheeded in Hosea, Joel, and Amos despite extended promises of YHWH's beneficent acts. As a result, the threat of punishment becomes increasingly prominent through Zephaniah. By contrast, actuated repentance takes hold in Haggai/Zechariah, though only for a time, during which YHWH moves to restore the land's fertility and reputation. Set after the rebuilding of the temple, Malachi returns to the situation with which the Book of the Twelve began. The infidelity of people and priests again affects what they are willing to bring as offerings to YHWH. The situation has largely returned to the paradigm of the people and priests described in Hosea. Still, YHWH remains ready to restore the fertility of the land in Malachi, if the people choose to bring the tithe into the storehouse as a test of YHWH's fidelity (3:8–12, a passage that once again echoes the images of Joel 1–2). As a result, YHWH promises to "open the windows of heaven for you and pour down for you an overflowing blessing" (Mal 3:10 NRSV; see Joel 2:14, 23–24), and to remove "the devourer" (Mal 3:11; see Joel 1:4; 2:25). The Book of the Twelve concludes with admonitions for the YHWH-fearers (3:16–18), with anticipation of a day of YHWH when the wicked will be punished (3:19–21 [Eng. 4:1–3]), and with an exhortation to live in accordance with YHWH's *torah* and *nebi'im* ("prophets;" 3:22–23 [Eng. 4:4–5]).

The fate of God's people thus involves several thematic elements interwoven through the corpus, elements that often play heavily upon one's knowledge of the story of Israel and Judah. These elements include distinctions between the Northern and Southern Kingdoms (esp. in Hosea, Amos, Micah, and Zephaniah), the relative sparsity of references to human kings in any of the prophetic material, God's use of other nations to punish Israel and Judah, God's compassion toward the nations, and God's restoration of the centrality of Zion. {131}

From near the beginning, the Book of the Twelve distinguishes between the Northern and Southern Kingdoms, in a manner reminiscent of the attitude found in 1 Kgs 12–2 Kgs 17. The similarity is not created by linguistic formulations so much as by conceptual similarities. Hosea and Amos focus on the fate of the Northern Kingdom, but one periodically finds notes embedded in the text, either organic to the context or from a redactor, that incorporate Judah (Hos 1:7, 11; 4:15; 5:13–14; 6:4, 11; 8:14; 10:11; 11:12; 12:2), or add warnings for Judah (Amos 2:4–5; 5:5 [Beersheba]). Even promises given to Israel in Hosea and Amos have an edge to them because the promises indicate a Judean preference (Hos 1:11; 3:5; Amos 9:11–15). By the time one gets to Micah, the reader is reminded that the Northern Kingdom has been destroyed (Mic 1:2–7) and that Judah had better pay attention if it hopes to avoid the same fate (3:12 which alludes to 1:5–7). Zephaniah functions for Judah much like Amos did for Israel. The time of decision has largely passed, and Judah's destruction becomes unavoidable.

In the Book of the Twelve, kings play a decidedly smaller role in the action of the writings than in other prophetic corpora except, perhaps, Ezekiel. Despite their role in the chronological pattern of the superscriptions, kings rarely appear as characters in the oracles themselves.[4] This

---

4. See Paul L. Redditt, "The King in Haggai-Zechariah 1–8 and the Book of the Twelve," in *Tradition in Transition: Haggai and Zechariah 1–8 in the Trajectory of*

contrasts markedly with Jeremiah and Isaiah, both of which contain several narratives portraying the prophet engaging the king directly. In the Book of the Twelve, only the brief account in Amos 7:10-17 comes close to this kind of engagement, but even there the king is absent, and the prophet only deals with the king's representative, Amaziah the chief priest at Bethel. Hosea contains a few oracles directed against the king or the king's family (5:1; 7:3; 10:7), and several which reject kingship for the Northern Kingdom as punishment (3:4; 7:7; 8:4; 8:10; 11:5; 13:10-11). Micah has only one clear reference to the king of Judah (4:9), but this reference concerns the exile of that king in an oracle directed to Lady Zion who will be exiled to Babylon (see 4:10). Zephaniah makes an interesting transition in that the coming day of YHWH will affect "the officials and the king's sons" (1:8). Later, in the eschatological, salvific additions to the book (3:14-20), YHWH enters Jerusalem as king (3:15). This change from a human king to YHWH as king largely replaces language about kingship in the remainder of the Twelve (Zech 9:9; 14:9, 10, 16, 17; Mal 1:14). Thus, the Book of the Twelve exhibits a dynamic similar to that found in the Psalms, where royal connotations in books 4 and 5 (Pss 90-106, 107-150, respectively) are associated with YHWH, not with human kings.

The movement from Micah to Nahum to Habakkuk to Zephaniah anticipates God's use of Assyria to punish Judah (Micah), followed by the destruction of Assyria (Nah 2-3) by the {132} Babylonians, who then will be used by YHWH to punish Judah and the surrounding nations (Hab 1-2; Zeph 1:1-3:8), before YHWH intervenes against Babylon (Hab 3:1-15). Words of prophetic hope in these sections (Hab 3:16-20; Zeph 3:11-20) presume that the hope they offer is directed only to the remnant that survives the coming judgment. This section of the Book of the Twelve, it must be borne in mind, is neither the beginning nor the end of the story.

In addition, this punishment by other nations appears in the recurring taunts and promises of restitution. God's people will be taunted by other nations seeking to take advantage of Judah's status (Mic 6:16). These nations will come to see that God will once again come to the aid of God's people (Joel 2:17, 19, 25; 4:1-21 [Eng. 3:1-21]; Obad 10-14, 15-21; Zeph 2:8; 3:18; Zech 1:9-17; 12-14). This motif occasionally intersects with the day of YHWH. Related to this promise that the nations who have taunted

---

Hebrew Theology, ed. Mark J. Boda and Michael H. Floyd, LHBOTS 475 (New York: T&T Clark, 2008), 56-82.

and taken advantage of Judah will be punished are periodic promises of the return of the possessions/captives (Hos 6:11; Joel 4:1 [Eng. 3:1]; Amos 9:14; Zeph 2:7; 3:20). With the exception of Joel, these other passages are often treated as editorial additions to the books in which they appear, but they provide sustaining elements of hope to the corpus as a whole.

The Theodicy Problem

The theodicy problem, especially as framed by Exod 34:6–7, raises questions about justice and retribution, and about grace and recompense on God's part.[5] In addition, the role of human responsibility reverberates with concepts of righteousness and justice. Exodus 34:6–7 forms the literary backdrop for several texts that explore issues surrounding judgment of the nation and God's justice. Four texts in the Book of the Twelve take up portions of Exod 34:6–7 explicitly: Joel 2:13; Nah 1:3; Jonah 4:2; and Mic 7:18–20. Joel 2:13 forms part of the culmination of an extended call to repentance in 2:12–17. It represents the theological rationale for why Joel 1–2 extends the call to repent, namely, by interpreting YHWH's response against a tendency to show grace and mercy toward those who petition YHWH to do so. In so doing, Joel 2:13 focuses only upon YHWH's positive attributes discussed in Exod 34:6–7a. Joel 4:21 (Eng. 3:21), the concluding verse of the book, comments upon the judgment against the nations on the day of YHWH described in Joel 4:9–20 (Eng. 3:9–20) by evoking the theme of Exod 34:7b. Joel 4:21 changes the recipient by reflecting upon the day of YHWH as a day of punishment for the nations *after* Judah has been punished. Together, Joel 2:13 and 4:21 combine both parts of Exod 34:6–7, highlighting YHWH's patience and wrath. {133}

Nahum 1:3 alludes to Exod 34:6–7 for other reasons. Nahum 1:3 mentions YHWH's patience (YHWH is slow to anger, Exod 34:6), emphasizes YHWH's power (not present in Exod 34:6–7), and then describes YHWH's recompense (using Exod 34:7b). These selections are not accidental, but fit the message of Nahum where Assyria, the political power that destroyed Israel at YHWH's behest, now has the tables turned. Nahum assumes Assyria has overstepped its mandate from YHWH by oppressing Judah and Jerusalem (Amos 6:14; see also Isa 9–10). Nahum's prophetic message

---

5. The first to make this connection was Van Leeuwen, "Scribal Wisdom," 31–49. See also James L. Crenshaw, "Theodicy in the Book of the Twelve," in Redditt, *Thematic Threads*, 175–91.

is that YHWH's *patience* has now run out and that Assyria will be *held to account*. These are precisely the two points highlighted by Nah 1:3 in the selective citation of Exod 34:6-7.

Jonah 4:2 (like Joel 2:13) draws upon YHWH's positive attributes described in Exod 34:6-7, but for yet another theological purpose. Jonah 4:2 uses Exod 34:6-7 to satirize the theological position that YHWH only exercises these positive attributes in relationship to Israel. The comic portrayal of Jonah, who would rather die from heat stroke than see Assyrians benefit from God's grace, mercy, and loving-kindness, upholds the appropriateness of YHWH's compassion "even for the nations" by satirizing the character of Jonah, thereby undercutting one reading of the theology of much of the Book of the Twelve.

Micah 7:18-20 draws upon Exod 34:6-7 more obliquely. YHWH

> *pardons iniquity,* passes over *transgression* ... and does not retain his anger forever, because he delights in showing *clemency* [*ḥesed*]. He will again have compassion upon us. He will tread our *iniquities* under foot. You will cast our sins into the depths of the sea. You will show *faithfulness* to Jacob and *unswerving loyalty* [*ḥesed*] to Abraham as you have shown to our ancestors from the days of old. (emphasis added)

The words, phrases, and combinations suggest that Mic 7:18-20 draws upon Exod 34:6-7. In addition, Mic 7:19 alludes to Jonah 2:4 (Eng. 2:3).

The framework created by these Exodus allusions highlights theodicy, but other texts in the Twelve also raise these issues without direct citation of Exod 34:6-7. Habakkuk 1:2-4 opens the book with a cry to YHWH typical of personal complaints, "How long, O Lord, shall I cry for help...?" The subject matter of the passage is often classified as wisdom related. The prophet complains about the injustice and violence (1:2-3) perpetrated by Judeans against other Judeans. This petition leads to a surprising response from YHWH in 1:5-11 wherein YHWH promises to send the Babylonians to punish the country so that the current violence will seem mild by comparison (1:9). By itself, this response appears out of proportion, especially because the genre of 1:2-4 makes one think of personal attacks, but {134} the response from YHWH is corporate and national. Thus, the complaint and response are typically interpreted as representing the state of the nation as a whole. Two issues from the Book of the Twelve reinforce this interpretation. First, the location of Habakkuk between Nahum and Zephaniah means that the movement of these three books deals in broad strokes with the end of the Assyrian empire, YHWH's sending of Babylon as a military force, and the destruction of Judah, respectively. Second, the pronouncement that YHWH is about to send the Babylonians as punishment parallels a similar pronouncement by YHWH (Amos 6:14) against the Northern Kingdom. While the Amos text does not mention Assyria by name, the identity of the nation whom YHWH promises to raise can hardly be interpreted as any nation other than Assyria.

The book of Malachi is structured around several disputations that culminate in a statement of purpose (3:16–18). In between, the disputations portray a postexilic situation where the people behave in a manner quite similar to the way that Hosea began. Neither the people nor the priests have learned how to worship YHWH properly. Malachi 3:16–18 changes YHWH's response to the nation's recalcitrance.

The concluding sections of Malachi move from judgment against the entire nation to a presumption that YHWH will punish the wicked while "those who fear YHWH's name" will fight on YHWH's behalf (Mal 3:19–21 [Eng. 4:1–3]). With Mal 3:16–18, the disputation genre ceases. In its place, the reader finds a report:

> Then those who revered the Lord spoke with one another. The Lord took note and listened, and a book of remembrance was written before him for those who revered the Lord and thought on his name. So that they shall be mine says the Lord of hosts, my special possession on the day when I act, and I will spare them as parents spare their children who serve them. *So that you shall again distinguish between the righteous and the wicked,* between one who serves God and one who does not serve him. (Mal 3:16–18, emphasis added)

Two issues are important for bringing some resolution to the motif: the nature of the "book of remembrance" and the purposive syntactical relationship of these three verses. Most English translations misrepresent the actions of these verses because they presume that the "book of remembrance" is essentially identical to the "book of life," meaning that it contains the names of those whom YHWH will remember at the time of judgment. However, the closest parallel appears in Esth 6:1, where the "book of remembrances" was read to the king when he could not sleep. The content of this book contained records of past events that the king wanted to recall later. It was not a list of names. Moreover, the book of remembrance {135} in Mal 3:16 was written before YHWH (*ləpānāyw*) for those revering him (ləyir'ê yhwh). In other words, the book was not for YHWH but for the YHWH fearers. Again, most English translations miss the purpose of the book because they assume it functions like the book of life recording the names of the pious until the time of the final judgment. In actuality, 3:18 states the purpose of the book: it was written for those fearing YHWH. It allows the YHWH fearers to distinguish between the righteous and the wicked. In other words, this book has an instructional purpose for the faithful. In this instance, this book is not recorded for the king (YHWH) to read later but for the subjects (the YHWH fearers), and it does not "remember" their deeds, but records the word of YHWH about which they are to contemplate in order to distinguish between righteousness and wickedness and to encourage them to continue to serve YHWH. It is no great stretch to conceptualize the Book of the Twelve as a book of remembrance, remembrance of YHWH's patience (ḥesed) and grace, as well as YHWH's commitment to punish the guilty.

Implications for Readers of the Book of the Twelve

Reading the Book of the Twelve provides a context to hear an ongoing dialogue, a dialogue between God and God's people mediated through twelve prophetic voices. This dialogue highlights God's righteousness, God's compassion, and God's expectations of justice. It challenges people to return to YHWH, who is the source of all that is good, and to recognize the gifts that YHWH has bestowed in the form of the land's fertility. It presents God as king of the world, whose power to manipulate nations (both friend and foe) for divine purpose is beyond dispute. It reminds God's people that God's beneficence has a contingent quality that demands they demonstrate their recognition of YHWH as king, benefactor, protector, and judge.

Reflection upon this message provides information to "those who fear YHWH," since this book of remembrance teaches YHWH's people how to "distinguish between the righteous and the wicked" (Mal 3:18). In modern parlance, perhaps, the Book of the Twelve offers an antidote to the old adage that whoever does not learn the lessons of history is condemned to repeat them.

Righteousness and justice—how one relates to God and human beings—are the hallmarks by which humanity in general, and God's people in particular, shall be evaluated. The prophets challenge God's people in times of crises in order to elicit a change in behavior. When people worship gods who do not control the world, consequences ensue. When {136} people treat the poor as commodities, consequences ensue. These two foci remind readers of the Twelve of their own responsibility to behave as those who fear YHWH, who learn to distinguish between the righteous and the wicked, and who live accordingly.

Repentance, not pride, in the face of calamity and threat offers the only hope that YHWH will intervene to thwart, stall, stop, or repair a damaged people. Hosea, Joel, Amos, Jonah, Zechariah, and Malachi all underscore the need to repent before YHWH, to change behavior, and to change attitudes toward God and humanity. The Book of the Twelve presumes that calamity comes from YHWH as punishment for rebellion against YHWH, or mistreatment of other human beings. The crimes for which God's people must repent include the use of idolatrous elements in worship (Hosea, Micah, Zephaniah, and Malachi), not paying attention to worship/temple issues (Haggai), and issues surrounding social ethics (Hosea, Amos, and Habakkuk).

Restoration begins when proper attention is paid to YHWH. From the resignation of Habakkuk (3:16-19), which sees hope, but only after devastation, to the responsibility and accountability underscored by Amos and Zephaniah, the writings in the Book of the Twelve pronounce judgment, but also end in hope for life beyond punishment, hope that life can improve. Repentance leads to rebuilding in Haggai/Zech 1-8, then to reconstituting relationships and realities in Zech 9-14. Refertilization of the land plays a major role, as well, in Hosea (2; 14), Joel, Amos, Habakkuk, Haggai, Zechariah, and Malachi.

Remembering is the theme at the beginning and end of Malachi. Remembering God's promise to punish Edom (Mal 1:2-5), reflecting upon what God has done in this book of remembrance (3:16-18), and recalling an even bigger story involving Moses and Elijah (4:4-5 [Eng. 3:22-23]) offers hope for those who fear YHWH. This hope, in Malachi, is not a naïve optimism, but a reminder that God has not abandoned God's people, even though the people have returned to acting much like the people in Hosea. Thus, judgment and hope remain in tension at the end of the Book of the Twelve, a tension that is never resolved, because it deals with the human condition and the relationship of humans to the deity. Those who fear YHWH, who remember what YHWH has done, and who turn to YHWH for help and strength, will find instruction and hope in the midst of life, while those determined to go their own way should know that this God of compassion does not leave the guilty unpunished. The great and terrible day of YHWH functions as both warning and comfort, depending upon what one has learned from this story (Mal 4:5 [Eng. 3:23]).

Jerusalem, Samaria, and Bethel in the Book of the Twelve

One of the recurring motifs in the Book of the Twelve concerns the fate of the nation, or perhaps better said, the fate of YHWH's people.[1] The fate of the nation can be treated either explicitly or implicitly in prophetic literature. Explicit references to Judah and/or Israel in the Book of the Twelve are certainly present and require attention. However, implicit references to the fate of Judah and/or Israel in the Book of the Twelve should not be overlooked. Redditt has already explored the role of the king in various stages of the collection that comes to be known as the Book of the Twelve,[2] but less work has been done on the extent to which the cities of Jerusalem, Bethel, and Samaria function to signify the fate of YHWH's people.[3] Before turning to the Book of the Twelve specifically, a few words are in order about the distribution of terms across the Hebrew canon when distinguishing the Southern and Northern Kingdoms from one another.

Distribution

These terms of identity are not evenly distributed across the canonical parts of the Hebrew Bible. Nevertheless, the presence or absence within canonical sections tells a story that says something about the literature comprising the Hebrew canon as a brief survey of the terms Judah, Jerusalem/Zion, Bethel, and Samaria will show. {252}

---

1. See Nogalski, "Recurring Themes in the Book of the Twelve," 125-36.
2. Redditt, "King in Haggai-Zechariah 1-8," 56-82.
3. Here I wish to extend my thanks to Aaron Schart for the opportunity to contribute to this volume celebrating the city of Essen as *Kulturstadt Europas* during the year 2010.

-195-

Judah

Judah appears only forty-seven times in the Pentateuch, and more than half of those (twenty-six) appear in the book of Genesis, with all but two of those (29:35; 35:23) appearing in the Joseph cycle referring to the son of Jacob and his descendants. The term never appears in Leviticus, while it appears only four times in Deuteronomy and in Exodus, and it appears thirteen times in Numbers.

By contrast, Judah appears 231 times in the Deuteronomistic History (or Former Prophets), but over half of those (139x) appear in the narrative about the monarchy, 1–2 Kings. Relatedly, Joshua and Judges combined account for only slightly more explicit references to Judah (49x) than does Samuel by itself (43x).

Equally significantly, Judah is mentioned 289 times in the Latter Prophets, but again the distribution is by no means consistent: Jeremiah mentions Judah 180 times; the Book of the Twelve mentions Judah 63 times; the book of Isaiah refers to Judah 31 times (but 27 of those appear in chapters 1–39); and Ezekiel mentions Judah only 15 times explicitly.

Judah appears some 255 times in the Ketuvim, but 224 of those appear in Chronicles (183x) and Ezra-Nehemiah (14x and 27x respectively). Most of the references in Chronicles occur in parallels to Kings material.

In summary, "Judah" plays a much more prominent role in the Neviim (Former and Latter Prophets) than in the other parts of the canon. This emphasis becomes even more prominent when one considers the distribution of Jerusalem and Zion, two terms used for the capital city of Judah.

Jerusalem

Jerusalem was the capital of Judah, and in many respects, represents the center—politically, religiously, and ideologically—for the entire Hebrew canon, despite the fact that the city is never mentioned explicitly in the Torah.

While "Jerusalem" does not appear explicitly in the Pentateuch, its presence is felt implicitly in several ways. First, Moriah represents the distant mountain site in Gen 22:2 to which Abraham took Isaac in the famous scene of the binding of his young son to offer him for sacrifice before YHWH withdrew the command. Yet, according to 2 Chr 3:1, this very mountain represents the place where Solomon ultimately built the temple.

Second, most readers, ancient and modern, would intuitively associate the commands for building the tabernacle and the narrative report of the building in Exod 25–31 and 35–40 as an oblique allusion to the temple in Jerusalem, or perhaps more accurately, to the Second Temple in Jerusalem.

Third, while Jerusalem is never mentioned, one of the Torah's key ideological passages appears in Deut 12, which describes the ultimate goal {253} of the wilderness wandering. This passage anticipates that the goal will be to find the "place that YHWH will choose." This place will be the place that will bear YHWH's name; it will become the site upon which to build a temple fit for YHWH. The fact that this temple is not built until the time of Solomon (1 Kgs 5–8) according to the epic narrative that extends from Genesis to Kings is of little consequence for the reader of Deut 12. Jerusalem's central place becomes the focus for the combined wilderness and conquest traditions because it represents the apex of the David and Solomon story, in the form of a divine fiat that drives Israel across the Jordan, that motivates the taking of the land, and that helps to explain the selection of a second king, David, whose decision to locate the palace in Jerusalem (2 Sam 4–6) paves the way for his son to build the temple (2 Sam 7; 1 Kgs 8).

Jerusalem appears explicitly far more frequently in the Former Prophets (137x), but the vast majority of those references (122/137) occur in the narrative between 2 Sam 5–2 Kgs 25, or from the time David takes Jerusalem until its destruction. On one level, this distribution is not surprising, given that the narrative episodes of the patriarchs, the Exodus stories, the conquest accounts, and the tales of the Judges largely recount stories that are either based upon local etiological traditions or upon narratives literarily set outside the land. On another level, though, given the fact that the larger narrative runs from Genesis through 2 Kings, this distribution is somewhat surprising: prior to 2 Sam 5, the epic narrative of Israel and Judah contains only fifteen explicit references to the city that would become the capital of the Davidic dynasty for roughly four hundred years.

As a group, the Latter Prophets demonstrate a more prominent and more sustained interest in Jerusalem than any other part of the canon, as evidenced by the 250 times the city is mentioned explicitly (51x in Isaiah, 66x in the Book of the Twelve, 107x in Jeremiah, and only 26x in Ezekiel whose literary setting in Babylon causes the narrator to refer to Jerusalem by name only periodically). These references nearly double those of the Former Prophets.

The 283 explicit references to Jerusalem in the Ketuvim are more numerous than the Former Prophets or the Latter Prophets individually, but once again this number does not tell the whole story since all but 43 of these references appear in three books: the narrative that runs from Chronicles (149x) to Ezra (49x) to Nehemiah (38x). By contrast, only Psalms (16x) and Daniel (10x) explicitly mention Jerusalem 10 or more times in the Ketuvim.

In summary, explicit reference to "Jerusalem" occurs more frequently in the Latter Prophets than in any canonical section of the Old Testament, though the 122 references to Jerusalem in the narrative block from 2 Sam–2 Kgs 25 or in the 236 references in the Chronicler's narrative (149x in 1–2 Chr; {254} 49x in Ezra; 38x in Nehemiah) also show a pronounced interest in the city.

Zion

One finds that the term "Zion" displays many of the same distribution patterns as the explicit references to Jerusalem, except that the term appears far less frequently and it appears primarily in poetic contexts. Consequently, "Zion" never appears in the Pentateuch and appears only four times in the Former Prophets (and none of these appear prior to 2 Sam 5). By contrast, "Zion" appears in the Latter Prophets (92x) more than the Writings (57x), the Former Prophets (4x), and the Pentateuch (0x) combined. In the Ketuvim, the poetic character of Zion can also be noted clearly in the Chronicler's narrative which refers to Jerusalem explicitly 236 times while those same writings refer to "Zion" only twice (1 Chr 11:5; 2 Chr 5:2). By contrast, the 39 references to "Zion" in Psalms more than doubles the 16 references to Jerusalem in the same book. Similarly, Lamentations refers to Jerusalem explicitly only 7 times while it refers to "Zion" more than twice as frequently (15x).

Distribution of the term "Zion" in the Latter Prophets is a bit different than those of "Jerusalem" in that Ezekiel never uses "Zion" while the frequency of the term in the other three prophetic books is inverted in comparison to "Jerusalem."

Jerusalem *Zion*
Jeremiah: 107x   Isaiah: 45x
The Twelve: 66x   The Twelve: 30x
Isaiah: 51x   Jeremiah: 17x

Ezekiel: 26x   Ezekiel: 0x
Total: 250   **Total: 92**

The two terms are almost evenly divided in Isaiah, but *Jerusalem* appears just over twice as many times in the Book of the Twelve as does *Zion*. *Jerusalem* appears more than three times as often than *Zion* in Jeremiah.

Bethel

The city of Bethel manifests quite an interesting distribution pattern. It appears almost as many times in the Pentateuch (12x in the Abraham and Jacob cycles) as it does in the Latter Prophets (11x, but ten of those are in the Book of the Twelve). By contrast roughly four times as many references appear in the Former Prophets (45x times) as in either of those canonical sections, while the Ketuvim refer to Bethel only five times (2x in Chronicles and Nehemiah; 1x in Ezra). The scarcity of references in the Ketuvim is largely {255} related to the Chronicler's editorial decision not to include material concerning kings from the Northern Kingdom in the narrative portions that parallel Samuel and Kings. The majority of the twenty-two references in Kings appear in the editorial condemnations of the northern kings for building and maintaining sanctuaries at Bethel and Dan that rival the temple in Jerusalem. These references are omitted in Chronicles systematically.

The appearance of ten of the eleven references to Bethel among the Latter Prophets within the Book of the Twelve is both statistically significant and literarily distinctive for this prophetic corpus. And yet, Bethel appears in only three of the Twelve: Hosea (2x), Amos (7x), and Zechariah (1x). In addition, though, Hosea uses the name Beth-aven three times (4:15; 5:8; 10:5) to condemn Bethel in a play on words. Bethel means house "house of God," while "Beth-aven" means "house of wickedness."

Samaria

The distribution pattern of explicit references to Samaria, which can refer to the city or the region surrounding it, reflects the narrative structure of the Torah, the Former Prophets, and the Ketuvim as well as a decidedly negative ideology toward the Northern Kingdom in the Deuteronomistic history. The Pentateuch contains no explicit mention of "Samaria," and all 69 references to "Samaria" in the Former Prophets appear in the book of

Kings, specifically after 1 Kgs 13:32, where the judgment oracle against Bethel by the anonymous "man of God" foreshadows doom for all the "cities of Samaria." From there, most of the remaining references refer to the capital city established by Omri (1 Kgs 16:23-24), which soon became the location of the temple and an altar dedicated to Baal that was established by Omri's son Ahab according to 1 Kgs 16:29-32.

All eleven of the explicit references to "Samaria" in the Ketuvim appear in the Chronicler's History (8x), Ezra (2x), and Nehemiah (1x). As in the Deuteronomistic History, most of these references assume some kind of negative assessment of Samaria, but the number of direct connections between the edited units in Chronicles and Kings is rather limited because the Chronicler systematically omits stories about the northern kings.

The majority of references to Samaria in the Latter Prophets assume the city as the referent, though a few passages more likely assume the region. In the Book of the Twelve, Samaria is both a region and a city. For example, Hos 10:5 refers to the "inhabitants of Samaria" who tremble before "the calf of Beth-aven." Literally, Beth-aven means "house of guilt," but it is a derogatory term to refer to Bethel, the location of one of the alternative shrines established by Jeroboam I (922-901 BCE). In Hos 10:5, "the inhabitants of Samaria" probably intends the broader region and not merely the city, because Bethel is {256} located within the region Samaria and the specific reference in 10:5 to the "inhabitants of Samaria" includes condemnation of the calf of Beth-aven (= Bethel). Similarly, the term "mountain of Samaria" (Amos 3:9; 4:1; 6:1) could refer to the broader region (as the phrase "mountains of Samaria" almost certainly does in Jer 31:5), but since the city stood atop a mountain, the phrase could intend only the city and its immediate environs.

Conclusion

From this survey of distribution patterns for Judah, Jerusalem, Zion, Samaria, and Bethel, two things should be clear. First, reference to these entities changes depending upon the literary context within the two grand canonical narratives (Genesis-Kings; Chronicles-Nehemiah) or in the individual prophetic scrolls. Second, outside the narrative literature, the prophetic books have a decided emphasis on (some of) these terms more than the remainder of the canonical writings. The remainder of this paper will now look at the role of Jerusalem, Bethel, and Samaria in the Book of the Twelve.

The Fate of Samaria, Bethel, and Jerusalem in the Book of the Twelve

In the Book of the Twelve, the fates of Samaria and Bethel, on the one hand, and Jerusalem/Zion, on the other hand, change as one moves across the corpus. In part, these changes reflect the interests of the individual writings wherein they appear, but they also periodically interact with other writings in the Twelve in ways that suggest editorial involvement. Consequently, these changes should have an effect upon the reader of the Book of the Twelve.

Samaria and Bethel

Samaria and Bethel function within significant portions of the Book of the Twelve as ciphers, or metaphors, for the Northern Kingdom. The metaphorical function connecting these cities with prophetic condemnation and the fate of the kingdom is not surprising since their prominence in the biblical text results from the fact that Samaria was the political capital and Bethel was the primary religious center of the Northern Kingdom, located not far from the capital Samaria in Ephraimite territory.

It is also not surprising to find Samaria and Bethel explicitly mentioned in Hosea and Amos, the two writings in the Book of the Twelve that deal prominently with the fate of the Northern Kingdom. Surprisingly, perhaps, both Bethel and Samaria play a more prominent role in the Book of the Twelve than in {257} any other prophetic corpus. Bethel appears eleven times in the Latter Prophets, and all but one of them occur in the Book of the Twelve. Samaria appears fifteen times in the Book of the Twelve, while no other prophetic writing mentions Samaria more than eight times.[4]

The fate of Samaria and Bethel in Hosea and Amos is clearly driven by the events of 722 and the Assyrian overthrow of the Northern Kingdom. Most of the references to Samaria or Bethel anticipate their destruction as punishment from YHWH for religious or political failures. Hosea and Amos condemn religious practice in Samaria and Bethel for the failure of

---

4. Samaria appears eight times in Isaiah, almost exclusively in chs. 7–10 (only 36:19—a text that parallels 2 Kgs 18:34—refers to Samaria outside of these chapters). Ezekiel mentions Samaria six times, but only in two chapters (16:46, 51, 53, 55 and 23:4, 33) where Samaria is personified as the sister of Lady Jerusalem. Samaria is mentioned only three times in Jeremiah (23:13; 31:5; 41:5).

the Northern Kingdom to worship properly (which means the failure to recognize that only worship conducted in the Jerusalem temple is legitimate).

Hosea

Implicitly, in many cases, the political system of the Northern Kingdom is assumed to be illegitimate in the eyes of the prophet, or the tradents who compiled the prophetic sayings. Hosea 8:4-6 illustrates both the religious and political aspects of this prophetic condemnation. Israel created kings whom YHWH did not recognize, and these kings created idols (8:4). YHWH will destroy the "calf of Samaria" (8:5-6). This text mentions Samaria explicitly, but the condemnation also includes Bethel since it is Bethel in Samaria where Jeroboam I erected a calf statue to keep the residents of the Northern Kingdom from traveling to Jerusalem to worship and to keep the inhabitants of Israel from looking to the descendants of David for political allegiance (1 Kgs 12:25-30).

Hosea 10:1-15 also brings these dual emphases of guilt created by a non-Davidic king and by Israel's religious practices. Several references to Israel's illegitimate religious practices appear: altars and pillars (10:1-2), the calf of Beth-aven (= Bethel, 10:5), the high places of Beth-aven (= Bethel, as noted by the descriptive phrase "the sin of Israel") and their altars (10:8). The impotence and guilt of Israel's king (10:3) leads to Israel's exile by Assyria's king (10:6) and the death of Samaria's king (10:7). The chapter concludes with a summary statement condemning the wickedness of Bethel and the king of Israel (10:15), who lives in Samaria. In fact, the wicked deeds of Samaria (רעה plural in 7:1) and the wickedness of Bethel (רעה singular in 10:15) are intertwined as the first and last references to these two places in Hosea, with the exception of the literary allusion to Bethel as the place of Jacob's dream in Hos 12:4. {258}

Amos

In Amos, the guilt of Bethel and Samaria also plays a major role in sealing the fate of the Northern Kingdom. In many of the references to Samaria in Amos (3:9, 12; 4:1; 6:1; 8:14), Samaria refers to the region more than the city, but presumes a devastating destruction is coming. Amos 3:9; 4:1; 6:1 all use the term "mountain of Samaria" to refer to the region, while 3:12 refers to the people of Israel who live in Samaria. Most of the Amos references to Samaria presume ethical misconduct as the primary cause for judgment,[5] but in a couple of places cultic impropriety seems to connect Samaria and Bethel with condemnation of the cult or the king. Amos 8:14 refers to the "Ashimah of Samaria" in parallel to Dan, which obviously condemns Bethel since Bethel and Dan represent the two sanctuaries of Jeroboam I and "Ashimah" means "guilt."

Explicit references to Bethel in Amos also condemn religious practices associated with the northern shrine. Particularly noteworthy in this respect is the rejection of the "altars [plural] of Bethel" that results in a pronouncement of punishment in Amos 3:14. This punishment essentially echoes the pronouncement of Hos 10:8 which anticipates the destruction of the "high places of Aven" (= Bethel) whose "altars" (plural) will be overrun with weeds.

Religious practices at Bethel and Gilgal are explicitly condemned in Amos 4:4 and 5:5. The condemnation of Bethel in 5:5 is followed in 5:6 by a call to "seek YHWH and live" before YHWH, like fire, devours Bethel.

Finally, the narrative of the confrontation between Amos and Amaziah in 7:10–17, inserted between the third and fourth vision, also demonstrates the close connection of Bethel with the condemnation of the king of Israel. In this brief narrative episode Amaziah, the chief priest at Bethel, rejects the word of YHWH delivered by Amos. In so doing, Amaziah commands Amos never to prophesy at Bethel again, because "it is the *king's sanctuary*, and it is a temple of the kingdom" (7:13 NRSV, emphasis added).

Elsewhere in the Book of the Twelve

Outside of Amos and Hosea in the Book of the Twelve, Samaria and Bethel also play a significant role. First, Samaria's role in Micah plays a purely editorial function whose purpose is to link the pronouncements of Amos and Hosea against Samaria with Micah's warning to Jerusalem that it will face a similar fate to Samaria. The superscription in Mic 1:1 labels Micah as the word of YHWH "concerning Samaria and Jerusalem." Yet Samaria is only mentioned {259} in Mic 1:5–6 where Samaria's destruction is used as a warning to Jerusalem. These references in 1:5–6 echo the language of Amos and Hosea.[6] Further, Mic 1:6 announces that Samaria will/has

---

5. Note the condemnation of the "cows of Bashan who live in Samaria" (4:1) who are condemned for oppressing the poor and crushing the needy.

6. The "transgression" of Jacob in Mic 1:5 recalls the language of the refrain "for three transgressions and for four" that appears prominently in Amos 1–2 and the lan-

become a pile of rubble in the field, an image which forms the culmination of the first part of the book in 3:12, when that image is applied to Zion/ Jerusalem which will be plowed like a field and become a heap of ruins.

The only other reference to Samaria in the Book of the Twelve appears in Obad 19, in which the "field of Samaria" appears in the promise to reconstitute the Davidic kingdom. Obadiah 19–20, or portions thereof, have often been treated as later supplements to one of the two primary oracular collections that comprise the book (1–14, 15b; 15a, 16–21). This is the only reference to the "field of Samaria" in the entire Hebrew Bible, which makes its appearance so close to Micah quite intriguing.[7] At any rate, there is little doubt that the reference to Samaria in Obad 19 concerns a promise for the reconstitution of the ideal borders of the united kingdom. Lands that had been depopulated from the time of the Assyrians onward would be repopulated and Jerusalem would be the center of this kingdom.

Bethel appears only once outside Hosea and Amos in the Book of the Twelve. Significantly, the lone reference to Bethel appears in Zech 7:2 which reports that a delegation from Bethel approached the priests and prophets in Jerusalem to determine whether it was time to stop bemoaning the destruction of Jerusalem, since temple reconstruction had begun in earnest. This question frames the sayings that make up the bulk of Zech 7–8, and consequently one has to go nearly all the way to the end of chapter 8 to find a definitive response to this question, but 8:18–19 makes clear that the question is answered affirmatively. There is no context to understand the motives of this {260} delegation, but this enigmatic question and response seems at least to

---

guage of "the wages of a prostitute" echoes the language of Hos 2:14 [Eng. 2:12]. For more complete treatment of these allusions see Schart, *Entstehung des Zwölfprophetenbuchs*, 177–81; and Nogalski, *Literary Precursors*, 137–41.

7. In most of the models attempting to describe the redactional history of the Book of the Twelve, Jonah appears quite late in the process. If the relatively late addition of Jonah is correct, then Obadiah presumably appeared between Amos and Micah for some time. See Nogalski, *Redactional Processes*, 255–62; Schart, *Entstehung des Zwölfprophetenbuchs*, 289–91, 305–6; Wöhrle, *Abschluss des Zwölfprophetenbuches*, 393–96, 400–419. Given the prediction in Mic 1:6 that Samaria would become a heap of ruins in the "field," it's conceivable—though admittedly not provable—that the phrasing in Obad 19 could be influenced by Mic 1:6. If so, the phrase "field of Samaria" should not be understood as a neutral designation of the area so much as a term indicating a devastated region.

open the possibility for religious reconciliation between Bethel and Jerusalem with the reconstruction of Jerusalem temple. The lack of negative pronouncements against Bethel here stands out in prophetic literature. It suggests that the compilation took place at a point when prospects for harmonious relations between Samarian territory and Judah seemed more hopeful than they would be later in the Persian period (or during the time of the divided monarchy).

In summary, Bethel and Samaria function primarily as ciphers for the religious and political problems of the Northern Kingdom in Hosea and Amos, and these problems threaten Jerusalem itself in Micah. By contrast, the two later references to Samaria (Obad 19) and to Bethel (Zech 7:2) open the door for political reincorporation and religious reconciliation in a reconstituted Davidic kingdom.

The Fate of Jerusalem and Zion in the Book of the Twelve

Lady Zion as a Signifier for Jerusalem

Surveying the fate of Jerusalem in the Book of the Twelve requires that one recognize where the subject of Jerusalem appears in the form of an explicit reference or in the presence of Lady Zion—the city of Jerusalem personified—even when she is not mentioned by name.

Jerusalem is signified by name as a city, by the eponym "Zion," and as a personified female entity. The first two of these significations show up readily in any concordance search, but the personification of Jerusalem as Lady Zion is not always introduced by name.

Lady Zion refers to the Hebrew term בת ציון (*bat Zion*), which literally translates "daughter Zion," and a significant number of investigations have demonstrated the tradition historical background of this phrase lies in the West Semitic conceptual milieu whereby cities were often envisaged as goddesses who were the consorts of patron deities.[8] Of course, in the Old Testament, Lady Zion is not deified. She does, however, carry many of the other attributes {261} of her ancient Near Eastern counterparts that make the metaphor of Lady Zion quite appropriate for describ-

---

8. See Fitzgerald, "Mythological Background for the Presentation of Jerusalem," 403–16; Schmitt, "Motherhood of God and Zion as Mother," 557–69; Biddle, "Figure of Lady Jerusalem," 173–94; Christl Maier, *Daughter Zion, Mother Zion: Gender, Space, and the Sacred in Ancient Israel* (Minneapolis: Fortress, 2008).

ing the fate of Jerusalem. First, she has a special relationship with YHWH that is frequently described or presumed as the relationship between husband and wife. Second, she is also mother, and her children represent the inhabitants of the city and, by extension in some texts, inhabitants of the kingdom as a whole. Third, poets describing the status of Jerusalem can utilize a wide array of metaphors to characterize the situation of Lady Zion in the Latter Prophets, Psalms, and Lamentations. For example, her clothing can be described as one would describe city walls (Isa 54:11–13) that have either been destroyed or are about to be rebuilt. Her marital relationship can be described in the most tender of terms (e.g., Jer 2:2; Isa 54:1–3) or condemned because Lady Zion has taken other lovers (Jer 4:30–31).

Lady Zion makes her first appearance in the Book of the Twelve in Micah, where she appears four times explicitly (Mic 1:13; 4:8, 10, 13). In addition to the explicit references to Lady Zion, she also appears as the speaker in Mic 7:8–10, a text where one feminine entity (Lady Zion) addresses another feminine entity (who should be interpreted as Lady Nineveh).[9]

After Micah, Lady Zion appears explicitly in three other passages within the Book of the Twelve (Zeph 3:14; Zech 2:14–15 [Eng. 2:10–11]; 9:9). She is also addressed, but not by name, in Zeph 3:7, 11, 15–16. These Lady Zion appearances function as implicit references to Jerusalem and must be taken into account in any delineation of the fate of Jerusalem.

Synthesis of Jerusalem's Fate in Three Stages

So, what happens to Jerusalem in the Book of the Twelve? To answer this question meaningfully, one needs to appreciate both diachronic and synchronic vantage points in order to ascertain the range of responses. For this reason, I will attempt to sketch the fate of Jerusalem in three steps that follow roughly the order in which significant parts of the corpus were edited together at various stages. These three steps include (1) the fate of Jerusalem in the Book of the Four Prophets (Hosea-Amos-Micah-Zephaniah); (2) in Haggai and Zech 1–8; and (3) in the extended eschatological

---

9. James D. Nogalski, "Micah 7:8–20: Re-evaluating the Identity of the Enemy," in *The Bible as a Human Witness to Divine Revelation: Hearing the Word of God through Historically Dissimilar Traditions*, ed. Randall Heskett and Brian Irwin, LHBOTS 469 (London: T&T Clark, 2010), 125–42.

dimensions of the day of YHWH. In so doing, I am attempting to simplify what I believe is a complicated process but one which these three perspectives may nevertheless illuminate. {262}

Jerusalem in the Book of the Four Prophets

The fate of Jerusalem in the Book of the Four Prophets (Hosea-Amos-Micah-Zephaniah) probably constituted an early form of what would become the multivolume corpus known as the Book of the Twelve.[10] It begins with only intermittent references to Jerusalem or Judah because the first two books deal largely with the fate of the Northern Kingdom—including Samaria and Bethel. Nevertheless, probably during the exilic period, these four books began to be edited together with an eye toward one another. While the fate of the Northern Kingdom is the primary focus of Hosea and Amos, periodic references in these two writings already begin to suggest to the reader that the fate of Judah and Jerusalem is somehow connected with the fate of Israel, Samaria, and Bethel (e.g., see Hos 1:7, 11; 4:15; 5:5, 12–14; 6:4, 11; 8:14; 10:11; 11:12; 12:1–2; Amos 2:4–5). Both the structure of the four books and periodic statements make these connections clear and often explicit.

The structure of the book of Hosea alternates between judgment sayings against the Northern Kingdom and promises of potential restoration. Each of the first three chapters starts with judgment and ends with restoration, while longer sections of judgment (chs. 4–10; 12–13) are punctuated by shorter, but powerful statements that hold open the possibility of restoration for Ephraim (Hos 11; 14). As a result, the writing of Hosea testifies ambivalently regarding the ultimate outcome for Israel.

---

10. The growing consensus that these four writings underwent common editing from the exilic period into the Persian period has been explored by various redactional studies, though the name of this corpus has changed. Nogalski originally called it the Deuteronomistic Corpus, though problems with that term were soon suggested by Schart, who preferred the term D-Korpus. Rainer Albertz suggested a more neutral term (*Vierprophetenbuch*) and he was followed by Jakob Wöhrle even though, paradoxically, Wöhrle's own work strengthened the argumentation for relating the story of Judah and Israel found in the book of Kings to the conceptual framework of this corpus. See Nogalski, *Literary Precursors*, 278–80; Schart, *Entstehung des Zwölfprophetenbuchs*, 157, 218–33; Albertz, *Exilszeit*, 154–85; Wöhrle, *Frühen Sammlungen des Zwölfprophetenbuches*, 51–53, 241–84.

By contrast, Amos offers no such ambivalence. From the beginning of Amos (1:2) and the surprising culmination of the oracles against the nations that are directed against Israel (2:6-16) until nearly the end of the book, the steady drumbeat of judgment oracles directed against Israel leave the reader with no alternative but to assume the prophet anticipates the annihilation of the Northern Kingdom. This same pattern reappears when prophetic speeches first alternate judgment and restoration speeches against Judah and Jerusalem (in {263} Micah) followed by Zephaniah which, from the beginning, articulates the idea that judgment against Jerusalem and Judah is unavoidable.

The shift in focus from the Northern Kingdom to the Southern Kingdom finds its fullest expression in these four writings near the beginning of Micah (1:5-7), where the destruction of Samaria and the Northern Kingdom functions as a paradigm for what will happen to Jerusalem. This warning to Jerusalem breaks off very briefly (2:12-13) before the pronouncement of judgment continues and then culminates in Mic 3:12 with the pronouncement that Zion/Jerusalem will be destroyed. Micah 3:12 uses the same images as 1:5-7: Jerusalem will be plowed like a field and become a heap of rubble.

At this point Mic 4-5 obfuscates the judgment by making a series of pronouncements regarding distant events that ultimately restore Jerusalem even though they also anticipate attacks from both Babylon (4:10) and Assyria (5:5-6). At this point, the modern critical reader must distinguish between how the prophetic voice functions within Micah and how the text came to be.[11] In its current form, Mic 4-5 is a composite, redacted entity, containing material from a much later time than the eighth century prophet for whom the writing is named. Nevertheless, these speeches are intended to be read as the word of YHWH for the distant future (indicated by the redactional framing of the units created by the eschatological formulas "in days to come" [4:1], "in that day" [4:6; 5:10]).

Micah 6 returns to the present generation and provides a series of accusations against YHWH's people that culminates in the prophet's rejection of this people (7:1-7). At this point Lady Zion speaks in 7:8-10 to an unnamed woman (but who must surely be understood as Lady Nineveh). In this speech Lady Zion recognizes that she will "bear the indignation of

---

11. For a discussion of this distinction in prophetic literature, see Seitz, "How Is the Prophet Isaiah Present," 219-40; Steck, *Prophetic Books*, 7-13, 22-25.

YHWH" (7:9), but that she will see the ultimate downfall of her enemy (7:10). The remainder of Mic 7 contains several speeches again offering promises to YHWH's people for life beyond Zion's indignation. Micah 7 ends the writing ambivalently, much like Hosea. Zion is given a reprieve—a time to build her walls (7:11)—but these promises do not revoke the "indignation" which Zion will bear (7:9, 13).

The Book of the Four concludes with Zephaniah. Whereas Micah is set in the eighth century (see 1:1), Zephaniah jumps forward to the time of Josiah (639–608) who reigned in the last third of the seventh century. Like Amos, Zephaniah leaves little doubt regarding the inevitable nature of the impending judgment. Like Micah, however, this judgment is directed primarily toward {264} Judah and Jerusalem. Zephaniah begins, in its current form, with pronouncements of judgment upon Jerusalem on the impending day of YHWH whose effects will be nothing short of the reversal of creation itself. These images of judgment dominate 1:2–2:3 and one can hardly interpret them as anything other than pronouncements of Jerusalem's destruction by Babylon in 587. Zephaniah's middle section (2:4–15) contains a series of oracles against foreign nations. These oracles against foreign nations culminate in 3:1–8 with a woe oracle addressed to an unnamed city. Like Amos, however, whose oracles against foreign nations surprisingly conclude with an extended judgment against Israel, the reader of Zeph 3:1–8 very soon realizes that this text has left behind the topic of foreign nations and instead directs judgment toward Jerusalem itself, because its people have refused to return to YHWH (3:7). For this reason, Jerusalem will now bear YHWH's wrath against the nation (3:8). This indignation will take the form of a purifying judgment that leaves behind only a remnant (3:9–13). Subsequently, Lady Zion will be restored (3:14–20) as YHWH returns as king (3:15, 17); her enemies will be removed (3:19); and her wounded and rejected inhabitants will come back to her (3:19).

The Book of the Four Prophets thus shows quite a bit of internal coherence, even within the midst of the use of very diverse source material. The structure of these four writings leads the reader toward the inevitable conclusion that Jerusalem must be destroyed because it failed to heed the warning sent by God first to Samaria and Israel and then to Judah and Jerusalem. Nevertheless, a remnant for Jerusalem will remain and will experience restoration. This collection of four probably experienced more than one redactional reworking from the exilic period into the postexilic period. In all likelihood, the core of this collection even predates the exile with the common transmission of Hosea and Amos.[12] Its chief characteristic, however, is that it largely focuses upon the fate of Israel and Judah from middle of the eighth century forward, attempting to document the failure of Israel and Judah to live up to the expectations—ethically, politically, and religiously—that YHWH had for YHWH's people.

Haggai and Zechariah 1–8

A second multivolume corpus presumes a very different attitude toward Jerusalem. These two writings are long thought to have been published together near the time of the appearance of the prophets in the late sixth century. Both writings assume a setting in Jerusalem, both assume Jerusalem's destruction lies in {265} the past, and both assume a significant turning point begins with the reconstruction of the temple.

The chronological structures of the two writings overlap with one another. A series of five dated appearances in Haggai from September to December in the year 520 BCE (1:1, 15; 2:1, 10, 20) overlap with three similar date formulas in Zechariah (1:1, 7; 7:1) so that Zechariah's first recorded speech (1:2–6) precedes the last two speeches in Haggai. This overlap is significant since the last two speeches in Haggai are dated to the day on which the temple foundation began (Hag 2:15), while the first speech in Zechariah articulates the repentance of the people of Jerusalem about one month earlier (cf. Zech 1:1; Hag 2:10). This positive response to the word of YHWH from Zechariah by the people stands in stark contrast to their ancestors who refused to repent when challenged to do so by earlier prophets. The next superscription introduces a series of eight vision reports that are dated approximately three months later than 1:2–6. The third and final section of Zech 7–8 contains a superscription dated some two years later still (7:1). These sayings portray a scenario that assumes the reconstruction of the temple is well under way, and they seek to encourage the people of Jerusalem to maintain diligence, even though the full effect of YHWH's blessing is not yet evident (see esp. 8:9–12).

The fate of Jerusalem in Haggai and Zechariah is quite different than the fate anticipated in Micah and Zephaniah because rather than a sense of impending judgment, Haggai and Zech 1–8 convey a sense that Jerusalem's situation is on the verge of changing in positive ways. In Haggai,

---

12. See especially Jeremias, "Anfänge des Dodekapropheton," 34–54.

economic woes are a sign of YHWH's continuing displeasure that will change only when the temple is rebuilt—once the foundation is laid. Haggai challenges the people to remember the day and see whether their fate changes (2:18–19).

In Zechariah, the fate of Jerusalem in the political realm is about to change. After the people repent in 1:2–6, Zechariah's first two visions announce that YHWH is about to punish the nations who have taken advantage of Jerusalem (1:8–17, 18–21), and the third vision (2:1–13) speaks about the enlargement of Jerusalem, so that it will be a city built without walls because so many people will come. The remaining visions have more to do with organizing leadership in the temple and in the land.

Certain portions of Haggai and Zech 1–8 lead one to conclude that the compilers of these writings, if not the prophets themselves, were aware of other prophetic writings, most notably allusions in Hag 2:17 to Amos 4:9 as well as reference to the "former prophets" in Zech 1:4. Moreover, certain portions of the vision reports, or the commentary that follows them, echo the phrasing found in other prophetic texts (most notably the reference in Zech 1:12 to the seventy years of punishment that comes from Jeremiah [cf. 25:11–12; 29:10]); YHWH's statement that he is jealous for Jerusalem and Zion in 1:14 that resonates very closely with language of Joel (2:13, 18); and in the command {266} to Lady Zion to sing and rejoice (Zech 2:14) because YHWH will dwell in her midst, a command that comes very close to the language of Zeph 3:14–15.

The Fate of Jerusalem/Zion in the Remainder of the Book of the Twelve

In Nahum and Habakkuk, as with the Book of Four, the question of the fate of Jerusalem has a dual focus: explanation of the rise and fall of Assyria and Babylon on the one hand; and the impending events of Jerusalem's destruction in 587 on the other hand.

The primary purpose of Nahum is to rejoice in and to theologize about the downfall of Assyria—essentially expanding upon the ideas expressed in Mic 7:8–10. Jerusalem is not mentioned explicitly in Nahum, but Judah is mentioned in one verse (2:1 [Eng. 1:15]). This verse actually comes from Isa 52:7, however, where it is addressed to Zion specifically. The second-person feminine singular forms of address in Nahum confirm that the reference to Judah in Nah 2:1 was added secondarily because Judah normally takes masculine pronouns. Nevertheless the point remains that Nahum begins with a poem affirming YHWH's punishment of YHWH's enemies

(1:2–8) before moving more explicitly to pronouncements of Assyria's downfall. This one verse (Nah 2:1) briefly provides a moment of hope for Judah, but that hope is soon dashed in Habakkuk.

Habakkuk begins with a prophetic complaint about the state of society, one that is very similar to the way that Judean society is described in Mic 7:1–7. The prophet complains of having to continue to look upon violence, wrongdoing, strife, contention, and the lack of justice. Consequently, YHWH responds to the prophet's complaint, beginning in 1:5, by announcing his intention to send the Babylonians to punish the land. To be sure, by the end of Habakkuk (3:3–15), the prophet is assured that Babylon itself will also be punished, but only after it has punished YHWH's people. The fact that Nahum and Habakkuk together account for the gap between Micah and Zephaniah show that whoever placed these two writings into their current location did so for two reasons: to affirm the role of YHWH in using Assyria and Babylon to punish Judah; and to expand the perspective of the Book of the Four Prophets to emphasize YHWH's universal dominion and power.

The fate of Jerusalem in Nahum and Habakkuk thus presumes that the reader knows where they are in the ongoing story. These writings presume the reader knows the context of Micah on the one hand even while anticipating the destruction of Jerusalem on the other hand (a central topic in Zephaniah).

Three of the remaining writings (Joel, Obadiah, Malachi) along with Zech 9–14 relate the fate of Jerusalem, in various ways, to events associated {267} with the day of YHWH. The day of YHWH already appeared in the Book of the Four Prophets, but primarily in Zephaniah where the day of YHWH describes YHWH's intervention against Jerusalem and Judah (note esp. 1:7–8, 14–18; 2:1–3). Joel, Obadiah, and Zech 9–14 in various ways depict day of YHWH traditions that extend beyond the destruction of Jerusalem.

Joel manifests the broadest array of traditions concerning the day of YHWH. The day of YHWH in Joel constitutes the day of judgment against Jerusalem/Zion (1:15–20), and a day of judgment against Jerusalem in which YHWH leads a cosmic army (2:1–11). In Joel, however, this day of YHWH's wrath against Jerusalem can still be avoided if the people repent (2:12–17), after which YHWH promises to restore the land (2:18–27) and make Zion/Jerusalem a place of refuge in the midst of cosmic signs concerning the day of YHWH (3:3–5 [Eng. 2:30–32]). Joel concludes, however, with depictions of the day of YHWH as a day of judgment against all the nations following Jerusalem's punishment (4:1, 14 [Eng 3:1, 14]), against all the surrounding nations (4:11-12 [Eng. 3:11-12]), and against specific nations (4:4-8 [Eng. 3:4-8]). Cumulatively Joel presents a composite portrayal of the day of YHWH, but one in which the day of YHWH first affects Jerusalem and then the other nations.

In Obadiah, the day of YHWH functions similarly, although the rhetoric of this short book is primarily directed against Edom. Nevertheless, the day of judgment will come against Edom (Obad 7-8) because of what Edom has done on the day of Jerusalem's destruction (Obad 10-14). These events initiate a day of YHWH against all nations who have taken advantage of Jerusalem during its time of punishment (15a, 16-21). The latter part of Obadiah also depicts this day of YHWH as a day when all the nations will swallow the same "cup of wrath" (Obad 16) that Jerusalem was forced to drink.

Zechariah 9-14, or more specifically 12-14, depicts a time of turmoil in the future for Jerusalem when YHWH will make Jerusalem a "cup of reeling" and a "heavy stone" for all the nations (12:3-4). The chapters emphasize the future orientation by the recurring phrase "on that day" (Zech 12:3, 4, 6, 8, 9, 11; 13:1, 2, 4; 14:4, 6, 8, 9, 13, 20, 21). The remaining portions of chapters 12 and 14 depict several scenarios whereby nations attack Jerusalem only to experience defeat at the hands of YHWH. Zechariah 14, in particular, anticipates a "day belonging to YHWH" (14:1) and a "day of battle" (14:3) when the nations will attack. Subsequently, "on that day" YHWH will defeat the nations (14:4, 6, 8, 9, 13, 20, 21).

Finally, Malachi also envisions a day of YHWH that will affect Jerusalem (the assumed literary location of Malachi by virtue of the proximity of the action to the temple), but this day is simultaneously more universal and less collective than in the other writings. To be sure, the day of YHWH in Malachi {268} will be a purifying time of purging Judah and Jerusalem (3:1-4). Nevertheless, it will not affect entire countries indiscriminately. Rather, the day of YHWH in Malachi comes as a day of judgment against the wicked which only the righteous can hope to endure (3:19-21). It matters little whether the wicked live in Judah or among the nations.

To summarize, these five writings (Joel, Obadiah, Nahum, Habakkuk, Malachi) combine with Zech 9-14 to broaden the implications for Jerusalem's encounter with the days of YHWH. Joel provides the paradigm where Jerusalem's encounter with numerous calamities sent by YHWH will ultimately lead Jerusalem to repent. That repentance will inaugurate the day of YHWH against the nations. Obadiah condemns Edom for its treatment of Judah and Jerusalem and anticipates Edom's own punishment on the day of YHWH that will follow the punishment of Jerusalem. Nahum and Habakkuk document the arrival and downfall of Assyria and Babylon respectively, who both serve as YHWH's tools of wrath against Judah, but who will both experience punishment by YHWH's intervention against them. Zechariah 9–14 offers extended reflections about the coming day of YHWH as a time of attack by the nations which YHWH will repel. Malachi announces that the punishment of Edom has begun (1:2–5), but changes the focus of the coming day of YHWH to one of judgment on the wicked (and escape for the righteous). In so doing, the impending day of YHWH serves a continuing function to warn the people of YHWH of every generation that their choices and their behavior have consequences.

Conclusion

While the fate of Jerusalem is frequently described in terms of the impending day of YHWH, what is meant by this day of YHWH differs within the collections and groups of writings that come to make up the Book of the Twelve. Sometimes these differences reflect ideas concerning the impending events of 587, while elsewhere the day of YHWH represents more complex images that assume judgment against Jerusalem will initiate a series of judgments against other nations, first against Assyria and Babylon, but then against all the nations, or all the surrounding nations who have taken advantage of Jerusalem's situation during its time of punishment.

Intertextuality

Intertextuality and the Twelve

Ancient traditions irrefutably establish that the writings of the twelve prophets were copied onto a single scroll and counted as a single book from at least 200 BCE.[1] Naturally, one presumes that someone intended these twelve writings to be read together. Unfortunately, the conventions for reading this entity called the Twelve were not transmitted with the writings themselves. In order to speak meaningfully of "unity" with respect to the Book of the Twelve, one must first establish that the texts of the Twelve relate to one another. Second, one must begin to evaluate what the intertextual relationships offer as clues for reading the Twelve as a "united" piece of literature.

The term "intertextuality," particularly in English language discussions, can mean many things. Here, "intertextuality" means the interrelationship between two or more texts which *evidence suggests* (1) was deliberately established by ancient authors/editors or (2) was presupposed by those authors/editors.[2] Such delimitation intentionally avoids the question {103} of readings which are oriented toward the modern reader. Such reader-oriented intertextual studies are avoided not because they have

---

1. For more thorough treatments of the ancient traditions reflecting the Twelve as a corpus, see Nogalski, *Literary Precursors*, 2–3; and esp. Jones, *Formation of the Book of the Twelve*, 1–13; and Fuller, "Form and Formation of the Book of the Twelve," 86–101.

2. For a thorough discussion and illustration of the variety of approaches dealing with intertextuality and related topics, see Danna Nolan Fewell, *Reading between Texts: Intertextuality and the Hebrew Bible*, LCBI (Louisville: Westminster John Knox, 1992), esp. 11–39. The primary distinction between definitions of intertextuality is the source of the intertextuality. One end of a rather long spectrum can be represented by Derrida, Kristeva, Barthes, and others, whose understanding of intertextuality orients itself toward the "modern reader." At the other end of the spectrum, those like Fishbane opt for an approach tied more concretely to Old Testament texts and the deliberate use of earlier traditions.

nothing to offer, but because this study reflects my own ongoing attempt to try to understand the foundational stimuli behind the compilation of the Book of the Twelve. To do so, one must *attempt* to recapture the intentions of those responsible for the development of the Book of the Twelve. Of course, any attempt to rediscover the development enters the realm of the hypothetical, and contains its own risks. Safeguards should be established to avoid idiosyncratic re-creations which do not exhibit some reasonable likelihood of having actually occurred.

However, even by limiting intertextuality to intentional and/or cognizant interrelationships, not every instance of intertextuality contributes equally to the question of understanding the conventions of reading the Book of the Twelve. For this reason, this investigation will focus on two aspects simultaneously: (1) illustrating types of intertextuality in the Book of the Twelve which suggest some implications for reading the Twelve, and (2) reflections about a methodology of working with intertextuality. For reasons of ongoing research, I have chosen to illustrate these types of intertextuality using Joel as the primary, though not exclusive, focal text.

Recognition of types of intertextuality adds significantly to one's ability to reconstruct reading strategies intended by those who developed the Book of the Twelve; however, it complicates one's understanding of the unity of the Book of the Twelve considerably. The Book of the Twelve exhibits at least five different types of intertextuality: quotes, allusions, catchwords, motifs, and framing devices. Some of these devices overlap with one another, and in a very real sense some are more objective than others. Nevertheless, each type of intertextuality offers an evaluable perspective for the reading of the Twelve as a corpus.

Quotations

The use of a preexisting *phrase, sentence, or paragraph* that is taken from another source constitutes a quotation.[3] Several factors complicate the recognition of quotations. First, Old Testament writers rarely footnote {104} the source of their quotations.[4] Second, modern exegetes often work with a narrow focus of a book or a passage within a book and thus do not

---

3. In practical terms, one should not label the use of a single word as a quotation. Instead, one should more accurately treat the use of a single word as an allusion or a catchword, both of which will be discussed below.

4. See Fishbane, *Biblical Interpretation in Ancient Israel*, 530–43.

evaluate the possibility that one text quotes another. Recognition of quotations often depends upon painstaking concordance work or the use of secondary literature. Third, quotations may come from sources no longer at our disposal.[5] Finally, a quotation may not be easily recognized because the words are not identical, a fact which requires further explanation.

An author may "quote" another text inexactly. An author may work from memory and simply record a slightly different version of the text, or an author may also deliberately alter the quotation to fit the context or to make a different point. One should attempt to make a decision regarding these alternatives since the presupposition of an intentional change or an oversight can directly impact how one interprets the function of the quotation. A few examples will illuminate the use of quotations of various lengths in the Book of the Twelve.

Obadiah 1–5 extensively quotes Jer 49:14–16 and 49:9, but the texts are not precise duplicates. The imprecise nature of the quotation naturally creates questions: Which is the source text and which is the receiving text, or is there an unknown source text from which both Obadiah and Jer 49 draw?[6] A perspective of the Book of the Twelve as a literary work sheds considerable light on these questions. Previously, I have documented in detail how the differences in the parallel texts allow some relatively specific conclusions.[7] Space does not permit replication of those details, but the conclusions can be summarized. The vast majority of the differences between Obad 1–5 and Jer 49:9, 14–16 can be plausibly explained as adaptations to the context of the Book of the Twelve. Obadiah 1–5 shows a remarkable tendency to imitate the structural {105} components of Amos 9:1–15 by modifying the quotation from Jeremiah. However, the similarities do not end with the quotation of Jer 49:9, 14–16 since virtually the entire book of Obadiah exhibits the same structural elements as Amos 9.[8] How does one explain these structural similarities?

The first step toward explaining the similarities requires one to eliminate the possibility that the similarities are unintentional. In this case, the

---

5. For this reason, one must necessarily limit the study of quotations to those whose source can be documented with some degree of certainty.

6. Cf. discussions in the following: Wolff, *Obadiah and Jonah*, 38–40; Wehrle, *Prophetie und Textanalyse*, 12–15; Stuart, *Hosea–Jonah*, 414–16.

7. See Nogalski, *Redactional Processes*, 61–68.

8. Ibid., 61–74, esp. 71–72.

evidence that the quotation from Jer 49:9, 14–16 was adapted offers significant evidence that the changes were made deliberately.

Given the deliberate changes, one must ask: Why would someone go to the trouble of structuring Obadiah similarly to Amos 9, and, just as importantly, why would these two writings appear sequentially in the Book of the Twelve? Again, thorough investigation of these questions is not the purpose of this discussion, but one can make a strong case that the compiler of the anti-Edom sayings of Obadiah wanted to communicate the conviction that the same fate which befell the Northern Kingdom would befall Judah's "brother" to the south. Context (Amos 9:2b and Obad 4b; cf. also Amos 9:12; Obad 18) supports this suggestion in addition to the structural arguments. The implications of this intertextual relationship for understanding Obadiah are not insignificant. Obadiah studies often treat this booklet as just another foreign prophecy. It is not. Edom receives special treatment because it should have been an ally.

The length of the Obadiah quotation is unusual. Direct citations typically appear as considerably smaller units. For example, scholars have long recognized Joel 4:16 as a quotation of Amos 1:2, and there is no reason to doubt this consensus. Rarely, however, do scholars ask why Joel 4:16 cites Amos 1:2. Several possibilities could explain the citation. For methodological reasons, one should always attempt to eliminate (1) accidental occurrence. In this instance, significant rationale all but preclude this possibility.[9] Given the great probability that Joel 4:16 quotes Amos (and not the other way around), one should consider two {106} additional possibilities.[10] (2) Joel quotes Amos but the citation functions apart from the literary horizon of the Twelve. (3) Joel deliberately anticipates Amos as part of the Book of the Twelve.

---

9. For several reasons, one can reject the notion that the phrase in Joel merely reflects a common saying rather than a quotation. First, the saying is not that common. Second, the quotation is rather precise. Third, literary observations indicate a significant probability that the compiler of Joel 4 combined several short preexisting pieces by quotations and allusions to other parts of Joel and the Twelve (see Bergler, *Joel als Schriftinterpret*). Fourth, Joel 4:16 is not the only quotation of Amos in the context (cf. Joel 4:18 and Amos 9:13).

10. Virtual consensus about the respective dates of the two texts eliminates the possibility that Amos quotes Joel. Scholars almost universally date Joel 4 later than Amos 9:11–15. See full discussion in Wolff, *Joel and Amos*, 81; Allen, *Joel, Obadiah, Jonah, and Micah*, 120.

Making a decision between the second and third possible explanations requires a broader perspective than just the immediate context. To summarize: the compositional technique for Joel indicates a tendency to unite preexisting text units by quotations and allusions.[11] These intertextual linking devices manifest two primary literary foci—the book of Joel and the Book of the Twelve. One must draw careful distinctions, however, between Joel's use of other writings (especially in the Twelve) and citations/allusions to Joel in other parts of the Twelve.[12] Joel demonstrates considerable awareness of the adjacent writings (Hosea and Amos), and, to a lesser degree, an awareness of other writings as well.[13] This tendency suggests that Joel's direct quotation of Amos 1:2 likely intends some type of linking function for the Book of the Twelve.

Two avenues present themselves when considering the rationale for Joel's citation of Amos 1:2. These possibilities need not be mutually exclusive and both must be evaluated. First, authorial intention may derive from the content of the actual quotation, or second, as with the Obadiah text above, the significant clue may be gleaned from the divergence in the quotation. For the first possibility, the quotation manifests a significant theological concept: "Yahweh roars from Zion, and from Jerusalem he utters his voice." The Jerusalem orientation of this pronouncement marks a substantive theological perspective: Jerusalem is {107} the place from which Yahweh acts. Joel 4:16 could thus be strengthening the Jerusalem orientation of the Twelve, particularly since the books on either side of Joel (Hosea and Amos) focus on the fate of the Northern Kingdom. Joel 1–4 focuses on Jerusalem, but "anticipating" Amos by quoting one of the less numerous Jerusalem texts in Amos encourages the reader of the Twelve not to forget to read Amos in light of Joel. One would then expect to find other touchstones between the two writings which would assist this process (e.g., compare the eschatological judgment against the

---

11. Bergler, *Joel als Schriftinterpret*, esp. 153–80, 295–326, 338–39.

12. In the case of the former, see discussions below regarding catchwords and allusions to Joel inserted into other literary contexts which refer back to Joel, especially with regard to the locust imagery designating the conquering nations motif and the motif of agricultural bounty to refer to the restoration of Israel's relationship to Yahweh.

13. This awareness is not limited to the Twelve. Joel apparently draws from the Pentateuch (Bergler, *Joel als Schriftinterpret*, 247–94), other prophetic writings (Bosshard, "Beobachtungen zum Zwölfprophetenbuch," 30–62, esp. 31–32, 37–42), and from the Twelve (e.g., Joel 2:2 cites Zeph 1:15).

nations in Joel 4 with Amos 1–2; or the locust imagery of Joel 1 with Amos 4:9).

For the second possibility, it is necessary to evaluate how Joel modifies the quotation. Here one enters a less objective realm. Nevertheless, a few remarks provide a starting point for interpreting the quotation.

Amos 1:2

ויאמר יהוה מציון ישאג ומירושלם יתן קולו ואבלו נאות הרעים ויבש ראש הכרמל

Joel 4:16

ויהוה מציון ישאג ומירושלם יתן קולו ורעשו שמים וארץ ויהוה מחסה לעמו ומעוז לבני ישראל

The first line of the verse contains virtually an exact quote.[14] However, the next lines of Joel 4:16 depart significantly from Amos 1:2. The second line of Amos 1:2 depicts the results of Yahweh's roar of judgment as the withering of the top of Carmel, a reference to the Northern Kingdom. By contrast, the second line of Joel 4:16 broadens the effect to include the trembling of "heaven and earth" rather than the Northern Kingdom. In addition, the third line introduces a very different outcome. "Yahweh will be a refuge for his people, and a stronghold for the sons of Israel."

Joel's adaptation thus broadens Amos 1:2 into a universal theophanic portrayal of judgment, the purpose of which is to encourage Yahweh's people. This adaptation fits well with the overall purpose of Joel 4, which describes a universal judgment scene where Yahweh acts on behalf of Jerusalem and Judah (cf. Joel 4:1, 9–17, 20), however, it also subtly reinterprets Amos in the process, if one is reading the Twelve in canonical succession. Because Joel precedes Amos, the sensitive reader of the Twelve will filter Amos 1:2 through Joel 4:16. In so doing, lines two and {108} three of Joel 4:16 acquire more significance because they illustrate larger thematic developments which Joel introduces and which continue to "play out" in the Twelve. Specifically, the themes of universal eschatological (apocalyptic?) judgment of the nations (line two) and Yahweh as refuge for his people (line three) recur relatively frequently in the

---

14. Amos 1:2 structures the text as statement from Amos (the "he" in ויאמר refers back to Amos in 1:1), while Joel's quotation receives no special introduction. Nevertheless, Joel does modify the text by adding the ו before Yahweh.

Twelve.¹⁵ Given Joel's tendency for thoughtful intertextual nuances, it seems quite plausible to suggest that Joel deliberately frames the oracles against the nations in Amos 1–2 as part of Yahweh's ongoing actions on behalf of his people. Simultaneously, the explanation of the identity of Yahweh's people for whom Yahweh will be a refuge develops rather more subtly across the Twelve.¹⁶

Allusions

Without doubt, defining a term as diversely used as allusion creates more difficulty, and involves more subjectivity, than defining a quotation.¹⁷ Those difficulties aside, most commentators recognize the use of {109} allusions as a significant compositional technique.¹⁸ An allusion consists of one or more words whose appearance intends to elicit the reader's recol-

---

15. While space does not permit full exploration, note that the Twelve treats the theme of universal judgment in various ways. Some of these variations derive from the particular prophetic book (e.g., the day of Yahweh in Zephaniah) while others may be part of motifs deliberately implanted by a redactor working with more than one writing. Note, e.g., that the root רעשׁ occurs ten times in the Twelve (Joel 2:10; 4:16; Amos 1:1; 9:1; Nah 1:5; 3:2; Hag 2:6, 7, 21; Zech 14:5), always in the context of Yahweh's judgment or the earthquake in the time of Uzziah (Amos 1:1; Zech 14:5).

16. The identity of Yahweh's people shifts as one reads the Twelve. One can detect a decided tendency to broaden the understanding beyond a political orientation. The Northern Kingdom is destroyed for its lack of faithful response to Yahweh (Hosea/Amos), leaving only a remnant. Judah experiences a similar judgment (Zephaniah). In the Twelve, Yahweh's people periodically face significant points which call for a decision (e.g., Hos 14; Joel 1–2; Hag 1:2–4; Zech 1:2–6), and which increasingly imply an awareness that only some inside (Mic 4:6–7; Zeph 3:18–20; Zech 8:3–12) and outside (Zech 8:21–23) Judah will be delivered. By the end of the Twelve, Malachi leaves the reader with the impression that the people in Judah still have not understood the message that Yahweh requires faithful obedience (cf. Mal 1:6–9), so that Yahweh will distinguish between the righteous and the wicked (Mal 3:16–18)—a remnant based upon one's attitude toward Yahweh, not one's political pedigree.

17. Allusions deserve treatment separately, but in many respects the general term is used for several techniques of referring to another text, particularly catchwords and motifs.

18. E.g., note the following discussions about dependence upon other texts and/or traditions: Utzschneider, *Künder oder Schreiber*, esp. 17–22, 42–44; Fishbane, *Biblical Interpretation in Ancient Israel*, 283–91; Steck, *Bereitete Heimkehr*, esp. 13–29; Herbert Donner, "'Forscht in der Schrift Jahwes und lest!': Ein Beitrag zum Verständnis der israelitischen Prophetie," *ZTK* 87 (1990): 285–98, esp. 288; Thomas Willi, *Die*

lection of another text (or texts) *for a specific purpose*. In practice, various types of allusions appear with some frequency in exegetical treatments, but exegetes should approach each of these with care to evaluate the likelihood of intentionality and/or cognizance by the author/redactor. In some respects, allusions are more readily discussed by techniques (catchword, motif, etc.), but all of these techniques share some common aspects which can be addressed to all types of allusions.

When working with allusions, caution dictates that one perform several subjectivity crosschecks. First, one must carefully distinguish between allusions and formulas. Formulas, especially introductory and concluding formulas, play an essential role in understanding a text, but unless they appear in conjunction with other criteria, they may or may not constitute an allusion.[19]

Second, what evidence suggests that the suspected words/ideas do not simply represent random recurrence? Addressing this question necessitates careful evaluation of at least five factors: word frequency, word pairings, motif development, literary homogeneity, and specific text combinations. The *frequency* of the word(s) involved in the alleged allusion affects the degree to which one can expect to convince others that an allusion is present. For example, arguing that the verb בוא alludes to another text is not a strong argument because that verb is simply too common in too many texts to make a convincing argument. Evidence of {110} typically recurring *word pairings* also decreases the likelihood of a deliberate allusion if no other criteria exist. For example, the presence of the antonyms "light" and "darkness" in two texts does not offer very strong evidence that one text alludes to another. By contrast, one cannot simply assume that an author could not allude to another text(s) using only uncommon words, and thus one should, even in the case of common words or word pairs, evaluate the extent to which other criteria might be present. For example, if one finds that a common word pair appears regularly in a specific writing, and actually helps to develop a *continuing motif* (see discussion of motifs below), then the likelihood that the word pair alludes to another

---

Chronik als Auslegung; Untersuchungen zur literarischen Gestaltung der historischen Überlieferung Israels, FRLANT 106 (Göttingen: Vandenhoeck & Ruprecht, 1972).

19. E.g., the formulas ביום ההוא and נאם יהוה by themselves do not constitute allusions, but in Amos 9:11–15, these formulas appear as part of a series of structural imitations of Amos 8, thus implying a deliberate attempt to call that text to mind. See detailed treatment in Nogalski, *Literary Precursors*, 117–18.

text(s) increases substantially, even though the burden of proof will still fall to the one arguing for the presence of an allusion.[20] One should evaluate evidence to determine the text's *literary homogeneity*. Does literary critical analysis indicate significant rationale for suggesting the word is part of a unit which was edited for the book (e.g., a literary introduction, conclusion, or a redactional gloss)? Finally, concordance studies could indicate that several words (common and/or uncommon) recur in two *specific texts* so that one suspects that the two texts were somehow related in the mind of the writer.[21]

Within the Twelve, one can illustrate allusions whose literary horizon focuses on another part of the same writing (internal allusions) and allusions which anticipate or reach back to another text (external allusions). Illustrating internal allusions is not difficult. For example, Wolff has presented a strong case that the end of the book of Joel (4:18–20) specifically alludes to texts in the first two chapters (using catchwords and themes).[22] This allusion deliberately reverses the situation of need {111} in Joel 1–2, creating a potent promise of abundance.[23]

External allusions are more complicated but equally important for discovering meaningful reading strategies and for speculating about the formative development of the Book of the Twelve. As with internal allusions, external allusions employ catchwords, motifs, and aggregate associations as the primary techniques to "reference" another text(s). Two recurring allusions to Joel, locust imagery and the motif of agricultural bounty, are

---

20. See, e.g., Peter D. Miscall, "Isaiah: New Heavens, New Earth, New Book," in Fewell, *Reading between Texts*, 49. Miscall argues that the significance of "light" in Isa 1–66 (used in a variety of meanings) and Gen 1:1–2:4a provide a touchstone between the two texts. Note that Miscall does not attempt to argue for deliberate allusions between these two texts, opting instead to explore a "poetic reading" without arguing for "a particular historical priority" (p. 47). However, if one wishes to bring allusions into the discussion of the development of a corpus, one cannot avoid the question of priority.

21. E.g., see Utzschneider, *Künder oder Schreiber?*, 50–53, who argues that Mal 1:8b–11 alludes to Gen 32–33, as well as other intertextual relationships. See also Nogalski, *Literary Precursors*, 155–58, for the argument that Mic 7:8–20 alludes to Isa 9–12, and that this intertextuality supplies some of the missing logic necessary to follow Mic 7:8–20.

22. Wolff, *Joel and Amos*, 83.

23. Hence the עסיס (juice) which is cut off (1:5) will drip from the mountains (4:20), and the אפיקים which are dried up (1:20) will flow with water (4:18).

mentioned here as illustrations. These will be explored more fully below in the respective sections related to catchwords and motifs. The Twelve periodically alludes to locusts as invading armies. These locust allusions constitute one hallmark of what I have elsewhere labeled the Joel-related layer. They appear at significant junctures in the Twelve, and often appear to have been inserted into existing units.[24] Similarly, allusions to coming agricultural bounty, or the lack thereof, recur with regularity in the Twelve using language which one readily recognizes from Joel.[25] One can document these allusions and speculate about their role in the literary intentions of the Twelve, but they also illustrate that the term allusion actually encompasses several techniques, some of the most significant of which now require discussion.[26] {112}

Catchwords

Old Testament studies have long recognized catchwords as a device utilized by those who "arranged" various transmission units, especially when col-

---

24. The locusts first appear in Joel 1:4, where the reader learns of their associations with invading armies (Joel 1:7). Catchwords continue this association for the reader of the Twelve. Amos 4:9 contains several words "reminiscent" of Joel. Amos 4:9 likely predated Joel, and may even have influenced Joel's compilation. Nahum 3:16b contains an inserted redactional gloss (Nogalski, *Redactional Processes*, 125–26) which, using catchwords, associates Assyria as one of the series of locusts mentioned in Joel 1:4, who will now pass from the scene. Habakkuk 1:9 alludes to the locust-like characteristics of Babylon, drawing upon the motif without using specific catchwords. Malachi 3:11 also draws upon the locust motif in a manner recalling Joel 1–2 (ibid., 204–6).

25. Following the decimation of the land mentioned in Joel, the Twelve keeps the promise of agricultural bounty alive by quotations (Amos 9:13 cites Joel 4:18, see Nogalski, *Literary Precursors*, 117–19), redactional glosses (Hag 2:19aβ; Zech 8:12; see ibid., 228–29, 263–65), and thematic development (Obad 5; see Nogalski, *Redactional Processes*, 66–67).

26. The allusions to locusts and to agricultural bounty illustrate the variety of techniques utilized to allude to texts, but by no means should one presume these two elements constitute the only allusions which transcend the writings of the Twelve. E.g., note the essay by Margaret S. Odell {112} which traces the view of the prophet as it develops from Hosea. The Twelve also offers several perspectives on the Day of Yahweh which must be evaluated for their relationship to one another, as well as for the potential for understanding the development of the Twelve ("The Prophets and the End of Hosea," in Watts, *Forming Prophetic Literature*, 158–70).

lecting wisdom sayings, legal sayings, psalms, and prophetic logia. Catchwords played a significant role in the arrangement of developing collections during both oral and written stages of transmission. More recently, however, the discipline has recognized that, in some texts, catchwords also play a significant role in a text's internal logic.[27] Thus, catchwords function as a type of allusion by using/reusing significant words to refer to another text(s). Intertextual work in the Twelve must recognize that catchwords play a significant role in the literary logic of the Twelve as both an ordering principle and a logical principle in light of significant evidence that catchwords recur consistently across neighboring writings, and that many of these catchwords have been deliberately (redactionally) implanted into existing texts to highlight these connections. In addition, catchwords also reach across nonadjacent writings in the Twelve, thereby serving as potential guides to any potential reading strategy.[28]

As with allusions, key questions must be resolved, as far as possible, regarding the likelihood that the catchwords were intentionally created for the sophisticated reader of these texts (see subjectivity cross-checks under allusions). Having established the plausibility and/or likelihood that someone deliberately created these links, one then turns to the most significant (and perhaps the most difficult) question: Why? The answer to this question will vary from text to text but requires careful evaluation. A specific, though certainly not isolated, example will serve to {113} highlight catchwords used in juxtaposition and in the explication of paradigmatic intentions.

Examination of the catchwords which appear in the "seams" (i.e., the concluding and opening passages) of the writings of the Twelve reveals a notable tendency. These words often appear in contexts which offer contrasting messages. Take the Hosea-Joel connection as an example, where "inhabitants" (Hos 14:8; Joel 1:2), "vine" (Hos 14:8; Joel 1:7, 12), "wine" (Hos 14:8; Joel 1:5), and "grain" (Hos 14:8; Joel 1:10) offer specific catchword connections which deliberately strengthen the "agricultural" ties between the two passages.[29] However, the words do not convey the same

---

27. See Nogalski, "Redactional Shaping of Nahum 1," 193–202; note also Steck, *Bereitete Heimkehr*, 13–37; Utzschneider, *Künder oder Schreiber?*, 42–44.

28. See Nogalski, *Literary Precursors*, 20–57, for translations highlighting the "catchword phenomenon" in the Twelve. The remainder of *Literary Precursors* and *Redactional Processes* then evaluate evidence of redactional implantation in those texts.

29. Because the words involved are relatively common, one should initially be

message. Hosea 14:8 functions within the *positive* promise of *future* agricultural bounty. By contrast, Joel 1:2–20 paints a *negative* picture of *current* agricultural disaster. One must broaden the investigation at this point to understand this juxtaposition more fully. First, many of the catchword connections utilize a similar technique—juxtaposing a promise of weal with a situation of suffering.[30] Second, these catchwords appear as part of a larger pattern in the Twelve of catchword associations to Joel 1–2. Third, the catchwords related to Joel 1–2 often appear to be redactionally inserted.[31] Fourth, one can detect significant literary development of the motif associated with these catchwords. This final statement requires further illustration.

In Hos 2:10–15, the reader of the Twelve first learns that these agricultural images (with others that appear in Joel 1) serve as a significant point of tension between Yahweh and his bride. As a result of this tension Yahweh will punish her by the removal of these elements (2:14), in the hope of getting her to recognize that these elements are gifts which come from Yahweh. The end of Hosea contains the promise of the future restoration of these elements (but the text still implies their loss {114} before their restoration). Joel 1–2 depicts the devastation of the locust/enemy as the loss of these agricultural elements, but further explicates how Yahweh will restore agricultural bounty (2:18–19) if the people repent (2:12–17). From this point, the agricultural elements come back into play at significant junctures (Hab 3:17; Hag 2:17, 19; Zech 8:12; Mal 3:10–11). One can make a strong case that these texts know the Joel passage, and that each of these texts are likely redactionally related to one another (either as part of compositional material or redactional glosses oriented toward the Book of the Twelve). Finally, one can document a consistent, developed point of view operating in the logic uniting these texts.

---

cautious regarding intentionality. Note, however, that all of these words appear in one verse in Hosea. Careful literary analysis reveals a strong likelihood that three of these words (inhabitants, grain, vine) entered Hos 14:8 as a "redactional gloss," presumably by editorial hands working on the Twelve. See Nogalski, *Literary Precursors*, 67–68.

30. See my discussions of the Zephaniah/Haggai connection (ibid., 207–9, 212–15), and the Zech 8/Malachi connection (Nogalski, *Redactional Processes*, 199–200), in particular.

31. See my literary analysis of Nah 1:2–10; Hab 3:17; and Zech 8:12 (Nogalski, *Redactional Processes*, 115–17, 176–79; Nogalski, *Literary Precursors*, 228–29, 262–67).

Briefly summarized, Hab 3:17 anticipates the coming Babylonian invasion, but specifically anticipates Judah's destruction through references to the agricultural images from Joel 1-2.

> [17]Though the fig tree will not blossom, nor fruit be on the vines, the produce of the olive will fail, and the fields will not produce food, the flock will be cut off from the fold, and there will be no cattle in the stalls, [18]yet I will rejoice in Yahweh, I will exult in the god of my salvation.

Inserted into a typical affirmation of confidence in Yahweh (Hab 3:16, 18-19),[32] this allusion to Joel in the context of the coming Babylonian invasion emphasizes the certainty of the coming destruction (as proleptically stated in Joel), but reminds the sophisticated reader that this (literarily imminent) action should be seen as part of Yahweh's activity. The righteous need not fear (cf. Mal 3:17). By contrast, the context of Haggai (and the historical framework of the Twelve as a whole) presumes that the reader of Hag 2:19 knows that the generation which returned from exile stands at an important crossroad. This "generation" must decide whether to obey Yahweh or to act as earlier generations had done by breaking covenant with Yahweh (cf. also Zech 1:2-6). When work on the temple begins, Haggai's message asks the people to take note of their fate after the foundation of the temple has been laid to see whether Yahweh remains true to his promise. Again, agricultural catchwords from Joel 1-2 come back into play in a phrase which is literarily suspect:[33] "Is the seed yet in the storehouse? (*or the vine, the fig* {115} *tree, the pomegranate?*), or the olive tree not producing? From this day I will bless you." Zechariah 8:12 validates this challenge by affirming Yahweh's faithful dealing with that generation in a speech set two years later (Zech 7:1). After calling upon the people to recall the days before the laying of the foundation (note the connection back to the context of Hag 2:19), Zech 8:11-12 asks the *current* generation to consider their own situation since that point.[34]

---

32. Nogalski, *Redactional Processes*, 176-79.
33. See Nogalski, *Literary Precursors*, 228-29. If studies of מגורה are correct, the hyperbole of placing a vine, a fig tree, or a pomegranate into underground storage makes more sense as a literary reference back to Joel than a literal statement.
34. For the temporal significance of the phrase "but now" as a reference to the current generation, see ibid., 262-65.

¹¹But now I am not like the previous days to the remnant of this people, says Yahweh Sebaoth. ¹²For a seed (there) is peace. The vine gives its fruit, and the land gives its produce, and the heavens give dew, and I have caused the remnant of this people to inherit all these things.

Within this passage, Yahweh asserts that he has kept his part of the bargain to the generation which began building the temple, but following the thread of these catchwords through the Twelve reveals that in Malachi Yahweh's people return to the cultic abuses of the earlier generations by offering less than their best to Yahweh (1:6–14) which prompts Yahweh to send a messenger to prepare for the day of his coming. Again, Yahweh's speeches in Mal 3:6–12 reference the language of Joel. Consider Mal 3:7 in light of Joel 2:12–14 and Amos 4:6–11: "From the days of your fathers you have turned aside from my statutes and have not kept them. *Return to me and I will return to you*, says Yahweh Sebaoth." (emphasis added). Note how Mal 3:10–11 reflects the language of Joel in a new challenge similar to Hag 2:19:

¹⁰Bring the full tithes into the *storehouse*, that there may be food in my house; and put me to the test in this, says Yahweh Sebaoth, to see whether I will not open the windows of heaven for you and pour down for you until there is no sufficiency. ¹¹And I will rebuke the *devourer* for you, so that it will not destroy the fruits of your soil. And the *vine of the field* will not stop producing for you. (emphasis added)

Even though most commentators have not previously interpreted this text in light of Joel 1–2, it is significant how many times the devourer in 3:11 has been treated as a locust.[35] {116}

When the catchwords are recognized, one can see how these passages work together to develop an agricultural motif based on allusions back to Joel 1–2. Common words may certainly occur naturally between two writings. If one speaks of catchwords, however, one should make an effort to determine the extent that one can speak of recurring words as intentionally created vehicles of meaning across the writings of the Twelve. The examples of catchwords could be multiplied, but space does not permit a more complete listing. Instead, it will be beneficial to use the agricultural

---

35. E.g., see Rudolph, *Haggai - Sacharja 1–8, Sacharja 9–14, Maleachi*, 284–85; Pieter A. Verhoef, *The Books of Haggai and Malachi*, NICOT (Grand Rapids: Eerdmans, 1987), 308–9; Redditt, *Haggai, Zechariah and Malachi*, 180.

motif as a springboard into a discussion of motifs as an intertextual device in the Twelve.

Themes and Motifs

Literary works naturally develop themes and motifs as devices used for "telling the story," or conveying meaning. The ability to recognize, analyze, and assimilate these devices will necessarily depend upon the level of sophistication of both author and reader. Thematic development in the Twelve requires one to presume a sophistication of author and reader, a presumption which constitutes a fairly recent development in Old Testament studies. In addition, similar types of literature will naturally share certain themes and motifs, and this similarity drastically complicates any attempt to trace the intentionality of themes and motifs within the Twelve. For example, judgment is a constitutive motif of prophetic literature, so judgment alone offers little help as an intertextual theme in the Twelve, if one wishes to consider the question of intentionality. Conversely, however, one cannot ignore the motif of judgment if one hopes to address the question of intentional literary development within the Twelve.

To say that Hosea, Joel, and Amos pronounce judgment on Israel is a true statement but offers little help regarding the purpose of the formation of the Twelve as a corpus. However, analyzing and comparing the type of judgment, the presuppositions, the metaphors, and the recipients of that judgment may lead one to isolate specific line(s) of thought more concretely. For example, the locust metaphor in Joel provides the unifying imagery for the instrument of judgment in Joel 1–2. Locust imagery unites diverse material presupposing threats from locust plague, drought, and enemy attack.[36] Later in the Twelve, several passages (Amos 4:9; {117} Nah 3:16b, 17; Hab 1:9; Mal 3:10) use locust metaphors to refer to divinely initiated threats to Yahweh's people. Notably, Nah 3:16b, 17 and Hab 1:9 associate the locust metaphors with nations which invade the land, a connection which has explicit connections to Joel 1–2. Both texts exhibit other tendencies which orient them to the Book of the Twelve, not just to the literary horizon of the particular writing in which they appear.[37] Amos 4:9

---

36. See Bergler, *Joel als Schriftinterpret*, 45–68. E.g., cf. Joel 1:7 (locust as nation-enemy) with the effects of a drought in Joel 1:17–20.

37. Nahum 3:16b, 17 represents two "redactional glosses" explicitly connoting Assyria as one of the invading locusts mentioned in Joel (see Nogalski, *Redactional*

plays a key role in Hag 2:17 where the context exhibits other Joel-related vocabulary that appears to be deliberately inserted.[38] Finally, the context of Mal 3:10–11 also appears to be one which deliberately references Joel.[39] Thus, all of these passages have plausible links to the same editorial movement which spans several writings of the Twelve. Not only can each of these texts be explained as part of the development of the Book of the Twelve, but they point to a consistent hermeneutic which interprets the locusts of Joel as the political superpowers (Assyria, Babylon, Persia) who "devour" the land.

Simultaneously, these images are interwoven with the promise of agricultural bounty which threads its way through the writings of the Twelve. As noted in the discussion of catchwords, the promise of agricultural bounty reappears at significant points using the language of Joel. Thus, both the locust and agricultural bounty motifs recur throughout the Twelve by catchwords and allusions to the language of Joel. The locust motif represents the "continuing threat" to the "agricultural bounty" which Yahweh promises if the people repent. Joel 1:4 speaks of a series of locust plagues, each devouring the leftovers from the previous plague. Joel 1:7 associates the "locusts" with an enemy attack. Joel 2:1–11 depicts the threat of that locust/army in more detail. Following an invitation to repentance (Joel 2:12–17), Joel 2:18–25 promises the removal of the enemy from the north (2:20), restoration of agricultural bounty (2:19, 22–24), and a reversal of the effects of all the predicted locust plagues (2:25).

These motifs continue to develop and to intertwine as one progresses {118} through the writings of the Twelve. In Amos 4:9, Yahweh laments that the Northern Kingdom refused to head warnings (drought, locust) and refused to repent. This refusal effectively discontinues Yahweh's attempts to lure Israel back to him (Hos 2:14). Nahum 3:16–17 portrays the destruction of one "locust" by another which in turn becomes an even larger threat to Judah (Hab 1:5–17).[40] By the end of Habakkuk

---

Processes, 124–27). Habakkuk 1:9 appears in the Babylonian commentary which imitates Nah 3:1–19 (see ibid., 140–42, 146–50).

38. Note 226 n. 25, which demonstrates how Hag 2:19 restates the promise of Joel while drawing upon the agricultural bounty motif. Note also the discussion of Amos 4:9 below.

39. See 226 n. 24 above.

40. For arguments delineating Hab 1:2–17 as a deliberate intensification of the Babylonian threat in comparison to Assyria, see Nogalski, *Redactional Processes*, 146–

the destruction of Jerusalem is anticipated in terms of the threat to the agricultural bounty (note 3:17).[41] Following the return of the exiles, the book of Haggai (note also Zech 1:2-6) documents the repentance of the people and their leaders which results in the rebuilding of the temple. At that point, the promise of agricultural bounty reappears (Hag 2:17, 19) using language from Amos 4:9 and Joel 1-2. Zechariah 8:12 confirms that Yahweh has begun answering the promise of bounty. However, the optimism of Zech 7-8 is short-lived. Malachi presumes the people have reverted to the practices which led to the locust attacks in the first place. They no longer recognize Yahweh's faithful actions. As a result the devourer remains a threat to the agricultural bounty (Mal 3:10-11).

This thematic development does not simply illustrate a modern reading of the Twelve. Several of these texts have likely been inserted into their respective contexts as redactional glosses. The book of Joel contains several of the major themes and/or motifs which recur in the Twelve (in addition to agricultural bounty and locusts, note especially the day of Yahweh). The threads of the motif recur in significant and appropriate locations within the Twelve. Thus, one can and should pay careful attention to the question of thematic development as a means for analyzing possible motives for the editing of the Twelve as a single (albeit composite) literary work.

Framing Devices

Having illustrated quotations, allusions, catchwords, and themes, one should also note the occurrence of framing devices as significant vehicles for developing meaning in the Twelve. Framing devices constitute a {119} somewhat broader category than the previously discussed types of intertextuality. The questions raised by these devices require more complex treatment than can be accomplished here, but for the sake of completeness, they must at least be mentioned briefly. Within the Twelve, at least five types of framing devices can be illustrated: superscriptions, genre similarities, structural parallels, juxtaposition of catchwords, and canonical allusions. Questions of intentionality become significantly

---

50. Note especially the reference to the face of the (locust) horde moving forward in Hab 1:9.

41. Zephaniah, the next writing, moves from the destruction of Jerusalem and Judah (chs. 1-2) to the anticipated return. See Nogalski, *Literary Precursors*, 198-200.

more difficult to ascertain when evaluating the texts, but these devices demand evaluation.

Superscriptions play a key role in the macrostructure of the Twelve.[42] Six superscriptions provide the chronological framework to the Twelve and represent the largest group which influences the reading of the Twelve. The superscriptions of Hosea, Amos, Micah, Zephaniah, Haggai, and Zechariah all contain chronological indicators, and, very significantly, *all six* appear in a literarily constructed chronological order.

The chronological presentation of the first four superscriptions derives from the patterned combination of the kings and the kingdoms mentioned in the superscriptions.

Hos 1:1	Amos 1:1	Mic 1:1	Zeph 1:1
Uzziah (Judah)	Uzziah (Judah)		
Jotham (Judah)		Jotham (Judah)	
Ahaz (Judah)		Ahaz (Judah)	
Hezekiah (Judah)		Hezekiah (Judah)	(Hezekiah)
Jeroboam (Israel)	Jeroboam (Israel)		↑
			Josiah (Judah)

This pattern encompasses the eighth and seventh centuries. It focuses upon the kings of Judah, but both Hosea and Amos also list Jeroboam, probably due to the fact that these messages of these writings relate {120} primarily to Yahweh's dealings with the Northern Kingdom. Micah 1:2–7 already presumes the destruction of Samaria, and even though the Northern Kingdom still existed during the reigns of Jotham, Ahaz, and part of the reign of Hezekiah, Mic 1:1 does not mention the kings of the Northern Kingdom. Zephaniah 1:1 places the prophet's ministry in the reign of

---

42. For a more thorough analysis of the varieties of superscriptions, see: John D. W. Watts, "Superscriptions and Incipits in the Book of the Twelve," in Nogalski, *Reading and Hearing the Book of the Twelve*, 110–25.

Josiah and traces the prophet's ancestry back to Hezekiah, thus linking the two most significant Judean kings (outside of David and Solomon) in the Deuteronomistic History.

In a separate grouping, Haggai and Zechariah also contain an interrelated chronological presentation. Haggai and Zechariah contain multiple chronological references.[43] These references are stylized, but manifest a radically different linguistic pattern from the first group of four. Within each book, these dated speeches appear in chronological order. The last three dated references in Haggai postdate the first dated reference in Zech 1:1 which causes the time periods of those two prophets to overlap.

Literary analysis suggests neither chronological schema is accidental nor simply the result of completed writings being placed next to one another.[44] However, both sets of chronologies appear to have been created prior to incorporation of the respective writings into the Twelve. Nevertheless, when these six writings were incorporated into the larger corpus, they were kept in chronological order.[45] As a result, one may state with relative confidence that the chronological order of these six writings constitutes an intentionally created framework which casts a historical perspective on the collection of the Twelve.

A second notable group of related superscriptions creates a threefold division at the conclusion of the Book of the Twelve. Zechariah 9:1; 12:1; and Mal 1:1 introduce groups of texts with the phrase "the burden (or oracle) of the word of Yahweh," which appears only in these three places within the entire Old Testament. As with the chronologies, this pattern appears to have been created deliberately.[46] These {121} superscriptions link blocks of material which focus on the fate of Ephraim and Judah (Zech 9-11); Judah and Jerusalem (Zech 12-14); and the postexilic community (cf. Mal 3:16-18).

A third category of superscriptions is more difficult to evaluate. Most of those writings which do not contain chronological superscriptions

---

43. Haggai 1:1; 1:15; 2:1; 2:10; 2:18; 2:20; Zech 1:1; 1:7; 7:1.

44. Likely, these superscriptions grew in two stages, as indicated by the redactional shaping of the Deuteronomistic superscriptions (Hos 1:1; Amos 1:1; Mic 1:1; Zeph 1:1) and the superscriptions of Haggai and Zechariah which are likewise very similar to one another. See Nogalski, *Literary Precursors*, 84-87.

45. Note that the LXX rearranges the order of the first six, but still keeps the dated superscriptions in their proper order.

46. See Nogalski, *Redactional Processes*, 217.

demonstrate an affinity to their contexts or to neighboring superscriptions. The superscription in Joel 1:1 mirrors the word of Yahweh superscriptions of Hosea (1:1), but without the chronological indicators. Obadiah's superscription labels the booklet as "the vision of Obadiah," which appropriately follows the visions of Amos. Nahum 1:1 and Hab 1:1 both make reference to the burden/oracle. Malachi 1:1, in addition to the phrase "burden of the word of Yahweh," contains reference to the message coming "by the hand" of Malachi, which appears elsewhere only in Haggai within the Twelve. It is difficult to draw any firm conclusions from this phenomenon, but these similarities do at least add to the impression of deliberately created linkages noted elsewhere within the texts.

Genre repetition provides a second framing device which can be illustrated in the Twelve. In at least two instances, one can note distinctive recurrences of genres which, if not intentionally created for the larger corpora, certainly serve an appropriate literary function within the respective writings. The first example of genre repetition appears with the occurrence of the "vision" of Obadiah which follows the five visions of Amos. The fact that Obadiah patterns itself after Amos 9 strengthens the impression that this reference to the vision of Obadiah is intentionally created at the point Obadiah was composed for its place next to Amos.[47]

In the Twelve, portrayals of theophanies of judgment begin or end four successive works.[48] Micah begins with a portrayal of a theophany which threatens Judah with the same fate as Samaria. Nahum begins with a semiacrostic theophany of universal judgment (1:2–9) which introduces the book's major theme of the destruction of Assyria. Habakkuk concludes with a theophany announcing the future destruction of the enemy, which in the context of the book implies Babylon. Zephaniah begins with a theophanic portrayal of judgment on Jerusalem. {122} All four theophanies contain at least hints of universal judgment while also pointing to judgment upon specific entities.[49] In previous discussions, I have suggested that Nahum and Habakkuk were expanded considerably for their

---

47. Ibid., 61–68, esp. 64.

48. See discussions of the origin and development of Old Testament theophanic portrayals by Jörg Jeremias, "Theophany in the OT," *IDBSup*, 896–98; Jeremias, *Theophanie: Die Geschichte einer alttestamentlichen Gattung*, WMANT 10 (Neukirchen-Vluyn: Neukirchener Verlag, 1965).

49. Note the universal elements of Mic 1:2a and Zeph 1:2–3 come prior to the specific judgments. Nahum 1:2–8 and Hab 3:1–20 convey a much larger portion of

place in the Twelve by the addition of these theophanic poems. It seems likely that the shorter theophanic material in Micah existed prior to the Joel-related layer, while the universal theophanic portrayal of Nah 1:2–8; Hab 3:1–20; and Zeph 1:2–3 all show strong linguistic and paradigmatic connections to Joel.[50]

Structural parallels constitute the third category of framing devices. Occasionally, adjacent passages in the seams of the Twelve exhibit significant parallels in the text markers and themes within the passages. Two examples (Amos 9/Obadiah; Nah 3/Hab 1) will illustrate this device. In both cases, the concluding chapters of Amos and Nahum have a similar structure to the previous chapters of those books.[51] It is not illogical then that the structural parallels of the context are continued in the editorial work of the following book. First, as noted above, Obadiah manifests most of the same structuring devices as Amos 9. These devices likely intend to equate (hence the parallel) Edom's fate with the fate of the Northern Kingdom.[52] The presence of an extended quotation in Obad 1–5 provides a cross-reference which increases the likelihood that this structural imitation was accomplished deliberately.

Second, Hab 1:5–17 utilizes catchwords and word plays to point back to Nah 3:1–8 but the connections also demonstrate a tendency to heighten the threat of Babylon in comparison to the threat which Assyria had posed previously. For example, Nineveh is attacked by horsemen (3:3), while Babylon attacks with horsemen (Hab 1:8); Nineveh will go into captivity (Nah 3:10) while Babylon collects captives (Hab 1:9). Nineveh becomes a mockery whose fortifications are ready to be destroyed (Nah 3:12, 14), while Babylon laughs at the fortifications of rulers (Hab 1:10). Nineveh's shepherds and king are defeated (Nah 3:18) while Babylon mocks rulers and kings (Hab 1:10). {123} In evaluating the possibility of intentionality in this example, the Babylonian commentary material in Habakkuk expands a previously existing wisdom piece about the prosperity of the wicked, making it plausible (but admittedly less objectively so), that Habakkuk was

---

universal imagery, although the context of the two books imply Assyria and Babylon are the primary targets of Yahweh's judgments.

50. Nogalski, *Literary Precursors*, 198–200.

51. For Amos 9 as the structural parallel to Amos 8, see ibid., 117–18. For the manner in which the structure of Nah 3 parallels Nah 2, see Nogalski, *Redactional Processes*, 123.

52. See above.

edited to create this parallel.[53] Thus, the literary transition from Nahum to Habakkuk implies that Judah endures the threat of Assyria only to hear that it will fall to the Babylonians.

The juxtaposition of catchwords represents the fourth framing device which needs to be brought into a discussion of intertextuality in the Twelve. Frequently, the catchwords which appear between two writings heighten the tension between a promise to Yahweh's people and the reality of the current situation. The Hosea-Joel connection illustrated this tendency in the discussion above. In addition, the end of Zephaniah relates Yahweh's promise to the people that he will gather the people "in that time" (3:18–19), while Hag 1:2 confronts "this people" who says "the time" has not yet come. Haggai ends with a promise to overthrow the nations with their chariots, horses, and riders while Zechariah's first night vision (1:6–17) portrays the nations at rest while the horses and riders of Yahweh patrol the earth. Zechariah 8:9–23 manifests more than twenty words and phrases in common with the beginning of Malachi.[54] In most cases, the word or phrase in Zechariah is used positively while the counterpart in Malachi appears as part of the prophet's confrontation of the people's lack of obedience to Yahweh.

Canonical allusions constitute a fifth type of framing device which deserves attention. This device serves an important function in at least one series of texts: Zech 13:9; Zech 14:1–21; Mal 3:22–24. Zechariah 13:9 reads: "And I will bring the third part through the fire, refine them as silver is refined, and test them as gold is tested. They will call on my name, and I will answer them; I will say, 'They are my people.' And they will say, 'The Lord is my God'" (NASB). The first half of this verse clearly alludes to Mal 3:3 while the second half draws from Hos 2:25 [Eng. 2:23]. The second text of this series combines a series of allusions to Isa 2 and 66.[55] Finally, it has frequently been noted that Mal 3:22 alludes to Josh 1:2, 7. The canonical implications of these three series of allusions and partial quotes may be graphically illustrated: {124}

---

53. Nogalski, *Redactional Processes*, 138–44.
54. See Nogalski, *Literary Precursors*, 53–55.
55. See Nogalski, *Redactional Processes*, 244–52.

INTERTEXTUALITY AND THE TWELVE   239

Beginning of Former Prophets	Beginning and end of first book of Latter Prophets	Beginning and end of the Twelve (last book of the Latter Prophets)	Alluding Texts	
		Hos 2:25 and Mal 3:3	Zech 13:9	
	Isa 2 and 66			Zech 14
Josh 1:2, 7				Mal 3:22

The canonical allusions move outwardly across the entire prophetic canon. Could this framing device be accidental? It is possible since the allusions are of different types, but the number of persons working independently who have noted these allusions argues strongly for the intentionality of the individual allusions. The meaningful order of the series certainly raises one's suspicions that the three passages belong to the same editorial movement.

Evaluating framing devices in the Twelve admittedly requires much more work before making definitive statements on the intentionality of all these devices. Still, the presence of these categories raises questions which deserve treatment about the possibility that editors intended readers to note them when reading the Twelve.

This paper has illustrated several intertextual devices which can help to develop reading strategies for the Book of the Twelve. Many of these devices can be attributed with some confidence to ancient editorial work on more than one writing within the Book of the Twelve. Others provide intriguing insights, but raise more questions than can be answered in this paper. The presence of such a wide variety of techniques begs for more study.

Zephaniah's Use of Genesis 1–11

A sea change has taken place in recent years in the study of prophetic literature through the recognition of the implications of the art of scribal allusion as a significant factor in the compilation of prophetic corpora. The book of Zephaniah represents a case in point. Since the 1980s a series of scholarly works have noted that this short book contains three subtle, but distinct allusions to texts and/or traditions located in Gen 1–11. What is more, these three passages in Zephaniah (1:2–3; 2:12–15; and 3:9–10) allude to texts in Gen 1–11 in sequential order by recalling Gen 1, 10, and 11 respectively. Unfortunately, while the individual allusions have drawn attention by various scholars, their cumulative effect has been considered less frequently.[1] Consequently, it remains somewhat a mystery {352} that the function and the motivation of these three pairings have not drawn more attention. Their presence has implications, both historical and literary, for understanding the hermeneutical and theological intentions of those who compiled and/or edited Zephaniah. They also shed light upon

---

1. For a definition of allusion, see Nogalski, "Intertextuality and the Twelve," 102–24. The use of the term "allusion" in this context refers to the use "of one or more words whose appearance intends to elicit the reader's recollection of another text (or texts) *for a specific purpose*" (109, emphasis original). Of course, validating criteria need to be considered for assessing the plausibility of an allusion as an author generated reference (as opposed to a purely reader-generated reference). For a more detailed discussion of the role played by allusion in biblical studies, see Richard L. Schultz, *The Search for Quotation: Verbal Parallels in the Prophets*, {352} JSOTSup 180 (Sheffield: Sheffield Academic, 1999), 183–207. Schultz documents the difficulty in finding consistent definitions of terms like citation, allusion, echo, and imitation, but he also correctly identifies the multiplicity of functions played by these devices. He argues one must reckons seriously with both authorial intent and reader competency when assessing the use of prophetic quotation and he ultimately seems to use quotation as a general term that also includes many functions typically associated with intentional allusions.

some of the scribal processes and conversations that were taking place in Persian period Yehud.

This essay will address this lacuna in three parts: (1) a synchronic presentation of the allusions themselves and a response to some of the objections raised in recent scholarship about treating these verses as allusions; (2) diachronic observations that evaluate the role of these allusions among the currently competing redactional models for Zephaniah; and (3) a constructive proposal for understanding the function and the motivation for these allusions in Zephaniah.

Zephaniah's Allusions to Genesis 1–11

Zephaniah 1:2–3

> I will utterly destroy everything from the face of the ground, says YHWH. I will destroy humanity and beasts. I will destroy the birds of the sky and the fish of the sea; and the ruins[2] with the wicked. And I will cut off humanity from the face of the ground, says YHWH.

The intentional use of Gen 1 in Zeph 1:2–3 was noted in 1980 by Michael De Roche.[3] De Roche argued that these verses deliberately recall both the creation account in Gen 1 and, more obliquely, the flood narrative of Gen 6–9. De Roche astutely observed that not only did the language in Zeph 1:3 mention the major categories of the created order of living beings in Gen 1, but it did so in precisely the reverse order that the elements were created according to that account. This reversal of the created order, according to De Roche, deliberately underscores the severity of the judgment to come by effectively portraying that judgment as the {353} reversal of creation itself. Moreover, he also infers echoes of the flood narrative at work in the *inclusio* created by the phrase "from the face of the earth" in Zeph 1:2 and 1:3.[4]

---

2. The word והמכשלות is often translated as "stumbling block" or emended to a verbal form, but see the singular in Isa 3:6, where it clearly means the place destroyed.

3. Michael De Roche, "Zephaniah 1:2–3: The 'Sweeping' of Creation," *VT* 30 (1980): 104–9.

4. Variations of this phrase (מעל פני האדמה) appear six times in the flood narrative in two different forms, three of which are the same variation as Zeph 1:2, 3. "From upon the face of the ground" (מעל פני האדמה) appears three times (Gen 6:7; 7:4;

The observations of de Roche have found a significant number of supporters in subsequent studies.[5] The allusions to the mythic past (creation and the flood) in Zeph 1:2–3 not only adds solemnity to the judgment pronouncement, it accounts for the order of the "list of the doomed,"[6] essentially selecting those elements that appear at the apex of the creation story (Gen 1:26) in order to convey the uniqueness of the judgment to follow. The list of targets includes humanity, beasts, birds, and fish respectively. In so doing, 1:2–3 conveys the impression that the divine act of judgment will in some way be as significant as the undoing of creation itself. What follows, of course, are pronouncements about the coming destruction of Judah and Jerusalem (Zeph 1:4–13).

Despite wide acceptance of the intentionality of 1:2–3, three lines of objection to De Roche's claims have been suggested. First, De Roche uses these two verses as the basis for claiming a very early date for the existence of the Pentateuch that already contained Priestly material. He suggested that this opening unit of Zephaniah provides compelling evidence that the Pentateuch (complete with priestly material) already existed in the seventh century because Zeph 1:1 places the prophet in the time of Josiah.[7] Even among those who accept that 1:2–3 contain allusions to Gen 1, this suggestion has found few followers. Two verses, in a book whose compilation and development are as complex as those of Zephaniah, do not provide a strong evidentiary foundation to overturn the consensus that the Priestly document stems largely from the exilic or early postexilic period.[8] Further, since De Roche wrote his article the general trend of pentateuchal research has indicated that the combined version of P and {354} non-P materials in Gen 1–11 were almost certainly not combined until long after the time of Josiah.[9] Zephaniah 1:2–3 is only the

---

and 8:7—as well as Zeph 1:2, 3) while the nearly synonymous phrase "from upon the earth" (מעל הארץ) appears in 7:4; 8:11, 13.

5. E.g., see Berlin, *Zephaniah*, 81–82. See also the survey in the essay for which I am indebted to the author: David P. Melvin, "Making All Things New (Again): Zephaniah's Eschatological Vision of a Return to Primeval Time," in *Creation and Chaos: A Reconsideration of Hermann Gunkel's Chaoskampf Hypothesis*, ed. JoAnn Scurlock and Richard H. Beal (Winona Lake, IN: Eisenbrauns, 2013), 269–81. See also Nogalski, *Book of the Twelve: Micah–Malachi*, 713.

6. Berlin, *Zephaniah*, 81.
7. De Roche, "Zephaniah 1:2–3," 106.
8. See Nogalski, *Literary Precursors*, 106.
9. See the discussion in Nogalski, *Book of the Twelve: Micah–Malachi*, 705.

first of three literary allusions to Gen 1–11. The fact that the other two exhibit awareness of P and non-P materials suggests that a combined P and non-P version of Gen 1–11 already existed for the editor of Zephaniah. This awareness undercuts the suggestion of De Roche for overturning the date of the Priestly source.

Ben Zvi offers a second line of objections to De Roche, this one based upon methodological principles. According to Ben Zvi, in Zeph 1:2, the phrase "I will utterly remove" has important thematic and linguistic connections to Jer 8:13 and Hos 4:3.[10] Ben Zvi tends to treat these, and other lexical pairings, as common traditions and stereotypical formulations rather than explicit utilization of one text by another. For him, the word "all" is too vague to be defined, but the explanatory note in 1:3 provides more definitive limits. The phrase "from upon the face of the earth" is always related to destruction, though by itself it does not always imply universal destruction (see esp. Exod 32:12; Deut 6:15; 1 Sam 20:15; 1 Kgs 9:7; 13:34; Jer 28:16; Amos 9:8). The phrase "utterance of YHWH" follows the phrase "I will destroy" (as it does in Jer 8:13). These four phrases lead Ben Zvi to conclude that the meaning of 1:2 implies total destruction from YHWH.[11] Subsequently, Ben Zvi clarifies that this destruction is "total but not necessarily universal destruction."[12]

Regarding 1:3, Ben Zvi takes issue with the assertions that expressions in 1:3 evoke the creation account and the flood story. He considers the expressions "man and beast" and "the birds of heaven and fish of the sea" as inconclusive evidence for the presence of allusions to Gen 1. "Man and beast" represents a common merism that occurs dozens of times in the Hebrew Bible. For Ben Zvi, "birds of heaven" appears relatively frequently in the Hebrew Bible, though it appears in conjunction with "fish of the sea" only in Zeph 1:3 and Hos 4:3. Further, Ben Zvi notes that "fish of the sea" only appears in Gen 9:2 in relationship to the flood tradition and never occurs in the two creation stories of Genesis. He does recognize a very close parallel in Ps 8:9 that uses the word צפור for bird. Ben Zvi does not accept the idea that the phrase "I will cause the wicked to stumble" is a secondary addition. Ben Zvi approaches the question of dependence from a very minimalist position, so in an attempt to avoid all {355} circular reasoning, he enforces almost mechanical evaluations of

---

10. Ben Zvi, *Historical-Critical Study of the Book of Zephaniah*, 271.
11. Ibid., 55.
12. Ibid., 271.

the relationship between intertexts that virtually eliminate any possibility of recognizing literary allusions, even while seeking to evaluate the social settings of the various formulations. In so doing, for him, the lack of conclusive evidence allows him to ignore 1:2-3 as an allusion to Gen 1. His insistence upon incontrovertible criteria cannot be met, and though it does provide some helpful cautions for jumping too quickly to find parallels between texts, he not only fails to take account of the creative way that allusions function but he also does not consider the presence of "memory variants" in citations.[13]

In a third line of objection, Sweeney takes issue with the implications of the allusions for treating Zephaniah as the product of a late redaction in light of Gen 1-11.[14] He does not always deny the existence of the allusions per se, but he argues that they could be the result of traditional material that would have been available to the compiler of Zephaniah close to the time of Josiah as noted in the book. He argues against 1:2-3 containing an allusion to the "Genesis flood tradition and the concomitant claim that

---

13. See Carr, *Formation of the Hebrew Bible*, 13-101 (esp. 25-36). Carr illustrates numerous instances when—in both oral and written contexts—"memory variants" factor significantly in citations. Further, the fact that the fish, e.g., are included in Zeph 1:3 does not eliminate the allusion to the flood narrative since that is part of the point. The destruction imagined in Zeph 1:2-3 is worse than the flood. It undoes all of creation. Ben Zvi notes Pss 69:36; 96:11; Job 12:7-8; and Deut 30:11-13 also refer to the cosmos for different rhetorical purposes using some of these phrases. The first two just mention the three parts (heavens, earth, and sea). Job 12:7-8 contains language much closer to the priestly creation account and recounts a debate about the role of wisdom in creation. See Norman C. Habel, *The Book of Job: A Commentary*, OTL (Philadelphia: Westminster, 1985), 218; David J. A. Clines, *Job 1-20*, WBC 17 (Dallas: Word, 1989), 292-93; Samuel E. Balentine, *Job*, SHBC 10 (Macon, GA: Smyth & Helwys, 2006), 201-4. Nevertheless, the allusion in Job 12:7-8 uses a lexical cluster of terms (animals [cf. Gen 1:24-26], birds of the air [cf. Gen 1:26, 28, 30], the [living things of the] earth [cf. Gen 1:10, 28; 9:2], fish of the sea [cf. Gen 1:26; 9:2]) that does not follow the exact order of Gen 1. That does not mean, however, that the author of Job 12 is not evoking Gen 1. Deuteronomy 30:11-13 mentions the heavens and the sea as places considered beyond the reach of humans (implying that they live on the dry land, but not using that term). In short, while these objections underscore the conceptual world of ancient Israel regarding a tripartite cosmos, they do not eliminate the likelihood that Zeph 1:2-3 draws artistically upon the creation account in Gen 1 specifically.

14. Marvin A. Sweeney, *Zephaniah: A Commentary*, Hermeneia (Minneapolis: Fortress, 2003), 14-15.

Zeph 1:3 (and 1:2) is the product of a postexilic eschatologizing redaction."[15] He applies the same logic for arguments concerning the creation account. Sweeney, while relying upon Ben Zvi in places, does not appear to be as methodologically rigorous as Ben Zvi. For example, {356} Sweeney recognizes the language in Zeph 3:9 as an allusion to Gen 11, but this allusion is considerably more oblique than the list of created beings in Zeph 1:3. However, since Gen 11 is typically classified as a J text, Sweeney argues that J would have predated Zephaniah and thus been available to the author of 3:9 in the seventh century. Consequently, rather than methodology, Sweeney appears to be driven by chronological concerns in 1:2–3. He otherwise finds ways to interpret the book of Zephaniah as largely stemming from the seventh century, early in the reign of Josiah.[16] If Sweeney were to follow De Roche, he would have even more difficulty dating Zephaniah in its final form to the seventh century. Sweeney does not make the mistake of De Roche by using these two verses to challenge the date of the Priestly editing of the Pentateuch. Rather, Sweeney's concern attempts to disassociate Zeph 1:2–3 from explicit use of Gen 1 because this would argue against his early dating of Zephaniah.

The three lines of objection (dating Priestly material to the seventh century, overly rigid methodological controls, and chronological conflicts with Zeph 1:1) do not effectively counteract the convincing power of De Roche and others who argue that Zeph 1:2–3 specifically recalls Gen 1 and more obliquely incorporates language that evokes the flood story. Scholarly consensus continues to treat the Priestly material as later than the seventh century, making De Roche's claims suspect. Ben Zvi's insistence upon a mechanical set of criteria does not do justice to the way that allusions work. On the other hand, while acknowledging a more oblique allusion in Zeph 3:9 to Gen 11, Sweeney's rejection of the allusion in 1:2–3 appears intent upon avoiding association of Zephaniah with material later than the seventh century. The evocation of the Priestly creation story in Zeph 1:2–3 carries considerable significance literarily and historically since it interprets what follows as judgment that is nothing short of the undoing of the created order and since it means that these verses, in all likelihood, do not come from the seventh century (despite 1:1).

---

15. Ibid., 63.
16. Ibid., 14.

Zephaniah 2:12-15

The second passage that draws upon Gen 1-11 appears at the conclusion of Zeph 2:4-15, that is, at the end of Zephaniah's oracles against the nations (OAN). Zephaniah 2:12-15 constitute the oracles against Cush (2:12) and Assyria (2:13-15), and they provide the penultimate climax of the OAN before the rhetoric shifts to a pronouncement against Jerusalem (3:1-7). A brief survey of recent treatments of the collection will elucidate {357} the function of Zephaniah's OAN in general, and the selection of *these* nations in particular. Thereafter, a closer look at the use of the table of nations (esp. Gen 10:5-14) in Zeph 2:12-15 will document the allusive language and its function.

The selection of nations in Zephaniah's OAN include oracles against the Philistines (2:4-7), Moab and the Ammonites (2:8-11), the Cushites (2:12), and Assyria (2:13-15). Recent studies have indicated that the driving hermeneutic for selecting these nations has to do with the socio-political situation of the late seventh century, though it is explained in different ways. At their core, these entities represent groups who suffered significant loss with the demise of Assyria.

Christensen and Sweeney illustrate the arguments of those who see the OAN as a collection that arose in the early years of Josiah's reign.[17] They believe that the selection of nations represents enemies of Josiah's reform movement or else they threaten the territorial expansion that Josiah planned. Two significant problems arise with this interpretation. First, the time they propose makes little sense for the denunciation of Cush (= Ethiopia) since the Cushite dynasty that had controlled Egypt was defeated in 663 BCE by Assyria itself. Cush was not a viable threat in the time of Josiah. Second, dating the collection to the early reign of Josiah does not explain the omission of Egypt and Edom from the list of nations. Both entities at this point would have stood in the way of Josiah's expansionism, but Zephaniah makes no mention of them.

Ben Zvi makes a more compelling case that the oracles against the nations in Zephaniah make sense in the early postmonarchic period because they display a consistent hermeneutic that would have understood the oracles against these nations to have been fulfilled in the latter

---

17. Duane L. Christensen, "Zephaniah 2:4-15: A Theological Basis for Josiah's Program of Political Expansion," *CBQ* 46 (1984): 669-82; Marvin A. Sweeney, "A Form-Critical Reassessment of the Book of Zephaniah," *CBQ* 53 (1991): 388-408.

decades of the seventh century.[18] This hermeneutic also explains the omission of Edom and Egypt, neither of whom would have been destroyed in the early postmonarchic period. For Ben Zvi, these oracles show a keen sense of history as well as a theological expectation regarding the collection of prophetic oracles, especially those anticipating the punishment of foreign nations. Nevertheless, Ben Zvi has an interesting take upon 2:12 (the oracle against {358} Cush). He notes that Cush was destroyed in 664 BCE, which does not fit his time in frame of the last decades of the seventh century. Ben Zvi offers an unusual explanation:

> But the Cushite unit is unique among the OAN units because of its brevity, but also and more importantly for the present case, because it is the only one that does not clearly point to future events. To the contrary, it seems likely that it refers to a present condition or even to a status that originated in the past.[19]

For him, then, the role of the oracles for the reader points to future events from the perspective of the reader of the book, with the exception of the oracle against Cush. Ben Zvi also notes that while Cush and Assyria had been at odds with one another prior to 664 BCE, Egypt and Assyria were allied, or at least not on hostile terms for the remainder of the seventh century until Nineveh's destruction in 612 BCE. Hence, while Ben Zvi's arguments are stronger, they still do not explain the inclusion of Cush with complete satisfaction.

Berlin, while finding the evidence for a preexilic or postmonarchic dating of 2:4–15 to be inconclusive, does point to a way forward by noting how the formulations of 2:11b–15 function as allusions to the table of nations material in Gen 10.[20] The evidence that Berlin provides concerns the following: (1) the phrase "islands of the nations" appears only in Zeph 2:11b and Gen 10:5; (2) both texts also contain the unusual combination of Cush (Zeph 2:12; Gen 10:6–7) and Assyria (Zeph 2:13; Gen 10:11); (3) the line of Cush (a son of Ham) specifically includes Assyria, founded by

---

18. Ben Zvi, *Historical-Critical Study of the Book of Zephaniah*, 298–306. See also the largely positive assessment in Berlin, *Zephaniah*, 34–43. Despite her sympathies toward his arguments, she ultimately decides the evidence for either preexilic or postmonarchic dating is inconclusive.

19. Ben Zvi, *Historical-Critical Study of the Book of Zephaniah*, 304.

20. Berlin, *Zephaniah*, 111–13, 120–24. See also Nogalski, *Book of the Twelve: Micah–Malachi*, 704–6.

Nimrod, as well as other ancient Mesopotamian kingdoms from the distant past;[21] (4) the line of Ham in Gen 10 also includes the descendants of Canaan (10:6, 15-20) and this line includes the Philistines (10:19) who are also condemned in Zephaniah (2:5, "Canaan, land of the Philistines"); (5) the condemnation of the entities in Zeph 2:4-15 essentially condemns the descendants of two of Noah's three sons: Japheth (labeled as the islands of the nations) and Ham (the descendants of Cush and Canaan); (6) and the nonmention of Edom makes sense since Edom comes from another genealogical line. {359}

When combined with the observations of Ben Zvi, Berlin's notation of the allusion to Gen 10 strengthens the sense that the specific combination of nations have been deliberately singled out as those whose fate diminished as a result of events of the seventh century. In keeping with the allusion to the creation story of Gen 1, Zephaniah's allusions to Gen 10 also invert the rhetorical purpose of the source text. Genesis 1 describes creation, while Zeph 1:2-3 describes the coming judgment as the undoing of creation. Similarly, Gen 10 describes the founding of the lines of Japheth and Ham, while Zeph 2:4-15 describes their undoing. As with the allusion to Gen 1, the allusion to Gen 10 complicates any attempts to date the final form of Zephaniah to the seventh century since the material in Gen 10:5-20, to which the Zephaniah material alludes appears to include both P and non-P material.[22] This combination of sources suggests a point in the formation of Genesis after which the bulk of the P and non-P material would have been woven together in these chapters.

The inclusion of specific neighboring peoples and allusions to the mythical line of Cush (who sired Nimrod, who founded the ancient Mesopotamian powers and built Nineveh [Gen 10:10-11]) anticipate the power structure of the seventh century. In other words, Zephaniah's inclusion of Cush and Assyria culminates Zephaniah's judgment oracles against

---

21. Berlin, *Zephaniah*, 111-13, 120-24. She interprets Cush as a mythic name for Mesopotamia in Zeph 2:12 and she may very well be correct, but the confusion of Cush with Ethiopia appears to be a consistent pattern in the reception history of these verses (as she documents very well), so that even in ancient times, it is impossible to know whether the Zephaniah author intended Cush to be a reference to Mesopotamia in general or to Ethiopia.

22. See the summary of several recent treatments of Gen 10 in relation to various models of the development of the Pentateuch in Nogalski, *Book of the Twelve: Micah–Malachi*, 704-6.

Assyria and its allies. As Sweeney, Berlin, and Ben Zvi have demonstrated, the surrounding peoples (Philistines, Moabites, Ammonites) were closely allied with Assyria in the seventh century and suffered devastating losses at the hands of Babylon in the change of power from Assyrian to Babylonian hegemony.[23] Hence, the Philistines were dealt a severe blow at the hands of Egypt (Gaza in 609 BCE; Ashdod by 616 BCE) and by the Babylonians (Ekron in 602–598 BCE; Ashkelon in 604 BCE; the Moabites and the Ammonites in 582/581 BCE). Conversely, this same dynamic accounts for why Edom and Egypt are not mentioned. Edom appears to have joined forces with Babylon more closely so that it is mentioned as aiding Babylon when it sacked Jerusalem (see Obad 10–14; Lam 4:21–22; Ps 137:7–8). Egypt also escaped Babylonian devastation to a large degree. To be sure, Egypt's hopes for controlling the Mediterranean coast and the inward trade routes were dashed at the battle of Carchemish in 605 BCE, when {360} Babylon essentially forced Egypt to retreat back to its own territory, but Babylon never succeeded in taking control of Egypt itself.

The removal of the two lines of the descendants of Noah, combined with the chronology of Zephaniah, makes a theological statement that provides clues for understanding why the nations in Zeph 2:4–5 receive attention in the first place. They do not represent a random collection of nations, but those whose fate was dramatically affected when Assyria was defeated in the last quarter of the seventh century. In this sense, the portrayal of the message of Zeph 2:4–15 reflects a scribal correlation: the events of the seventh century are interpreted as experience of the day of YHWH whose importance is nothing short of the reversal of Gen 10 and its founding of the order of Assyria and its allies after the flood.

Zephaniah 3:9–10

Zephaniah 3:9–10 contains a widely recognized allusion to the story of the tower of Babel (Gen 11:1–9).[24] This allusion in Zeph 3:9–10 inverts

---

23. Sweeney, *Zephaniah*, 17; Berlin, *Zephaniah*, 118–19; Ben Zvi, *Historical-Critical Study of the Book of Zephaniah*, 298–306.

24. A partial list of those who recognize this allusion includes: Julia M. O'Brien, *Nahum, Habakkuk, Zephaniah, Haggai, Zechariah, Malachi*, AOTC (Nashville: Abingdon, 2004), 123; Smith, *Micah–Malachi*, 141–42; Steck, "Zu Zef 3:9–10," 94; Berlin, *Zephaniah*, 14; Sweeney, *Zephaniah*, 182; Nogalski, *Book of the Twelve: Micah–Malachi*, 705–6, 743–45; Melvin, "Making All Things New (Again)."

the curse of multiple languages that leads to confusion at precisely the point in the book where the salvific section of Zephaniah begins. The phrasing of these verses is awkward, but the verses display a distinct perspective in Zephaniah:

> ⁹For then I will change *(their speech)* into pure speech for the peoples so that all of them will call on the name of YHWH to serve him with one shoulder. ¹⁰From beyond the rivers of Cush, my worshipers will bring my offering, O Daughter of my dispersed ones.

Several elements in these verses stand out. The idioms are unusual and something has to be added in 3:9 for the construction to make sense in English. Also, the reference to "Daughter of my dispersed ones" is treated here as a vocative, contrary to most English translations. The personified city has already been the subject of the woe oracle in 3:1–7, the second-person feminine single references in 3:11–12 also refer to her,²⁵ and a specific address to "Daughter Zion" appears in 3:14. This reading makes sense of the phrase in context, though the phrase has often been treated as an otherwise {361} obscure insertion into the text. Its odd formulation as a reference to Jerusalem helps to link the verse with Gen 11:1–9 by tying Lady Zion to the root פוץ (scatter). Zephaniah 3:9–10 anticipates the reconciliation of foreign peoples to YHWH—both by reference to the bringing of offerings and the worship of YHWH, and by allusions to the tower of Babel story. The allusions to Gen 11:1–9 have been recognized by a number of exegetes.²⁶ Zephaniah 3:9 says, "I will change" the speech of the peoples to "a pure speech" (שפה ברָרה), and the result, addressed to the "Daughter of my scattered ones" (בת פוצי) will be that those worshiping YHWH from "beyond the rivers of Cush" will bring YHWH's offerings.²⁷ This phrasing, in a short space, also produces quite a large concentration of lexical clusters shared with the language of Gen 11 where the whole earth had "one language" (שפה אחת, 11:1, 6) and was "one people" (עַם אחד, 11:6) until YHWH "confused [בלל] the language of the entire earth [שפת כל־הארץ]" (11:9) and they became "scattered" (פוץ) over the face

---

25. Zephaniah 3:11–12 refers to a feminine entity in direct address. In this sense, treating "Daughter of my dispersed ones" as a vocative in 3:10 connects the 2fs verb forms in 3:7 with the 2fs verb forms of 3:11–12.
26. See Berlin, *Zephaniah*, 14.
27. See Nogalski, *Book of the Twelve: Micah–Malachi*, 744–45.

of the earth (11:9). The word "pure" in Zeph 3:9 comes from the root ברר, and creates a word play on the root בלל (confused) in Gen 11:9 (which is also recognized as a word play on בבל).[28] As with the other two allusions to Gen 1 and 10, the allusions in Zeph 3:9-10 also reverse the message of the Genesis text to which it alludes (11:1-9). The tower of Babel story recounts how humanity was scattered across the world and lost the ability to be one people as well as the ability to communicate. The pronouncement in Zeph 3:9-10 anticipates a time when YHWH's worshipers from distant lands will come together in Zion to worship in purified speech. This imagery brings together the nations and YHWH's people in Zion to provide offerings to YHWH.

Genesis 11:1-9 is not the only text to which Zeph 3:9-10 alludes. Steck sees Zeph 3:9-10 as a *Fortschreibung* of Zeph 3:8 that is part of a larger redaction of the prophetic corpus.[29] He does not extrapolate why Zeph 3:8 entered the corpus. He only briefly mentions the allusion to Gen 11 in Zeph 3:9,[30] but he sees the formulation of 3:9-10 as highly influenced by Isa 18-19 even while it draws upon Gen 11:1-9. Steck notes several significant verbal connections to Isa 18-19 in Zeph 3:9-10: {362}

	Zeph 3:9-10		Isaiah 18-19
3:9	they will call on the *name of* YHWH	18:7	the place of *the name of* YHWH
	they will serve [עבד] YHWH	19:23	they will make [עבד] sacrifices and cereal offerings [מנחה]
	speech [שׂפה] as allegiance to YHWH		
		19:23	they will serve [עבד] YHWH
		19:18	speech [שׂפה] as allegiance to YHWH
3:10a	"beyond the rivers of Cush"	18:1	"beyond the rivers of Cush"

---

28. See Claus Westermann, *Genesis 1-11*, CC (Minneapolis: Fortress, 1997), 553-54; Gordon J. Wenham, *Genesis 1-15*, WBC 1 (Waco, TX: Word Books, 1987), 241; etc.

29. Steck, "Zu Zef 3:9-10," 90-95.

30. Ibid., 94.

3:10b	they will bring [יבל] cereal offerings [מנחה; see Isa 19:21] to YHWH	18:7	they will bring [יבל] gifts [שׁי] to YHWH in Mount Zion
	Addressed to the Daughter of my Dispersed ones [בת פוצי = Zion]		
	my entreaters [עתרי]	19:22	he will be entreated [עתר] by them

For Steck, the connections to Isaiah 18-19 are conceptual and highly connected to late scribal prophecy at a point in the time of the Diadochoi, since he also sees Isa 18-19 reflective of this later milieu. Other treatments of Isa 18-19 do not place these chapters as late.[31]

Zephaniah 3:9-10 assumes two distinctive issues are combined: the restoration of Jerusalem (as the presumed destination of peoples bringing offerings) and the reconciliation of foreign peoples to YHWH. The material in Zeph 3:9-10 thus anticipates a restored Jerusalem that will be aided by foreign worshipers of YHWH. The assumption of restoration means two things simultaneously: (1) judgment against Jerusalem and Judah is not denied, since the bringing of offerings happens after Jerusalem's punishment and conterminously with the gathering of the nations described in 3:8;[32] and (2) the material addressed to the restored Jerusalem looks beyond the time of Zephaniah to a time after the destruction of Jerusalem.

By alluding to Gen 11:1-9 and the story of the tower of Babel, Zeph 3:9-10 portrays this restoration as the undoing of human dispersion. Rather than the tower of Babylon as the epitome of human accomplishment, Jerusalem operates as the center of the utopian imagery—the place {363} to which YHWH's offerings are brought by those among the nations who speak in a purified language.

---

31. Williamson and Blenkinsopp are among those who do not question an early date for Isa 18. Williamson focuses only upon Isa 13-14 and 24-27 as later accretions to the Isaiah OAN. See Hugh G. M. Williamson, *The Book Called Isaiah: Deutero-Isaiah's Role in Composition and Redaction* (Oxford: Oxford University Press, 2005). Blenkinsopp argues that Isa 18 makes sense in the events surrounding 701 BCE; see Joseph Blenkinsopp, *Isaiah 1-39: A New Translation with Introduction and Commentary*, AB 19 (New York: Doubleday, 2000), 310.

32. Hence: "for then..." that begins 3:9 puts this action of 3:9-10 on the same chronological time frame as the judgment of the nations in 3:8.

Diachronic Proposals and the Genesis Allusions

While the previous section outlined the synchronic evidence that Zeph 1:2-3; 2:11b, 12-15; and 3:9-10 all allude to Gen 1-11 in a meaningful way, it also suggested that the presence of these allusions in Zephaniah had significant implications for dating their inclusion into Zephaniah. The evidence suggests that a single editor is responsible for these allusions because of their subtle, yet sophisticated and consistent, hermeneutical treatment of the Genesis texts. Yet, this scribal art also has to be factored into explanations of how the book of Zephaniah reached its final form. Several redactional models have been proposed for Zephaniah, some related and others not related to the development of the Book of the Twelve, but none to date have taken these allusions fully into account.[33]

As already noted, Ben Zvi and Sweeney struggle for different reasons with how to incorporate these allusions into their treatments of Zephaniah because they see the book as essentially the work of a single compiler.[34] While their compositional models imply a single creative act of composition, this composition does not account adequately for the divergent elements within Zephaniah. By contrast, Wöhrle's most recent treatment takes seriously the syntactical and thematic shifts in order to postulate a developmental model of Zephaniah that grows over time, but as will be shown, it does not adequately account for some of the unifying elements of literary framing such as one finds in the allusions to Gen 1-11. No consensus has been reached, however, on how to describe the development of Zephaniah, as can be illustrated by a brief survey of two diachronic models by Schart and Wöhrle. {364}

Wöhrle analyzes Zephaniah and finds five layers of composition and redactional growth.[35] In relative chronological order, he labels these layers

---

33. See Schart, *Entstehung des Zwölfprophetenbuchs*, 204-18; Wöhrle, *Frühen Sammlungen des Zwölfprophetenbuches*, 198-224.

34. Sweeney's compositional model presumes an early date that is too early to account for the interplay of priestly and nonpriestly material present in these verses. Ben Zvi assiduously avoids speculation about redactional development based upon his scepticism that the processes can be accurately described and his overly rigid methodological cautions. By contrast with Sweeney, Ben Zvi insists that the book of Zephaniah betrays a postmonarchic perspective.

35. Wöhrle, *Frühen Sammlungen des Zwölfprophetenbuches*, 198-228.

as: the foundational layer,[36] the Deuteronomistic layer,[37] the Joel layer,[38] the foreign nations layer I,[39] the salvation for the nations layer,[40] and isolated additions[41] that cannot be placed within systematic redactional layers. Apart from the foundational layer and the isolated additions, the other three layers relate to redactional layers that transcend an isolated Zephaniah corpus.

Wöhrle's layers are largely thematic in nature, so it is little wonder that the allusions to Gen 1–11 play a minor role in his analysis. For these allusions to function meaningfully in Zephaniah one has to recognize that the redactor using them to frame the three sections of the book is combining three thematic elements that Wöhrle does not think belong together as part of a single editorial agenda: judgment against Jerusalem, judgment against the nations, and the eventual restoration of both. Further, all of these allusions to Gen 1–11 function within a compositional setting that puts Zephaniah in the reign of Josiah (according to Zeph 1:1). Yet, despite the care with which Wöhrle proceeds with his literary-critical analysis, he ends up with a model in which he attributes the three sets of Genesis allusions to four different hands. According to Wöhrle, Zeph 3:9–10 belongs to a layer advocating the salvation of the nations, while Zeph 1:2–3 belongs to the foundational layer (minus the phrase "and those stumbling with the wicked"—a phrase he, and others, see as an isolated addition). Wöhrle treats the OAN (2:4–15) as coming from three different hands, with the initial layer entering as part of the work of the Deuteronomistic layer (1:4–6, 13b; 2:1–6*, 8–9a; 3:1–4, 6–8a) while 2:7, 9b–10, 13–15 function as part of his *Fremdvölkerschicht* I (which also includes 3:8b, 18–19). He sees 2:11–12 (the oracle against the Cushites) as an isolated addition, but Zeph 2:11–12 contains the strongest lexical connections to the Gen 10 parallel.

Schart comes at the literary-critical analysis implicitly emphasizing a different set of criteria, two of which stand out in comparison to the presentation of Wöhrle. First, Schart takes internal and external

---

36. 1:2, 3* (without את־הרשעים והמשכלוה), 7–9, 12–13a, 14–18.
37. 1:1, 4–6, 13b; 2:1–2, 3* (without כל־ענוי הארץ אשר משפטו פעלו), 4–6, 8–9a; 3:1–4, 6–8a, 11–13.
38. 3:14–17.
39. 2:7, 9b–10, 13–15; 3:8b, 18–19.
40. 3:9, 10*(without עתרי בת־פוצי).
41. 1:3* (והמשכלוה את־הרשעים), 10–11; 2:3* (כל־ענוי הארץ אשר משפטו פעלו), 11, 12; 3:5, 10* (עתרי בת־פוצי), 20.

citations from {365} other writings (e.g., quotations, allusions, echoes) into account more deliberately than does Wöhrle. Schart's presentation demonstrates that echoes of expressions from Hosea, Amos, and Micah play a more significant role in his reading of Zephaniah than they do for Wöhrle. Second, Schart ascribes significantly more of Zephaniah to the foundational core of the compilation than does Wöhrle. For Wöhrle, only a small portion of Zeph 1 belongs to his foundational layer,[42] while Schart assumes that the core collection represents smaller units preserved by the Zephaniah tradents and grouped for thematic and rhetorical purposes.[43] Hence, the Zephaniah corpus is, according to Wöhrle, a gradually unfolding document while for Schart, Zephaniah is a collection of speeches and sayings that has been updated with insertions that point toward the influence of other writings (Hosea, Amos, and Deuteronomy in particular).

These tendencies affect how one treats the underlying text. Thus, while both Schart and Wöhrle analyze formal criteria such as change of speaker, Wöhrle more often assumes that deviations from these criteria must point to a new hand while Schart allows more freedom for vacillation between the prophetic and divine voices used for rhetorical effect.[44] Similarly, both scholars recognize thematic similarities as unifying elements, but Schart tends to treat thematically similar texts with more suspicion when they contain what he feels to be resonances from Hosea, Amos, or other identifiable texts.[45] {366}

---

42. Wöhrle's foundational layer includes only material from Zephaniah 1: 1:2–3*, 7–9, 12–13a, 14–18.

43. Schart's foundational layer includes most of 1:4–3:7: 1:4–5, 7–13a; 14–18a (except the phrase "for they sinned against YHWH" in 1:17); (2:1–2?), 4–6, 8–9, 12–15; 3:1–7. For Schart, then, many of the places that Wöhrle suggests indicate tensions with surrounding verses, Schart would see as signs of independent sayings collected and arranged by the Zephaniah tradents.

44. See the treatment of the prophetic voice versus divine voice in Wöhrle regarding the change between 3:14–17 and 3:18 (*Frühen Sammlungen des Zwölfprophetenbuches*, 214–15) and Schart's explanation of the vacillating speakers in 1:2–18 (*Entstehung des Zwölfprophetenbuches*, 205–6).

45. E.g., Wöhrle treats 1:4–6 as a homogenous unit even though it changes speaker in 1:5 because of its close association with the charges against idolaters punished by Josiah in 2 Kgs 23:4–14 (*Frühen Sammlungen des Zwölfprophetenbuches*, 34, 201–2) while Schart seems to assume the verses reflect an underlying speech in the time of Josiah, but he separates 1:6 as a later insertion because of expressions that sound as

And yet, despite the variations between the two, one should not ignore some of the significant points of agreement as well. First, when one evaluates the first two layers of their proposals, the corpora they propose appear very similar. Second, both conclude that Zephaniah experienced redactional work that is best accounted for in the context of reflection upon texts in the Deuteronomistic History. Third, both see the origins of this Deuteronomistic editing in the context of the Book of the Four Prophets (Hosea, Amos, Micah, Zephaniah). These commonalities deserve a closer look.

If one looks at the Zephaniah corpus as described by both Wöhrle and Schart—that is, involving the foundational layer and the editing done under the influence of Deuteronomistic scribes—the textual profile of Zephaniah includes the following:

Schart	Wöhrle
1:1, 4–18a	1:1–9, 12–13a, 14–18
2:1–6, 8–9, 12–15	2:1–6, 8–9,
3:1–7 (3:11–13 represents Schart's next layer)	3:1–4, 6–8a, 11–13

By comparing these proposals at this stage of their development, one finds remarkable agreement in terms of the relative sequence in which the core of Zephaniah came together, despite these interpreters' differences regarding the underlying process. They only disagree about the following texts: 1:2–3, 13b, 18b; 2:12–15; 3:5, 8a, 11–13. Almost all of these differences can be explained by decisions based upon the larger model that the two presuppose. Wöhrle believes that 1:2–3 belongs to the foundational layer while Schart sees this text as part of his third layer, which is a universal eschatologizing frame that entered at the point of 3:11–13 (related to Nahum and Habakkuk). Significantly, this means that 1:2–3 and 3:11–13 represent a third step in the development of Zephaniah—the next stage

---

though 1:6 draws upon Amos (esp., "and who did not seek YHWH"; *Entstehung des Zwölfprophetenbuches*, 208–9.). By contrast, Wöhrle believes the purported connections to Amos represent too common of an idiom to claim dependence, even though the phrase does not appear in 2 Kgs 23 and even though the idea of "seeking YHWH" appears with בקש in Hosea (3:5; 5:6; 7:10), Amos (in a varied form—"to seek the word of YHWH", cf. 8:12), and Zephaniah (1:6; 2:3) and with דרש in Hosea (10:12), Amos (5:4–6, 14), and Micah (6:8).

after Schart's D-Corpus. Relatedly, Schart puts 1:18b after 1:2–3, so the fact that 1:18b cites 1:2–3 makes it necessary for him to account for that citation, while 1:18b does not stand out literarily for Wöhrle because 1:2–3 is part of his foundational layer. In 3:1–7, Schart and Wöhrle disagree only on the literary homogeneity of 3:5, which Wöhrle believes is an isolated addition unrelated to the editorial structuring of the book while Schart does not see the literary disjunctures to be so striking as to remove them. Schart and Wöhrle also disagree about how to interpret Zeph 3:8. Schart sees the entire verse as part of a universal frame with an eschatological {367} orientation while Wöhrle thinks the verse comes from two different hands (with 3:8a part of the Deuteronomistic editing and 3:8b part of the Foreign Nations I layer). Finally, Schart and Wöhrle disagree over the question of whether the material in 2:12–15 was part of the original collection of oracles against the nations. Schart sees no reason to doubt the oracles against Cush and Assyria were part of that collection while Wöhrle thinks that the Assyria oracle (2:13–15) entered later. Interestingly, both agree that 2:10–11 was not part of the original collection of oracles, though they explain the tensions differently. They disagree on the brief oracle against Cush (2:12), however, in that Wöhrle sees it (along with 2:11) as an isolated insertion.

Remarkably, for the purposes of this essay, not only do Wöhrle and Schart agree on the relative sequencing of the text for a major portion of Zephaniah, but most of the places where they disagree concerning the growth of the text at this point relate in a significant way to the Genesis allusions. Given what was noted above concerning how the resonances of intertexts affect one's understanding of the development of the text, a fresh look at the role of these allusions in light of an intermediate stage of development for Zephaniah would appear to be in order.

A Constructive Proposal

A few remarks about the current state of discussions regarding the scribal world in postmonarchic Judah are in order. In an attempt to reconcile the forces that produce both the unifying and the disjunctive elements in biblical texts, recent works have begun looking for new models by which to explain the role of scribes in the production of biblical literature. One common theme that has emerged from several of these studies concerns the extent to which the scribes who had both knowledge of and access to these texts were not mere copyists. In fact, evidence is mounting that scribal conversations developed as a result of both training and ideology. Van der Toorn[46] speaks of the development of a scribal culture while Carr develops a model of the growing body of literature as a curriculum.[47] {368} Texts, including biblical texts, were used as the source of education. Students, including those who would later become master scribes, would have learned from these texts from a very early age. The education required for scribal work would have extended well beyond memorization of a few key passages. These texts were studied and formed the knowledge base and the foundational theological testimony of the professional and religious commitments. In the words of Carr, these texts and traditions were "written on their heart," not merely texts that they were paid to copy.[48] And yet, the internalizing of these texts did not mean that every citation reflects perfect agreement of the text being cited because even "memorized" texts would likely include "memory variants" which reflect adaptation of the text, sometimes intentionally, sometimes unintentionally.[49]

Against the background of these discussions, which often deal with epigraphy, archaeology, and social realities of Judah in the postexilic period, certain biblical texts take on greater significance for understanding how training, theological perspectives, and actualizations of texts based upon other texts may well have come about. For example, consider the portrait of Ezra that develops in the Ezra-Nehemiah corpus. In Neh 8:13–14 one finds a significant, but frequently overlooked, passage that implies

---

46. Van der Toorn, *Scribal Culture*. See especially his treatment of the development and closure of canon, pp. 233–64.

47. Carr, *Writing on the Tablet of the Heart*, 156–73. Carr describes the nature of the process as the creation of an "education-enculturation curriculum." For an assessment of models of this lengthy development in the development of the canon, see also van der Toorn, *Scribal Culture*, and his discussion of canon as a "library catalogue" (236–44) and "curriculum" (244–47).

48. Carr describes a process in which texts were both memorized and consulted: "Long-duration texts ... were transmitted dually—in written media and in the minds and hearts of those who had ingested them. On one level, written copies were stored in a scribal workshop or temple sanctuary.... Nevertheless, a primary focus of long-duration textuality was the inscribing and preserving of texts in the people they were used to educate. Stored written copies, holy though they were, were merely the technology and tangible written talisman for a broader process of passing on to the next generation of leaders the values, views, and less tangible qualities of the ancient, revered tradition" (Carr, *Writing on the Tablet of the Heart*, 160).

49. Ibid., 57–65.

260 THE BOOK OF THE TWELVE AND BEYOND

a type of educational seminar for the religious and familial leadership that involved studying the Torah and acting upon it.

> [13] On the second day the heads of ancestral houses of all the people, with the priests and the Levites, *came together to the scribe Ezra in order to study the words of the law.* [14] And *they found it written in the law,* which the Lord had commanded by Moses, that the people of Israel should live in booths during the festival of the seventh month, [15] and that they should publish and proclaim in all their towns and in Jerusalem as follows, "Go out to the hills and bring branches of olive, wild olive, myrtle, palm, and other leafy trees to make booths, *as it is written*." (NRSV, emphasis added) {369}

Further, in the same chapter one finds an account of a group who instruct the people on the meaning of the law:

> [7] Also Jeshua, Bani, Sherebiah, Jamin, Akkub, Shabbethai, Hodiah, Maaseiah, Kelita, Azariah, Jozabad, Hanan, Pelaiah, and the Levites, helped the people to understand the law, while the people remained in their places. [8] So they read from the book, from the law of God, *with interpretation. They gave the sense, so that the people understood the reading.* [9] And Nehemiah, who was the governor, and Ezra the priest and scribe, and the Levites *who taught the people* said to all the people, "This day is holy to the Lord your God; do not mourn or weep." For all the people wept when they heard the words of the law. (NRSV, emphasis added)

Together these texts imply both the study and teaching of the law and its meaning was a responsibility of the leadership. These tasks, however, required training. Not only does this scenario imply the use of the skill of reading, it also implies a functional and systematic transmission of knowledge based upon that reading. Of course, historically, Neh 8 is difficult to date with certainty.[50] The chapter is highly stylized and could well be a retrojection of an idealized form of training back into the past, but it

---

50. On the difficulties of dating Ezra and Nehemiah, see the summary in Joseph Blenkinsopp, *Ezra-Nehemiah: A Commentary*, OTL (Philadelphia: Westminster, 1988), 41–69; Lester L. Grabbe, *Yehud: A History of the Persian Province of Judah*, vol. 1 of *A History of the Jews and Judaism in the Second Temple Period*, LSTS 47 (London: T&T Clark, 2005), 70–83 (esp. 72). The *terminus ab quo* would be the middle of the fifth century since Ezra's mission is dated typically to 458 BCE and Nehemiah's building of the wall took place in 445 BCE. The *terminus ad quem* would be tied to the critical

does reflect presuppositions of what the religious training of the people involved. It is not a huge step to suggest that this retrojection reflects the kind of scenario wherein someone read from the Torah and *interpreted* the text's meaning based upon transmitted knowledge.

Herein lies the background for a scenario that helps to explain the mythopoeic Genesis allusions in Zephaniah. A scribe reflecting upon the material in Zephaniah decides that the largely existing collection reflects events of cosmic significance: the destruction of Jerusalem and its temple equates with the undoing of creation as previously designed by YHWH. The coming destruction of Jerusalem and Judah, when read from the time of Josiah (1:1), is closely associated with YHWH's divine intervention against his own people.[51] Adding Zeph 1:2–3 as an introduction to the {370} depiction of Jerusalem's destruction draws this parallel forcefully, as already described, but it also alludes to the flood narrative precisely because this undoing of the cosmic order must have implications beyond Judah.

In fact, the OAN of Zeph 2 comprise the warning to the nations allied with Assyria that they too will be undone. Zephaniah 1:18aβ, b makes this connection explicit by associating the day of YHWH (1:7–18a) with the destruction of the inhabitants of the land/earth (כל ישבי־הארץ).[52] This day of wrath combines the destruction of Judah with the destruction of

---

question of the date of composition for the combined corpus of Ezra-Nehemiah which a number of critical scholars now put in the third or second century.

51. Here it should be noted that Ben Zvi and Sweeney correctly warn against understanding the day of YHWH as an eschatological event in Zephaniah. Ben Zvi argues correctly that the phrase in Zephaniah assumes for the postmonarchic community that the Day of YHWH refers to the coming destruction of Jerusalem in 587 BCE. Sweeney attempts to locate the warning to earlier events in the seventh century. See Ben Zvi, *Historical-Critical Study of the Book of Zephaniah*, 277–28; Sweeney, "Form-Critical Reassessment," 390. Ancient readers far more likely would have associated the coming judgment against Judah and Jerusalem on the day of YHWH with the events of 587 BCE than with some distant eschatological event. The larger context of the chronological structure of both the Book of the Four Prophets and the Book of the Twelve would only have strengthened this association with the "future" events when seen from the time of Josiah.

52. Schart correctly notes this connection as well as the parallel created for the Northern Kingdom destruction in Hos 4:1–3 using the language of Gen 1 (*Entstehung des Zwölfprophetenbuchs*, 204). Because these allusions use synonyms, however, Schart sees 1:18aβ, b as a later imitation of 1:2–3. Given the proximity of 1:2 and 1:18, this imitation could easily have been corrected by checking the source. It would appear

the nations. The OAN then provide explicit illustrations of this coming destruction of nations whose fate suffered with the changing epoch, when Assyria was replaced by Babylon as the ruling force in the region. At this point the addition of Cush and Assyria (2:12–15) along with the reference to the "islands of the nations" (2:11) could have been added to the end of the OAN in order to create the connections to the table of nations in Gen 10.[53] The resulting allusion reverses the Genesis text in that the birth of the nations described there will now lose their power. The resulting description of the destroyed city of Nineveh thus parallels the devastation of Jerusalem which it then introduces (3:1–7).

Here, it should probably also be noted that the inclusion of the Assyria/Nineveh material most likely took place at a point within the literary context of the Book of the Four before it was expanded with Nahum and Habakkuk. The brief anticipation of the destruction of Assyria makes sense within the context of this collection, but hardly seems necessary if Nahum was already included. By contrast those incorporating Nahum/Habakkuk were interested in filling a gap from the time of {371} Hezekiah (Mic 1:1) and Josiah (Zeph 1:1), a gap that saw the rise and fall of Assyria (Nahum) and the emergence of Babylon (Habakkuk).[54]

The same combination of a day of YHWH that leads to destruction for Judah *and* the nations appears in Zeph 3:8. It builds upon the destruction of Jerusalem in 3:1–7 by reconnecting with the threads of 1:18 and 1:2–3 at the precise point in the corpus where the collection changes from judgment to reconciliation for Jerusalem. Schart correctly notes the similarity of these texts even though he attributes them to two different stages.[55]

What is not typically recognized, however, is the way in which 3:9–10 makes the same combination of Judah and the nations, but now anticipates a way in which the peoples can be incorporated into life after the impending destruction. The oneness motif of 3:9–10 and the purified lan-

---

more likely that 1:18aβ, b simply opts for a different combination of words for stylistic and contextual reasons.

53. See Wöhrle, *Frühen Sammlungen des Zwölfprophetenbuchs*, 218–20. Wöhrle makes a convincing case on formal and stylistic grounds that 2:11, 13–15 come from a different hand than the foundational collection. Contrary to Wöhrle, these verses should be seen as a climax to the OAN and not as interpreting 3:1–8 as directed against Nineveh.

54. See Nogalski, *Book of the Twelve: Micah–Malachi*, 494–95, 601–6, 644–49, 652–54.

55. Schart, *Entstehung des Zwölfprophetenbuchs*, 212–13.

guage demonstrates that the situation after the tower of Babel (scattering of the nations and the creation of confusion of multiple languages) will be reversed in this new era. The nations will (again) learn to recognize YHWH and those from beyond the rivers of Cush will bring offerings to YHWH in Jerusalem. This combination of judgment *and* restoration appears to be thematically odd, and thus is frequently ascribed to different redactional layers. Recognition of the reversal of Gen 1-11 suggests that 3:9-10 is best seen as a commentary upon the existing collection, a collection which already combined elements of restoration of a remnant in Jerusalem (3:11-13) and perhaps the centrality of YHWH's dominion in Zion (3:14-17), along with YHWH's decision to remove oppressors from her midst (3:18-19). In the view of 3:9-10, which assumes the removal of the oppressors by the punishment of the nations, the creation of a framework from Gen 1-11 provides an interpretive lens with which to read Zephaniah. One can anticipate the reconstruction of life as it was intended—with Jerusalem at the center of the world and the glorification of the name of YHWH as the purpose of the kingdom. These themes of judgment *and* reconciliation for *both* Judah and the nations simply draw together those elements already in Zephaniah and Genesis. A scribe trained in the heady years after the publication of a Torah curriculum that included the combined P and non-P materials would have undoubtedly been exposed to training in these texts and consequently would have had the wherewithal to note the pattern implied in the transferal from Gen 1-11 (creation and judgment of the world order) to Zephaniah (judgment and recreation of the world order). {372}

Conclusion

The results of this study demonstrate that key texts in Zephaniah, which reverse texts in Gen 1-11, play a meaningful role in structuring the collection of Zephaniah at an intermediate stage of its composition. These allusions recognize that the day of YHWH against Judah and Jerusalem (literally) anticipates the events of 587 BCE and that Zephaniah's OAN predict the reversal of fortune for Assyria and its allies at the end of the seventh century. Certainly Zephaniah was not composed in a single setting from scratch, but a careful analysis of two detailed redactional studies provides corroborative evidence that at a significant point of Zephaniah's development, a form of Zephaniah existed wherein the incorporation of these allusions makes good sense.

This penultimate stage of editing assumes a form of Zephaniah wherein the interests of the compiler and the Deuteronomistic editing were already combined. The focus on Judah and Jerusalem's destruction as the coming day of YHWH (1:4–6, 7–18a) leads to an exhortation to seek YHWH (2:1–3) before the fate of the surrounding nations who were Assyrian allies (2:4–10) becomes the fate of Jerusalem as well (3:1–7) resulting in a judgment where only a few would survive (3:11–13). The Genesis allusions (1:2–3, 18*; 2:11*–15; 3:8*) together frame this collection by insertions at the seams of the thematic shifts so as to put the underlying text into a context that witnesses to its importance—that is, nothing short of the undoing and re-creation of the cosmic order. These texts focus *simultaneously*, not sequentially, upon judgment and reconciliation because they attest to a restructuring of the socio-political world at YHWH's leading. For these texts, it is not a question of either judgment or restoration but judgment and reconciliation for YHWH's people in Judah and beyond, when seen from the time of Josiah (1:1). For the scribe who interpreted Zephaniah in light of Gen 1–11, these texts make sense as the result of a scribal reading, reflection, and access to Zephaniah, incidentally fitting in well with recent discussions of texts as scribal curriculum. In this case, we see one source of that curriculum (Gen 1–11) shaping another curriculum text (Zephaniah in the context of the Book of the Four Prophets).

Job and Joel: Divergent Voices on a Common Theme

Method and Task

The current essay will utilize a synchronic, reader-oriented intertextual approach to enter into a comparative analysis of the ways in which the verb שוב functions differently within Job 8–10 and Joel. For an excellent summary of the backgrounds and difficulties associated with the term intertextuality, see Miller's 2011 study.[1] Miller surveys the use of the term in Old Testament scholarship and offers descriptive categories (reader-oriented and author-oriented) to avoid pejorative connotations and long-standing debates when talking about the methods as diachronic or synchronic. His calls for clarity and transparency should be heeded, but his preference stated at the end of the article that "intertextuality" should be reserved for the synchronic, reader-oriented approach appears short-sighted.[2] Many diachronic, author-oriented studies will continue to use the term intertextuality because ancient composers were also readers and rereaders of precursor texts.[3] In many respects, attempts to document, characterize, and interpret ancient authors' use of existing texts parallel the synchronic, reader-oriented task.[4] Diachronic, author-oriented studies may attempt to describe an *ancient* reader's intertextual reading (as well as to extrapolate historical implications from this reading). For this reason, scholars will continue to use "intertextuality" for both tasks.[5]

---

1. Miller, "Intertextuality in Old Testament Research," 283–309.
2. Ibid., 303–5.
3. Ben Zvi, *Historical-Critical Study of the Book of Obadiah*, 3–6.
4. Richard J. Bautch, "Intertextuality in the Persian Period," in *Approaching Yehud: New Approaches to the Study of the Persian Period*, ed. Jon L. Berquist, SemeiaSt 50 (Atlanta: Society of Biblical Literature, 2007), 25–35.
5. In shedding light on the thought world of ancient authors: a diachronic, author-

My approach, however, exhibits no interest in the intentions of the author but is rooted in two convictions of postmodern literary studies: (1) no text has meaning until it is read in relationship to other texts; and (2) every text holds a plurality of meanings based upon the texts with and {130} against which it is read.[6] This reader-oriented approach thus decries reading a text in isolation and resists any attempt to find *the* definitive meaning for a text. By reading Job 8–10 and Joel together, the rhetorical function of the verb שוב will generate an exploration of literary and theological implications for interpreting the claims of Job, Bildad, and Joel in their respective contexts and in "response" to one another. In so doing, the conversation that arises from this synchronic approach puts into relief the theological claims of these three characters.

This essay will evaluate the first Bildad speech (Job 8) and Job's response (Job 9–10) for their intertextual echoes with the book of Joel, especially chapters 1 and 2. Six times (9:12, 13, 18; 10:9, 16, 21) Job's response to Bildad draws upon the verb שוב, the same verb that forms the interpretive crux of Joel's extended call to repentance that culminates in Joel 2:12–14. Rereading the Bildad speech heightens other motifs that resonate with the imagery of Joel. And yet, the ideological perspectives of these three characters hardly fit neatly with one another. Nevertheless, this trialectic reading (from Bildad to Job, to Joel, and back) offers a fresh venue for hearing the broad range of voices as comments upon one another. These three voices continually raise points of contrast as they move between the language of the individual versus the community, between calls for accommodation versus protest, and between voices of wisdom versus prophets. Joel (a prophetic voice) and Bildad (the "wise friend" of Job) deliver calls for changes in action and attitude to enable God to act beneficently. The community's silence in Joel creates ambiguity while Job's rejection of Bildad's critique challenges the easy answers of orthodoxy. To understand the dynamics involved in reading these passages intertextually, it will be necessary to situate Job 8–10 in its larger context, to compare the use of the verb שוב between Job 9–10 and Joel, and to create a conversation between Job, Joel, and Bildad.

---

oriented approach to intertextuality overlaps considerably with the tasks of tradition history and redaction history, as defined in comprehensive treatments of exegetical methodology. See Odil Hannes Steck, *Old Testament Exegesis: A Guide to the Methodology*, trans. James D. Nogalski, 2nd ed., RBS 39 (Atlanta: Scholars Press, 1998), 15–20.

6. See Fewell, *Reading between Texts*.

The Literary Context of Job 8–10

Bildad's Response (Job 8) to Job's Speech (Job 6–7): A Literary Dilemma

The response of Bildad to Job creates a dilemma for the reader. The narrator/editor gives strong signals of connectedness to push the reader to relate the speeches of Job and Bildad to one another (chs. 6–7, 8, 9–10) using ויען ("and he answered") in 8:1 and 9:1 and in the characters' initial references to something that has gone before at the beginning of {131} both speeches.[7] However, the relative dearth of lexical commonalities between these passages and the lack of specific references to the argumentation from the preceding speech force the reader to create some kind of thematic coherence to fill in the gaps. When the reader seeks to understand *how* these speeches respond to one another, the task quickly becomes complicated because the "responses" lack specific lexical or rhetorical links and because the few lexical similarities that are present tend to push the reader to other parts of Job than the immediate context.

Consider the following illustrative examples. First, the phrase "How long?" represents the first of only three occurrences in Job (8:2; 18:2; 19:2), and all three relate to Bildad/Job interchanges.[8] Second, the topic of the punishment of the children in 8:4 evokes the Job narrative to many readers, but this association does not respond directly to the speech of Job in chapters 6–7 since "children" are not mentioned there. Instead, any invocation of the punishment of the children motif relates to the narrative frame. Third, and similarly, the terms "pure" (זך) and "upright" (ישר) applied to Job in 8:6, evoke the narrative introduction which characterizes Job three times (1:1, 8; 2:3) as "blameless" (תם) and "upright" (ישר). Hence, the phrase is similar, but the words used for "pure" and "blameless" are different.[9] Finally, "sin" and "transgression" appear at the end of Job's

---

7. Bildad asks in Job 8:2, "How long will you say *such things?*"; Job responds to Bildad in 9:2, "Indeed, I know that *this* is so" (emphasis added).

8. The first two references appear at the beginning of Bildad's first two speeches while the third one appears at the beginning of Job's second response to Bildad's second speech. This phrase suggests that impatience characterizes the interaction between Bildad and Job.

9. Even the word "upright" is not typical for the poetic sections of Job, appearing once more (23:7) in the singular and twice in the plural form (4:7; 17:8). The noun "uprightness" (יֹשֶׁר) also appears three times in the speech of Elihu (33:3, 23, 27).

speech (7:20-21) and near the beginning of Bildad's response (8:4), but even these key words are not readily linked since Job asks rhetorical questions that presume *he* does not sin or transgress, while Bildad refers to the sin and transgression of *someone's* children. The situation which Bildad's speech addresses is so different from Job's situation that most commentators treat Bildad's speech as sarcastic or ironic.[10] Bildad's speech condemns the children (8:4), but the narrative indicated no sin of which the children were guilty. Rather, Job acted on their behalf to make certain that they had not inadvertently sinned (1:5). {132}

The Message of the Bildad Speech

Despite the lack of verbal connections between Job's speech in chapters 6-7 and Bildad's response in chapter 8, scholars find creative ways to link the two speeches, frequently supplying Bildad with motives that would help account for the shift in topics. For example, Habel and Crenshaw portray Bildad as a defender of divine justice motivated by the incompatibility of God's very nature and the implications of Job's claim to innocence.[11] Consequently, Bildad's speech functions largely as a new thematic chapter in the larger drama. The rhetorical flow of Bildad's speech begins with a defense of divine justice (8:2-7) that assumes calamity must derive from sin. The opening salvo (8:2) makes the transition by dismissing the words of Job as "a great wind" who has spoken for too long. The following rhetorical question (8:3) brusquely rejects any notion that God could act in a manner that was not just and righteous. The second half of this defense, though, conveys the impression that Bildad offers Job a way to resolve the dilemma by suggesting the children's demise was caused by their own behavior (8:4) while Job has the option of making supplication to God (8:5) and living uprightly (8:6) so that the future will bring a greatness that makes the problems of the past seem trivial (8:7).

---

10. See the irony described in Habel, *Book of Job*, 174, or the sarcasm as interpreted by John E. Course, *Speech and Response: A Rhetorical Analysis of the Introductions to the Speeches of the Book of Job (Chaps. 4-24)*, CBQMS 25 (Washington, DC: Catholic Biblical Association of America, 1994), 53. Others see the "if" clauses as signs of hypothetical formulation that suggest Bildad is sincere but indirect. See James L. Crenshaw, *Reading Job: A Literary and Theological Commentary*, ROT (Macon, GA: Smyth & Helwys, 2011), 71; Clines, *Job 1-20*, 202-3.

11. Habel, *Book of Job*, 174; Crenshaw, *Reading Job*, 71.

The logic of the second portion (8:8-22) turns from the theoretical to the illustrative as Bildad underscores his conviction by drawing upon ancestral tradition (8:8-10) and a series of botanical metaphors (8:11-19) before returning to the two motifs of 8:2-7 with which the speech began: (1) God's justice involves rewarding the righteous and punishing the wicked (8:20); and (2) a blameless life offers hope for a better future (8:21-22).

The logic of the illustrations may not always be easy to follow, but their essential function reflects the twin themes that surround them. Moreover, precisely these two themes convey the inherent logic that makes Bildad's speech understandable as a "response" to Job since chapters 6-7 convey numerous examples where Job implies his life has been above reproach but the consequences of his righteous behavior have left him in despair, not with hope. The unstated implications of Job's extended recitation of good behavior are left to the reader to deduce: if good behavior does *not* result in reward, then God has not played fair. By supplying these implications, the reader can make sense of Bildad's thematic shift. Job has not said that God is unjust, but Bildad's response assumes this accusation and comes to God's defense. {133}

Job's Response to Bildad: More Monologue than Retort

Also, Job's response (chs. 9-10) hardly displays an integral connection to the statements of Bildad, even though the narratival/editorial frame invites the reader to see Job's speech as a response (9:1). Further, 9:2 cannot begin an entirely independent poem since it refers back to something: "Truly, I know that *such is the case,* but how can a man be right with God?" (emphasis added). Functionally, Job 9:1-2a creates a narrative transition to the following poetic monologue (whether originally independent or not).[12]

Scholars have put forth various proposals concerning the structure and unity of these two chapters as a response to Bildad. They argue the chapters contain between two and seven sections, whose interrelatedness to and independence from one another likewise varies from scholar

---

12. Job 9:1-2a, however, could serve as the introduction to a previously independent poem (9:2b-24) whose theme is "How can a man be right with God?" So also, Raik Heckl, *Hiob: Vom Gottesfürchitigen zum Repräsentaten Israels; Studien zur Buchwerdung des Hiobbuches und zu seinen Quellen,* FAT 70 (Tübingen: Mohr Siebeck, 2010), 69.

to scholar.[13] Those opting for two main units see the primary breaking point between 9:2–24 and 9:25–10:22 based upon form-critical criteria. The former speaks about God in the third person while the dominant form of address in the latter speaks directly to God (with the exception of 9:32–35). Debate exists concerning the addressees of 9:2–24 because the text never addresses anyone directly. Hence, 9:2–24 functions like a monologue—in context, a text spoken by Job to Job—placed here to function as Job's response to Bildad. Since God does not respond to Job's address in 9:25–10:22, the second half of this response essentially remains a monologue even though it uses the style of a prayer.

The content of this speech, when read in relation to the twin themes of Bildad's speech (divine justice and righteous living), functions meaningfully as an extended reframing of Bildad's accusations. Job admits Bildad's first point and affirms God's just character (9:2) but rejects the accusation of guilt implied by Bildad. Job assumes his own innocence (9:20–21). He also rejects Bildad's argumentation that a blameless life {134} benefits the righteous (9:22–24). Similarly, Job's prayer implicitly challenges God to make good on the promises to reward the righteous rather than turn a blind eye.

The Verb שוב in Job and Joel

The role played by שוב in Job's response to Bildad functions as a good case study for an intertextual reading since the six examples in Job 9–10 (9:12, 13, 18; 10:9, 16, 21) appear in two different sections of the speech's structure, no matter whether one divides the response into two or more units. The verb שוב appears more frequently in this speech than in any other speech in Job. Virtually every Job speech contains the verb, suggesting it functions as a kind of leitmotif for the character, but its range of meanings is by no means uniform in the sixteen times that the verb occurs in the

---

13. Those proposing three units (9:2–24; 9:25–35; 10:1–22) tend to explain the 3ms references to God in 9:32–35 as more consistent with the preceding verses (9:25–31) than with the verses that follow (10:1–22). A smaller number suggest four or more units make up this response. These scholars subdivide 9:2–24 into two sections (9:2–13, 14–24) and understand 10:1–6 as more closely related to the unit which precedes (9:25–35) than that which follows (10:7–22). Clines correctly refers to these distinctions as "more subtle and more debatable" than the form-critical differences related to speaking about God or speaking to God (*Reading Job*, 223).

mouth of Job.[14] Still, the use of שוב in Job 9–10 coheres in one sense. The verb appears in support of the related motifs of dire threat and death to the speaker. God's "restraint" in these three instances threatens the speaker.

The first three examples of שוב appear in the soliloquy (9:2b–22), and the verb's meaning concerns "restraint" using hiphil forms in 9:12, 13, and 18. In the first two instances, no one can restrain God's wrath. In the final instance, God "restrains my breath," making it difficult for the speaker to breathe.

The verb שוב also appears three times in the prayer (10:9, 16, 21). These verbal forms use שוב in three different ways: "to send back" (10:9), "to repeat" (10:16), and "to return" (10:21). All three of these nuances represent an expression of death for the speaker. In 10:9, the speaker asks God whether God intends to *send* the speaker *back* to the dust from which God created the human (a subtle allusion to the Yahwistic creation story [Gen 2:7; 3:19]). Job 10:16 depicts God as a lion who *repeatedly* (שוב) hunts down its prey (the speaker) whenever the prey steps out of line. Given the metaphor, the hunting lion can only imply a recurring threat to the speaker's life. In 10:21, the speaker asks God to leave him alone to find solace because the days of his life are few before he goes to "the land of gloom and deep darkness" from which the speaker will *not return* (a clear reference to the speaker's death). Consequently, the verb שוב consistently conveys a sense of threat and death in Job's "response" to Bildad.

Unlike Job, Joel uses the verb שוב (2:12–14; 4:1, 4, 7) in response to calamity to convey hope. The use of שוב in Joel functions as the primary {135} concept in the major literary transition in Joel by calling the community to return to YHWH in hopes of turning from devastation to deliverance.

Joel 2:12–14 marks the turning point of the writing. Joel 1 calls the community to lament, addressing specific groups, including elders (1:2), drunkards (1:5), farmers (1:11), vintners (1:11), priests (1:13), and the land personified (1:8). In addition, the prophet prays to YHWH (1:19–20). Subsequently, 2:1–11 depicts the threat of the day of YHWH coming against Jerusalem. This depiction implies the arrival of a cosmic army, led by YHWH, to destroy the land. At this point 2:12–14 implores the people to change before it is too late:

---

14. Job 6:29; 7:7, 10; 9:12, 13, 18; 10:9, 16, 21; 13:22; 14:13; 16:22; 17:10; 23:13; 30:23; 31:14.

> Yet even now, says the Lord, return [שוב] to me with all your heart, with fasting, with weeping, and with mourning; rend your hearts and not your clothing. Return [שוב] to the Lord, your God, for he is gracious and merciful, slow to anger, and abounding in steadfast love, and relents from punishing. Who knows whether he will not turn [שוב] and relent, and leave a blessing behind him, a grain offering and a drink offering for the Lord, your God?

Joel 2:12–14 uses שוב to depict a very different set of actions than Job 9–10. These verses employ שוב positively, twice commanding the people to return to YHWH, and once holding out the prospects that YHWH will return to the people and bless them. These actions are contingent upon one another. Only if the people שוב to YHWH is there a chance that YHWH will שוב to them. YHWH responds by offering a series of blessings (2:18–27), contingent upon the response to the call to repent in 2:12–17.

The remaining uses of שוב in Joel (4:1, 4, 7), though less pivotal, also offer promises to Judah and Jerusalem. The use of שוב in Joel 4:1 is written as a qal, but the sense of the verb (as well as the spoken *qere* tradition) treats the verb as a hiphil form ("cause to return" or "bring back"). YHWH promises to "restore" or "return" the possessions of Judah and Jerusalem. Similarly, Joel 4:4 anticipates YHWH punishing those who have acted against Judah (i.e., returning their own deeds against them). Joel 4:7 also uses a hiphil form in this same way. Thus, the long-term promise to Judah and Jerusalem expressed in Joel 4 implies that possessions will be returned, and that the aggressive acts of enemies will be returned upon them, but only after (cf. 4: 1) the people have returned to YHWH (2:12–17).

Using the verb שוב in these two books as a starting point, one finds that Bildad, Job, and Joel provide some intriguing points of comparison and contrast. Observing these similarities and differences sheds new light on all three characters. {136}

Creating a Conversation between Joel and Job 8–10

Joel and Job

Two realities deserve notice when comparing Joel and Job. First, the analysis of שוב in Joel and Job 9–10 exhibits quite a contrast of meanings, but, second, the underlying logic of Bildad's speech (Job 8) shows considerable affinity with assumptions about the rhetorical logic of Joel 1–2. These points of similarity help one to create a productive intertextual conversation between Joel 1–2 and Job 8–10 that helps shape one's understanding of each passage. Consider what has already been noted concerning the use of שוב in Job 9–10. The verb appears in contexts that threaten death for an individual, while the same verb in Joel promises relief and restoration for a collective group (Judah and Jerusalem).

The prophetic text in Joel 1–2 implores Judah and Jerusalem to return to YHWH in order to allow YHWH the chance to restore the nation. Joel 2:12–14, in particular, implies the guilt of the community can only be overcome by corporate repentance (in the sense of turning to God). As such, these verses tend to presuppose the same lines of argumentation implied in Bildad's speech, but the three-fold logic is applied to the people as a whole: (1) God is just and must punish the recalcitrant; (2) since the community has experienced (Joel 1) and is about to experience (Joel 2:1–11) disasters of epic proportions, then one must assume that the group has turned from God; (3) a return to God is the only means available to stop the deity's wrath.[15]

By contrast, the wisdom text in Job 9–10 uses the verb שוב to resist the application of cause and effect theology to the character Job. The verb שוב in Job appears, then, in the context of a *via negativa*. Job does not use the verb to express a desire to "return" to God. Rather, the character uses the verb to express YHWH's unrestrainable wrath (9: 12, 13) and the refusal to "restore" breath to Job (9: 18).

The context of Job's response (Job 9–10) undercuts the logic of Bildad. The first Bildad speech (Job 8), when reread, strengthens the impression of the ineffectuality of Bildad, who represents traditional teachings. For the careful reader, the "pure and upright" formulations in Bildad's speech (8:6) challenge the reliability of Bildad to assess the issue of divine punishment since the reader of Job already knows that the calamities experienced by Job have nothing to do with punishment. {137} Rather, the reader knows that Job's plight results not from being punished for wickedness, but as a test because of his righteousness. From the very first verse of the book, the reader learns that Job is blameless and upright (1:1, 8; 2:3), which earns him the attention of the satan. Consequently, Bildad's accusation (8:6) that Job's character has caused God to punish him, undercuts Bildad's author-

---

15. Crenshaw argues the case in light of justice and mercy: "For Joel ... YHWH's repentance forms a bridge between divine wrath and mercy" (*Joel*, 137). Crenshaw correctly observes that in the ancient world, Joel would have been heard as assuming guilt, but Joel does not indicate the nature of the guilt (146).

ity as a wise counselor in the eyes of Job's readers. The subversion of Bildad's authority also creates suspicion for the reader when Bildad's speech implies that the sin of Job's children caused God to punish them (8:4), even though such a claim remains unstated in the narrative frame of the book.

The artist who composed Job, however, was not recounting a historical report of one righteous man. The role of Job serves as paradigm for a righteous man faced with the human condition. As often noted, Job protests against easy answers, but the power of these protests derives from the many ways in which Job makes his point by challenging accepted wisdom and traditional teachings. In a very real way, Job takes on religious orthodoxy as an insufficient means to express the complexity of life. Job protests against the reduction of tradition into simplistic cause and effect theology. By contrast, Joel starts from the calamities against the nation as the motivation for an orthodox response.

Joel and Bildad

What happens when one brings the dialectic of tradition and protests in Job 8-10 into conversation with the rhetoric of Joel 1-2? Job's protest and the undercutting of Bildad's authority created in Job 8-10 raise questions about the efficacy of Joel's pronouncements precisely because, as typically interpreted, Joel essentially presupposes the same cause and effect theology espoused by Bildad.

Joel 1 depicts a scenario of cataclysmic devastation by conveying a series of calls to lament the desolation of the land caused by locusts, drought, and military invasion. Cumulatively, these calls to the community portray a situation as dire as any situation faced by Judah and Jerusalem depicted in biblical texts. The rhetoric calls for a response from the community, but the devastation leaves the reader with a portrait of the land that makes Job's plight appear tame by comparison because of the corporate nature of the disasters. Whereas Job faces personal tragedy that affects him and his family, the devastation of Joel 1 affects everyone in the land: the elders, the children, the farmers, the priests, and all the inhabitants. This scenario magnifies exponentially the problems faced by Job individually. Following this extended call to different groups (1:2-18), the prophet petitions YHWH in 1:19-20 by summarizing {138} the situation in which the fields, the trees, and the brooks have been devastated. They provide nothing in the way of sustenance for the animals, much less human society.

In addition to this devastation, the reader learns in 2:1-11 that the land faces an even greater threat. Joel 2:1 sounds the military alarm that the day of YHWH is at hand that will bring an attack from a cosmic army led by YHWH himself (2:11). Considering the plight of Judah and Jerusalem in Joel, one can hardly miss the parallels to Job in which calamity follows calamity to the point where it seems all hope is lost (Joel 1), and then even greater calamity threatens the land (Joel 2:1-11). Only then does the prophet use the language of repentance, calling for the people to return (שוב) to YHWH (2:12-14). This action is followed by a call for a fast (2:15-16) that begins identically to 2:1 ("blow the trumpet"). Joel 2:17 then reports a plea for mercy from the priests. These responses in 2:12-17 are typically (and probably correctly) interpreted as presuming the same cause and effect theology that Bildad articulates in Job. Namely, the prophet issues a call for repentance and fasting *because* the prophet *assumes* that the devastation of the land reflects YHWH's punishment because of the guilt of the people.

The word "assumes" in the previous sentence is significant because nowhere does Joel 1-2 specify this guilt, a fact that has generated a great variety of explanations.[16] Rather, in a classic case of turning to God as one's last resort, Joel 2:12-14 and 2:15-17 call for a change of heart and acts of contrition. Hence, the prophet in Joel 1-2 asks of the community what Bildad asks of Job as an individual. Bildad does not need to convince Joel to follow Bildad's advice, because the prophet shares his perspective. The underlying logic can be described clearly enough. Calamity of this magnitude cannot have escaped the attention of YHWH, so it must come from YHWH. YHWH does not act arbitrarily; ergo this calamity must result from the sin of the people. Only by returning to YHWH can the people hope to persuade YHWH to remove the punishment. Repentance is the only choice left to the people in the rhetoric of Joel. Bildad would be pleased. Job, however, would protest.

Job and Joel

At the very least, Job would challenge Joel to make the case. Job would refuse to assume that the calamities afflicting the country resulted from sin. He would demand to know what he or his countrymen had done to

---

16. For discussion of these possibilities, see ibid., 40-42. Although Crenshaw's own assertion that Joel does not necessarily presume guilt appears rather forced despite his desire to take account of the innocent victims.

{139} cause YHWH to make them suffer. He would likely intercede on behalf of the people in a very different way. If Job were a prophet, Job might speak past Joel in much the way that he speaks past Bildad and challenge YHWH directly. The words of Job's response in chs. 9–10 sound very different if read as a response to the calamities of Joel 1–2.

Job contends that no human can respond to God in a way that would justify humanity before God. Job avers that the power of the God who created the world makes it impossible for humans to contend with God (9:1–12). Job acknowledges God's power, but also argues that God's overwhelming judgment leaves the question of innocence out of the discussion (9:13–24). In Job's eyes, by sending devastation and calamity God destroys the wicked and the innocent. This charge is only magnified if read in light of the corporate catastrophes in Joel. Job recognizes the futility of challenging God if the battle concerns only power (9:25–35) and even wonders aloud why cleansing himself makes any sense at all if God is only going to plunge him into the muck of life (9:30–31). Job challenges God to take account of Job's own innocence since God created Job and Job's current plight makes God look bad (10:1–22). This last line of reasoning even finds its way into the priests' plea for mercy in Joel: "Spare your people, O Lord, and do not make your heritage a mockery, a byword among the nations. Why should it be said among the peoples, 'Where is their God?'" (Joel 2:17 NRSV). Yet, Job offers no such plea. Rather, Job challenges God concerning the fate of the innocent and the pious. Joel does not take this bold step.

The rhetoric of Job's speech, as shown above, radically undercuts the reader's confidence in the reliability of Bildad through connections to the broader literary context. Bildad accuses Job of sin when the reader knows better. This undercutting is lacking, however, if one asks whether Joel's assumptions are supported in the broader literary context. When read as an isolated prophetic text, Joel presumes the guilt of the people, but never makes the case. At this point, if one asks about the broader literary context, Joel's presuppositions about the guilt of the people receive support when compared to the presumptions of Bildad.

Recent investigations into the Book of the Twelve have suggested that Joel—more than any other writing in the collection—was compiled from existing sources with the intention from the outset that it be read in its position between Hosea and Amos.[17] These investigations make the case

---

17. See Nogalski, "Joel as 'Literary Anchor,'" 91–109; Aaron Schart, "The First

that the book of Joel takes on new meaning when read in its location in the Book of the Twelve because of the intricacy of the connections to the {140} writings on either side of Joel. These connections are created by catchwords, overlapping genres, explicit citations, and other constellations. These connections involve accusations of cultic abuse (such as Hos 2:7–8, 19 [Eng. 5–6, 17]; 4:7–9, 12–13) and ethical violations (as in 4:1–2) that threaten (2:10–11 [Eng. 8–9]; 4:3, 9–10) or make promises (2:14 [Eng. 12]) about the fertility of the land. Whereas both the threat and the promise in Hosea lie in the future, Joel 1 uses these images to portray the current reality. The agricultural symbols of a fertile land represent the images of the calamity facing the people.

Consequently, in the same way that Bildad's speech draws upon and presumes the narrative frame of Job, Joel presupposes Hosea and Amos. Specifically, Joel 1–2 contains connections to Hosea that invite the reader of the Book of the Twelve to read Joel as both a continuation of the message of Hosea and a reappropriation of that message for Judah and Jerusalem (whereas Hosea primarily concerns the Northern Kingdom).[18]

In short, the reader of Joel 1 who begins reading from Hosea receives a very different impression of the prophet's reliability than does the reader of Job who encounters the speech of Bildad. This reader of Joel does not experience the cognitive dissonance between what the prophet says and the larger context. To the contrary, Hosea describes behavior that would be punished by removing agricultural fertility. Joel describes a situation in terms quite similar to the threatened punishment of Hosea. The reader of the Twelve connects the punishment in Hosea with the current reality of Joel and thus equates Joel's situation with the punishment of sin from Hosea. Thus, the reader of Joel would not immediately judge Job's questions concerning the innocence of the victims to have the same relevance as they do in the book of Job.

And yet, Job's protest against Bildad's assumptions cannot be ignored if one wishes to compare the two texts in order to deal seriously with the implications of cause and effect theology for the community of faith today. Bildad and Joel represent, in many respects, the dominant theological perspective of Deuteronomy and Proverbs: do well and God will bless you.

Section of the Book of the Twelve Prophets: Hosea—Joel—Amos," *Int* 61 (2007): 138–52; see also the section labeled "Repentance, Guilt, and Punishment," in Nogalski, *Book of the Twelve: Hosea–Jonah*, 205–6.

18. Schart, "First Section of the Book of the Twelve Prophets," 142–43.

Nevertheless, Job's protest against the facile association of reward and a righteous life also resonates with other texts in the canon. Within the Book of the Twelve, Jonah portrays God as one who is eager to find ways to exercise compassion, even against the wicked (3:10; 4:2) and to protect the ignorant and innocent animals (4: 11). Even this opposing position does not, however, do complete justice to Job's protest since Jonah still essentially presumes the same need for repentance in the {141} face of divine wrath. Job, by contrast, wrestles at length with the problem of innocent suffering in ways that still work to subvert the notion that divine judgment offers adequate explanations for calamity on either the personal or the corporate level. Canonically, Job serves as an important corrective in this respect to the dominant theological voices in the Torah, the Prophets, and the Writings.

Conclusion

Reading and rereading Job 8–10 in conversation with Joel 1–2 has illuminated several dynamics that underscore the difference between the wisdom of Job as protest literature and the function of Joel as prophetic literature. The verb שוב conveys messages of death in Job 9–10 but implies hope in Joel. Conversely, Job's "friend" has much in common with the presuppositions of Joel. Nevertheless, while connections to the broader literary context in Job cause the reader to mistrust the message of Bildad, the broader literary horizon of Joel conveys confidence to the reader of the Book of the Twelve that Joel's message can be trusted. Of course, this reading should not be terribly surprising in light of the purpose of the two books. Job is protest literature that seeks to make traditional theological paradigms problematic, while Joel anchors the major recurring themes of the Book of the Twelve and, as such, instructs its readers in corporate versions of the very traditions against which Job protests. Reading the two together displays how intricately the characters of the two books are tied to their own competing theologies.

Textual Criticism and Tradition History

The Problematic Suffixes of Amos IX 11

The MT of Amos 9:11 in its present form contains three incongruous suffixes which seemingly defy explanation. These three distinct suffixes used in the second half of the verse refer back to the unique phrase "booth of David." The MT may be literally translated:

> On that day I will raise up the fallen booth of David;
> And I will wall up their [fp] breaches [*pirṣêhen*],
> And I will raise his [ms] ruins [*wahărīsōtāyw*],
> And I will build it [*ûbənîtîhā*: fs] as in the days of old. {412}

The problem is clear enough. The use of the feminine plural, masculine singular, and feminine singular suffixes cannot be readily explained grammatically as references to the feminine singular construct "booth of David." The normal solution follows the LXX and reads all three suffixes in the third-person feminine singular (τὰ πεπτωκότα αὐτῆς; τὰ κατεσκαμμένα αὐτῆς; ἀνοικοδομήσω αὐτήν). The vast majority of commentators have welcomed the LXX as the means of avoiding the problem, either through their unqualified acceptance or with the hesitant admission that no better suggestion has adequately explained the incongruity.[1] In the light of such

---

1. A selection of those following the LXX is impressive: Julius Wellhausen, *Die kleinen Propheten: Übersetzt mit noten* (Berlin: Reimer, 1892), 94; Bernhard Duhm, "Anmerkungen zu den Zwölf Propheten I," *ZAW* 31 (1911): 17; Artur Weiser, *Das Buch der zwölf kleinen Propheten I: Die Propheten Hosea, Joel, Amos, Obadja, Jona, Micha*, 8th ed., ATD 24 (Göttingen: Vandenhoeck & Ruprecht, 1985), 203; Theodore H. Robinson and Friedrich Horst, *Die Zwölf Kleinen Propheten*, HAT 1/14 (Tübingen: Mohr Siebeck, 1938), 106; Richard S. Cripps, *A Critical and Exegetical Commentary on the Book of Amos*, 2nd ed. (London: SPCK, 1955), 270–71; Edmond Jacob, Samuel Amsler, and Carl-Albert Keller, *Osée, Joël, Amos, Abdias, Jonas*, CAT 11a (Neuchâtel: Delachaux & Niestlé, 1965), 245; Hans Walter Wolff, *Dodekapropheton 2, Joel und Amos*, BKAT 14.2 (Neukirchen-Vluyn: Neukirchener Verlag, 1969),

unanimity it would appear superfluous to suggest an alternative reading were it not for the fact that scholars have generally proceeded from two incorrect assumptions when treating this text. First, most authors implicitly or explicitly presume that the LXX represents the "more original" reading;[2] and second, they presume that the solution must explain away one or more of the problematic suffixes. There are good reasons for rejecting both these presuppositions.

The LXX need not represent the "original reading" of Amos 9:11; rather, it may harmonize the MT. Mays and Rudolph call the LXX reading into question but offer no grounds for doing so; nor do they offer clarification of the meaning or explanation of the so-called corruption of the MT.[3] In reality, the LXX is no different from the other ancient versions. The LXX, Syriac, and Vulgate all read the same text but attempt a solution to the suffixes in their own way. Whereas the LXX eliminates the problem by ignoring the change of number and gender in the suffixes, the Syriac and Vulgate offer some help both in the verification of the MT and, more indirectly, toward a solution.

A comparison of the Vulgate with the MT and LXX reveals an attempt to avoid the problem through phraseology, as well as the creation of further problems with the use of an otherwise unattested third-person masculine singular suffix for the feminine suffix in the phrase "I will rebuild *it.*" The Vulgate may be read: "I will raise the tent of David which is destroyed, and

---

403; Ina Willi-Plein, *Vorformen der Schriftexegese innerhalb des Alten Testaments: Untersuchungen zum literarischen Werden der auf Amos, Hosea und Micha zurückgehenden Bücher im hebräischen Zwölfprophetenbuch,* BZAW 123 (Berlin: de Gruyter, 1971), 57; Rudolph, *Joel, Amos, Obadja, Jona,* 278-79; Stuart, *Hosea-Jonah,* 395-96.

2. Note especially Willi-Plein, *Vorformen der Schriftexegese,* 57, who not only accepts the LXX but offers a suggestion as to how MT came about. Willi-Plein argues that dittography caused the final *nun* as a result of the following *waw.* The only explanation she offers for changing "his ruins" to "her ruins" is that the fs form of "her ruins" was simply displaced, for psychological reasons, by the more frequently attested masc. suffix. The problem with this suggestion is that it fails to account for the fact that the feminine is already attested twice (s and p). Her argument about dittography is more plausible, but does not solve the problem by itself.

3. Rudolph acknowledges the priority of the MT over the LXX, but he translates with the LXX for lack of a better alternative (*Joel, Amos, Obadja, Jona,* 278-79). James Luther Mays preserves the tension of the MT, but offers no explanation for the significance of the suffixes (*Amos: A Commentary,* OTL [Philadelphia: Westminster, 1969], 163-64).

I will rebuild the holes of *its* walls; and *those things* which they destroyed I will repair; and I shall rebuild *him* as in the days of old." In the first occurrence of the suffix, the word "its" (*eius*) can be masculine, neuter, or feminine, but since the antecedent is neuter (*tabernaculum*), *eius* must be neuter as well. The Vulgate has been formulated according to {413} the gender of the Latin and not the Hebrew. The Vulgate avoids the second suffix. The Vulgate obviously has problems translating the Hebrew, since it changes the plural noun "ruins" into a masculine plural verb as though reading *hārəsû*. One may legitimately explain this variation as an intentional change for two reasons. First, it is doubtful that two letters (*tav* and *yod*) would have fallen away from the MT. Second, the Vulgate preserves echoes of a suffix attached to "ruins" in the phrase "those things which" (*ea quae*). The Vulgate treats the third suffix uniquely. The use of the third-person masculine singular suffix must grammatically refer back to David, and the connection of the verb "rebuild" with David indicates the translator has understood David symbolically. More importantly for the eventual understanding of the MT, the Vulgate interprets both "booth" and "David" as antecedents to the suffixes.

The Syriac likewise struggles with its translation. The pertinent portions of the verse read: "I will raise the fallen tent of David, and I will close their [mp] breaches, and I will raise their [mp] ruins, and I will build it [fs] as in the days of old." The Syriac, like the MT, attests both "booth" and "fallen" as singular, but it uses the masculine plural for both of the next two suffixes ("their breaches" and "their ruins") rather than feminine plural and masculine singular as in the MT. The reason for this variation is twofold. First, the use of "tent" in the Syriac version means that the translator used a masculine noun rather than a feminine noun as in the MT. Second, the masculine plural suffixes indicate that the translator understood the entire phrase "fallen booth of David" as a collective expression. The final suffix in the Syriac version reverts to a literal translation of the third-person feminine singular suffix of the MT. Given the use of the collective in the first two instances, this return to a literal rendering of the MT is striking, but in spite of the deviations mentioned above, it is highly unlikely that the Syriac presupposes a different *Vorlage*. The tension reflects an attempt to comprehend the MT. This tension is the more notable since the Syriac does not revert to the LXX reading, a practice it follows elsewhere with some regularity.

A comparison of the MT with the LXX, Syriac, and Vulgate versions of Amos 9:11 demonstrates that none of the three suffixes {414} appears in the same form in every version. These results may be summarized as follows:[4]

	Breaches Suffix	Ruins Suffix	I will rebuild "it" suffix
MT:	fp	ms	fs
LXX:	fs	fs	fs
Syriac:	mp	mp	fs
Vulgate:	ns	np	ms

Of all these readings, only the LXX reading is consistent within itself. However, given the evidence of the other versions, the principle of *lectio difficilior* suggests that the LXX merely smooths over the problems of a very difficult MT.

One may not, therefore, presume that the LXX represents the "more original" reading. Other solutions must be sought which are more in keeping with the MT and which simultaneously shed light on the intended significance of these suffixes. To accomplish this task, it is necessary to question the second presupposition that the problem lies in the corruption of the suffixes. Two further alternatives should be explored: (1) the problem lies in the corruption of the antecedent "booth of David"; or (2) the variation of suffixes represents a deliberate device on the part of the author.

Over one hundred years ago, Geo Hoffmann argued that the problem could be solved by separating the first two of the parallel statements from the third and fourth and by supposing that the original antecedent to "their breaches" was the plural "booths of David."[5] Hoffmann's suggestion has gone largely unnoticed, but prudence and precision demand a closer evaluation of this possibility, although several crucial obstacles argue against its acceptance.[6] Hoffmann treats the phrase as an example of haplography caused by the omission of the *mater lectionis waw* from the consonantal text of Hebrew *Vorlage*, which originally read: *sukkôt dāwîd hannōpelôt*. It must be admitted that several observations make this reading possible. *Waw* is one of the more frequent letters involved in scribal errors. The fact that the letter was situated between the letters *kaph* and *tau* increases

---

4. "f" = feminine, "m" = masculine , "n" = neuter, "s" = singular, "p" = plural.

5. Geo Hoffmann, "Versuche zu Amos," *ZAW* 3 (1883): 125–26.

6. Only Friedrich Schwally takes up Hoffmann's suggestion favorably ("Das Buch Ssefanjâ: Eine historisch-kritische Untersuchung," *ZAW* 10 [1890]: 226).

the likelihood of haplography, since this ending often appears with two spellings. The feminine plural absolute *sukkōt* is well attested both with defective and with *plene* spellings, often within neighboring verses.[7] This interchangeable form would add to the susceptibility {415} of the word to the accidental omission of the *waw*. In addition, the omission of the *waw* in the consonantal text changed the number from plural to singular, but left a word which made sense in its context. Relatedly, only one other word would have been affected by this omission, namely, *hnplt*, but this word would have appeared exactly the same in the consonantal text whether the word was plural (*hannōpəlōt*) or singular (*hannōpelet*).

In spite of the admission that Hoffmann's reading is possible, several problems result from it. First, no ancient version attests a plural "booths" in place of the singular "booth." Second, while his reading alleviates the problematic feminine plural suffix of "their breaches," it does not solve the problem of the variation of suffixes (3ms and 3fs) in the remainder of the verse.[8] Third, Hoffmann's reading does not adequately explain the significance of the plural "booths" in the context. He understands "booths" as a derogatory reference to the high palaces of the north which should now be rebuilt in the simple style of a hut from the Davidic period. So understood, the verse runs counter to the promissory nature of 9:11–15, whose unbridled positive character, is beyond dispute. Thus, one may safely eliminate Hoffmann's reading of "booths" on textual, syntactical, and contextual grounds.

When one eliminates textual corruption of both the problematic suffixes and the antecedent as explanations for the divergent suffixes, one is forced to grapple with Amos 9:11 as it stands in the MT. The verse,

---

7. Genesis 33:17; Neh 8:15; Deut 16:13; and Lev 23:42 have no *mater lectionis* to represent the vowel ō, whereas other passages have the *plene* spelling. Second Samuel 22:12; Neh 8:14, 16, 17; Lev 23:34, 43; Deut 16:16; 31:10; Zech 14:16, 18, 19; Ezra 3:4, 2 Chr 8:13; 2 Sam 11:11; 1 Kgs 20:12, 16. Interestingly, with the exception of Gen 33:17 all the other defective spellings appear in the context of verses where the *plene* spelling is used.

8. Hoffmann correctly suggests that the 3ms suffix could refer back to David but stretches the point when he argues that the 3fs suffix in the phrase "I will build it" relates to "the land" ("Versuche zu Amos," 226). He ignores the fact that the closest example of "land" appears two verses away (9:9). If the 2fs suffix intended "land" as the antecedent, it would have to bypass three other feminine nouns in the MT (not only "booth" in 9:11, but "sword" and "calamity" in 9:10). Such a syntactical oversight appears highly unlikely.

as noted already, contains four statements, yet the formulation of these statements is enlightening. If we ignore the problem of the suffixes for the moment, these four consecutive statements appear in synonymous parallelism. The combination of verbs (raise, wall up, raise, rebuild) twice articulates YHWH's action of lifting and repairing in beautifully constructed synonymous parallelism.[9] Taking the cue from this structural formulation, one must ask if it is possible to make any sense of the suffixes in the light of the parallel expressions. When so viewed, one may answer that the suffixes do play a role in the parallelism.

The syntactical key to unlocking the understanding of these suffixes appears in the expression of collective ideas via the combination of feminine singular nouns with plural adjectives.[10] This phenomenon occurs with enough regularity to enable us to presume that the collective idea could as well be expressed via the combination of a feminine singular noun and a plural suffix.[11] Thus, it is {416} possible to view the second statement as a collective parallel to the first statement. Moreover, the third and fourth statements are even easier to explain in the light of the parallel structure, since the suffixes relate specifically back to the constituent elements of the phrase "booth of David." The third-person masculine singular suffix of the third statement pertains specifically to David when it mentions "his" ruins, and the third-person singular feminine suffix of the fourth statement refers explicitly back to the feminine noun "booth." The parallel structure and the function of the enigmatic suffixes may thus be graphically displayed:

I will raise up	I will wall up	I will raise	I will rebuild
the fallen booth			it
of David		his ruins	
	their breaches		

---

9. Amos 9:11 twice uses "I will raise," and uses the synonyms "I will wall up" and "I will rebuild" to create the second half of the AB/A'B' schema.

10. Cf., e.g., Gen 30:43 and 1 Sam 25:18, where the feminine singular "sheep" takes a plural adjective. See also Wilhelm Gesenius, *Gesenius' Hebrew Grammar*, ed. E. Kautzsch, tran. A. E. Cowley, 2nd ed. (Oxford: Clarendon, 1910), §132g and §145c.

11. See, e.g., Num 27:17, where the feminine singular noun appears with the plural pronoun.

Having detailed the elements of this verse it is now necessary to turn to the question how this understanding of Amos 9:11 relates to the larger context of 9:11–15.

The salvation oracle at the end of the book is clearly separated from what precedes it by both theme and style. The positive tenor of 9:11–15 contrasts sharply with the message of the remainder of the book, and the situation presumed by these verses is most understandable in exilic and postexilic times. For this reason the verses are correctly assumed to be a later addition to the book.[12]

It has been argued above that the writer of Amos 9:11 used the metaphor "booth of David" for a collective entity. Not only does the use of the feminine plural pronoun "their" treat this phrase collectively, but the remainder of the nouns in the verse (breaches, ruins), which function identically in the parallelism, are also plural, further adding to the impression of a collective identity. On its own, Amos 9:11 does not clearly impart the identity of this "fallen booth of David," but an evaluation of the larger context reveals that the real key for understanding the metaphorical language of Amos 9:11 on a more concrete level is found in Amos 9:14, where the destruction imagery appears once again. "I will return the captivity of my people Israel, and they will rebuild the ruined cities." The recurrence of the verb "to build" and the use of "ruined" (which expresses the same meaning as "ruins" in 9:11) relate back to the situation in 9:11. Thus, it is clear that the ruined cities of 9:14 and the fallen booth (= David's ruins) of 9:11 are intended to be one and the same. The metaphorical use of "booth" as a reference to a city is attested elsewhere.[13] The "fallen booth" of 9:11 does not {417} reflect a polemic against the divided kingdom in the time of Amos but refers collectively to the destruction of the cities of David's kingdom.[14] The frequent assumption of an exilic or postexilic date for these verses makes perfect sense, since the desolate state of the cities

---

12. For a classic example of this opinion, as well as a more detailed summary of the arguments, see Wolff, *Dodekapropheton 2, Joel und Amos*, 405–6. For a dissenting opinion, see Rudolph, *Joel, Amos, Obadja, Jona*, 284–85.

13. Isaiah 1:8 uses this metaphor to refer to Jerusalem.

14. While one must acknowledge that the context does not provide precise definitions of the extent of territory and people involved in the metaphorical "booth," it must nevertheless be stated clearly that the collective attributes of the MT within the larger context do not allow the supposition of the consonants *skt* as the Transjordanian city as suggested by commentators such as H. Neil Richardson, "Skt (Amos 9:11) : 'Booth' or 'Succoth'?," *JBL* 92 (1973): 375–81; and Stuart, *Hosea–Jonah*, 398.

during that period, resulting from the Babylonian destruction of the entire area, makes this extended metaphor intelligible.

In summary, it has been argued that the LXX does not reflect the "original reading" of Amos 9:11 but is itself a harmonization of problematic suffixes. Likewise, the argument of a textual corruption in the antecedent does not withstand critical scrutiny. It has been argued here that attention to the parallel structure of the verse as it appears in the MT can account for the suffixes by noting how they function in the verse and in the larger context.

Obadiah 7:
Textual Corruption or Politically Charged Metaphor?

Obadiah 7 presents difficulties for translators both modern and ancient. For the last century, one phrase in this verse has been treated almost universally as textually corrupt.[1] However, careful investigation reveals avenues of conceptual reasoning which illuminate the disputed phrase as a meaningful metaphor which should not be emended.

The Problem

Obadiah 7 contains four syntactically coherent lines, translated literally from the MT as follows:

עד־הגבול שלחוך כל אנשי בריתך	All the men of your covenant send you to the border.
השיאוך יכלו לך אנשי שלמך	The men of your peace deceive you; they overpower you.
לחמך ישימו מזור תחתיך	They place your bread as a trap beneath you.
אין תבונה בו	There is no understanding in him.

The third line raises questions. Modern scholars argue that the line manifests a meaningless sentence, when it says, "They place your bread as a trap beneath you."[2] As evidence, when it is given, many cite ancient translations. For example, the LXX deliberately omits the whole word "your

---

1. See, e.g., Rudolph, *Joel, Amos, Obadja, Jona*, 304; Hans Walter Wolff, *Dodekapropheton 3, Obadja und Jona*, BKAT 14.3 (Neukirchen-Vluyn: Neukirchener Verlag, 1977), 17; Stuart, *Hosea–Jonah*, 412; Allen, *Joel, Obadiah, Jonah, and Micah*, 150.
2. See, e.g., Rudolph, who says that the MT "gibt keinen Sinn und wird deshalb von G weggelassen" (*Joel, Amos, Obadja, Jona*, 304).

-289-

bread."[3] In reality, these versions more likely confirm the difficulty of the phrase for later minds than offer strong evidence of a different text.

One emendation dominates the suggestions regarding how the verse should be read. Its proponents postulate that a י was omitted through a copyist error. They argue that reinserting this י allows the resulting consonantal text to be repointed as a plural participle with a second-person masculine singular suffix (לֹחֲמֶיךָ). Thus, they translate the phrase, "Those eating your bread place a trap beneath you." At first glance, this suggestion evokes favorable reaction. Changing {68} the singular noun ("your bread") to a plural participle ("those eating your bread") changes the syntactical function of the word from the object to the subject of the verse, and provides a third explicit subject involving a collective entity (All the men of your covenant; the men of your peace; those eating your bread). This subject repetition harmonizes well with the synonymous parallelism one expects from this poetic line. Further, the resulting image conforms readily to our own conceptual realm, by presenting a picture of betrayal from within. Edom will suffer at the hands of those whom it has befriended. Those who enjoy the hospitality of Edom will turn on them in the end. The suggestion appears plausible since it requires minimal change to the text, and the intelligibility of the resulting phrase provides a simple solution to a strange text. Despite the attractiveness of this suggestion, there are insurmountable problems which virtually preclude its acceptance as a viable alternative.

At least twice this century, short notes have been published which demonstrate conclusively that this suggestion is highly problematic.[4] However, these articles receive virtually no treatment in recent commentaries. Normal syntax and other instances of the verb לחם with an attached suffix

---

3. Evidence that the LXX *deliberately* omits לַחְמְךָ derives from the fact that Akiva, Symmachus, and Theodotion all attest the presence of the disputed word. Akiva and Theodotion both have αρτον σου, while Symmachus has οι συνεσθιοντες σοι.

4. Godfrey Rolles Driver, "Studies in the Vocabulary of the Old Testament. VII," *JTS* 35 (1934): 391; and Graham I. Davies, "New Solution to a Crux in Obadiah 7," *VT* 27 (1977): 484–87. Despite the pointedness of Davies's observations on the syntactical construction, his own suggestion of emendation on the basis of dittographical error is unconvincing. Allen objects to Driver's observations by relying on Gesenius (Allen, *Joel, Obadiah, Jonah, and Micah*, 150; cf. Gesenius, *Hebrew Grammar*, §116h). This paragraph only confirms, however, that, as a rule, participles can form genitive objects in poetic texts. Davies's point remains strong that the verb לחם does not exhibit this construction anywhere else in the Hebrew Bible.

require that the suffix functions as the direct object to the verb. However, the י emendation causes the suffix to be treated as an indirect object in Obad 7. These observations thus imply that the emended phrase in Obad 7 could not be translated "those eating *with* you" as most would presume. In reality, the emended phrase would have to be translated, "Those eating you will place a trap beneath you." The absurdity of this statement requires no further exploration. Thus, the slight emendation, which *seemingly* solved so many problems, in reality creates a construction even more obtuse than the MT it seeks to explain. We are thus forced back to the MT to attempt an explanation of the text as it stands. Syntactical observations, coupled with a search for a conceptual framework within the Hebrew Bible, open a path to understanding the MT in its present form as a coherent construct.

Syntactically, one cannot avoid the presence of the synonymous parallelism in the first two lines: "All the men of your covenant send you to the border;" and "The men of your peace deceive you; they overpower you." The subjects "men of your peace" and "men of your covenant" intend one and the same group. The problem comes in trying to explain the relationship of the third line to the first two. One cannot avoid two paradoxical observations. On the one hand, one gets the distinct impression that the *content* of the third line demands a continuation of the synonymous parallelism of the first two lines. On the other hand, the current syntactical form of the MT *does not provide an explicit parallel subject* as in the first two lines. If one does not emend the MT, then the singular phrase "your bread" (לחמך) cannot function as the subject of the plural verb "they place" (ישימו). Syntactically, the most natural reading of the third line would be to presume "your bread" to be the *direct object* of the clause, and to presume that the verbal phrase "they place" requires an antecedent. In this case, a plural antecedent is readily available in the {69} parallel subjects from the previous two lines: "the men of your covenant" and the "men of your peace." Thus, *syntactically*, the simplest grammatical reading of the MT could be stated: "They (the men of your covenant/peace) place your bread as a trap beneath you."

Recognizing this simple syntax underscores the problem which causes so many commentators to emend the text in the first place. This sentence creates tremendous *conceptual* difficulties for the modern reader (and ancient translators). However, the Hebrew Bible provides tradition-historical clues which illuminate this line greatly. As a point of departure, note that the parallels of the first two lines (men of your covenant/men of your peace) place one squarely in the conceptual realm of treaty language.

This fact causes one to ask whether this treaty background could help to explain the use of bread in the third line.

The Political Implications of "Bread"

Several Hebrew Bible passages (Judg 8:4–7; Josh 9:11–14; 1 Sam 22:13; 25:11) demonstrate a combination of political alliances and treaties in which "bread" plays more than a peripheral role. In Judg 8:4–7, Gideon asks the men of Succoth to provide his people with loaves of bread while he is pursuing Zebah and Zalmunna, the kings of Midian. The response to Gideon's request demonstrates their awareness that consent to Gideon's request carried *political implications*:

> [6]And the leaders of Succoth said, "Are the hands of Zebah and Zalmunna already in your hands that we should give bread to your army?"

The leaders imply that providing sustenance for Gideon's army would open them to punishment from the kings of Midian, because they would have aided the enemy. Gideon's unsympathetic reaction confirms the political nature of the request from the other perspective:

> [7]And Gideon said, "All right, when the Lord has given Zebah and Zalmunna into my hand, then I will thrash your bodies with the thorns of the wilderness and with briers."

Gideon's response exemplifies the adage, "The one who is not with me is against me." Gideon thus warns the men of Succoth that their decision not to provide bread to his army was an act of nonalliance. The account thus presupposes the reader's knowledge that providing "bread" to the leader of an army carried political implications.

A second example where a narrative presupposes the political implications of "bread" surfaces in the story of the Gibeonite deception of Joshua and the men of Israel (Josh 9:1–15). This story narrates how the Gibeonites disguised messengers to come to Joshua and the men of Israel so that it appeared they had traveled a long distance to make a covenant with Joshua. The distance was significant since the Israelites were under orders to kill the people of the land (9:6–7; cf. Deut 3:21; 7:2; Josh 24:18; etc.). The Gibeonites put on old clothes and packed *old bread* to take with them. Joshua and the men of Israel were skeptical when this group first arrived, but the Gibeonites explain that they are on an official mission from their homeland.

> ¹¹So our elders and all the inhabitants of our country spoke to us, saying, "Take provisions in your hand for the journey, and go to meet them and say to them, 'We are your servants; now make a covenant with us.' ¹²This *our bread* was warm when we took it for our *provisions* out of our houses on the day that we left to come to you; but now behold it is dry and has become crumbled. ¹³And these wineskins which we filled were new, and behold, they are torn." (NASB, emphasis added) {70}

Their explanation satisfied the Israelites and Joshua, so that they did not seek divine counsel but allowed themselves to be tricked into making the covenant. Notice the description of this covenant:

> ¹⁴So the men of Israel took some of their *provisions*, and did not ask for the counsel of the Lord. ¹⁵And Joshua made *peace* with them, and made a *covenant* with them to let them live; and the leaders of the congregation swore an oath to them. (NASB, emphasis added)

The men of Israel *accepted* their provisions, and Joshua made an alliance with them. The fact that these provisions were not fit to eat, especially the bread, implies strongly that the acceptance of their provisions had ceremonial or contractual overtones beyond the simple satisfaction of human needs. Significantly, this passage explicitly combines three concepts which also appear in Obad 7, namely, covenant (9:11, 15), peace (9:15), and bread (Josh 9:12).

Two other passages also deserve brief mention because they demonstrate the pervasiveness of the presupposition that providing bread carried political implications. First Samuel 21–22 recounts David's flight from Saul. When David fled, Ahimelech the priest at Nob gave him bread and a sword because David said he was on a mission for Saul (1 Sam 21:2). Even though David deceived Ahimelech, Saul executed all the priests at Nob together with all the inhabitants of that city (1 Sam 22:16–19). The stated reason for Saul's decision cited the priest's act of providing David with *bread*, a sword, and counsel (1 Sam 22:13).

The final passage also comes from the narratives surrounding David's flight from Saul. First Samuel 25 relates the story of a wealthy man, Nabal, who refused to give bread and other provisions to David's men (25:11). This refusal angered David, and he prepared to attack Nabal and his household. Nabal's wife Abigail realized the consequences of Nabal's refusal. She arranged that *bread*, wine, and meat be sent to David, and then she went to David to plead for mercy. Her plea (25:23–31) is full of statements which demonstrate her awareness of the religious *and* political implications of her actions.

These four passages (Judg 8:4–7; Josh 9:11–14; 1 Sam 22:13; 25:11) provide documentary evidence that, in certain situations, the simple provision of a normally innocuous item, "bread," constituted a political action binding two parties in a formal or informal alliance. One of these passages (Josh 9:11–14) specifically ties three terms together which appear in successive lines in Obad 7 (covenant, peace, and bread). With the recognition of this conceptual framework, it is now possible to return to Obad 7 to demonstrate that the MT is by no means unintelligible as it stands.

"Bread" as a Politically Charged Metaphor in Obadiah 7

As many have correctly presumed, the first three poetic lines in Obad 7 should be read in synonymous parallelism. However, the passages noted above allow a simple explanation for the third line without resorting to textual emendation. One need merely understand that the "bread" functions as a politically charged metaphor. In this poetic context, "bread" is used as a synonym to "covenant" and "peace." This simple suggestion solves the *conceptual* problems by recognizing that the combination of "covenant," "peace," and "bread" conforms well to the semantic field of treaty language which is elicited in the first two lines. Providing sustenance to an army cemented an alliance with that army.

Syntactically, recognizing this metaphor allows one to read the MT the way one would most logically expect it to be read. "Bread" functions as the object of the verb "they place" and was never intended to be the subject. The verbal form "they place" {71} (ישימו) merely presumes the synonymous expressions "men of your covenant" and "men of your peace" as the collective antecedent for the subject. If "bread" is to be understood as the object, one must then explain how the author continues the synonymous parallelism of the first two lines. Again, the answer is not complicated. One must merely recognize that "your bread" is not used as a synonym for the entire phrase "all the men of your covenant" or "the men of your peace." Rather, "your bread" functions explicitly as a metaphorical synonym to "your covenant" and "your peace." The third line could thus be paraphrased: "These men have placed your covenant (or your alliance) as a trap beneath you."

This metaphorical understanding of "your bread" falls into a documentable conceptual frame, thereby allowing one to read the sentence in its expected syntactical construction. Moreover, the wider *context* of Obadiah provides additional evidence that Obad 7 reflects the condemnation of a political alliance. Obadiah 10–14 refers explicitly to Edom's role in the Babylonian destruction of Jerusalem in 587 BCE. The text is not entirely consistent with regard to the extent of Edom's active role, but these verses denounce the duplicity of Edom for conspiring in Judah's misfortune.[5] Obadiah 7 also presupposes that Edom has entered some type of alliance.

When all of the evidence is taken into account, it is possible to say that the MT of Obad 7 makes sense conceptually, syntactically, and contextually. One need only recognize "your bread" as a politically charged metaphor which parallels the expressions "your covenant" and "your peace" in the previous two lines. Colloquially paraphrased, the third line could be restated: "Your alliance will come back to haunt you."

Conclusion

Although usually emended, several observations support the MT in Obad 7, specifically in the phrase which reads: "They place your bread beneath you as a trap." First, the most common emendation creates syntactical problems. Second, the MT contains no syntactical problems once one recognizes "your bread" as the direct object. Third, the treaty language of Obad 7 provides the conceptual avenue for understanding the disputed phrase, since several Old Testament passages demonstrate that providing bread to an army constituted an act of political alliance. "Bread" in Obad 7 should thus be understood as a metaphorical synonym for "covenant" and "peace" explicitly mentioned in the first part of the verse and implicit in Obad 10–14.

---

5. Obadiah 11 implies that Edom's main crime was its apathy, its refusal to aid Judah in the conflict. By contrast Obad 13 implies the Edomites entered the city to loot it following the destruction. Obadiah 14 accuses the Edomites of hindering the flight of the people of Judah who tried to escape.

Reading David in the Psalter:
A Study in Liturgical Hermeneutics

In 1986, James Mays began his essay "The David of the Psalms" with the following statement:

> An essay on a subject like "The David of the Psalms" is a sign of what is going on in biblical studies in our time. The subject suggests that there is a David whose reality and importance lies in his connection with psalms and psalmody. The subject assumes that it is legitimate and useful to be interested in this figure who exists as a literary reality—and may never have existed in any other way. The subject is a way of claiming that such a figure is a proper matter for Old Testament study and research.[1]

Indeed, Mays demonstrates that the association of "David" with psalms occurs differently in Samuel, Chronicles, and the Psalms. Mays concludes that

> the notion of the David of the Psalms is an intra-textual reality. The notion arises from looking at the text in terms of certain relations to which the texts themselves guide the reader. It is a product of the Old Testament, not just separate books, and its function and effect is hermeneutic; its usefulness has to do with the interpretation of the text as Scripture and in liturgy.[2]

The following analysis will evaluate several psalms, attempting to draw modern readers into conversation with ancient interpreters of David.[3]

---

1. James Luther Mays, "The David of the Psalms," *Int* 40 (1986): 143.
2. Ibid., 155.
3. Thirteen psalms contain superscriptions relating the psalm to the life of David (3, 7, 18, 34, 51, 52, 54, 56, 57, 59, 60, 63, 142). Of these, only 7:1 refers to an episode not clearly related to the Samuel narratives. However, only one of these superscrip-

{169} This essay evaluates seven superscriptions relating the attached psalm to specific instances in David's life. These so-called biographic superscriptions are often noted as scribal additions to the psalm, but the implications of these notations for understanding David's portrayal in the Psalter and the use of Davidic traditions in ancient worship are seldom treated in any detail. This essay will explore how the superscriptions, and the psalms which they introduce, create an image of David when read with the various narratives. The association of David with many of these narrative episodes also provides insights into the hermeneutical trajectories of the person(s) responsible for associating each psalm with the narrative in ways that transcend both the psalm and the narrative. The connections suggest that the psalms were used at key moments in the telling of the story of David to clarify and sharpen the narrative episode in ways that would make the episode, or sometimes even the character of David himself, more suitable for use in a communal worship setting.[4]

Several guiding questions will help illustrate how the superscriptions connect the individual psalms to the narrative episodes:

1. To what text or tradition does the superscription refer?
2. What is the nature of the linguistic connections from the superscription to the psalm or from the superscription to the source?
3. How does the genre affect the connection?
4. Can one detect tensions or similarities between the psalm and the narrative context?

From these questions, observations will arise which can help to explain how someone would have made the connection between the psalm and the narrative. {170}

---

tions (60:1) points to an episode that also appears in the narratives of Chronicles. For reasons of space, only seven will be treated.

4. Caution is advised since it is not clear what this worship setting would have entailed. For a sample of some of the complexity of the topic of worship in ancient Israel, see Paul J. Achtemeier, "The Praise of God in Psalm and Hymn," *Int* 39 (1985): 3–74; Hans-Joachim Kraus, *Worship in Israel: A Cultic History of the Old Testament* (Richmond: John Knox, 1966); John H. Eaton, "The Psalms and Israelite Worship," in *Tradition and Interpretation: Essays by Members of the Society for Old Testament Study*, ed. George W. Anderson (Oxford: Clarendon, 1979), 238–73.

Psalm 3:1

A Psalm of David, when he fled from his son Absalom.[5]

Source

The psalm's superscription points to the story of Absalom's revolt in 2 Sam 15–19, and more specifically to the point of David's flight (chs. 16–17). However, no specific instance in the narrative states that David prayed to YHWH during this flight. Relating this psalm to the narrative, however, requires a point where David would utter this psalm as a prayer.

Linguistic Connections

The superscription (3:1) displays no linguistic connections to the psalm, although one can find thematic connections by choosing to read the psalm with the narrative of Absalom's revolt. Linguistic connections do exist from the superscription to the narrative of Absalom's revolt. The reference to Absalom refers the reader to 2 Sam 15–19. The verb (to flee) appears twice in those accounts: 15:14 and 19:10. Second Samuel 15:14 appears in the mouth of David after David has just been told of Absalom's intent. David speaks to "those with him in Jerusalem," later described as "his servants" (15:15) and "his household" (15:16). Second Samuel 19:10 is a summary of the events described after Absalom's death.

Genre Associations

Scholars have long classified Ps 3 as an individual complaint song.[6] As such, its structure is readily discernible.[7] The amount of material dedicated to the complaint (3:2–3 [Eng. 3:1–2]) and affirmation of confidence (3:4–7 [Eng. 3:3–6]) takes up the bulk of the psalm. However, these elements culminate

---

5. Unless otherwise noted, all scripture quotations in this chapter are taken from the NRSV.
6. See Hermann Gunkel and Joachim Begrich, *Introduction to Psalms: The Genres of the Religious Lyric of Israel*, trans. James D. Nogalski, MLBS (Macon, GA: Mercer University Press, 1998), 121; Erhard S. Gerstenberger, *Psalms: Part 1; with an Introduction to Cultic Poetry*, FOTL 14 (Grand Rapids: Eerdmans, 1988), 50.
7. Gerstenberger, *Psalms: Part 1*, 50.

in the petition to smite the enemies (3:8 [Eng. 3:7]). The petition is thus a more significant element for this psalm than its size would suggest. Gerstenberger assumes that the petition is the reason that the superscription was added.[8] The heavy {171} emphasis upon confidence in YHWH implies that the psalmist relies heavily on past experience to know that YHWH will come to his aid.

Narrative Tensions and Connections

Apart from the superscription, several points of contact allow the reader to associate Ps 3 with the narrative about Absalom's revolt. First, the theme of a threat from enemies, though vaguely formulated (cf. 3:2, 8 [Eng. 3:1, 7]), creates a general affinity with the Absalom revolt narrative where David's son leads a revolt so powerful that it drives David from Jerusalem. Second, the phrasing of verse 5 (Eng. 3:4) is also ambiguous enough to allow the reader to assume that the speaker of the psalm is not in Jerusalem, since YHWH "answers me from his holy hill." This phrasing does not state that the author is or is not in Jerusalem, but it does allow the assumption that the author is thinking of YHWH responding from a distance. In this respect, it allows the reader to associate this distance with David's flight. Third, while the psalm acknowledges YHWH's frequent help in the past, the culmination of the psalm lies in the petition concerning the threat that is, as yet, unresolved. Of course, an unresolved problem is an essential ingredient of any complaint psalm. So, in at least these aspects, the psalm and the narrative can be connected by the reader, but these similarities are ambiguous and only created by the reader of the superscription. Without the superscription, the psalm would have no indisputable links to the Absalom narrative.

However, several significant tensions also exist between Ps 3 and the Absalom revolt narrative. First, the psalm speaks of the threat from enemies, a common term for individual complaint psalms, while the superscription speaks specifically of Absalom. Plural forms are used in verses 2, 8 (Eng. 3:1, 7) to refer to these persons. This tension can be discounted to a degree, since the narrative also refers to the defeat of David's s enemies (plural) when news of Absalom's defeat and death is relayed to the king (2 Sam 18:19, 32). Second, the psalm contains no sense of internal tension

---

8. Ibid., 51.

with respect to the psalmist's attitude toward these enemies. The psalmist appears completely resolute in his anger toward the enemies and calls for YHWH to deliver violent vengeance upon them. The psalm does not provide any sense of the betrayal one might expect from a king whose son was attempting a coup. Also, the psalm contains no hint of the internal conflict of David as described in {172} 2 Samuel when the news of Absalom's death is reported (2 Sam 18:5, 12, 33–19:8). Third, the threat implied by the psalm, if the superscription is not considered, appears to have a defensive quality. The psalmist describes life as usual in the face of the threat: "I lie down and sleep; I wake again, for the Lord sustains me" (3:6 [Eng. 3:5]). There is no sense of flight in the body of this psalm.

The psalm adds something that is not present in the narrative, a prayer from David. By reading this psalm at a point in the narrative when David is fleeing, David's plight and his dependence upon God are dramatized.

Relying upon the verbal links and the genre associations allows one to suggest how the person who added the superscription understood the psalm in relation to the narrative. The genre and the superscription suggest a threat in progress, which in turn intimates that the psalm was intended to be associated with a point in the narrative when David is still on the run from Absalom. Second, the genre reinforces Joab's point of view in the narrative that David should be righteously indignant at the rebellion and ignore the fact that it is his son Absalom who is leading the revolt (cf. 2 Sam 19:1–7). The psalm underscores the threat faced by the psalmist.

Psalm 34:1

Of David, when he feigned madness before Abimelech, so that he drove him out, and he went away.

Source

Psalm 34:1 refers to the episode recounted in 1 Sam 21:13–15, 22:1, despite the fact that the Philistine king mentioned in that episode is named Achish rather than Abimelech, as in Ps 34:1.[9] In {173} the narrative episode, while

---

9. The difference in the name is readily explained as a mistaken association of the priest's name (Ahimelech) from the previous chapter with the Philistine king (Abimelech of Gerar) mentioned in Gen 20 and 26. According to Jewish tradition, however, Achish is called Abimelech in honor of the king of Gerar because "Achish, though a

fleeing persecution from Saul, David escapes to Gath, where he is seen by the king's servants as a threat to King Achish. The servants of Achish recognize David as more powerful than Saul (21:11). Fearing for his life, David decides to act like a madman. David's behavior convinces Achish that David is no threat: Achish says to his servants, "Look, you see the man is mad; why then have you brought him to me? Do I lack madmen, that you have brought this fellow to play the madman in my presence?" (21:14–15). David then escapes to the cave of Adullam, where he is joined by his family and followers (22:1). This narrative episode never mentions a prayer (or any response from David), nor does it mention YHWH. By contrast, Ps 34 asks the reader to place this psalm within the framework of this narrative. How is the connection made?

Linguistic Connections

Psalm 34:1 presumes that the narrative episode occurred in the past. The superscription and the words of Achish in 1 Sam 21:14 contain the only two instances of the particular idiom for going mad in the Old Testament (שנה + טעם) thus creating a very strong link between the two texts. Still, there are no strong linguistic connections from the superscription to the psalm itself. Apart from the superscription, the psalm proper contains no strong verbal links to the narrative episode.

Genre Associations

The genre of Ps 34 is an individual thanksgiving psalm, but it is also an acrostic poem. The genre of the thanksgiving psalm presumes the threat about which the psalmist speaks has already passed. The psalmist offers thanks to YHWH for deliverance, but the perspective of Ps 34 takes on a decidedly didactic tone. Moreover, the psalm's acrostic style shows considerable thought went into the composition of this psalm. Before exploring the associations one can perceive by reading this psalm in conjunction with 1 Sam 21, one should acknowledge several tensions between the

---

heathen, was pious, for which reason he is called Abimilech in the Psalms after the king of Gerar who was also noted for his piety" (Louis Ginzberg, *Bible Times and Characters from the Joshua to Esther*, vol. 4 of *The Legends of the Jews*, trans. Henrietta Szold and Paul Radin [Baltimore: Johns Hopkins University Press, 1998], 89).

psalm and the narrative that make it unlikely that the psalm was originally composed for the narrative.

Narrative Tensions and Connections

Several tensions demonstrate that the original setting of Ps 34 does not fit the context of 1 Sam 21:13–15. Psalm 34 implies a congregational/group setting, whereas the narrative episode occurs during David's lonely flight from Saul. Not {174} only is the setting of a thanksgiving psalm generally presumed to have been a worship setting, but the psalmist speaks directly to others in several places (note especially the plural forms of direct address in 34:4, 9–12, and the second-person address of someone other than God in 34:14 [Eng. 34:3, 8–11, 13]). In addition, the didactic nature of the psalm makes it highly likely that this psalm was composed to be performed before a worshiping group (cf. the teaching about the righteous in 34:16–19 [Eng. 34:15–18]). Finally, the psalm contains no specific references to the situation described in the narrative.

Why, then, would a scribe attach a superscription to this psalm which associates the psalm with the narrative of David pretending to be mad in order to escape the clutches of the king of Gath? First, it should be noted that the narrative episode never mentions YHWH. By contrast, from the opening line, the psalm mentions YHWH sixteen times. The psalm adds a dimension that presumes a role for God in the narrative episode. This inclusion of God where God does not appear in the narrative recurs several times with the "biographic" superscriptions of the Psalter. Second, the use of the thanksgiving genre would make "David" fittingly grateful for God's active help in this situation, but it seemingly ignores the fact that God plays no active role in the narrative episode as recorded in 1 Samuel. For this interpretation to make sense, one would have to presume that YHWH is somehow involved with David's display of insanity. In the case of Ps 34, however, Jewish tradition offers precisely this type of reading:

> David once said to God: "The world is entirely beautiful and good, with the one exception of insanity. What use does the world derive from a lunatic, who runs hither and thither, tears his clothes, and is pursued by a mob of hooting children?" "Verily, a time will come," said God in reply, "when thou wilt supplicate me to afflict thee with madness." Now it happened when David, on his flight before Saul, came to Achish.... In his distress, David besought God to let him appear a madman in the eyes of Achish and his court. God granted his prayer.... Thus it was that

David was rescued. Thereupon, he composed the Psalm beginning with the words, "I will bless the Lord at all times," which includes even the time of lunacy.[10] {175}

Naturally, one cannot know whether this tradition already circulated at the time when the superscription was added to the psalm, but clearly this tradition was told in midrashic style to help explain the connection between the narrative and the thanksgiving offered in Ps 34.

The "biographic" superscription of Ps 34 thus accomplishes two tasks: it presumes an interpretation, or a tradition, about the narrative episode that creates a role for God in this episode of David's life where none exists in the narrative, and second, it emphasizes a "David" who is more overtly pious and grateful to YHWH than is evident from the episode as portrayed in Samuel. It is not the only time that the "biographic" superscriptions function in this manner.

Psalm 51:1–2

"¹To the leader. A Psalm of David, ²when the prophet Nathan came to him, after he had gone in to Bathsheba."

Source

The superscription in this psalm references a particular point in the story of David and Bathsheba (2 Sam 11–12). The superscription refers specifically to the prophet Nathan's confrontation of David, as described in chapter 12, after David has arranged the death of Uriah, Bathsheba's husband (11:14–27). In this episode, Nathan confronts the king by telling David of two men, one rich and one poor (12:1–4). The rich man takes the property of the poor man to suit his own purpose. Incensed, David demands that the rich man be killed for his insolence (12:5–6). Nathan then turns the story on David and announces YHWH's four-fold punishment: David will always face battles to protect his kingdom (12:10); David's own family will rebel against him (12:11); David's own wives will be taken from him by

---

10. Ibid., 4:89–90. Ginzberg is summarizing material from several sources. See Louis Ginzberg, *From Moses to Esther: Notes for Volumes 3 and 4*, vol. 6 of *The Legends of the Jews*, trans. Henrietta Szold and Paul Radin, (Baltimore: Johns Hopkins University Press, 1998), 253 n. 46.

another (12:11); and the child of the affair with Bathsheba will die (12:14). Nathan's confrontation elicits a brief note of confession from David, but this confession merely states the obvious: "I have sinned against the Lord" (12:13). It offers no sense of the extent of David's contrition. YHWH, through Nathan, accepts this confession and offers forgiveness to David, but does not remove the punishments. {176}

After the child becomes ill, David fasts in the hope that YHWH will change his mind (12:15-19). After the child dies, David goes to YHWH's house, but he returns to business as usual very quickly (12:20-25). David explains this change as a recognition that nothing can change the boy's plight. The narrative implies that David's actions were entirely geared to help the boy live. It would seem that Ps 51 (with the superscription) is designed to change the impression of David left by the Samuel story, that David shows little remorse for his actions toward Uriah. His only real concern appears to have been to save the life of the child, and even after the child's death, David does not grieve as would be expected (12:20-23).

Psalm 51:2 suggests that the psalm be read at the point of the narrative after Nathan confronts David—presumably after 2 Sam 12:14. The psalm makes no allusion to the death of the child, the central concern of the narrative in 2 Sam 12:15-25. The psalm shows some linguistic connections, but the most important linking feature appears to be the genre elements of the penitential prayer and the individual complaint song.

Linguistic Connections

In addition to the superscription, three phrases within the psalm proper also evoke recognition of similar phrases in the Samuel narrative: "Have mercy on me [חנני], O God, according to your steadfast love" (51:3 [Eng. 51:1]; cf. 2 Sam 12:22); the confessional statement, "Against you, you alone, have I sinned" (51:6 [Eng. 51:4]; cf. 2 Sam 12:13); and the confession of the psalmist, "and done what is evil in your sight" (51:6 [Eng. 51:4]; cf. 2 Sam 11:27b). The first reference links only by a verbal root that occurs more than thirty times in the Psalter, making intentionality difficult to ascertain. However, the presence of two more extensive phrases in verse 6 [Eng. 51:4] that recall the beginning of the narrative episode (2 Sam 11:27b) and David's confession (2 Sam 12:13) at least suggest that the connections in verse 6 [Eng. 51:4] may have been adapted with the Samuel story in mind.[11]

---

11. The factor that complicates a decision on intentionality is that both parallel

However, several tensions between the psalm and the narrative (see below) make it unlikely that the bulk of Ps 51 was originally composed with an eye toward 2 Sam 12. {177}

Genre Associations

Psalm 51 exhibits the characteristic elements of an individual complaint song, but with a significant emphasis on the element of penitence. In fact, the core of the psalm functions as an extended penitential prayer.[12] This core contains an initial plea for mercy (51:3-4 [Eng. 51:1-2]), a confession of sin (51:5-8 [Eng. 51:3-6]), an extended petition for forgiveness (51:9-14 [Eng. 51:7-12]), and a vow to recount YHWH's forgiveness to others (51:15-17 [Eng. 51:13-15]). The worship setting can be seen in particular in the vow. The petition to rebuild the walls of Jerusalem suggest a postexilic setting, at least for these verses.[13]

The superscription of Ps 51 suggests that the genre and content of the psalm have influenced someone to suggest reading this psalm with the story of Nathan's confrontation of David. The emphasis on confession and a plea for forgiveness add a dimension to the "David" of 2 Sam 12 not present in the narrative. When this psalm is read with the narrative at the point where Nathan confronts David, David's brief statement of fact (2 Sam 12:13) takes on a pathos and sense of contrition that simply is not otherwise present in the Samuel narrative. It makes David a more admirable character for the worshiper who sees the "David" of Ps 51 in the narrative of 2 Sam 12.

Narrative Tensions and Connections

Despite the recurring phrases, certain tensions between the psalm and the narrative make it more likely that Ps 51 was not originally composed for the Samuel narrative. First, the psalm lacks any allusion to the death of the child, a primary focus in the Samuel narrative. Second, there is no mention of Uriah or Bathsheba, either by name or by clear inference. Third, the threat of bloodshed in Ps 51:16 (Eng. 51:14) makes no sense in the

---

phrases are rather idiomatic. Nevertheless, a case can be made that 51:6 (Eng. 51:4) is aware of the Davidic association implied by the superscription.

12. Gerstenberger, *Psalms: Part 1*, 211-15.

13. Gerstenberger sees these elements as additions to the psalm (ibid., 214).

narrative account. Fourth, explicit pleas to rebuild the walls of Jerusalem presuppose a far different historical reality than the time of David. Finally, the portrayal of "David" in the psalm differs from the "David" of the narrative. The Samuel narrative concludes ambiguously, without a clear sense of the extent to which the encounter changes David. By contrast, the psalm not only presents a contrite "David," but one who first, plans to {178} teach others from his mistakes (51:15 [Eng. 51:13]); second, longs to see the joy of salvation (51:14 [Eng. 51:12]); third, requests wisdom (51:8 [Eng. 51:6]) and cleansing from God (51:9-11 [Eng. 51:7-9]); and fourth, knows that internal change transcends external change (51:18 [Eng. 51:16-17]).

This last observation points to the most likely reason why the psalm would have been used liturgically to supplement the reading of the narrative episode. Psalm 51, when read at the point of 2 Sam 12:13, expands David's confession to portray an unmistakable sense of contrition and a request for forgiveness. No one reading Ps 51 after 2 Sam 12:13 could doubt whether David had shown remorse, no matter how ambiguously the narrative might unfold. This psalm becomes an affirmation of David's proper response to YHWH when David is confronted with the error of his ways.

Psalm 52:1-2

[1]To the leader. A Maskil of David, [2]when Doeg the Edomite came to Saul and said to him, "David has come to the house of Ahimelech."

Source

The source cited by the superscription of Ps 52 refers the reader/hearer to the episode recounted in 1 Sam 21:7; 22:9-22. In this episode, Doeg the Edomite is present (see 1 Sam 21:7) when David receives aid from Ahimelech during his flight from Saul. Later, in response to Saul's anger, Doeg tells Saul that he has seen Ahimelech inquire of YHWH for David and load him with provisions, including Goliath's sword (22:9-10). As a result, Saul summons Ahimelech before him, confronts the priest, then orders him killed. None of the Benjamites present will raise their hand against the priest, but Doeg, at Saul's command, kills Ahimelech and the priests at Nob (22:11-18). According to the narrative (22:19), Doeg all too willingly completes this task, killing eighty-five priests and wiping out almost the entire village of Nob and its inhabitants.

Linguistic Connections

The superscription of Ps 52:1–2 contains an adapted citation of 1 Sam 22:9, while assuming that the audience knows the rest of the story. The citation of 1 Sam 22:9 by Ps 52:2 {179} cannot truly be classified as a quotation because only the verb and the name of the priest appear in common. Nevertheless, several observations can illustrate how this superscription frames Doeg's actions. First, Ps 52:2 names David explicitly, while 1 Samuel uses the term "son of Jesse," a common term for David in Samuel. This change implies a distance from the narrative. Second, a subtle change emphasizes the castigation of Doeg more than the text of 1 Samuel. In Ps 52:2, Doeg goes to Saul and tells him that David had gone to "the house of Ahimelech." By contrast, in Samuel, Doeg does not seek out Saul. He responds only when asked by Saul. Finally, Ps 52:2 implies that Doeg implicates the entire house of Ahimelech, a detail that undoubtedly helps to explain Saul's retribution against Ahimelech's entire household rather than just the priest himself as the narrative would imply. Interestingly, both the narrative and the psalm seem, by implication, to ascribe more guilt to Doeg for telling Saul where David had been than for actually carrying out Saul's commands to kill the priest, his family, and the inhabitants of his village.

The most important linguistic connection between the superscription and the psalm proper appears as a thematic point of contact in Ps 52:3–6 [Eng. 52:1–4], with its accusations against one who causes trouble by opening one's mouth with evil intentions. This fits with the condemnation of Doeg for providing Saul with information he (presumably) knows would lead to death for Ahimelech.

Genre Associations

The genre of Ps 52 is notoriously difficult to determine, even though the individual elements of the psalm have numerous parallels with complaint psalms. The psalm begins with an impeachment of the enemy (52:3–7 [Eng. 52:1–5]), but its style of direct confrontation, accusation, and verdict has more in common with prophetic forms. Complaint psalms more typically use a prayer style.[14] The accusation of slander is common for

---

14. Ibid., 216–17; Artur Weiser, *The Psalms: A Commentary*, trans. Herbert Hartwell, OTL (Philadelphia: Westminster, 1962), 185.

complaint psalms, as is the affirmation that the evildoer will be punished by God (52:7 [Eng. 52:5]). The concluding sections of Ps 52 announce the impact of God's action against the wicked person. God's action will be seen as an affirmation to the {180} righteous (52:8–9 [Eng. 52:6–7]), and it evokes an individual's affirmation of confidence (52:10 [Eng. 52:8]) and thanksgiving (52:11 [Eng. 52:9]). The psalm is thus nearly evenly divided between accusation and verdict (52:3–7 [Eng. 52:1–5]) and affirmations of God's goodness for punishing the wicked (52:8–11 [Eng. 52:6–9]).

Narrative Tensions and Connections

Psalm 52 exhibits several tensions with the narrative that greatly limit the possibility that the psalm comes from the time of David or that the psalm was originally composed in response to the events described in 1 Sam 22. First, the psalm contains no mention of the slaughter of the priests or the village. Second, the psalm specifically refers to the temple (52:10 [Eng. 52:8]), eliminating the time of David before the temple was constructed. Third, the accusation of Ps 52 is against someone who tells falsehoods, but Doeg essentially tells the truth. One can certainly argue that Doeg should have withheld the information on David's whereabouts from Saul, but one cannot accuse Doeg of speaking falsely when he says that David had visited Ahimelech. The statement that the evil one trusted in his wealth (52:9 [Eng. 52:7]) plays no part in the Doeg narrative. It thus seems highly probable that the psalm was not originally composed with the Doeg episode in mind.

Nevertheless, the superscription raises the question, "How would someone have read this psalm in light of the Doeg story?" The answer to this question seems fairly obvious, based on the two parts of the psalm itself. First, even though slander is the primary charge against the person in the psalm, one can say that the person who added the superscription would have been drawn to the psalm by the fact that the wicked one causes trouble with his mouth and his evil intentions. Second, the heavy concentration of affirmations that God will punish the wicked, when read in light of the Doeg narrative, implies a belief that Doeg is punished despite the fact that the Samuel narrative never recounts Doeg's fate. Third, the fact that the punishment is carried out by YHWH further adds to the portrayal of David as one who relies on God for vengeance, not on his own need of retribution. Such an interpretation would require some folklore regarding Doeg's fate that confirmed YHWH's punishment. Jewish rabbinic sources record such a tradition. It is said that Doeg died of leprosy at the young age of thirty-four after being driven from the {181} house of study by his own disciples.[15] Moreover, even this gruesome death was deemed insufficient for his crimes so, according to Jewish tradition, angels burned Doeg's body and scattered his ashes to prevent him from experiencing the afterlife.[16] Reading this psalm with the narrative episode thus presumes that "David" called upon YHWH to punish Doeg for what he had done.

Psalm 54:1–2

¹To the leader: with stringed instruments. ²A Maskil of David, when the Ziphites went and told Saul, "David is in hiding among us."

Source

Psalm 54:2 refers the reader to a time when the Ziphites betray David to Saul. The David story narrates two accounts of betrayal by the Ziphites that are nearly identical with regard to the role of the Ziphites (1 Sam 23:15–29 and 1 Sam 26:1–25). In 1 Sam 23, the Ziphites offer to hand David over to Saul. Saul makes them return to set up a better trap. Saul is in the process of trapping David (23:26) when he receives word that the Philistines have raided the land, causing Saul to abandon pursuit of David and thereby allowing David to escape to the strongholds of En-Gedi. In 1 Sam 26, the Ziphites use the same language, but Saul immediately sends three thousand men after David. In this instance, David stealthily makes his way to Saul's camp and takes Saul's spear and water jar. David then uses these purloined items to humiliate Abner, who was responsible for protecting Saul. Neither episode contains an explicit reference to YHWH or YHWH's activity in delivering David from Saul's pursuit.

Linguistic Connections

The connection to the source text is accomplished by a close quotation of a portion of 1 Sam 23:19 and 1 Sam 26:1: "Is not David hiding among us?" This connection solidifies scholarly assumptions that the "biographic" superscriptions in the Psalms were not composed by David. For one thing,

---

15. Ginzberg, *The Legends of the Jews*, 4:76.
16. Ibid. For the references, see 6:242–43 n. 106.

the perspective of the {182} superscription presumes that the intended audience knows the story by the quotation. Relatedly, the perspective of the superscription reflects the third-person perspective of a narrator, not the perspective of the one fleeing from Saul.

Apart from the superscription, the psalm proper contains one phrase that offers a muted point of contact with the narrative episodes. Psalm 54:5 [Eng. 54:3] states "for strangers have risen against me."[17] The association of Ziphites with strangers would not be difficult, since the narrative traditions of David refer to them only in these two episodes. However, it should also be noted that while the Ziphites could be considered strangers, the Ziphites are not the ones who are pursuing David in either narrative (see the discussion of narrative tensions below).

Genre Associations

Scholars generally recognize Ps 54 as an individual complaint.[18] The initial plea (54:3-4 [Eng. 54:1-2]) contains four imperatives calling upon God for deliverance and attention. The complaint proper (54:5 [Eng. 54:3]) depicts the psalmist under threat from strangers. The remainder of the psalm contains an affirmation of confidence in YHWH's deliverance and destruction of the enemies (54:6-7 [Eng. 54:4-5]) followed by a vow and a note of (proleptic) thanksgiving (54:8-9 [Eng. 54:6-7]). Generally, complaint psalms presume that the danger indicated in the complaint still threatens the psalmist.[19] Nonetheless, it is not uncommon for complaint songs to include elements of thanksgiving in close association with the affirmation of certainty that God has heard one's cry for help.[20]

Narrative Tensions and Connections

Several tensions suggest that neither Ps 54 nor its superscription were originally composed during David's lifetime. The intriguing reference to "strangers" who "have risen up against me" does not fit the portrayal of either narrative where Saul and his men are the ones who actually pursue

---

17. NRSV translates "strangers" as "insolent ones."
18. Gerstenberger, *Psalms: Part 1*, 221-22; Weiser, *Psalms*, 415; Marvin E. Tate, *Psalms 51-100*, WBC 20 (Waco, TX: Word, 1990), 45.
19. Gunkel and Begrich, *Introduction to Psalms*, 169-70.
20. Ibid., 184.

David. Also, reference to a freewill offering (54:8 [Eng. 54:6]) suggests a later time with a functioning {183} temple, since the word used appears four times in the Psalter but never in Samuel.[21] The psalm's superscription points to the conversation between the Ziphites and Saul, a point when David is not present. Finally, the narrative contains no explicit reference to David praying, nor to YHWH's intervention on David's behalf.

Despite these tensions, or in one case because of these tensions, the person who added the superscription intended David to be the "I" in the psalm. When one reads this psalm in conjunction with the narrative episode(s), several things happen to the way one understands the narrative. First, "David" again appears more devout and pious in the psalm than in the narrative. David acts with cunning and bravado in 1 Sam 26, while the episode in 1 Sam 23:19–29 portrays David as merely acting with an eye toward self-preservation. The "David" of the psalm calls on God for help and makes a vow to God in grateful assurance that God will act. Second, God does not appear in the narrative episodes, but is mentioned or assumed in every verse of the psalm. The psalm was intended to support an interpretation whereby the Philistine attack that caused Saul to stop pursuing David (1 Sam 23:27) would have been instigated by YHWH to save David, although the narrative never states as much. In this interpretation, God would have intervened at David's behest. The reading of this psalm with the narrative thus creates several effects. It underscores the special relationship between David and YHWH, it highlights David's piety in a way not present in the Samuel narratives, and it emphasizes God's power to change threat to deliverance, even in dire situations.

Psalm 59:1

To the leader: Do not destroy. Of David. A *miktam*, when Saul ordered his house to be watched in order to kill him.

Source

The superscription refers to the narrative episode of 1 Sam 19:11–17. In this episode, David has just been forced to flee from Saul because Saul throws a spear at David while David is playing music for {184} Saul one

---

21. Psalms 54:8; 68:10; 110:3; 119:108.

evening. David returns home and Saul sends messengers to watch David's house because Saul plans to kill David in the morning. Michal, David's wife and Saul's daughter, helps David escape through a window, and then she covers a household idol with goat's hair and places it in David's bed. This ruse helps buy David time. Michal tells Saul's messengers that David is sick the first time they come to get him. Only when they return with a command from Saul to bring David anyway, do they learn that David has gone. When Saul confronts Michal, she claims that David threatened her with death if she did not go along with his plan. This narrative episode is remarkable for the passive role that David plays. Michal speaks, but there is no recorded reaction from David. Fleeing from Saul, David returns to his home, where he is urged by Michal to continue his flight because she deduces what her father has in store for David. God is never mentioned, nor is David's reaction.

Linguistic Connections

Psalm 59:1 refers to the narrative episode of 1 Sam 19:11–17 by using a slightly modified quotation of that verse:

1 Sam 19:11a: Saul sent [שלח] messengers to David's *house to keep watch* over him, planning *to kill him* in the morning.

Ps 59:1: To the leader: Do not destroy. Of David. A *miktam*, when *Saul ordered* [שלח] his *house* to be *watched* in order to *kill* him.

Since the citation in Ps 59:1 functions as a summary allusion to the narrative episode, it is quite clear that 59:1 changes from the narrative style to one more suited to its purpose.

Genre Associations

Psalm 59 is an individual complaint song, but it also contains clues that it was performed in a congregational setting. The psalm refers to "our shield" and "my people" in verse 12 [Eng. 59:11] in a manner that indicates a group context (note also references to Israel and Jacob in verses 6, 14 [Eng. 59:5, 13]).

The psalmist's claim of innocence (59:4b–5 [Eng. 59:3b–4]) represents a notable element of this complaint psalm. While this element is certainly a part of the arsenal of elements for this genre, the extent to which it is highlighted near the beginning of this particular psalm suggests a significant avenue for reading the psalm with the narrative, where Saul's attack on David is unprovoked. {185}

Narrative Tensions and Connections

Several tensions between Ps 59 and 1 Sam 19:11–17 reflect a different setting than implied in the superscription, but several touchstones suggest themselves as possible motivating factors for associating this psalm with 1 Sam 19:11–17. Naturally, the communal elements of this psalm already mentioned do not reflect the setting of David escaping from the window of his home. Second, the combination of complaint and thanksgiving elements (59:17–18 [Eng. 59:16–17]) create an effective worship element, but also create tension between the psalm and the narrative. Not only does David not speak in the narrative, but the narrative contains no account of a prayer. David's escape is accomplished by the plan hatched by Michal in the narrative. Third, the enemy mentioned in the psalm is "the nations" (59:6, 9 [Eng. 59:5, 8]), not Saul.

These, and other, tensions notwithstanding, one can detect several avenues for a reading strategy that would help to explain how this psalm could have been applied to help interpret the narrative episode of 1 Sam 19:11–17. First, this complaint psalm contains a strong affirmation of innocence at the beginning. When the psalm's superscription places this protestation in the mouth of David, it accentuates David's righteousness in comparison to Saul. It presumes an emphasis on Saul's arbitrary persecution of David, who in 1 Sam 19 has done nothing but play music to soothe Saul. Second, the refrain of the psalm (59:7, 15 [Eng. 59:6, 14]) depicts the threat that comes from a group gathered at night. In a vague sense, this reference coincides with the narrative setting where Saul's messengers wait outside David's house for daybreak to come so that they can take David back to Saul. The first two elements would then allow for the psalm to be placed in David's mouth as he ponders his next move, knowing that the king's messengers are waiting to take him to certain death. In so doing, the "David" of the psalm does something that the David of the narrative does not do. The "David" of the psalm prays to God for deliverance from his enemies. The resulting escape of the narrative, by implication, receives a divine imprimatur. The flight becomes part of God's plan, not merely the impromptu act conceived by Michal.

When this psalm is read in this way, it provides a voice to David not present in the narrative, where he never speaks. With the addition of the psalm, David prays to YHWH for deliverance, but he also pleads with {186} YHWH not to destroy his enemy (59:12 [Eng. 59:11]). The psalm helps solidify the impression of David's innocence, and the anticipated thanksgiving (59:17-18 [Eng. 59:16-17]) allows David to express his assurance that he will live to "sing aloud of your steadfast love in the morning" (59:17 [Eng. 59:16]).

Psalm 60:1-2

¹To the leader: according to the lily of the covenant. A *miktam* of David; for instruction; ²when he struggled with Aram-naharaim and with Aram-zobah, and when Joab on his return killed twelve thousand Edomites in the Valley of Salt.

Source

The superscription refers to events recorded in 2 Sam 8 and 1 Chr 18, but the references are hard to reconcile with either narrative precisely. The fact that the episodes to which the superscription refers appear in Chronicles and Samuel is unusual. None of the other "biographic" superscriptions has a parallel in Chronicles. The episodes appear in a prominent context in the narrative. The brief accounts summarize David's foreign campaigns, which extend the boundaries of Israel. Second Samuel 8 and 1 Chr 18 recount battles against the Philistines, Moabites, Edomites, and Syrians. However, neither chapter mentions the name of the Syrian kings in precisely the same form as Ps 60:2. Moreover, neither chapter cites Joab as the one who kills twelve thousand Edomites in the Salt Valley as the superscription states. According to 2 Sam 8:13, David "killed eighteen thousand Syrians in the Valley of Salt," while 1 Chr 18:12 claims that it was Abishai (Joab's brother) who "killed eighteen thousand Edomites in the Valley of Salt." Both texts, however, list Joab as the commander of the army (2 Sam 8:16 [=1 Chr 18:15]).[22] Thus, Ps 60:2 appears to refer to the defeat of the Syrians and Edomites (in the same order as 2 Sam 8:3-9 [=1 Chr 18:3-9] and

---

22. It is impossible to determine whether the deviation in numbers and identity of those killed in these three texts reflect an additional story not recorded in the biblical texts, or whether Ps 60:2 reflects variant traditions about the same event.

2 Sam 8:13-14 [= 1 Chr 18:12-13]). One can detect a certain lessening {187} of the portrayal of David's brutality in Chronicles. It omits reference to David's measuring of the Moabites to determine who would be slaughtered (2 Sam 8:2; cf. 1 Chr 18:2). This downplaying of the more brutal elements of David's campaigns is typical of the Chronicler's agenda of recasting David in a more positive, almost idealized, light.

To make matters more complex, a significant portion of the psalm (60:7-14 [Eng. 60:5-12]) appears in almost identical form in Ps 108:7-14 [Eng. 108:6-13]).[23] Psalm 108 contains a significantly different beginning than Ps 60. The superscription in Ps 108 contains no "biographic" note, although it does contain the brief note common to "Davidic" psalms. Moreover, Ps 108:2-7 [Eng. 108:1-6] opens far more triumphantly with a hymn of exhortation, although these verses are also incorporated from another psalm (108:2-6 = 57:8-12). It is the less confident beginning of Ps 60 that suggests how Ps 60 was utilized liturgically in conjunction with 2 Sam 8 (see the discussion below of the narrative tensions/connections).

Linguistic Connections

The connection between the narrative and the superscription is looser than most of the other "biographic" superscriptions because of the variations in names and numbers. Still, there is little doubt that Ps 60:2 has the events of 2 Sam 8 in mind. The superscription mentions Zobah (cf. 2 Sam 8:5), Joab (60:16), the "Valley of Salt" (60:13), and Edom (60:14).

Unlike many of the other psalms with "biographic" superscriptions, the body of Ps 60 also contains significant catchwords that could help to account for association of the psalm with the narratives. Most prominently, Ps 60:10 [Eng. 60:8] mentions three of the foreign lands that David defeats according to 2 Sam 8: Moab, Edom, and Philistia.

Genre Associations

Scholars generally classify Ps 60 as a communal complaint song or a communal complaint liturgy. The setting for the complaint appears to be a people's defeat at the hands of an enemy. In actuality, this psalm appears to

---

23. See the more detailed discussion of the parallel text in Erhard S. Gerstenberger, *Psalms: Part 2 and Lamentations*, FOTL 15 (Grand Rapids: Eerdmans, 2001), 253-56.

contain a dual complaint. The first {188} complaint (60:3-5 [Eng. 60:1-3]) portrays a people who are defeated in spirit as they survey their situation. This portion of the psalm leads to an unusual element for this genre: an extended YHWH speech (60:8-11 [Eng. 60:6-9]). This speech functions much like an affirmation of confidence, especially in light of the call for a divine response embedded in verse 7 [Eng. 60:5]. The second part of the psalm again calls for God to aid God's people (60:12-13 [Eng. 60:10-11]) and ends with an affirmation of confidence that God will bring about victory (60:14 [Eng. 60:12]). It is difficult, at first glance, to see why someone would have seen a connection between this psalm and the narrative of David's numerous victories over the surrounding nations. Still, consideration of the placement of the song in a liturgical setting may provide a key to understanding how this psalm could have been used in conjunction with the narrative.

Narrative Tensions and Connections

To be sure, apart from the superscription, the original setting of the psalm does not seem to have the narrative of 2 Sam 8 in mind. Too many tensions exist. The psalm anticipates defeat; the narrative recounts unbridled victory. This juxtaposition of these elements, however, may provide the very dynamic that can help to account for the association of the psalm with the victory narratives of 2 Sam 8, especially when compared to Ps 108. The desperate beginning of Ps 60, when read in conjunction with the David narrative, suggests that the use of this psalm implicitly reflects a significantly different interpretation of David's campaigns than is present in 2 Samuel. The narrative episodes, as portrayed in 2 Sam 8, give no indication of defeat for David, yet the psalm presupposes a threat to the people and the psalmist.

If one assumes, with Weiser and others, that the allusions to YHWH's promise of land to Israel in verses 8-10 [Eng. 60:6-8] helped to make the association with 2 Sam 8, then the issue of the threat to this promise's fulfillment present in the opening verses takes on dual significance. First, the psalm presumes an implicit rationale for David's campaigns against the surrounding nations. Specifically, these nations present a threat to David and Israel because of their attacks against YHWH's people. For this reason, "David" petitions YHWH for help and asks YHWH to remember his promise to give the land to Israel. As such, this psalm would probably have preceded the recounting of David's victories. These {189} victory narratives would then have functioned as evidence that God keeps promises. Second, the communal nature of Ps 60 should not be overlooked. The bleak beginning of Ps 60 would have resonated with the worshiping community from the exilic period onward. The postexilic community of Judah faced significant opposition to restoring the monarchy to its former idealized glory. The "David" of Ps 60 (unlike the "David" of 2 Sam 8) knows the depths of frustration and defeat, thus offering worshipers a subtle reminder that David also had to overcome insurmountable odds before he, with YHWH's help, established the kingdom.

Conclusion

Several conclusions can be drawn from the connections between certain psalms and narrative episodes created by the "biographic" superscriptions. These conclusions concern the Psalter and the hermeneutical principles presupposed in these headings. These superscriptions worked from traditions about David that are, with one exception (Ps 7) clearly related to material recorded in the book of Samuel. At the same time, the superscriptions do not demonstrate a slavish dependence upon those narrative traditions. The superscriptions sometimes contain incorrect names, or require that one recast the narrative with a different twist before connection to the psalm makes sense. Significantly, the superscriptions as a whole contain far more linguistic connections to the narratives than appear in the psalms. This observation reinforces the view that the psalms were neither originally written by David nor originally composed for the narrative episode to which they point. Rather, existing psalms were applied to the Davidic traditions.

In addition, only one of the narrative episodes mentioned in these biographic superscriptions appears in the Chronicler's account of David. On the one hand, this is not surprising, since most of the episodes to which the superscriptions allude point to internal strife between David and Saul or to problems within David's own family. The Chronicler's more idealized presentation of David assiduously avoids both of these topics. On the other hand, the fact that only one narrative episode from {190} the superscriptions even appears in Chronicles strongly suggests that the superscriptions arose in a time or a place where the Chronicler's account of David was not yet available. Otherwise, the idealized version of David in the Chronicler's account would have better suited the tendency to portray David in a better light. It appears plausible that these superscriptions reflect a point in the development of the Davidic traditions between time of the Deuteronomistic History and the Chronicler.

This analysis of the Psalter also demonstrates that the image of "David" facilitated by these psalms is not a literary character who develops across the Psalter. These biographic notes are designed to connect specific narrative episodes with particular psalms. Relatedly, these superscriptions do not appear to represent a redactional shaping of the Psalter. They do not appear in any particular order, and they appear in several different subcollections of the Psalter. This randomness suggests that the superscriptions were added to the psalms for a purpose other than the literary shaping of the Psalter. Despite the lack of strong linguistic connections, one can readily observe that as a group the psalms chosen for the narrative episodes are genre appropriate for the purpose. The didactic nature of some of these psalms, as well as the communal forms that appear frequently, suggest a worship setting of some type where David's story is told in a way that highlights David's piety and the role of YHWH in ways that the narratives alone do not.

Despite the fact that the biographic superscriptions were not created as part of a redactional program for the Psalter, they do share some hermeneutical tendencies. Not only do they draw upon narrative traditions about David rooted in Samuel and the Deuteronomistic History, they also react to the presentation of David in that corpus. They tend to do so in two ways. First, the combination of the psalm with the narrative tends to accentuate David's piety. The "David" of these psalms reacts to situations as one whom the reader should emulate. The character of "David" in these psalms does not exhibit the ambiguity of "David" in Samuel. Second, with the connection between the various psalms and the narrative traditions, YHWH takes on a more active role as protector, confidant, and avenger than the picture of YHWH that unfolds in the narrative alone. {191}

These two hermeneutical tendencies suggest some constructive avenues for reclaiming the connection between the psalms and the narratives of David in a modern worship setting. By recognizing how the superscriptions ask the congregation to read the psalm, one can begin to imagine homiletical approaches and dramatic readings that offer comfort to the modern worshiper. The psalms, when read with the Davidic episodes, highlight the need for utter dependence of YHWH in times of distress. They highlight the need for humility before God. They confidently affirm God's presence in times of persecution and trial.

Bibliography

Achtemeier, Paul J. "The Praise of God in Psalm and Hymn." Int 39 (1985): 3–74.
Albertz, Rainer. Die Exilszeit: 6. Jahrhundert v. Chr. BiE 7. Stuttgart: Kohlhammer, 2001.
———. "Exile as Purification: Reconstructing the Book of the Four (Hosea, Amos, Micah, Zephaniah)." Pages 213–33 in Society of Biblical Literature 2002 Seminar Papers. SBLSP 41. Atlanta: Society of Biblical Literature, 2002.
———. A History of Israelite Religion in the Old Testament. Translated by John Bowden. 2 vols. OTL. Louisville: Westminster John Knox, 1994.
———. "In Search of the Deuteronomists: A First Solution to a Historical Riddle." Pages 1–17 in The Future of the Deuteronomistic History. Edited by Thomas C. Römer. BETL 147. Leuven: Leuven University Press, 2000.
Allen, Leslie C. The Books of Joel, Obadiah, Jonah, and Micah. NICOT. Grand Rapids: Eerdmans, 1976.
Anderson, John E. "Awaiting an Answered Prayer: The Development and Reinterpretation of Habakkuk 3 in its Contexts." ZAW 123 (2011): 57–71.
Balentine, Samuel E. Job. SHBC 10. Macon, GA: Smyth & Helwys, 2006.
Barton, John. Joel and Obadiah: A Commentary. OTL. Louisville: Westminster John Knox, 2001.
Bautch, Richard J. "Intertextuality in the Persian Period." Pages 25–35 in Approaching Yehud: New Approaches to the Study of the Persian Period. Edited by Jon L. Berquist. SemeiaSt 50. Atlanta: Society of Biblical Literature, 2007.
Beck, Martin. Der "Tag YHWHs" im Dodekapropheton: Studien im Spannungsfeld von Traditions- und Redaktionsgeschichte. BZAW 356. Berlin: de Gruyter, 2005.

Bellinger, William H. "Reading from the Beginning (Again): The Shape of Book I of the Psalter." Pages 114–26 in *Diachronic and Synchronic: Reading the Psalms in Real Time: Proceedings of the Baylor Symposium on the Book of Psalms*. Edited by Joel S. Burnett, William H. Bellinger, and W. Dennis Tucker Jr. LHBOTS 488. London: T&T Clark, 2007.

Ben Zvi, Ehud. *A Historical-Critical Study of the Book of Obadiah*. BZAW 242. Berlin: de Gruyter, 1996.

———. *A Historical-Critical Study of the Book of Zephaniah*. BZAW 198. Berlin: de Gruyter, 1991.

———. "Twelve Prophetic Books or 'The Twelve': A Few Preliminary Considerations." Pages 125–56 in *Forming Prophetic Literature: Essays on Isaiah and the Twelve in Honor of John D. W. Watts*. Edited by James W. Watts and Paul R. House. JSOTSup 235. Sheffield: Sheffield Academic, 1996.

Bergler, Siegfried. *Joel als Schriftinterpret*. BEATAJ 16. Frankfurt am Main: Lang, 1988.

Berlin, Adele. *Zephaniah: A New Translation with Introduction and Commentary*. AB 25A. New York: Doubleday, 1994.

Beuken, W. A. M. *Haggai-Sacharja 1–8: Studien zur Überlieferungsgeschichte der frühnachexilischen Prophetie*. SSN 10. Assen: Van Gorcum, 1967.

Biddle, Mark E. "The Figure of Lady Jerusalem: Identification, Deification and Personification of Cities in the Ancient Near East." Pages 173–94 in *Biblical Canon in Comparative Perspectives*. Edited by William W. Hallo, K. Lawson Younger, and Bernard F. Batto. ANETS 11. Lewiston, NY: Mellen, 1991.

Blenkinsopp, Joseph. *Ezra-Nehemiah: A Commentary*. OTL. Philadelphia: Westminster, 1988.

———. *Isaiah 1–39: A New Translation with Introduction and Commentary*. AB 19. New York: Doubleday, 2000.

———. *Prophecy and Canon: A Contribution to the Study of Jewish Origins*. SJCA 3. Notre Dame: University of Notre Dame Press, 1977.

Bosshard, Erich. "Beobachtungen zum Zwölfprophetenbuch." *BN* 40 (1987): 30–62.

Bosshard, Erich, and Reinhard Gregor Kratz. "Maleachi im Zwölfprophetenbuch." *BN* 52 (1990): 27–46.

Bosshard-Nepustil, Erich. *Rezeptionen von Jesaia 1–39 im Zwölfprophetenbuch: Untersuchungen zur literarischen Verbindung von Propheten-*

büchern in babylonischer und persischer Zeit. OBO 154. Göttingen: Vandenhoeck & Ruprecht; Fribourg: Presses Universitaires, 1997.
Braaten, Laurie J. "God Sows: Hosea's Land Theme in the Book of the Twelve." Pages 104–32 in *Thematic Threads in the Book of the Twelve*. Edited by Paul L. Redditt and Aaron Schart. BZAW 325. Berlin: de Gruyter, 2003.
Bracke, John M. "Šûb šebût: A Reappraisal." *ZAW* 97 (1985): 233–44.
Braun, Roddy L. *1 Chronicles*. WBC 14. Waco, TX: Word, 1986.
Budde, Karl. "Eine folgenschwere Redaktion des Zwölfprophetenbuchs." *ZAW* 39 (1921): 218–29.
Burkitt, Francis Crawford. "Micah 6 and 7: A Northern Prophecy." *JBL* 45 (1926): 159–61.
Burnett, Joel S. "A Plea for David and Zion: The Elohistic Psalter as Psalm Collection for the Temple's Restoration." Pages 95–113 in *Diachronic and Synchronic: Reading the Psalms in Real Time; Proceedings of the Baylor Symposium on the Book of Psalms*. Edited by Joel S. Burnett, William H. Bellinger, and W. Dennis Tucker Jr. LHBOTS 488. London: T&T Clark, 2007.
Carr, David McLain. *The Formation of the Hebrew Bible: A New Reconstruction*. New York: Oxford University Press, 2011.
———. *Writing on the Tablet of the Heart: Origins of Scripture and Literature*. Oxford: Oxford University Press, 2005.
Cassuto, Umberto. "The Sequence and Arrangement of the Biblical Sections." Pages 1–6 in *Biblical and Oriental Studies*. Translated by Israel Abrahams. Vol. 1. Jerusalem: Magnes, 1973.
Childs, Brevard S. *Introduction to the Old Testament as Scripture*. Philadelphia: Fortress, 1979.
Christensen, Duane L. "Acrostic of Nahum Reconsidered." *ZAW* 87 (1975): 17–30.
———. *Transformations of the War Oracle in Old Testament Prophecy: Studies in the Oracles Against the Nations*. HDR 3. Missoula, MT: Scholars Press, 1975.
———. "Zephaniah 2:4–15: A Theological Basis for Josiah's Program of Political Expansion." *CBQ* 46 (1984): 669–82.
Clines, David J. A. *Job 1–20*. WBC 17. Dallas: Word, 1989.
Cook, Stephen L. "The Metamorphosis of a Shepherd: The Tradition History of Zechariah 11:17 + 13:7–9." *CBQ* 55 (1993): 453–66.
Cooper, Alan. "In Praise of Divine Caprice: The Significance of the Book of Jonah." Pages 144–63 in *Among the Prophets: Language, Image, and*

Structure in the Prophetic Writings. Edited by Philip R. Davies and David J. A. Clines. JSOTSup 144. Sheffield: Sheffield Academic, 1993.
Course, John E. *Speech and Response: A Rhetorical Analysis of the Introductions to the Speeches of the Book of Job (Chaps. 4–24).* CBQMS 25. Washington, DC: Catholic Biblical Association of America, 1994.
Crenshaw, James L. *Joel: A New Translation with Introduction and Commentary.* AB 24C. New York: Doubleday, 1995.
———. *Reading Job: A Literary and Theological Commentary.* ROT. Macon, GA: Smyth & Helwys, 2011.
———. "Theodicy in the Book of the Twelve." Pages 175–91 in *Thematic Threads in the Book of the Twelve.* Edited by Paul L. Redditt and Aaron Schart. BZAW 325. Berlin: de Gruyter, 2003.
Cripps, Richard S. *A Critical and Exegetical Commentary on the Book of Amos.* 2nd ed. London: SPCK, 1955.
Cross, Frank Moore. "Reconstruction of the Judean Restoration." *JBL* 94 (1975): 4–18.
Curtis, Byron G. "The Zion-Daughter Oracles: Evidence on the Identity and Ideology of the Late Redactors of the Book of the Twelve." Pages 166–84 in *Reading and Hearing the Book of the Twelve.* Edited by James D. Nogalski and Marvin A. Sweeney. SymS 15. Atlanta: Society of Biblical Literature, 2000.
Davies, Graham I. "New Solution to a Crux in Obadiah 7." *VT* 27 (1977): 484–87.
De Roche, Michael. "Zephaniah 1:2–3: The 'Sweeping' of Creation." *VT* 30 (1980): 104–9.
De Vries, Simon J. "Acrostic of Nahum in the Jerusalem Liturgy." *VT* 16 (1966): 476–81.
———. *From Old Revelation to New: A Tradition-Historical and Redaction-Critical Study of Temporal Transitions in Prophetic Prediction.* Grand Rapids: Eerdmans, 1995.
———."Futurism in the Pre-exilic Minor Prophets Compared with That of the Postexilic Minor Prophets." Pages 252–72 in *Thematic Threads in the Book of the Twelve.* Edited by Paul L. Redditt and Aaron Schart. BZAW 325. Berlin: de Gruyter, 2003.
Delitzsch, Franz. "Wann weissagte Obadja?" *ZTK* 12 (1851): 91–102.
Dever, William G. "Asherah, Consort of Yahweh: New Evidence from Kuntillet 'Ajrûd." *BASOR* 255 (1984): 21–37.
Donner, Herbert. "'Forscht in der Schrift Jahwes und lest!': Ein Beitrag zum Verständnis der israelitischen Prophetie." *ZTK* 87 (1990): 285–98.

Driver, Godfrey Rolles. "Studies in the Vocabulary of the Old Testament. VII." *JTS* 35 (1934): 380–93.
Duhm, Bernhard. "Anmerkungen zu den Zwölf Propheten I." *ZAW* 31 (1911): 1–43.
———. "Anmerkungen zu den Zwölf Propheten II." *ZAW* 31 (1911): 81–110.
Eaton, John H. "The Psalms and Israelite Worship." Pages 238–73 in *Tradition and Interpretation: Essays by Members of the Society for Old Testament Study*. Edited by George W. Anderson. Oxford: Clarendon, 1979.
Eissfeldt, Otto. "Ein Psalm aus Nord-Israel: Mi 7,7–20." *ZDMG* 112 (1962): 259–68.
Eszenyei Széles, Mária. *Wrath and Mercy: A Commentary on the Books of Habakkuk and Zephaniah*. Translated by George A. F. Knight. ITC. Grand Rapids: Eerdmans, 1987.
Everson, A. Joseph. "The Days of Yahweh." *JBL* 93 (1974): 329–37.
Ewald, Heinrich. *Die Propheten des alten Bundes*. Vol. 2. 2nd ed. Göttingen: Vandenhoeck & Ruprecht, 1868.
Fewell, Danna Nolan, ed. *Reading between Texts: Intertextuality and the Hebrew Bible*. LCBI. Louisville: Westminster John Knox, 1992.
Fishbane, Michael A. *Biblical Interpretation in Ancient Israel*. Oxford: Clarendon, 1985.
Fitzgerald, Aloysius. "Mythological Background for the Presentation of Jerusalem as a Queen and False Worship as Adultery in the OT." *CBQ* 34 (1972): 403–16.
Fuller, Russell. "The Form and Formation of the Book of the Twelve: The Evidence from the Judean Desert." Pages 86–101 in *Forming Prophetic Literature: Essays on Isaiah and the Twelve in Honour of John D. W. Watts*. Edited by James W. Watts and Paul R. House. JSOTSup 235. Sheffield: Sheffield Academic, 1996.
Galambush, Julie. *Jerusalem in the Book of Ezekiel: The City as Yahweh's Wife*. SBLDS 130. Atlanta: Scholars Press, 1992.
Gerstenberger, Erhard S. *Psalms: Part 1; with an Introduction to Cultic Poetry*. FOTL 14. Grand Rapids: Eerdmans, 1988.
———. *Psalms: Part 2 and Lamentations*. FOTL 15. Grand Rapids: Eerdmans, 2001.
———. "'Gemeindebildung' in Prophetenbüchern? Beobachtungen und Überlegungen zum Traditions- und Redaktionsprozeß prophetischer Schriften." Pages 44–58 in *Prophet und Prophetenbuch: Festschrift für Otto Kaiser zum 65. Geburtstag*. Edited by Volkmar Fritz, Karl-Fried-

rich Pohlmann, and Hans-Christoph Schmitt. BZAW 185. Berlin: de Gruyter, 1989.
Gesenius, Wilhelm. *Gesenius' Hebrew Grammar*. Edited by E. Kautzsch. Translated by A. E. Cowley. 2nd ed. Oxford: Clarendon, 1910.
Ginzberg, Louis. *Bible Times and Characters from the Joshua to Esther*. Vol. 4 of *The Legends of the Jews*. Translated by Henrietta Szold and Paul Radin. 6 vols. Baltimore: Johns Hopkins University Press, 1998.
———. *From Moses to Esther: Notes for Volumes 3 and 4*. Vol. 6 of *The Legends of the Jews*. Translated by Henrietta Szold and Paul Radin. Baltimore: Johns Hopkins University Press, 1998.
Grabbe, Lester L. *Yehud: A History of the Persian Province of Judah*. Vol. 1 of *A History of the Jews and Judaism in the Second Temple Period*. LSTS 47. London: T&T Clark, 2005.
Gruber, Mayer I. "The Motherhood of God in Second Isaiah." *RB* 90 (1983): 351–59.
Gunkel, Hermann. "Der Micha-Schluß: Zur Einführung in die literaturgeschichtliche Arbeit am Alten Testament." *ZS* 2 (1924): 145–78.
———. "The Close of Micah: A Prophetic Liturgy." Pages 115–49 in *What Remains of the Old Testament and Other Essays*. Translated by Alexander K. Dallas. New York: Macmillan, 1928.
Gunkel, Hermann, and Joachim Begrich. *Introduction to Psalms: The Genres of the Religious Lyric of Israel*. Translated by James D. Nogalski. MLBS. Macon, GA: Mercer University Press, 1998.
Gunneweg, Antonius H. J. *Leviten und Priester: Hauptlinien der Traditionsbildung und Geschichte des israelitisch-jüdischen Kultpersonals*. FRLANT 89. Göttingen: Vandenhoeck & Ruprecht, 1965.
Habel, Norman C. *The Book of Job: A Commentary*. OTL. Philadelphia: Westminster, 1985.
Hadley, Judith M. *The Cult of Asherah in Ancient Israel and Judah: Evidence for a Hebrew Goddess*. UCOP 57. Cambridge: Cambridge University Press, 2000.
Haran, Menahem. *Temples and Temple-Service in Ancient Israel: An Inquiry into the Character of Cult Phenomena and the Historical Setting of the Priestly School*. Oxford: Clarendon, 1978.
Heckl, Raik. *Hiob: Vom Gottesfürchitigen zum Repräsentaten Israels; Studien zur Buchwerdung des Hiobbuches und zu seinen Quellen*. FAT 70. Tübingen: Mohr Siebeck, 2010.
Hillers, Delbert R. *Micah*. Hermeneia. Philadelphia: Fortress, 1984.

Hoffman, Yair. "The Day of the Lord as a Concept and a Term in the Prophetic Literature." *ZAW* 93 (1981): 37–50.
Hoffmann, Geo. "Versuche zu Amos." *ZAW* 3 (1883): 87–126.
House, Paul R. *The Unity of the Twelve*. JSOTSup 97. Sheffield: Almond Press, 1990.
Ihromi. "Die Häufung der Verben des Jubelns in Zephanja 3:14f, 16–18: *rnn, rw', śmḥ, 'lz, śwś* und *gîl*." *VT* 33 (1983): 106–10.
Irsigler, Hubert. *Gottesgericht und Jahwetag: Die Komposition Zef 1,1–2,3, untersucht auf der Grundlage der Literarkritik des Zefanjabuches*. ATSAT 3. St. Ottilien: EOS, 1977.
Jacob, Edmond, Samuel Amsler, and Carl-Albert Keller. *Osée, Joël, Amos, Abdias, Jonas*. CAT 11a. Neuchâtel: Delachaux & Niestlé, 1965.
Japhet, Sara. *I & II Chronicles: A Commentary*. OTL. Louisville: Westminster John Knox, 1993.
Jenson, Philip Peter. *Obadiah, Jonah, Micah: A Theological Commentary*. LHBOTS 496. New York: T&T Clark, 2008.
Jeremias, Jörg. *Der Prophet Hosea*. ATD 24.1. Göttingen: Vandenhoeck & Ruprecht, 1983.
———. "Die Anfänge des Dodekapropheton: Hosea und Amos." Pages 87–106 in *Congress Volume: Paris, 1992*. Edited by J. A. Emerton. VTSup 61. Leiden: Brill, 1995.
———. "Die Anfänge des Dodekapropheton: Hosea und Amos." Pages 34–54 in *Hosea und Amos: Studien zu den Anfängen des Dodekapropheton*. FAT 13. Tübingen: Mohr Siebeck, 1996.
———. *Die Propheten Joel, Obadja, Jona, Micha*. ATD 24.3. Göttingen: Vandenhoeck & Ruprecht, 2007.
———. *Hosea und Amos: Studien zu den Anfängen des Dodekapropheton*. FAT 13. Tübingen: Mohr Siebeck, 1996.
———. "The Interrelationship Between Amos and Hosea." Pages 171–86 in *Forming Prophetic Literature: Essays on Isaiah and the Twelve in Honor of John D. W. Watts*. Edited by James W. Watts and Paul R. House. JSOTSup 235. Sheffield: Sheffield Academic, 1996.
———. *Kultprophetie und Gerichtsverkündigung in der späten Königszeit Israels*. WMANT 35. Neukirchen-Vluyn: Neukirchener Verlag, 1970.
———. *Theophanie: Die Geschichte einer alttestamentlichen Gattung*. WMANT 10. Neukirchen-Vluyn: Neukirchener Verlag, 1965.
Jerome. "Incipit prologus duodecim prophetarum." *Biblia Sacra Vulgata*. Vol. 2. Stuttgart: Württembergische Bibelanstalt, 1969.

Jones, Barry Alan. *The Formation of the Book of the Twelve: A Study in Text and Canon*. SBLDS 149. Atlanta: Scholars Press, 1995.
Jones, Douglas. *Jeremiah*. NCB. Grand Rapids: Eerdmans, 1992.
Kessler, Rainer. "'Ich rette das Hinkende, und das Versprengte sammle ich': Zur Herdenmetaphorik in Zef 3." Pages 93–101 in *Der Tag wird kommen: Ein interkontextuelles Gespräch über das Buch des Propheten Zefanja*. Edited by Walter Dietrich and Milton Schwantes. SBS 170. Stuttgart: Katholisches Bibelwerk, 1996.
Kratz, Reinhard Gregor. *The Composition of the Narrative Books of the Old Testament*. Translated by John Bowden. London: T&T Clark, 2005.
Kraus, Hans-Joachim. *Worship in Israel: A Cultic History of the Old Testament*. Richmond: John Knox, 1966.
Krinetzki, Günter. *Zefanjastudien: Motiv- und Traditionskritik + Kompositions- und Redaktionskritik*. RST 7. Frankfurt am Main: Lang, 1977.
Kuhl, Curt. *Die Entstehung des Alten Testaments*. SamDalp 26. Bern: Francke, 1953.
Langevin, Paul-Émile. "Sur l'origine du 'Jour de Yahvé'." *ScEccl* 18 (1966): 359–70.
Lau, Wolfgang. *Schriftgelehrte Prophetie in Jes 56–66: Eine Untersuchung zu den literarischen Bezügen in den letzten elf Kapiteln des Jesajabuches*. BZAW 225. Berlin: de Gruyter, 1994.
Lee, Andrew Yueking. "The Canonical Unity of the Scroll of the Minor Prophets." PhD diss., Baylor University, 1985.
Leeuwen, Cornelis van. "The Prophecy of the Yōm YHWH in Amos v 18–20." Pages 113–34 in *Language and Meaning: Studies in Hebrew Language and Biblical Exegesis*. Edited by James Barr. OTS 19. Leiden: Brill, 1974.
Lescow, Theodor. "Redaktionsgeschichtliche Analyse von Micha 6–7." *ZAW* 84 (1972): 182–212.
Lundbom, Jack. *Jeremiah 1–20: A New Translation with Introduction and Commentary*. AB 21A. New York: Doubleday, 1999.
———. *Jeremiah 37–52: A New Translation with Introduction and Commentary*. AB 21C. New York: Doubleday, 2004.
Maier, Christl M. *Daughter Zion, Mother Zion: Gender, Space, and the Sacred in Ancient Israel*. Minneapolis: Fortress, 2008.
Marti, Karl. *Das Dodekapropheton*. KHC 13. Tübingen: Mohr Siebeck, 1904.
Mason, Rex A. "Purpose of the 'Editorial Framework' of the Book of Haggai." *VT* 27 (1977): 413–21.

———. "The Use of Earlier Biblical Material in Zechariah 9–14: A Study in Inner Biblical Exegesis." Pages 1–208 in *Bringing Out the Treasure: Inner Biblical Allusion in Zechariah 9–14*. Edited by Mark J. Boda and Michael H. Floyd. JSOTSup 370. London: Sheffield Academic, 2003.
———. "The Use of Earlier Biblical Material in Zechariah IX–XIV: A Study in Inner Biblical Exegesis." PhD diss., University of London, 1973.
Mays, James Luther. *Amos: A Commentary*. OTL. Philadelphia: Westminster, 1969.
———. "The David of the Psalms." *Int* 40 (1986): 143–55.
———. *Micah: A Commentary*. OTL. Philadelphia: Westminster, 1976.
Melvin, David P. "Making All Things New (Again): Zephaniah's Eschatological Vision of a Return to Primeval Time." Pages 269–81 in *Creation and Chaos: A Reconsideration of Hermann Gunkel's Chaoskampf Hypothesis*. Edited by JoAnn Scurlock and Richard H. Beal. Winona Lake, IN: Eisenbrauns, 2013.
Mendecki, Norbert. "Deuteronomistische Redaktion von Zef 3,18–20?" *BN* 60 (1991): 27–32.
Meyers, Carol L., and Eric M. Meyers. *Haggai, Zechariah 1–8: A New Translation with Introduction and Commentary*. AB 25B. Garden City, NY: Doubleday, 1987.
———. *Zechariah 9–14: A New Translation with Introduction and Commentary*. AB 25C. New York: Doubleday, 1993.
Miller, Geoffrey David. "Intertextuality in Old Testament Research." *CurBR* 9 (2011): 283–309.
Miller, Patrick D. "Divine Council and the Prophetic Call to War." *VT* 18 (1968): 100–107.
Miscall, Peter D. "Isaiah: New Heavens, New Earth, New Book." Pages 41–56 in *Reading Between Texts: Intertextuality and the Hebrew Bible*. Edited by Danna Nolan Fewell. LCBI. Louisville: Westminster John Knox, 1992.
Nogalski, James D. *The Book of the Twelve: Hosea–Jonah*. SHBC. Macon, GA: Smyth & Helwys, 2011.
———. *The Book of the Twelve: Micah–Malachi*. SHBC. Macon, GA: Smyth & Helwys, 2011.
———. "The Day(s) of YHWH in the Book of the Twelve." Pages 192–213 in *Thematic Threads in the Book of the Twelve*. Edited by Paul L. Redditt and Aaron Schart. BZAW 325. Berlin: de Gruyter, 2003.
———. "Intertextuality and the Twelve." Pages 102–24 in *Forming Prophetic Literature: Essays on Isaiah and the Twelve in Honor of John D.*

W. Watts. Edited by John W. Watts and Paul R. House. JSOTSup 235. Sheffield: Sheffield Academic, 1996.

———. "Jeremiah and the Twelve: Intertextual Observations and Postulations." Paper presented at the Annual Meeting of the Society of Biblical Literature. Orlando, FL, 22 November 1998.

———. "Joel as 'Literary Anchor' for the Book of the Twelve." Pages 91–109 in *Reading and Hearing the Book of the Twelve*. Edited by James D. Nogalski and Marvin A. Sweeney. SymS 15. Atlanta: Society of Biblical Literature, 2000.

———. *Literary Precursors to the Book of the Twelve*. BZAW 217. Berlin: de Gruyter, 1993.

———. "Micah 7:8–20: Re-evaluating the Identity of the Enemy." Pages 125–42 in *The Bible as a Human Witness to Divine Revelation: Hearing the Word of God through Historically Dissimilar Traditions*. Edited by Randall Heskett and Brian Irwin. LHBOTS 469. London: T&T Clark, 2010.

———. "One Book and Twelve Books: The Nature of the Redactional Work and the Implications of Cultic Source Material in the Book of the Twelve." Pages 11–46 in *Two Sides of a Coin: Juxtaposing Views on Interpreting the Book of The Twelve/The Twelve Prophetic Books*. AnGor 201. Piscataway, NJ: Gorgias, 2009.

———. "The Problematic Suffixes of Amos ix 11." *VT* 43 (1993): 411–18.

———. "Reading the Book of the Twelve Theologically: The Twelve as Corpus; Interpreting Unity and Discord." *Int* 61 (2007): 115–22.

———. "Recurring Themes in the Book of the Twelve : Creating Points of Contact for a Theological Reading." *Int* 61 (2007): 125–36.

———. *Redactional Processes in the Book of the Twelve*. BZAW 218. Berlin: de Gruyter, 1993.

———. "The Redactional Shaping of Nahum 1 for the Book of the Twelve." Pages 193–202 in *Among the Prophets: Language, Image, and Structure in the Prophetic Writings*. Edited by Philip R. Davies and David J. A. Clines. Sheffield: JSOT Press, 1993.

———. Review of *Schriftgelehrte Prophetie in Jes 56–66: Eine Untersuchung zu den literarischen Bezügen in den letzten elf Kapiteln des Jesajabuches*, by Wolfgang Lau. *JBL* 116 (1997): 127–29.

———. "Teaching Prophetic Books." *PRSt* 36 (2009): 251–56.

Nogalski, James D. and Marvin A. Sweeney, eds. *Reading and Hearing the Book of the Twelve*. SymS 15. Atlanta: Society of Biblical Literature, 2000.

O'Brien, Julia M. *Nahum, Habakkuk, Zephaniah, Haggai, Zechariah, Malachi*. AOTC. Nashville: Abingdon, 2004.
Odell, Margaret S. "The Prophets and the End of Hosea." Pages 158-70 in *Forming Prophetic Literature: Essays on Isaiah and the Twelve in Honor of John D. W. Watts*. Edited by James W. Watts and Paul R. House. JSOTSup 235. Sheffield: Sheffield Academic, 1996.
Ottosson, Magnus. *Gilead: Tradition and History*. ConBOT 3. Lund: Gleerup, 1969.
Petersen, David L. "A Book of the Twelve?" Pages 3-10 in *Reading and Hearing the Book of the Twelve*. Edited by James D. Nogalski and Marvin A. Sweeney. SymS 15. Atlanta: Society of Biblical Literature, 2000.
———. *Haggai and Zechariah 1-8: A Commentary*. OTL. Philadelphia: Westminster, 1984.
———. *Late Israelite Prophecy: Studies in Deutero-Prophetic Literature and in Chronicles*. SBLMS 23. Missoula, MT: Scholars Press, 1977.
———. *Zechariah 9-14 and Malachi: A Commentary*. OTL. Louisville: Westminster John Knox, 1995.
Pierce, Ronald W. "Literary Connectors and a Haggai/Zechariah/Malachi Corpus." *JETS* 27 (1984): 277-89.
Pohlmann, Karl-Friedrich. *Das Buch des Propheten Hesekiel (Ezechiel): Kapitel 1-19*. ATD 22.1. Göttingen: Vandenhoeck & Ruprecht, 1996.
Raabe, Paul R. *Obadiah: A New Translation with Introduction and Commentary*. AB 24D. New York: Doubleday, 1996.
Rad, Gerhard von. "Origin of the Concept of the Day of Yahweh." *JSS* 4 (1959): 97-108.
Radday, Yehuda T., and Dieter Wickmann. "Unity of Zechariah Examined in the Light of Statistical Linguistics." *ZAW* 87 (1975): 30-55.
Redditt, Paul L. "The Book of Joel and Peripheral Prophecy." *CBQ* 48 (1986): 225-40.
———. *Haggai, Zechariah and Malachi*. NCB. London: HarperCollins, 1995.
———. "Israel's Shepherds: Hope and Pessimism in Zechariah 9-14." *CBQ* 51 (1989): 631-42.
———. "The King in Haggai-Zechariah 1-8 and the Book of the Twelve." Pages 56-82 in *Tradition in Transition: Haggai and Zechariah 1-8 in the Trajectory of Hebrew Theology*. Edited by Mark J. Boda and Michael H. Floyd. LHBOTS 475. New York: T&T Clark, 2008.

———. "The Two Shepherds in Zechariah 11:4-17." *CBQ* 55 (1993): 676-86.

Redditt, Paul L. and Aaron Schart, eds. *Thematic Threads in the Book of the Twelve*. BZAW 325. Berlin: de Gruyter, 2003.

Reicke, Bo. "Liturgical Traditions in Mic 7." *HTR* 60 (1967): 349-67.

Rendtorff, Rolf. "How to Read the Book of the Twelve as a Theological Unity." Pages 420-32 in *Society of Biblical Literature 1997 Seminar Papers*. SBLSP 36. Atlanta: Scholar's Press, 1997.

———. "How to Read the Book of the Twelve as a Theological Unity." Pages 75-87 in *Reading and Hearing the Book of the Twelve*. Edited by James D. Nogalski and Marvin A. Sweeney. SymS 15. Atlanta: Society of Biblical Literature, 2000.

Richardson, H. Neil. "Skt (Amos 9:11) : 'Booth' or 'Succoth'?" *JBL* 92 (1973): 375-81.

Robertson, O. Palmer. *The Books of Nahum, Habakkuk, and Zephaniah*. NICOT. Grand Rapids: Eerdmans, 1990.

Robinson, Theodore H., and Friedrich Horst. *Die Zwölf Kleinen Propheten*. HAT 1/14. Tübingen: Mohr Siebeck, 1938.

Roth, Martin. *Israel und die Völker im Zwölfprophetenbuch: Eine Untersuchung zu den Büchern Joel, Jona, Micha und Nahum*. FRLANT 210. Göttingen: Vandenhoeck & Ruprecht, 2005.

Rudolph, Wilhelm. *Haggai, Sacharja 1-8, Sacharja 9-14, Maleachi*. KAT 13.4. Gütersloh: Mohn, 1976.

———. *Hosea*. KAT 13.1. Gütersloh: Mohn, 1966.

———. *Joel, Amos, Obadja, Jona*. KAT 13.2. Gütersloh: Mohn, 1971.

———. *Micha, Nahum, Habakuk, Zephanja*. KAT 13.3. Gütersloh: Mohn, 1975.

Schart, Aaron. *Die Entstehung des Zwölfprophetenbuchs: Neubearbeitungen von Amos im Rahmen schriftenübergreifender Redaktionsprozesse*. BZAW 260. Berlin: de Gruyter, 1998.

———. "The First Section of the Book of the Twelve Prophets: Hosea—Joel—Amos." *Int* 61 (2007): 138-52.

———. "Reconstructing the Redaction History of the Twelve Prophets: Problems and Models." Pages 34-48 in *Reading and Hearing The Book of the Twelve*. Edited by James D. Nogalski and Marvin A. Sweeney. SymS 15. Atlanta: Society of Biblical Literature, 2000.

Schmitt, John J. "The Motherhood of God and Zion as Mother." *RB* 92 (1985): 557-69.

Schneider, Dale Allan. "The Unity of the Book of the Twelve." PhD diss., Yale University, 1979.
Schniedewind, William M. *How the Bible Became a Book: The Textualization of Ancient Israel*. Cambridge: Cambridge University Press, 2004.
Schultz, Richard L. *The Search for Quotation: Verbal Parallels in the Prophets*. JSOTSup 180. Sheffield: Sheffield Academic, 1999.
Schulz, Hermann. *Das Buch Nahum: Eine redaktionskritische Untersuchung*. BZAW 129. Berlin: de Gruyter, 1973.
Schunck, Klaus D. "Die Eschatologie der Propheten des Alten Testaments und ihre Wandlung in exilisch-nach-exilischer Zeit." Pages 116–32 in *Studies on Prophecy: A Collection of Twelve Papers*. Edited by Daniel Lys. VTSup 26. Leiden: Brill, 1974.
———. "Strukturlinien in der Entwicklung der Vorstellung vom 'Tag Jahwes.'" *VT* 14 (1964): 319–30.
Schwally, Friedrich. "Das Buch Ssefanjâ: Eine historisch-kritische Untersuchung." *ZAW* 10 (1890): 165–240.
Schwesig, Paul-Gerhard. *Die Rolle der Tag-JHWHs-Dichtungen im Dodekapropheton*. BZAW 366. Berlin: de Gruyter, 2006.
Scoralick, Ruth. "The Case of Edom in the Book of the Twelve: Methodological Reflections on Synchronic and Diachronic Analysis." Pages 35–54 in *Perspectives on the Formation of the Book of the Twelve: Methodological Foundations, Redactional Processes, Historical Insights*. Edited by Rainer Albertz, James D. Nogalski, and Jakob Wöhrle. BZAW 433. Berlin: de Gruyter, 2012.
Seitz, Christopher R. "How Is the Prophet Isaiah Present in the Latter Half of the Book? The Logic of Chapters 40–66 within the Book of Isaiah." *JBL* 115 (1996): 219–40.
Seybold, Klaus. *Die Psalmen: Eine Einführung*. KUT 382. Stuttgart: Kohlhammer, 1986.
———. *Profane Prophetie: Studien zum Buch Nahum*. SBS 135. Stuttgart: Katholisches Bibelwerk, 1989.
Smith, Ralph L. *Micah–Malachi*. WBC 32. Waco, TX: Word, 1984.
Snyman, S. D. "Yom (YHWH) in the Book of Obadiah." Pages 81–91 in *Goldene Äpfel in Silbernen Schalen: Collected Communications to the XIIIth Congress of the International Organization for the Study of the Old Testament, Leuven 1989*. Edited by Klaus D. Schunck and Matthias Augustin. BEATAJ 20. Frankfurt am Main: Lang, 1992.
Spieckermann, Hermann. "Dies irae: Der alttestamentliche Befund und seine Vorgeschichte." *VT* 39 (1989): 194–208.

Stade, Bernhard. "Streiflichter auf die Entstehung der jetzigen Gestalt der alttestamentlichen Prophetenschriften." *ZAW* 23 (1903): 153-71.
Steck, Odil Hannes. *Bereitete Heimkehr: Jesaja 35 als redaktionelle Brücke zwischen dem Ersten und dem Zweiten Jesaja.* SBS 121. Stuttgart: Katholisches Bibelwerk, 1985.
———. *Der Abschluß der Prophetie im Alten Testament: Ein Versuch zur Frage der Vorgeschichte des Kanons.* BibS(N) 17. Neukirchen-Vluyn: Neukirchener Verlag, 1991.
———. *Die Prophetenbücher und ihr theologisches Zeugnis: Wege der Nachfrage und Fährten zur Antwort.* Tübingen: Mohr Siebeck, 1996.
———. *Old Testament Exegesis: A Guide to the Methodology.* Translated by James D. Nogalski. 2nd ed. RBS 39. Atlanta: Scholars Press, 1998.
———. *The Prophetic Books and Their Theological Witness.* Translated by James D. Nogalski. St. Louis: Chalice, 2000.
———. Review of *Schriftgelehrte Prophetie in Jes 56–66: Eine Untersuchung zu den literarischen Bezügen in den letzten elf Kapiteln des Jesajabuches,* by Wolfgang Lau. *TLZ* 120 (1995): 782-86.
———. "Zion als Gelände und Gestalt: Überlegungen zur Wahrnehmung Jerusalems als Stadt und Frau im Alten Testament." *ZTK* 86 (1989): 261-81.
———. "Zu jüngsten Untersuchungen von Jes 56,9–59,21; 63,1–6." Pages 192-213 in *Studien zu Tritojesaja.* BZAW 203. Berlin: de Gruyter, 1991.
———. "Zu Zef 3:9–10." *BZ* 34 (1990): 90-95.
———. "Zur Abfolge Maleachi–Jona in 4Q76 (4QXIIa)." *ZAW* 108 (1996): 249-53.
Steuernagel, Carl. *Lehrbuch der einleitung in das Alte Testament: Mit einemanhang über die apokryphen und pseudepigraphen.* SThL. Tübingen: Mohr Siebeck, 1912.
Struppe, Ursula. *Die Bücher Obadja, Jona.* NSKAT 24.1. Stuttgart: Katholisches Bibelwerk, 1996.
Stuart, Douglas. *Hosea–Jonah.* WBC 31. Waco, TX: Word, 1987.
———. "The Sovereign's Day of Conquest." *BASOR* 221 (1976): 159-64.
Sweeney, Marvin A. "A Form-Critical Reassessment of the Book of Zephaniah." *CBQ* 53 (1991): 388-408.
———. "Sequence and Interpretation in the Book of the Twelve." Pages 49-64 in *Reading and Hearing The Book of the Twelve.* Edited by James D. Nogalski and Marvin A. Sweeney. SymS 15. Atlanta: Society of Biblical Literature, 2000.

———. *The Twelve Prophets*. 2 vols. Berit Olam. Collegeville, MN: Liturgical Press, 2000.
———. *Zephaniah: A Commentary*. Hermeneia. Minneapolis: Fortress, 2003.
Tate, Marvin E. *Psalms 51–100*. WBC 20. Waco, TX: Word, 1990.
Toorn, Karel van der. *Scribal Culture and the Making of the Hebrew Bible*. Cambridge: Harvard University Press, 2007.
Tuell, Steven Shawn. *Ezekiel*. NIBCOT 15. Peabody, MA: Hendrickson, 2009.
Utzschneider, Helmut. *Künder oder Schreiber? Eine These zum Problem der "Schriftprophetie" auf Grund von Maleachi 1,6–2,9*. BEATAJ 19. Frankfurt am Main: Lang, 1989.
Van Leeuwen, Raymond C. "Scribal Wisdom and Theodicy in the Book of the Twelve." Pages 31–49 in *In Search of Wisdom: Essays in Memory of John G. Gammie*. Edited by Leo G. Perdue, Bernard B. Scott, and William J. Wiseman. Louisville: Westminster John Knox, 1993.
Verhoef, Pieter A. *The Books of Haggai and Malachi*. NICOT. Grand Rapids: Eerdmans, 1987.
Watts, James W. and Paul R. House, eds. *Forming Prophetic Literature: Essays on Isaiah and the Twelve in Honor of John D. W. Watts*. JSOTSup 235. Sheffield: Sheffield Academic, 1996.
Watts, John D. W. "Superscriptions and Incipits in the Book of the Twelve." Pages 110–24 in *Reading and Hearing the Book of the Twelve*. Edited by James D. Nogalski and Marvin A. Sweeney. SymS 15. Atlanta: Society of Biblical Literature, 2000.
Wehrle, Josef. *Prophetie und Textanalyse: Die Komposition Obadja 1–21 interpretiert auf der Basis textlinguistischer und semiotischer Konzeptionen*. ATSAT 28. St. Ottilien: EOS, 1987.
Weimar, Peter. "Obadja: Eine redaktionskritische Analyse." *BN* 27 (1985): 35–99.
Weiser, Artur. *Das Buch der zwölf kleinen Propheten I: Die Propheten Hosea, Joel, Amos, Obadja, Jona, Micha*. ATD 24. Göttingen: Vandenhoeck & Ruprecht, 1949.
———. *Das Buch der zwölf kleinen Propheten I: Die Propheten Hosea, Joel, Amos, Obadja, Jona, Micha*. 8th ed. ATD 24. Göttingen: Vandenhoeck & Ruprecht, 1985.
———. *The Psalms: A Commentary*. Translated by Herbert Hartwell. OTL. Philadelphia: Westminster, 1962.

Wellhausen, Julius. *Die kleinen Propheten: Übersetzt mit noten.* Berlin: Reimer, 1892.
Wenham, Gordon J. *Genesis 1–15.* WBC 1. Waco, TX: Word, 1987.
Westermann, Claus. *Genesis 1–11.* CC. Minneapolis: Fortress, 1994.
Willi, Thomas. *Die Chronik als Auslegung; Untersuchungen zur literarischen Gestaltung der historischen Überlieferung Israels.* FRLANT 106. Göttingen: Vandenhoeck & Ruprecht, 1972.
Williamson, Hugh G. M. *The Book Called Isaiah: Deutero-Isaiah's Role in Composition and Redaction.* Oxford: Oxford University Press, 2005.
———. *Ezra, Nehemiah.* WBC 16. Waco, TX: Word, 1985.
Willi-Plein, Ina. *Vorformen der Schriftexegese innerhalb des Alten Testaments: Untersuchungen zum literarischen Werden der auf Amos, Hosea und Micha zurückgehenden Bücher im hebräischen Zwölfprophetenbuch.* BZAW 123. Berlin: de Gruyter, 1971.
Wilson, Gerald H. *The Editing of the Hebrew Psalter.* SBLDS 76. Chico, CA: Scholars Press, 1985.
Wöhrle, Jakob. *Der Abschluss des Zwölfprophetenbuches: Buchübergreifende Redaktionsprozesse in den späten Sammlungen.* BZAW 389. Berlin: de Gruyter, 2008.
———. *Die frühen Sammlungen des Zwölfprophetenbuches: Entstehung und Komposition.* BZAW 360. Berlin: de Gruyter, 2006.
Wolfe, Rolland Emerson. "The Editing of the Book of the Twelve." *ZAW* 53 (1935): 90–129.
Wolff, Hans Walter. *Dodekapropheton 2, Joel und Amos.* BKAT 14.2. Neukirchen-Vluyn: Neukirchener Verlag, 1969. Repr., 1975.
———. *Dodekapropheton 3, Obadja und Jona.* BKAT 14.3. Neukirchen-Vluyn: Neukirchener Verlag, 1977.
———. *Hosea: A Commentary on the Book of the Prophet Hosea.* Translated by Gary Stansell. Hermeneia. Philadelphia: Fortress, 1974.
———. *Joel and Amos: A Commentary on the Books of the Prophets Joel and Amos.* Translated by Samuel Dean McBride Jr. Hermeneia. Philadelphia: Fortress, 1977.
———. *Micah: A Commentary.* Translated by Gary Stansell. CC. Minneapolis: Augsburg, 1990.
———. *Obadiah and Jonah: A Commentary.* Translated by Margaret Kohl. Minneapolis: Augsburg, 1986.
Zenger, Erich, ed. *"Wort Jhwhs, das geschah—" (Hos 1,1): Studien zum Zwölfprophetenbuch.* HerBS 35. Freiburg: Herder, 2002.

Zimmerli, Walther. *Ezekiel: A Commentary on the Book of the Prophet Ezekiel, Chapters 1–24.* Translated by Ronald Clements. Hermeneia. Philadelphia: Fortress, 1979.

———. *Ezekiel: A Commentary on the Book of the Prophet Ezekiel, Chapters 25–48.* Translated by James D. Martin. Hermeneia. Philadelphia: Fortress, 1983.

———. "Vom Prophetenwort zum Prophetenbuch." *TLZ* 104 (1979): 481–96.

Ancient Sources Index

Genesis   241, 242, 245, 245 n. 13, 246, 249, 252, 254, 261 n. 52
1–11   241, 243–45, 247, 255, 263264
1:1–2:4a   225 n. 20
1:10   245 n. 13
1:24–26   245 n. 13
1:26   245 n. 13
1:28   245 n. 13
1:30   163, 245 n. 13
2:7   271
3:19   271
6–9   242
6:4   159 n. 6
6:7   242 n. 4
7:4   242 n. 4, 243 n. 4
8:7   243 n. 4
8:11   243 n. 4
8:13   243 n. 4
9:2   244, 245 n. 13
10   241, 248–49, 249 n. 22, 250, 252, 255
10:5   248
10:5–14   247
10:5–20   249
10:6   249
10:6–7   248
10:10–11   249
10:11   248
10:15–20   249
10:19   249
11   241, 246
11:1   251
11:1–9   250–53
11:6   251
11:9   252
19:27   31 n. 12
19:30–38   131
20   301 n. 9
22:2   196
26   301 n. 9
29:35   196
30:43   286 n. 10
32–33   225 n. 21
33:17   285 n. 7
35:3   176 n. 34
35:23   196
39:22   178 n. 41
43:17   178 n. 41
43:18   178 n. 41
43:19   178 n. 41
43:24   178 n. 41
44:14   178 n. 41
46:27   178 n. 42
50:8   178 n. 41

Exodus
2:11   159 n. 6
8:18   160 n. 9
13:8   160 n. 9
16:25   158 n. 5
19:3   178 n. 42
25–31   197
31:17   160 n. 9
31:18   160 n. 9
32:12   244
32:29   158 n. 5
33:9   31 n. 12
34–40   197
34:6   107, 108
34:6–7   95, 97, 107–8, 113, 153, 189–90
34:6–7a   189

-339-

Exodus (cont.)		18:5	178 n. 41
34:7	107–8	20:4	31 n. 12
34:7b	189	20:6	159 n. 6
		21	111 n. 63
Leviticus		21:3	111 n. 63
23:34	158 n. 5	21:8	111 n. 63
23:42	285 n. 7	21:27	111 n. 63
23:42	285 n. 7	21:34	111 n. 63
		21:41	111 n. 63
Numbers		24:18	292
27:17	286 n. 11		
		Judges	
Deuteronomy		1:22	178 n. 41
1:19	168 n. 21	1:23	178 n. 41
2:4	131	1:35	178 n. 41
2:4–5	131	5:4	130
3:21	292	7:13	75 n. 20
6:15	244	8:4–7	292, 294
7:2	292	9:52	75 n. 20
7:21	168 n. 21	17:6	159 n. 6
8:8	149	18–21	164
8:15	168 n. 21	18:1	159 n. 6
10:21	168 n. 21	19–21	164 n. 14, 165
12	197	19:1	159 n. 6
16:13	285 n. 7	20:18	164 n. 14
16:16	285 n. 7	20:18–20	165
17:9	159 n. 6	20:23	164 n. 14
19:7	159 n. 6	20:26–28	164 n. 14
26:3	158 n. 5, 159 n. 6	20:27	159 n. 6
31:10	285 n. 7	20:28	159 n. 6
30:11–13	245 n. 13	21:25	159 n. 6
33:2	130		
		1 Samuel	
Joshua		3:1	159 n. 6
1:2	238–239	3:12	160 n. 9
1:7	238–239	8:18	160 n. 9
9:1–15	292	19	314
9:6–7	292	19:11a	313
9:11	293	19:11–17	312, 314
9:11–14	292, 294	20:15	144
9:11–15	293	21	302
9:12	293	21–22	293
9:15	293	21:2	293
14:4	111 n. 63	21:7	307
17:17	178, 178 n. 41	21:11	302

21:13–15	301, 303	12:13	305–6
21:14	302	12:14	305
21:14–15	302	12:15–19	305
22	209	12:15–25	305
22:1	301–2	12:20–23	305
22:9	308	12:20–25	305
22:9–10	307	12:22	305
22:9–22	307	14:14	299
22:11–18	307	15–19	299
22:13	292–94	15:15	299
22:16–19	293	15:16	299
22:19	307	16:23	159 n. 6
23	310	18:5	301
23:19	310	18:12	301
23:19–29	312	18:19	300
23:26	310	18:32	300
23:27	312	18:33–19:8	301
25	293	19:1–7	301
25:8	286 n. 10	19:10	299
25:11	292–94	19:21	178 n. 41
25:23–31	294	22:12	285 n. 7
26	312		
26:1	310	1 Kings	
28:1	159 n. 6	5–8	197
		8	197
2 Samuel		9:7	244
4–6	197	11:28	178 n. 41
5	197, 198	12	187
7	197	12:25–30	202
8	315–18	13:32	200
8:2	316	13:34	244
8:5	316	16:23–24	200
8:3–9	315	16:29–32	200
8:13	315	20:12	285 n. 7
8:13–14	316	20:16	285 n. 7
8:16	315	22:25	160 n. 9
11–12	304		
11:11	285 n. 7	2 Kings	
11:14–27	304	10:32	159 n. 6
11:27b	305	11:28	178
12	304, 306	15:37	159 n. 6
12:1–4	304	17	86, 187
12:5–6	304	18:31	69
12:10	304	18:32b–35	69
12:11	304–5	18:34	201 n. 4

2 Kings (cont.)		5:12	110
18:35	69	7:6	110
19:3	176 nn. 34, 35	8:13	285 n. 7
20	86	8:14–15	110
20:1	159 nn. 6, 7	11:13–14	111
22–25	86	17:8	112
23	257 n. 45	18:24	160 n. 9
23:4–14	256 n. 45	20:1–30	74 n. 19
25	197	20:9	110
		20:14	110
1 Chronicles		20:19	110
6:31	110	29:4–19	110
6:48	110	29:25–26	110
6:64	111	29:30	110
9:18	109	29:34	111
9:26–27	109	30:6–9	112 n. 64
9:31	111	30:21–27	110
9:33	111	31:4–5	111
9:33–34	110	32:5	69
11:5	198	32:24	159 n. 6
13:2	111	32:28	111
15:16	111	34:12	110
15:16–24	110	34:13	112
15:27	111	35:3	112
16:4	110	35:5	110
18	315	35:11	111
18:2	316	35:14–18	110
18:3–9	315	35:15	111
18:12	315	36:22–23	88, 108
18:12–13	316		
18:15	315	Ezra	
23:24	111	1:1–2	88
23:26–32	109	1:1–3a	108
23:28	109–10	1:5	110
23:29	111	2:4	110
24:5–6	110	2:68–70	110
24:6	112	2:70	111
26:17	110	3:4	285 n. 7
26:20	110	3:8–9	110
29:5	158 n. 5	3:10	110
35:7–9	110	5:1	112 n. 65
		6:14	112 n. 65
2 Chronicles		7:7	111
3:1	196	7:13–18	111
5:2	198	7:24	111

8:29–30	110	Esther	
8:33	110	1:2	159 n. 6
9:1	110	2:21	159 n. 6
9:4–5	110	6:1	191
10:5	110		
10:15	110	Job	
		1:1	267, 273
Nehemiah		1:1–3	131
1:5	168 n. 21	1:5	268
4:8	168 n. 21	1:8	267, 273
5:1–11	111	2:3	267, 273
6:17	159 n. 6	4:7	267 n. 9
7:1	111	6–7	267–269
7:43–45	110	6:29	271 n. 14
7:73	111	7:7	271 n. 14
8	260	7:10	271 n. 14
8:7–9	260	7:20–21	268
8:7–11	112	8	266–67, 272–73
8:13–14	259–60	8–10	265–67, 272–74, 278
8:14	285 n. 7	8:1	267
8:15	285 n. 7	8:2	267, 267 n. 7, 268
8:15–20	112	8:2–7	268–269
8:16	285 n. 7	8:3	268
8:17	285 n. 7	8:4	267–68, 274
9:4–5	112	8:5	268
9:32	112	8:6	267–68, 273
9:32–37	113	8:7	268
9:38	110	8:8–10	269
10:9	110	8:8–22	269
10:28	110–11	8:11–19	269
10:30	110	8:20	269
10:31–39	111	8:20–21	269
11:22	111	9–10	266, 269–73, 276, 278
12:8	110	9:1	267, 269
12:24–25	110	9:1–2a	269, 269 n. 12
12:27	110	9:1–12	276
12:30	110	9:2	267 n. 7, 269, 270
12:47	111	9:2–13	270 n. 13
13	110	9:2–24	270, 270 n. 13
13:5	110–11	9:2b–24	269 n. 12, 271
13:10	110–11	9:12	266, 270–71, 271 n. 14, 273
13:15	159 n. 6	9:13	266, 270–71, 271 n. 14, 273
13:22	110	9:13–24	276
13:23	159 n. 6	9:14–24	270 n. 13
		9:18	266, 270–71, 271 n. 14, 273

Job (cont.)		23:4	76 n. 23
9:20–21	270	30	88 n. 30
9:22–24	270	34	297 n. 3, 302–4
9:25–31	270 n. 13	34:1	301–2
9:25–35	270 n. 13, 276	34:4	303
9:25–10:22	270	34:9–12	303
9:30–21	276	34:14	303
9:32–35	270, 270 n. 13	49:14	76 n. 22
10:1–6	270 n. 13	50:15	176 n. 34, 177
10:1–22	270 n. 13, 276	51	297 n. 3, 305–7
10:7–22	270 n. 13	51:1–2	304
10:9	266, 270–71, 271 n. 14	51:3	305
10:16	266, 270–71, 271 n. 14	51:3–4	306
10:21	266, 270–71, 271 n. 14	51:5–8	306
12:7–8	245 n. 13	51:6	305, 306 n. 11
13:22	271 n. 14	51:8	307
14:13	271 n. 14	51:9–11	307
16:22	271 n. 14	51:9–14	306
17:8	267 n. 9	51:14	307
17:10	271 n. 14	51:15	307
18:2	267	51:15–17	306
19:2	267	51:16	306
20:23	271 n. 14	51:18	307
23:7	267 n. 9	52	297 n. 3, 307–9
23:13	271 n. 14	52:1–2	307–8
31:14	271 n. 14	52:2	308
33:3	267 n. 9	52:3–6	308
33:23	267 n. 9	52:3–7	308, 309
33:27	267 n. 9	52:7	309
		52:8–9	309
Psalms		52:8–11	309
3	297 n. 3	52:9	309
3:1	299	52:10	309
3:2	300	52:11	309
3:2–3	299	54	297 n. 3, 311
3:3–6	299	54:1–2	310
3:5	300	54:2	310
3:6	301	54:3–4	311
3:8	300	54:5	311
7	297 n. 3, 318	54:6–7	311
7:1	297 n. 3	54:8	312, 312 n. 21
8:9	244	54:8–9	311
15	88 n. 13	56	297 n. 3
18	297 n. 3	57	297 n. 3
20:2	176, 176 n. 34	57:8–12	316

59	313–14	Isaiah	
59:1	312–13	1–31	159
59:4b–5	313	1–39	8, 196
59:6	313–14	1:8	287 n. 13
59:7	314	2	238, 239
59:9	314	2:2	160 n. 10
59:12	313, 315	2:2–4	15
59:14	313	2:5	178 n. 42
59:15	314	2:6	178 n. 42
59:17	315	2:12	158 n. 5
59:17–18	314–15	3:6	242 n. 2
60	297 n. 3, 316–18	7–10	201 n. 4
60:1–2	315	8:17	178 n. 42
60:2	315	9–10	189
60:3–5	317	9–12	66, 69–70, 76, 80, 225 n. 21
60:7	317	9:1–2	67–69
60:7–14	316	9:3	160 n. 10
60:8–10	317	9:9	67–69
60:8–11	317	10	103–4, 107
60:10	316	10:1	66
60:12–13	317	10:1–2	106
60:13	316	10:2	66
60:14	316–17	10:3	66–67, 160 n. 10, 164 n. 13
60:16	316	10:3–4	66
63	297 n. 3	10:5	67–68, 76, 103
68:10	312 n. 21	10:5–6	103
69:39	245 n. 13	10:5–12	104–105
77:3	176 n. 34, 177	10:6	67–69
86:7	176 n. 34, 177	10:6–12	104
90–106	188	10:8–11	104
96:11	245 n. 13	10:12	67, 104
99:3	168 n. 21	10:13	67
107–150	188	10:15	68, 76, 164 n. 13
108	316	10:16–18	77 n. 26
108:2–6	316	10:17	160 n. 10
108:2–7	316	10:18	67, 68
110:3	312 n. 21	10:19	67
114:1	178 n. 42	10:20	178 n. 42
119:108	312 n. 21	10:20–22	68, 69
137:7–8	250	10:23	67
142	297 n. 3	10:24	67–68, 76
		10:25	67–69
Proverbs		10:26	67–69
24:10	176 n. 34, 177	10:33	68, 80
25:19	176 n. 34, 177	10:33–34	80

Isaiah (cont.)

10:34	67
11:14–16	69
11:23	164 n. 13
12:1	68, 69
12:1–6	80, 80 n. 32
12:2	66
13–14	253 n. 31
13:6	158 n 3, 177 n. 39
13:9	158 n. 3
13:13	160 n. 10
14:1	178 n. 42
17:11	160 n. 10
18	253 n. 31
18–19	39, 252–53
18:1	252
18:1b	39
18:7	252–53
19:18	252
19:22	253
19:23	252
19:23–24	77 n. 26
22:5	160 n. 10
22:12	159 n. 8
23:12	164 n. 13
24–27	253 n. 31
29:17	77 n. 26
29:22	178 n. 42
30:25	160 n. 10
32:15–16	77 n. 26
33:9	30, 77 n. 26
34–35	130
34:1	132
34:5	132
34:5–6	50, 179
34:8	132, 160 n. 10, 164 n. 13, 178
36:16	69
36:18–20	69
36:20	69
37:3	160 n. 10, 176 nn. 34–35
37:24	77 n. 26
38:1	159 n. 7
38:14	30 n. 10
40–55	8, 130
46:3	178 n. 42
47:9	160 n. 10
48:1	178 n. 42
48:44	164 n. 13
49	41 n. 21
49:8	160 n. 10
50:1	41 n. 21
50:27	164 n. 13
51:17–23	129
51:18	164 n. 13
52	28
52:2	28 n. 7
52:4	28 n. 7
52:7	28 n. 7, 105, 211
54:1–3	206
54:11–13	206
55:4–5	128
56–66	8
58:1	178 n. 42
60	160 n. 12
60–62	71 n. 14
61:2	160 n. 10
63:1	132
63:1–6	130, 132, 179
63:3	132
63:4	132, 160 n. 10
63:6	132
66	62, 238–39

Jeremiah

2:2	206
2:4	178 n. 42
2:20	178 n. 42
3:16	159 n. 7
3:18	159 n. 7
4:30–31	206
5:18	159 n. 7
8:13	244
12:3	160 n. 10
16:9	176 n. 34
16:19	160 n. 10, 176 n. 35
17:16	160 n. 10
17:17	160 n. 10
17:18	160 n. 10
18:17	160 n. 10
23:1–6	56

23:13	201 n. 4	49:39	160 n. 10
23:20	160 n. 10	50:4	159 n. 7
25:11–12	211	50:17–19	77, 77 n. 26, 78
25:13	133	50:19	30
25:15–29	129	50:20	159 n. 7
25:34	160 n. 10	50:31	160 n. 10
26:18	72 n. 17	51:7	129
27:22	160 n. 10		
28:16	244	Lamentations	
29:10	211	2:22	158 n. 4
30:7	160 n. 10	4:21	65 n. 8, 129, 131
30:12–17	160 n. 12	4:21–22	250
30:24	160 n. 10	5:6	75 n. 20
31:5	200, 201 n. 4	5:9	75 n. 20
31:6	160 n. 10		
31:29	159 n. 7	Ezekiel	
33:15	159 n. 7	5	50
33:16	159 n. 7	5:3–4	50, 61 n. 36
39:10	159 n. 8	7:7	160 n. 10, 177 n. 39
39:16	160	7:12	160 n. 10
39:17	160	7:19	160 n. 10
41:5	201 n. 4	12:23	160 n. 10
46:10	160 n. 10	13:5	158 n. 3
46:11	39	16	71 n. 14
46:21	160 n. 10	16:46	201 n. 4
47:4	160 n. 10	16:51	201 n. 4
47:6	50	16:53	201 n. 4
48:11	31 n. 12	16:55	201 n. 4
48:47	160 n. 10	20:5	178 n. 42
49	132	20:6	159 n. 8
49:7	121, 132	21	50
49:7–8	132	22	162 n. 12
49:7–22	64 n. 7, 121, 124, 129 n. 20, 133, 133 n. 28	22:4	160 n. 10
		22:14	160 n. 10
49:9	15, 64 n. 8, 119–21, 124, 126, 219–20	22:17	61 n. 36
		22:17–22	50, 51, 61 n. 36
49:9a	119–20, 126	22:23	51
49:9b	119, 125–26	22:24	160 n. 10
49:12	129, 133 n. 27	23	71 n. 14
49:13	125	23:4	201 n. 4
49:14	64 n. 8, 125	23:33	201 n. 4
49:14–16	15, 64 n. 8, 119–21, 124, 219–20	23:38	159 n. 8
		23:39	159 n. 8
49:16	119, 125–26, 129 n. 19	23:31–32	129
49:22	121	25:12–14	132

Ezekiel (cont.)

26:18	160 n. 10
27:27	160 n. 10
30:2	160 n. 10
30:3	158 n. 5, 160 n. 10, 177 n. 39
30:9	160 n. 10
30:18	160 n. 10
30:21	39
31:15	160 n. 10
32:10	160 n. 10
33:12	160 n. 10
34:1–23	56
34:13	76 n. 22
35	64 n. 7, 133 n. 27
35–36	133 n. 27
35:5	132, 133 n. 27
35:10	133, 133 n. 27
35:10–11	133 n. 27
37:15–28	49
37:23	51, 51 n. 7
37:27	51, 51 n. 7
38:17	159 n. 7
39:8	160 n. 10
46:13	158 n. 5

Daniel

9:4	168 n. 21
10:2	159 n. 6

Hosea

1	95
1–2	61
1:1	31 n. 14, 234–35 n. 44, 236
1:1–9	163
1:5	160, 163
1:7	187, 207
1:11	187, 207
2	95, 149 n. 23, 162–63, 166–67 n. 18, 173, 184–85, 193
2:2	160 n. 10, 163, 172–73
2:2–25	174
2:5	163
2:7–8	277
2:9	162 n. 11
2:10	144, 149 n. 23, 150 n. 23, 185
2:10–11	164, 277
2:10–15	147, 228
2:10–25	147
2:11	149 n. 23
2:11–15	185
2:14	163, 173, 185, 204 n. 6, 228, 232, 277
2:15	144, 160 n. 10, 163
2:16	173
2:16–22	147
2:17	163
2:18	163
2:18–19	163
2:19	277
2:20	61, 163
2:22	165
2:23	163–64, 167
2:23–24	164
2:23–25	148, 163, 185
2:24	147, 149 n. 23, 150 n. 23
2:24b	164
2:25	51, 51 n. 7, 61, 238–39
3:4	188
3:5	187, 257 n. 45
4–10	207
4–13	95
4:1–2	277
4:1–3	261 n. 52
4:3	163, 244, 277
4:7–9	277
4:9–10	277
4:11	149 n. 23
4:12–13	277
4:13	244
4:15	187, 199, 207
5:1	188
5:5	207
5:6	257 n. 45
5:8	199
5:9	160 n. 10
5:12–14	207
5:13	141 n. 11
5:13–14	187
6:4	187, 207
6:11	46, 46 n. 35, 187, 189

ANCIENT SOURCES INDEX 349

7:3	188	12:1	141 n. 11
7:7	188	12:1–2	207
7:10	257 n. 45	12:2	187
7:11	141 n. 11	12:4	202
7:12	163	13:1	144
7:13	40 n. 21	13:2–4	141
7:13–14	147	13:4	141 n. 11
7:14	149 n. 23	13:10–11	188
7:16	141 n. 11	14	193, 207, 223 n. 16
8:1	40 n. 21	14:2–9	141, 143, 147
8:4	188, 202	14:3	141, 146
8:4–6	202	14:3–4	146
8:5–6	202	14:4	141, 143
8:9	141 n. 11	14:5–8	148
8:10	160 n. 10, 188	14:5–9	141–42, 142 n. 12, 144, 146 n. 19, 148
8:14	207		
9	164	14:7–8	149 n. 23, 185
9:1–2	148, 149 n. 23	14:8	149 n. 23, 227–28, 228 n. 29
9:2	145	14:8a	148
9:3	141 n. 11, 164	14:9	142 n. 12
9:5	164	14:10	40 n. 21, 142
9:6–8	165		
9:7	152, 160 n. 10, 164–65, 167 n. 19	Joel	
9:7–9	165–66, 167 n. 18	1	154, 156, 166, 166 n. 17, 182, 184, 222, 228, 271, 273–75, 277
9:9	164–65		
9:10	144	1–2	94, 96, 101, 143, 145 n. 16, 146, 149, 166, 169, 185, 187, 189, 223 n. 16, 225, 226 n. 24, 228–31, 233, 266, 272–78
10:1–2	202		
10:1–15	202		
10:5	199–200, 202		
10:6	141 n. 11, 202	1:1	31 n. 14, 236
10:7	188	1:2	143, 144, 144 n. 15, 146 n. 19, 153, 166, 227
10:8	202–3		
10:9	164	1:2–3	97
10:9–10	165	1:2–18	274
10:10	165	1:2–20	228
10:11	187, 207	1:2–2:11	144
10:12	257 n. 45	1:2–2:17	184
10:14	160 n. 10	1:4	150 n. 25, 155, 185, 187, 226 n. 24, 232
10:15	202		
11	172 n. 27, 207	1:5	166, 225 n. 23, 227, 271
11:2	144	1:5–20	155
11:5	141 n. 11, 188	1:6	146
11:11	141 n. 11	1:6–7	150 n. 25, 184–85
11:12	187, 207	1:7	154, 226 n. 24, 227, 232
12–13	207	1:8	271

Joel (cont.)

1:10	30 n. 10, 148, 149 n. 23, 227
1:10-11	170
1:11	166, 271
1:12	30 n. 10, 170, 227
1:13	166, 271
1:13-16	143
1:15	152, 158 n. 3, 166, 167 n. 19, 169, 177, 177 n. 38
1:15-20	212
1:17	151
1:19-20	274
1:20	225 n. 23
2	172, 182
2:1	146, 152, 158 n. 3, 166, 167 n. 19, 177, 177 n. 38, 275
2:1-11	143, 146, 151, 154-55, 168, 182, 184-85, 212, 232, 271, 273, 275
2:1-24	143
2:2	152, 160 n. 10, 166, 167 n. 19, 170-171
2:4-9	155 n. 35
2:4-10	185
2:10	169, 223 n. 15
2:10b	152, 167 n. 19, 168
2:10-11	166
2:11	152, 158 n. 3, 166-67, 167 n. 19, 182, 275
2:12	155 n. 32, 170-71
2:12-14	230, 266, 271-73, 275
2:12-16	143
2:12-17	182, 185, 189, 228, 232, 272
2:12-25	155
2:12-26	144
2:12-27	143, 185
2:13	30, 107, 189-90, 211
2:14	187
2:15-16	275
2:15-17	275
2:17	144, 149, 169, 188, 275-76
2:18	211
2:18-19	156, 228
2:18-25	232
2:18-27	144, 212, 272
2:19	144, 144 n. 14, 148, 149 n. 23, 155 n. 31, 164, 167, 188, 232
2:20	144, 232
2:21	144
2:21-23	155 n. 31
2:22	144
2:22-24	232
2:23	151, 156
2:23-24	187
2:24	144-45, 148, 149 n. 23, 151
2:25	144, 151, 155 n. 31, 185, 187, 188, 232
2:26-27	144
3-4	94
3:1	62, 167-69, 182
3:1-5	155
3:2	152, 159 n. 7, 166-67, 167 n. 19, 168-69
3:3-5	168, 212
3:4	152, 158 n. 3, 166-67 n. 19, 168-69
3:5	168, 179
3:13	185
3:18	186
4	32, 46-47, 62, 145, 168, 170, 182-83, 188, 220 n. 10, 222
4:1	46, 146, 152, 155, 159 n. 7, 166, 167 n. 19, 168-69, 182, 189, 213, 222, 271-272
4:1-21	145-46, 155
4:4	145, 271-72
4:4-8	97, 213
4:7	271-72
4:9-17	146, 222
4:9-20	189
4:9-21	185
4:11	145
4:11-12	213
4:12	145
4:14	152, 158 n. 3, 166, 167 n. 19, 169, 177, 177 n. 38, 213
4:14-16	169
4:15	169
4:16	84, 145-46, 155, 167, 220, 220 n. 9, 221-22, 223 n. 15

4:16a	169	5	172
4:16–20	146 n. 19	5:1	171
4:17	146, 155, 169	5:4–6	257 n. 45
4:18	84, 118, 145, 153, 155, 166–67, 167 n. 19, 169, 173, 220 n. 19, 225 n. 23, 226 n. 25	5:5	171, 187, 203
		5:6	178, 178 n. 41, 203
		5:12	40 n. 21
4:18–20	225	5:14	257 n. 45
4:18–21	145	5:16–17	170, 171
4:19	145, 179 n. 44, 185	5:18	158 n. 3, 171
4:20	222, 225 n. 23	5:18–20	162 n. 11, 170–71
4:21	30, 107, 146, 146 n. 19, 155, 189	5:20	158 n. 3, 171
		5:21–23	171–72

Amos

1–2	145, 203 n. 6, 222, 223	6:1	200, 202
1:1	31 n. 14, 222 n. 14, 223 n. 15, 234, 235 n. 44	6:3	160 n. 10
		6:14	106 n. 57, 189, 191
		7:1–4	146
1:2	84, 145–146, 167, 169, 208, 220–22, 222 n. 14	7:10–17	188
		7:13	203
1:3	40 n. 21	8	171, 224 n. 19, 237 n. 51
1:3–2:5	37	8–9	162 n. 11
1:3–2:16	37 n. 10	8:3	171
1:6	40 n. 21, 179 n. 44	8:4–14	170
1:6–8	37 n. 10	8:9	160 n. 10
1:9	40 n. 21, 179 n. 44	8:9–10	171–72
1:11	40 n. 21, 179 n. 44	8:10	171–72, 172 n. 27
1:11–12	132	8:11	171–72
1:13	40 n. 21	8:11–12	172
1:14	160 n. 10	8:12	257 n. 45
2:1	40 n. 21, 179 n. 44	8:13	171, 172
2:4	40 n. 21	8:13–14	172
2:4–5	187, 207	8:14	202, 203
2:6	40 n. 21	9	97, 117–18, 120, 124–26, 128, 129 n. 20, 134, 175 n. 33, 178, 220, 236–37, 237 n. 51
2:6–16	37		
3:3	178		
3:9	200, 202	9:1	118, 223 n. 15
3:12	202	9:1–4	64 n. 8, 117, 119, 121, 129
3:13	178 n. 42	9:1–10	120
3:14	40 n. 21, 165, 203	9:1–15	118
4:1	200, 202, 203 n. 5	9:2	118, 125
4:4	40 n. 21, 203	9:2b	220
4:6–11	146, 184, 230	9:2–4	118, 126
4:6–12	184	9:5–6	117
4:9	149, 149 n. 23, 150, 150 nn. 23, 25, 154–56, 211, 222, 226 n. 24, 231–32, 232 n. 38, 233	9:6	125
		9:7	118, 120–21
		9:7–10	117, 117 n. 4, 118, 120, 134

Amos (cont.)
9:7–15   117, 121
9:8   121, 178, 178 n. 42
9:8–10   120, 244
9:9   285 n. 8
9:10   285 n. 8
9:11   13, 118, 121–22, 172, 281–83, 285, 285 n. 8, 286 n. 9, 287–88
9:11–12   77 n. 26, 119, 123, 128, 173
9:11–15   46 n. 35, 117, 117 n. 4, 120, 134, 170, 172–74, 187, 224 n. 19, 287
9:12   84, 116, 118–19, 122, 172–73, 179 n. 44, 220, 220 n. 10, 285
9:12a   173
9:13   84, 118, 121–22, 145–46, 153, 155, 167 n. 19, 169, 186, 220 n. 9, 226 n. 25
9:13b   118, 173
9:13–14   185
9:14   46, 46 n. 35, 119, 124, 167, 184, 186, 189, 287
9:14–15   173
9:15   119, 124

Obadiah
1   64 n. 8, 118, 120, 125–126
1–4   119
1–5   15, 64 n. 8, 119–21, 124, 219, 237
1–9   97, 124, 129 n. 20
1–14   126–27, 127 n. 15, 204
1–15   173
4   118–19, 125–26
4b   220
4–5   118
5   118–19, 126, 226 n. 25
5a   119, 125–26
5b   119–20, 126
7   13, 132, 289, 291, 293–95
7–8   213
8   118, 121, 126, 174, 175
8–9   119–21, 124, 132
9   121, 174
10–14   97, 119, 121–22, 124, 126, 129, 129 n. 20, 132, 188, 213, 250, 295
10–15   174, 179
11   160 n. 10, 175, 295 n. 5
11–14   118, 183
11–15   175
12   160 n. 10, 176, 176 n. 34, 177
12–14   129, 175
13   132, 160 n. 10, 295 n. 5
14   160 n. 10, 176, 176 n. 34, 177, 295 n. 5
15   118, 158 n. 3, 174–75, 177
15a   97, 119, 122, 124, 126–27, 127 n. 15, 128, 129 n. 20, 204, 213
15b   97, 119, 122, 124, 126–27, 127 n. 15, 129 n. 20, 204
15–17   128
15–21   188
16   118, 122–23, 128, 213
16–17   127
16–18   127
16–21   97, 119, 122, 124, 126–27, 127 n. 15, 204, 213
17   123, 168, 178 n. 42
17–18   116, 119, 178
18   123, 127, 132, 173, 178, 178 nn. 41–42, 220
19   123, 177, 204, 204 n. 7, 205
19–20   119, 123, 127, 128, 204
19–21   77 n. 26, 127, 173
20   179
21   119, 124, 127

Jonah
1:1   31 n. 14
2   14, 25, 97, 101
2:4   190
3:10   278
4   25
4:2   189, 190, 278
4:11   278

Micah
1   25
1:1   31 n. 14, 72 n. 17, 80, 84, 105, 203, 234, 235 n. 44, 262
1:2a   236 n. 49

ANCIENT SOURCES INDEX 353

1:2–5	32	7:1–6	106
1:2–7	187, 234	7:1–7	32, 208, 212
1:5	40 n. 21, 203 n. 6	7:2	66
1:5–6	203	7:3	66, 165 n. 15
1:5–7	187, 208	7:3–4	165, 165 n. 15
1:5–9	155	7:4	66, 160 n. 10
1:6	203, 204 n. 7	7:5–6	66
1:7	73	7:7	66, 105, 106
1:9	73	7:7–8	155
1:13	40 n. 21, 73, 206	7:8	27 n. 5, 64, 67–69, 77 n. 24
1:16	172 n. 27	7:8–10	64, 64 n. 7, 65–66, 71–73, 76, 78, 105, 206, 208, 211
2:1–11	73		
2:4	162 n. 11	7:8–11	75
2:7	178 n. 42	7:8–13	64, 70, 81, 162 n. 12
2:12–13	208	7:8–20	26, 28, 63–64, 66, 69–70, 74, 80, 105, 162 n. 11, 171, 225 n. 21
3:1–12	73		
3:8	40 n. 21	7:9	65 n. 10, 67–68, 71, 77 n. 24, 79, 105, 209
3:9	178 n. 42		
3:12	89 n. 16, 155, 187, 204, 208	7:9–10	69
4–5	45 n. 34, 162 n. 11, 208	7:10	27 n. 5, 64, 65 n. 10, 67–69
4:1	160 n. 10, 208	7:11	27 n. 5, 67–69, 71 n. 14, 74, 77, 160 n. 10, 209
4:1–4	15, 155		
4:2–4	97	7:11–12	73, 81
4:4	149 n. 23	7:11–13	71–73
4:6	208	7:12	27 n. 5, 67, 72, 74–75, 75 n. 20, 79, 160 n. 10
4:6–7	43, 44, 44 n. 32, 45, 168, 223 n. 16		
		7:12–13	75
4:7	45, 45 nn. 32–34	7:13	27 n. 5, 31, 67–68, 72, 73 n. 18, 75–77, 81, 105, 209
4:8	206		
4:9	188	7:14	27 n. 5, 30, 67–68, 75–79
4:10	188, 206	7:14–15a	75–79, 81
4:13	206	7:14–15	70, 81
5:5	76	7:15	68–69
5:5–6	208	7:15b	75–76, 76 n. 21, 78–79, 81
5:10	208	7:16	68–69, 78, 29 n. 30, 80
6	208	7:16–17	79 n. 30, 81
6–7	105, 155	7:16–18	79
6:1–16	73	7:16–20	70, 78, 80–81
6:7	40 n. 21	7:17	27 n. 5, 71 n. 14, 78, 79 n. 30
6:8	257 n. 45	7:18	27 n. 5, 40 n. 21, 65 n. 10, 68–69, 78 n. 28, 79
6:15	149 n. 23		
6:16	66, 188	7:18–20	79–81, 189–190
6:16–7:6	105	7:19	68–69, 71 n. 14, 78 n. 28, 98, 108, 190
7	28, 107, 209		
7:1	66	7:19b	70, 71 n. 14, 78 n. 29

Micah (cont.)

7:20	79

Nahum

1	14, 26, 97, 100 n. 50, 101, 107
1:1	27, 236
1:2	27 n. 5, 39, 101
1:2–8	27–29, 101–3, 105, 212, 236 n. 49, 237
1:2–9	236
1:2–10	228 n. 31
1:2b–3a	29, 32, 107–8
1:3	27 n. 5, 189–90
1:3a	155
1:4	27 n. 5, 30
1:5	27 n. 5, 223 n. 15
1:6	27 n. 5, 39, 39 n. 14, 160 n. 10, 176, 176 n. 34
1:7	
1:8	27 n. 5
1:9–10	27, 28
1:9–14	27
1:9–2:1	103, 105
1:11	27
1:11–12a	27–28
1:12a	27
1:12b	28
1:12–13	27, 28 n. 8
1:12–14	27
1:13	28, 28 n. 7
1:14	27, 27 n. 5, 28
2	237 n. 51
2–3	27, 72, 103, 188
2:1	28 n. 7, 105, 211–12
2:1–3	27–28
2:4	160 n. 10
2:4–14	28
3	150, 237, 237 n. 51
3:1–8	237
3:1–15	28
3:2	223 n. 15
3:3	237
3:8	104
3:8–11	104
3:10	237
3:12	237
3:13	39 n. 14
3:14	237
3:15ab	32
3:15aγ	150
3:15–17	154–55, 185
3:15b–17	27
3:16–17	28, 232
3:16b	32, 150, 226 n. 24, 231, 231 n. 37
3:17	231, 231 n. 37
3:18	237
3:18–19	27–28

Habakkuk

1	107, 237
1–2	188
1:1	236
1:2–3	190
1:2–4	106, 190
1:2–17	232 n. 40
1:5	212
1:5–6	106
1:5–11	106, 190
1:5–17	232, 237
1:6	101, 106, 106 n. 57
1:6–11	151
1:7–10	155 n. 35
1:8	237
1:9	150, 154, 190, 226 n. 24, 231, 232 n. 37, 233 n. 40, 237
1:10	237
1:12–17	39 n. 15, 106
1:17	39 n. 15
2:1	165 n. 15
2:3	38 n. 14, 39 n. 15
2:3–5	39
2:5	39 n. 14
2:5b	39 n. 15
2:8	39 n. 15
2:12	129
3	14, 97, 100 n. 50, 101–2, 106–7, 236 n. 49, 237
3:1–15	188
3:2–15	39, 186
3:3	130

3:3–15	176 n. 37, 212	1:7–18a	261, 264
3:11	31 n. 12	1:8	160 n. 10, 188
3:16	39, 42, 101, 106, 176, 176 n. 34, 183, 229	1:10–11	255 n. 41
		1:12–13	42
3:16–17	185–86	1:12–13a	255 n. 36, 256 n. 42, 257
3:16–19	106, 176 n. 37, 193	1:13b	255, 255 n. 37, 257
3:16–20	188	1:14	152, 156, 158 n. 3, 167 n. 19, 172 n. 27, 177
3:17	149 n. 23, 150 n. 23, 155, 162 n. 11, 228, 228 n. 31, 229, 232	1:14–15	168, 170, 172
3:18	186	1:14–16	183
3:18–19	42, 229	1:14–18	38 n. 12, 177, 212, 255 n. 36, 256 n. 42, 257

Zephaniah

1	256	1:14–18a	256 n. 43
1–2	34, 233 n. 41	1:15	152, 156, 160 n. 10, 167 n. 19, 170 n. 25, 176 n. 34, 177
1:1	31 n. 14, 35, 37, 44, 234, 235 n. 44, 243, 246, 255, 255 n. 37, 257, 261, 264	1:16	160 n. 10
		1:17	256 n. 43
1:1–9	257	1:18	38–39, 39 n. 14, 262, 264
1:1–2:3	177, 209	1:18ab	261, 261 n. 52, 262 n. 52
1:1–3:8	188	1:18b	257–258, 261, 262 n. 52
1:2	241, 242 n. 4, 243 n. 4, 244, 246, 261 n. 52	2	261
		2:1–2	255 n. 37, 256 n. 43
1:2–3	38, 163, 236 n. 49, 237, 241–43, 245, 245 n. 13, 246, 249, 254–55, 255 n. 36, 256 n. 42, 257–58, 261, 261 n. 52, 262, 264	2:1–3	212, 264
		2:1–6	255, 257
		2:2	158 n. 4, 160 n. 10
		2:3	158 n. 4, 160 n. 10, 255 n. 37, 255 n. 41, 257 n. 45
1:2–18	256 n. 44	2:3–5	39
1:2–2:3	162 n. 11, 168 n. 22	2:4	37 n. 10
1:3	241, 242 n. 4, 243 n. 4, 244, 246, 255 n. 41	2:4–5	250
		2:4–6	255 n. 37, 256 n. 43
1:4–5	256 n. 43	2:4–7	247
1:4–6	255, 255 n. 37, 256 n. 45, 264	2:4–10	264
1:4–12	38	2:4–15	33, 37, 209, 247, 249–50, 255
1:4–13	243	2:5	37, 37 n. 10, 249
1:4–18a	257	2:7	46, 189, 255, 255 n. 39
1:4–2:3	37	2:8	188
1:4–3:7	256 n. 43	2:8b	42
1:5	256 n. 45	2:8–9	256 n. 43, 257
1:5–11	39	2:8–9a	255, 255 n. 37
1:6	256 n. 45, 257 n. 45	2:8–11	247
1:7	156, 158 n. 3, 177	2:9b–10	42, 255, 255 n. 39
1:7–8	183, 212	2:10–11	258
1:7–9	255 n. 36, 256 n. 42	2:11	255 n. 41, 262, 262 n. 53
1:7–13a	256 n. 43	2:11–12	255

Zephaniah (cont.)
2:11–15	264
2:11b	248, 254
2:11b–15	248
2:12	248, 255 n. 41, 258
2:12–15	39, 241, 247, 254, 256 n. 43, 257–258, 262
2:13	248
2:13–14	101
2:13–15	100 n. 51, 103, 247, 255, 255 n. 39, 258, 262 n. 53
3	34, 36–38, 45, 162 n. 11
3:1	100 n. 51
3:1–4	255, 255 n. 37, 257
3:1–7	37, 38, 40, 47, 247, 251, 256 n. 43, 257–58, 262, 264
3:1–8	33, 100 n. 51, 209, 262 n. 53
3:1–8a	33
3:1–19	101
3:2–4	42
3:2–15	50
3:5	255 n. 41, 257–58
3:6	34
3:6–8a	255, 255 n. 37, 257
3:7	34, 38, 206, 209, 251 n. 25
3:8	34, 38 n. 14, 40, 41 n. 21, 43, 160 n. 10, 209, 252–53, 253 n. 32, 258, 262, 264
3:8a	37, 38, 257–58
3:8b	33, 38, 40, 255, 255 n. 39
3:8–10	34 n. 1, 37
3:8–20	91
3:9	246, 251–253 n. 32, 255 n. 40
3:9–10	33, 39–40, 41 n. 21, 47, 241, 250–53, 253 n. 32, 254–55, 262–63
3:9–13	209
3:9–20	33
3:10	251 n. 25, 255 n. 40, 255 n. 41
3:10a	39, 252
3:10b	253
3:11	40, 40 n. 21, 41–42, 45 n. 34, 206
3:11–12	251, 251 n. 25
3:11–13	33, 40–41, 41 n. 21, 42, 47, 255 n. 37, 257, 263–64
3:11b–13	41
3:11–20	37, 71 n. 14, 188
3:12–13	40
3:13	40 n. 20, 45 n. 32, 101
3:14	41–43, 206, 251
3:14–15a	41 n. 24
3:14–15	33, 211
3:14–17	34, 41–42, 255 n. 38, 256 n. 44, 263
3:14–19	162 n. 12
3:14–20	188, 209
3:15	41, 45, 45 n. 33, 188, 209
3:15bα	41 n. 24
3:15bβ	41 n. 24
3:15–16	206
3:16	39, 41, 41 n. 24, 42, 101
3:16–17	33
3:17	41, 209
3:17a	41 n. 24
3:17b	41 n. 24
3:18	40 n. 20, 44, 188, 256 n. 44
3:18b	34 n. 1, 44 n. 29
3:18–19	33, 43, 47, 238, 255, 255 n. 39, 263
3:18–20	43, 43 nn. 26, 28, 223 n. 16
3:19	44, 44 nn. 30, 32, 45, 209
3:19–20	156, 168, 170
3:20	33, 34 n. 1, 40, 40 n. 20, 43, 45–47, 152, 167 n. 19, 189, 255 n. 41
3:20aβ	43 n. 26
3:20b	46

Haggai
1:1	31 n. 14, 210, 235 n. 43
1:2	44 n. 32, 238
1:2–4	223 n. 16
1:4	44 n. 32
1:6	184
1:10–11	148, 184
1:11	148–49, 149 n. 23, 156
1:15	210, 235 n. 43
2:1	210, 235 n. 43
2:6	223 n. 15
2:7	223 n. 15
2:10	169 n. 23, 184, 210, 235 n. 43
2:15	210

2:15–19	184, 186	7–8	183, 204, 210, 233
2:17	150 n. 25, 156, 211, 228, 232–33	8	25, 156, 162 n. 11, 228 n. 30
2:18	235 n. 43	8:3–12	223 n. 16
2:18–19	211	8:6	159 n. 7
2:19	148–49, 149 n. 23, 150 n. 23, 156, 228–30, 232 n. 38	8:8	51 n. 7
		8:9–12	186, 210
2:19aβ	226 n. 25	8:9–15	183
2:20	169 n. 23, 184, 210, 235 n. 43	8:9–23	238
2:21	223 n. 15	8:10	186
2:22	39 n. 14	8:11	186
		8:11–12	229

Zechariah

1	182	8:12	156, 186, 226 n. 25, 228, 228 n. 31, 229, 233
1–6	101	8:12–13	156
1–8	16, 86–87, 93, 99, 193, 206, 210–11	8:18–19	183, 204
		8:20–23	97
1:1	31 n. 14, 169 n. 23, 183–84, 210, 235, 235 n. 43	8:21–23	223 n. 16
		8:23	159 n. 7, 168
1:2–6	140 n. 7, 156, 169 n. 23, 182, 210–11, 223 n. 16, 229, 233	9–11	53, 54, 235
		9–14	51, 53–54, 56, 58–59, 62, 87 n. 10, 93, 98, 98 n. 48, 99, 193, 212–14
1:3–6	112 n. 64	9:1	235
1:4	211	9:1–10	53
1:6	182	9:9	188, 206
1:6–17	238	9:9–10	55
1:7	183–84, 210, 235 n. 43	9:9–13	183
1:8–17	211	9:11–10:1	53
1:9–17	188	9:13	43 n. 28
1:12	211	10:1	51
1:14	182, 211	10:2–3b	53
1:14–17	39	10:3b–12	53
1:15	156, 182	10:4	55
1:17	182	10:6	178 n. 41
1:18–21	211	11	62
2:1–13	211	11–14	59
2:14	211	11:1–17	53
2:14–15	206	11:4	56, 76 n. 22
2:15	162 n. 11	11:4–17	49–52, 54, 54 n. 18, 55, 55 n. 21, 56–62
3:8	55		
3:9	160 n. 10	11:15	56
6:10	159 n. 8	11:15–17	55
6:12–14	55	11:17	52, 56
7:1	186, 210, 229, 235 n. 43	12	53, 162 n. 11
7:1–3	183	12–14	53–55, 57, 183, 188, 213, 235
7:1–7	140		
7:2	204–5	12:1	235

Zechariah (cont.)
12:1–4a	53
12:1–9	55
12:1–13:6	49, 51–52, 54, 58 n. 34, 59–60, 62
12:2–9	183
12:3	213
12:3–4	213
12:4	213
12:5	53
12:6	213
12:6–7	53, 53 n. 12, 54
12:8	213
12:8–9	53
12:9	213
12:10	62
12:10–12	53 n. 12
12:10–13:1	55
12:10–13:6	53, 54
12:10–13:9	183
12:11	213
12:13	113
13	56, 57, 162 n. 11
13:1	51, 56, 56 n. 28, 57, 213
13:1–6	97
13:2	56 n. 28, 213
13:2–6	53 n. 12, 55–56, 56 n. 28, 57
13:4	213
13:6	53 n. 12, 54 n. 18
13:7	50, 52, 56–57
13:7–9	49–50, 52–56, 56 n. 28, 57–58, 58 n. 34, 59–60, 62
13:8	51, 54
13:8–9	51, 54, 61 n. 36
13:9	51, 51 n. 7, 60–62, 62 n. 37, 238, 239
13:9a	61
13:9b	61
14	25, 55, 58–60, 62, 162 n. 11, 183, 238–39
14:1	158 n. 5, 160 n. 10
14:1–13	53
14:2	58 n. 34
14:3	160 n. 10
14:4	213
14:5	223 n. 15
14:6	213
14:8	51, 213
14:9	45 n. 33, 58 n. 34, 188, 213
14:10	188
14:13	213
14:14b–21	53
14:16	188, 285 n. 7
14:16–17	45 n. 33
14:16–21	47
14:17	51, 188
14:18	285 n. 7
14:19	285 n. 7
14:20	213
14:21	213

Malachi
1	25
1:1	235, 236
1:2–5	64 n. 7, 129–30, 132, 134, 179, 193, 214
1:4	179 n. 44
1:6–9	223 n. 16
1:6–14	230
1:10–14	97
1:11	183
1:11–14	168, 179
1:14	45 n. 33, 183, 188
2:4	113
2:8	113
3	162 n. 11, 183
3:1	61
3:1–4	213
3:2	160 n. 10
3:2–3	183
3:3	61, 62 n. 37, 113, 238–39
3:6–12	230
3:7	153, 156, 230
3:7b	184
3:8–11	186
3:8–12	187
3:10	156, 187, 231
3:10–11	151, 185, 228, 230, 232–33
3:11	187, 226 n. 24, 230
3:16	184, 191

3:16–18	156, 187, 191, 193, 223 n. 16, 235
3:17	229
3:18	184, 192
3:19	160 n. 10
3:19–21	187, 191, 213
3:21	171
3:22	238–239
3:22–23	187
3:22–24	238
3:23	152, 158 n. 3, 167 n. 19, 168, 170, 179
4:1–3	183
4:4–5	193
4:5	194

Sirach
49:12	23

4 Ezra
14	23

Babylonian Talmud, Bava Batra
13b	89 n. 15
13b–15a	23

Jerome, *Incipit prologus in Librum Duodecim Prophetarum*   23 n. 2

Modern Authors Index

Achtemeier, Paul J.	298	Cook, Stephen L.	53, 54–56, 59
Albertz, Rainer	16–17, 86, 127, 207	Cooper, Alan	147, 153
Allen, Leslie C.	65, 72, 144, 220, 289, 290	Crenshaw, James L.	154, 189, 268, 273, 275–76
Amsler, Samuel	281	Cripps, Richard S.	281
Anderson, John E.	130	Cross, Frank Moore	3, 74
Balentine, Samuel E.	245	Davies, Graham I.	290
Barton, John	124, 126–28	De Vries, Simon J.	28, 98–99
Bautch, Richard J.	265	Delitzsch, Franz	24
Beck, Martin	87–88, 90–91, 99	De Roche, Michael	242–43, 246
Begrich, Joachim	299, 311	Dever, William G.	131
Bellinger, William H.	19, 88–89	Donner, Herbert	222
Ben Zvi, Ehud	11, 36, 44, 87–91, 124, 129, 244–46, 248, 250, 254, 261, 265	Driver, Godfrey Rolles	290
		Duhm, Bernhard	63, 281
Bergler, Siegfried	91, 96, 140, 148, 220–21, 231	Eaton, John H.	298
		Eissfeldt, Otto	63, 77
Berlin, Adele	35, 243, 248–51	Everson, A. Joseph	157
Beuken, Willem A. M.	87, 112	Ewald, Heinrich	24
Biddle, Mark E.	2, 71, 162, 205	Fewell, Danna Nolan	217, 266
Blenkinsopp, Joseph	24, 253	Fishbane, Michael	6, 7, 217–18
Bosshard-Nepustil, Eric	2, 24, 25, 41, 91, 93, 97–98, 100, 140, 176, 221	Fitzgerald, Aloysius	71, 162, 205
		Fuller, Russell	3, 85, 217
Braaten, Laurie J.	95, 184	Fulton, Deirdre	19
Bracke, John M.	46	Galambush, Julie	162
Braun, Roddy L.	74	Garton, Roy E.	83
Budde, Karl	24	Gerstenberger, Erhard S.	7, 299–300, 306, 308, 311, 316
Burkitt, Francis Crawford	77		
Burnett, Joel S.	19, 88	Gesenius, Wilhelm	286, 290
Carr, David	12, 18, 245, 259	Ginzberg, Louis	302, 304, 310
Cassuto, Umberto	24. 116	Gruber, Mayer I.	71
Childs, Brevard S.	5, 6, 10, 53, 100	Gunkel, Hermann	63–64, 299, 311
Christensen, Duane L.	28, 29, 30, 247	Gunneweg, Antonius H. J.	108, 113
Clements, Ronald	133	Habel, Norman	245, 268
Clines, David J. A.	245, 268, 270	Hadley, Judith M.	131
Curtis, Byron G.	34, 43	Haran, Menahem	109

Heckl, Raik	269	237–38, 241, 243, 248–51, 262, 266, 277	
Hillers, Delbert R.	63, 65–66		
Hoffmann, Geo	284–85	O'Brien, Julia M.	250
Hoffman, Yair	157	Odell, Margaret S.	226
Horst, Friedrich	281	Ottosson, Magnus	77
House, Paul R.	1, 3, 116	Petersen, David L.	36, 53, 58–60, 62, 74, 87, 92, 140
Ihromi	41		
Jacob, Edmund	281	Pierce, Ronald W.	87
Japhet, Sara	111	Pohlmann, Karl-Friedrich	133
Jeremias, Jörg	27, 46, 125, 140–41, 143, 165, 210, 236	Raabe, Paul R,	121, 124, 127–28
		Rad, Gerhard von	157
Jenson, Philip Peter	116	Radday, Yehuda T.	53
Jones, Barry	3, 85, 217	Redditt, Paul L.	3, 53–54, 59–60, 83, 113, 154, 187, 195, 230
Jones, Douglas	135		
Keller, Carl-Albert	281	Reicke, Bo	63
Kessler, Rainer	34, 41, 44	Reid, Steve	19
Kratz, Reinhard Gregor	2, 74, 98	Rendtorff, Rolf	157, 181
Kraus, Hans-Joachim	298	Richardson, H. Neil	287
Krinetzki, Günter	42	Robertson, O. Palmer	35
Kuhl, Curt	24	Robinson, Theodore H.	281
Lau, Wolfgang	35	Römer, Thomas	4
Lee, Andrew Yueking	24	Roth, Martin Roth,	98, 100
Leeuwen, Cornelis van	157	Rudolph, Wilhelm	24, 64–65, 126–27, 165, 230, 282, 287, 289
Lescow, Theodor	63–64		
Langevin, Paul-Émile	157	Saebø, Magne	74
Lundbom, Jack	125, 133	Schart, Aaron,	3, 15–17, 41, 83, 85–86, 89, 91, 95, 97–98, 100, 103, 124, 131, 137, 140, 145–46, 150, 169, 173, 176, 195, 204, 207, 254, 256–58, 262, 277
Maier, Christl	205		
Mallau, Hans	2		
Marti, Karl	63		
Mason, Rex	49–62, 87	Schmid, Hans Heinrich	1
Mays, James Luther	63–64, 282, 297	Schmid, Konrad	2
Melvin, David P.	243, 250	Schmitt, John J.	71, 162, 205
Mendecki, Norbert	43, 206	Schneider, Dale Allan	23, 85
Meyers, Carol L.	53, 54, 56, 57–60, 87	Schniedewind, William	127
Meyers, Eric M.	53, 54, 56, 57–60, 87	Schultz, Richard L.	241
Miller, Geoffrey David	13	Schulz, Hermann	27
Miller, Patrick D.	157, 265	Schunck, Klaus D.	157
Miscall, Peter D.	225	Schwally, Friedrich	284
Nogalski, James D.	3–4, 23, 35, 37, 40–41, 43, 44–45, 62–64, 71, 73, 77, 85–86, 90–92, 95–100, 103, 106, 115, 117, 119, 121, 124, 130–31, 137–38, 140–41, 145, 149–50, 155–56, 166–67, 173, 175–76, 178–79, 181, 195, 204, 206–7, 217, 219, 224–29, 231–33, 235,	Schwesig, Gerhard	99
		Scoralick, Ruth	130
		Seitz, Christopher R.	139, 208
		Sellin, Ernst	64
		Seybold, Klaus	27, 88
		Shepherd, Gerald	63
		Smith, Ralph L.	28, 65, 72, 250

Snyman, Fanie 174
Spieckermann, Hermann 2, 157
Stade, Bernhard 63
Steck, Odil Hannes 1, 2, 7–9, 12, 35–36, 39, 41, 44, 71, 85, 132, 138–39, 173, 208, 222, 227, 250, 252–53, 266
Steuernagel, Carl 24
Struppe, Ursula 116
Stuart, Douglas 116, 140, 157, 219, 287, 289
Stulman, Louis 133
Sweeney, Marvin A. 3, 65, 85, 125, 245–47, 250, 254, 261
Széles, Mária Eszenyei 34
Toorn, Karel van der 12, 18, 259
Tucker, Dennis 19
Tuell, Steven 133
Utzschneider, Helmut 140, 222, 225, 227
Van Leeuwen, Raymond C. 95, 107, 141, 146–47, 153, 189
Verhoef, Pieter A. 230
Watts, James W. 3
Watts, John D. W. 3, 5, 234
Wehrle, Josef 97
Weimar, Peter 24, 97
Weiser, Artur 125, 308
Wllhausen, Julius 281
Wenham, Gordon J. 252
Westermann, Claus 252
Wickmann, Dieter 53
Willi, Thomas 222
Willi-Plein, Ina 282
Williamson, Hugh G. M. 108–12, 253
Wilson, Gerald H. 88
Wöhrle, Jakob 16, 17, 86, 92–96, 99–100, 125, 131, 204, 207, 254–58, 262
Wolfe, Rolland Emerson 24
Wolff, Hans Walter 5, 6, 24, 64–65, 117, 126–27, 154, 219–20, 225, 281, 287, 289
Zenger, Erich 89
Zimmerli, Walther 7, 37, 133

www.ingramcontent.com/pod-product-compliance
Lightning Source LLC
Chambersburg PA
CBHW021930290426
44108CB00012B/794